Tracts of Action

Library of the Written Word

VOLUME 127

The Handpress World

Editors-in-Chief

Andrew Pettegree (*University of St Andrews*)
Arthur der Weduwen (*University of St Andrews*)

Editorial Board

Trude Dijkstra (*University of Amsterdam*)
Falk Eisermann (*Staatsbibliothek zu Berlin – Preußischer Kulturbesitz*)
Shanti Graheli (*University of Glasgow*)
Katherine Halsey (*University of Stirling*)
Earle Havens (*Johns Hopkins University*)
Ian Maclean (*All Souls College, Oxford*)
Angela Nuovo (*University of Milan*)
Malcolm Walsby (*ENSSIB, Lyon*)
Alexander Wilkinson (*University College Dublin*)

VOLUME 104

The titles published in this series are listed at *brill.com/lww*

Tracts of Action

Material, Visual, and Practical Dimensions of Early Modern How-to Books

Edited by

Stefan Laube

BRILL

LEIDEN | BOSTON

Cover illustration: Excerpt from the frontispiece designed and produced by Thomas Cross, in [John White], *A rich cabinet, with variety of inventions: unlock'd and open'd, for the recreation of ingenious spirits at their vacant hours. Being receits and conceits of severall natures, and fit for those who are lovers of natural and artificial conclusions. As also variety of recreative fire-works both for land, air, and water. And fire-works of service, for sea and shore. Whereunto is added divers experiments in drawing, painting, arithmetick, geometry, astronomy, and other parts of the mathematicks.* / Collected by J.W. a lover of artificial conclusions. (London: printed for William Whitwood at the sign of the Golden Lion in Duck-Lane near Smith-field, 1668), fourth edition (first published: 1651). Courtesy University of Glasgow Library, Ferguson Collection, Ak – e.31.

The Library of Congress Cataloging-in-Publication Data is available online at https://catalog.loc.gov
LC record available at https://lccn.loc.gov/2024007068

Typeface for the Latin, Greek, and Cyrillic scripts: "Brill". See and download: brill.com/brill-typeface.

ISSN 1874-4834
ISBN 978-90-04-68337-2 (hardback)
ISBN 978-90-04-68338-9 (e-book)
DOI 10.1163/9789004683389

This book is printed on acid-free paper and produced in a sustainable manner.

Contents

PART 3
Text and Image Simultaneity

PART 4
Prescription and Improvisation

Figures and Tables

Figures

Tables

Notes on Contributors

Laura Balbiani
is associate Professor of German Language and Linguistics at the Università Cattolica del Sacro Cuore in Milan (Italy). She studied in Milan and Heidelberg, got her PhD in Historical Linguistics working on Books of Secrets and scientific literature in the Early Modern Age and received the international award 'Luigi De Franco' for the best doctoral dissertation (2001): *La magia naturalis di Giovan Battista della Porta: lingua, cultura e scienza in Europa all'inizio dell'età moderna.* Laura is author of several essays on alchemy and medicine in the 16th and 17th centuries and her research interests focused on the cultural transfer between Germany and Italy in the fields of science and philosophy. Historical lexicography is the subject of her next project, a study on phraseology in bilingual dictionaries. She is working also as a translator and has published editions of several classics of German literature (Goethe, Hesse, Hauptmann, Hölderlin) and philosophy (Kant, Spalding) in Italian translation.

Petra Feuerstein-Herz
Dr. phil., Herzog August Bibliothek Wolfenbüttel, since the early 1990s librarian and researcher in Wolfenbüttel, head of the Department of Early Printed Books (until autumn 2022). Main research interests: Book and science history of the early modern period, with a focus on natural history and alchemy history. Publications (selection): – 'Von heimlichkeit der Natur. Benutzungsspuren in alchemischen Anleitungsbüchern', in Ute Schneider (ed.), *Praxeologische Studien zur historischen Buchwissenschaft* [= Medium Buch. Wolfenbütteler interdisziplinäre Forschungen 1 (2019)], pp. 45–68; – 'Solve et Coagula. Handschriften und Drucke zur Alchemie in der Herzog August Bibliothek Wolfenbüttel', in *Imprimatur* N.F. XXV (2017), pp. 195–220; – 'Weiße Seiten. Durchschossene Bücher in alten Bibliotheken', *Zeitschrift für Ideengeschichte,* 11 (2017), pp. 101–114, see also *Ephemera. Abgelegenes und Vergängliches in der Kulturgeschichte von Druck und Buch.* Festschrift für Petra Feuerstein-Herz, eds. by Hartmut Beyer and Peter Burschel, Medium Buch 3 (2021) (Wiesbaden: Harrassowitz, 2022).

Laurence Grove
is Professor of French and Text/Image Studies and Director of the Stirling Maxwell Centre for the Study of Text/Image Cultures at the University of Glasgow. His research focuses on historical aspects of text/image forms, and in particular 'bande dessinée'. He is President of the International Bande Dessinée

Society. As well as serving on the consultative committees of several journals, he is co-editor of *Glasgow Emblem Studies* (book series) and of *European Comic Art*. Laurence (also known as Billy) has authored (in full, jointly or as editor) twelve books and approximately seventy chapters or articles. He co-curated *Comic Invention* (Hunterian, Glasgow), *Frank Quitely: The Art of Comics* (Kelvingrove, Glasgow) and *Demon Drink* (Hunterian) and is co-author of their accompanying books. He is currently working towards exhibitions for Brussels and for the Western Isles on comics and their iconography. His ongoing book project, *The Collapse of the Canon*, looks at shifts in cultural norms away from 'Great Books' listings and asks why this should be so.

Britta-Juliane Kruse

is associate Professor (PD Dr.) at the Free University Berlin, research focus on Literature and Cultural History for the Late Medieval and Early Modern Era. Studies of Ancient and Modern German Literature, Art History and Classical Archaeology in Bonn and Berlin, PhD and Habilitation at the Free University Berlin. Her doctoral thesis dealt with recipes of gynecology: *'Die Arznei ist Goldes wert' – Mittelalterliche Frauenrezepte* (Berlin, New York: de Gruyter, 1997). For 15 years she has been active in various research projects for the Herzog August Bibliothek Wolfenbüttel. This has resulted in two monographs in recent years: *Korrespondenznetzwerke am Wolfenbütteler Hof. Briefwechsel von Julius und Hedwig von Braunschweig-Lüneburg (1550–1600)*, to be published 2024 by de Gruyter; *Gelehrtenkultur und Sammlungspraxis. Architektur, Akteure und Wissensorganisation in der Universitätsbibliothek Helmstedt (1576–1810)* (Berlin/Boston: de Gruyter, 2023).

Stefan Laube

is associate Professor (PD Dr.) at the Institute for Cultural Studies at the Humboldt University Berlin; since 2006 various research tasks at the Herzog August Library Wolfenbüttel, development of a research focus on alchemy, the monograph *Alchemie&Augenschein. A History of Knowledge and Media* will be published shortly by Matthes&Seitz Berlin, research interests: Visual Languages of Knowledge, Media History and Material Cultures, Collection and Museum History. Publications in selection: *Einladende Buch-Anfänge. Titelbilder des Wissens in der frühen Neuzeit* (Wolfenbüttel: Herzog August Bibliothek, 2022); '„Wer langweilig ist, der kauffe mich". Beiläufiges zum 'Büchlein", in *Ephemera. Abgelegenes und Vergängliches in der Kulturgeschichte von Druck und Buch*. Festschrift für Petra Feuerstein-Herz, eds. by Hartmut Beyer and Peter Burschel, Medium Buch 3 (2021) (Wiesbaden: Harrassowitz, 2022), pp. 115–136; *Der Mensch und seine Dinge. Eine Geschichte der Zivilisation erzählt von 64 Objekten,* (Munich: Hanser, 2020); 'Medium & Magie. Wandlung und Wirkung in der Aufklärung', *Das Achtzehnte Jahrhundert,* Zeitschrift der Deutschen Gesellschaft für die Erforschung des achtzehnten Jahrhunderts 43 (2019) (Göttingen: Wallstein, 2019). Further information at www.stefanlaube.de.

Andrea van Leerdam

is curator of printed works at the Special Collections of Utrecht University Library. As a book historian, she has a special interest in early modern visual cultures and reading practices, and in digital approaches of print culture. A revised version of her dissertation *Woodcuts as Reading Guides: How Images Shaped Knowledge Transmission in Medical-Astrological Books in Dutch (1500–1550)* has been published by Amsterdam University Press in 2024. She co-edited, with Anna Dlabačová and John J. Thompson, *Vernacular Books and Their Readers in the Early Age of Print (c. 1450–1600)* (2023).

Sven Limbeck

Dr. phil., Herzog August Library Wolfenbüttel, Deputy Head of the Department Manuscripts and Special Collections; research interests in cultural, gender, and media history of the late Middle Ages and Early Modern Age (piety and liturgy, pictoriality of knowledge, mediology of manuscripts). Co-initiator of the network *Historische Wissens- und Gebrauchsliteratur* [https://hwgl.hypo theses.org/]. Publications (selection): with Rainer Falk (eds.), *Casta Diva. Der schwule Opernführer,* Berlin: Querverlag, 2019, 'Alchemische Überlieferung in Kodex und Manuskript. Mediologische Aspekte ihrer Erschließung', in *Alchemie – Genealogie und Terminologie, Bilder, Techniken und Artefakte. Forschungen aus der Herzog August Bibliothek,* eds. by Petra Feuerstein-Herz and Ute Frietsch, (Wolfenbüttel: Herzog August Bibliothek, 2021), pp. 27–48; with Rainer Schmitt and Sigrid Wirth (eds.): *Musik im Umbruch. Studien zu Michael Praetorius* (Wolfenbüttel: Herzog August Bibliothek, 2022); for more information see https://www.hab.de/author/dr-sven-limbeck/.

Robert Maclean

is a rare books librarian in University of Glasgow's Archives & Special Collections' Engagement Team. His current role sees him responsible for learn-ing & teaching engagement, historical bibliography and book history enquiries, and rare book cataloguing. He has worked in University of Glasgow Library for the last twenty years. He occasionally publishes articles on the collections, the most recent being on the library's eighteenth- and early-nineteenth-century legal deposit acquisitions, with another article forthcoming on the library of a seventeenth-century Scottish sea captain.

Tillmann Taape
is a lecturer and postdoctoral researcher in history of medicine and science at the Charité in Berlin. He obtained his PhD in History and Philosophy of Science from Cambridge University in 2017 and was subsequently a post-doctoral scholar at the Making and Knowing Project at Columbia University and Senior Editor of the Project's digital critical edition, *Secrets of Craft and Nature*. Tillmann has published on early modern alchemy, artisanal knowledge, and visual culture. His first monograph, *Crafting Medicine*, presents the first in-depth study of the Strasbourg surgeon Hieronymus Brunschwig and his influential printed books, published around 1500, which articulate a new way of knowing and practicing medicine. At present, Tillmann is working on a new history of distillation and is studying the Berlin physician and alchemist Leonhart Thurneisser.

Sergei Zotov
is a PhD student at the Centre for the Study of the Renaissance of the University of Warwick. His thesis focuses on the analysis of alchemical allegorical images from European, mainly German and English treatises of the fifteenth and sixteenth century. He received his Bachelor of Arts in Philology and Literature in Saratov State University (Russian Federation), and his Master of Cultural Studies from Russian State University of the Humanities (Moscow). Sergei authored and co-authored five monographs and popular books on European medieval and early modern religious art, icons, votives, magic, and alchemy (in Russian). In 2017–2022 he worked at the Herzog August Library in Wolfenbüttel as a junior researcher in Stefan Laube's and Gia Toussaint's projects on iconography of alchemy and medieval nuns.

Simone Zweifel
is a independent researcher in the field of Early Modern History and Book History. She received her Master of Arts in History and German Studies from Basel University, and her PhD in 'Organisation and Culture' with a focus on history from the University of St. Gallen. Her doctoral research focused on the production of early modern 'Books of Secrets' in a case-study on the publications of Johann Jacob Wecker (1528–1586) and his collaborators. Her dissertation was published in 2021 by De Gruyter: *Aus Büchern Bücher machen: Zur Produktion und Multiplikation von Wissen in frühneuzeitlichen Kompilationen.*

Introduction: How-to Books – the Birth and Development of an Understudied Genre

Stefan Laube

How do I make soap? How do I dye textiles? What ingredients do I need for an effective medicine? How do I find and mine mineral resources? How do I prepare food that is as tasty as it is wholesome? Manuals of instructions and recipes offered a way out of awkward life situations. The proliferation of this book genre from the first centuries of printing is striking: instructional literature flooded the book market; printers and other versatile lay people made specialist knowledge accessible to a wider public in as catchy a way as possible. What does it mean when the handling of substances and devices was accompanied by a new medium that was supposed to enable people to understand a practical process and apply such knowledge to their own actions? Actually, they are two processes of producing: at the end of the production process there is not only a product, but in the description of the process another product, the instruction manual. An international workshop on this rather unassuming book genre was held between September 27 and 29, 2021, at the Duke August's Library (Herzog August Bibliothek) in Wolfenbüttel and, because of Covid-19, in virtual space. 'Why were these books so popular? Who used them and how? Do they even represent a clearly defined genre?' These questions were at the heart of the discussions.[1]

1 How-to Knowledge Is Different

Simple how-questions related to concrete problems keep society going: they have advanced and refined civilization. The corresponding medium is guides, instructions and recipes, a perennial favorite of mankind, from the manuscripts of the third century (e.g. Papryus Leidensis X) to the YouTube videos of our days.[2] There is hardly an area of life that cannot be cast in the form of

---

[1] The German Research Community (DFG) provided the funding in the form of a pilot year launched on July 1, 2021 to initiate international cooperation. The Ferguson Collection housed at the University of Glasgow Library is probably the world's best early modern collection in this field.

[2] The Papyrus Leidensis X (Leiden University Library) from the third century is considered the first written documentation of alchemy/chemistry and consists of more than a hundred

a best-selling how-to book: from Kathleen Meyer's *How to Shit in the Woods* (Conrad Stein 1998) to Clancy Martin's *How Not to Kill Yourself* (Pantheon 2023), to name just two recent examples that address the all-too-human. Just as communicates as a human being, even if he remains silent, there is also a constructive moment in every piece of advice, even if one refuses it.[3]

Instructions and their manuals have become a key tool for finding one's way in an increasingly complex society. It is hardly surprising that flourished at the beginning of the modern era in the sixteenth century. Instruction manuals were ubiquitous at that time, in agriculture, astrology, culinary arts, economics, educational books, etiquette and courtesy, games and recreations, medical texts, military handbooks, mathematics and botany, to call upon the classification scheme of the Universal Short Title Catalogue (USTC), which at the same time conjure up the wealth of these sources on the screen in seconds with a click.[4] Furthermore there are instruction manuals as academic literature and not least as piety literature. Martin Luther wrote down the how-to of his new faith in *Enchiridion. Der kleine Catechismus* (Wittenberg: Lufft, 1529), where the basics of the Protestant church are dealt with in simple questions and answers, which everyone, especially young people and schoolchildren, should understand.[5]

What is so exciting and innovative about how-to literature? They transport concrete instructions for action from an inexhaustible variety of topics, which even non-experts can follow. Sometimes hard to grasp philosophically, practices of know-how are omnipresent in past and present.[6] Our smart phones

---

recipes in Greek dealing with the imitation of precious materials. See Lawrence M. Principe, *The Secrets of Alchemy* (Chicago: The University of Chicago Press, 2013), pp. 10–12.

3　Paul Watzlawick's *Anleitung zum Unglücklichsein* [Instructions for Unhappiness] (Munich: Piper, 2009, first 1983) appears as an advice parody, an anti-advice book. Yet many readers were to lead less unhappy lives after reading it.

4　https://www.ustc.ac.uk/search.

5　Andrew Pettegree, *Brand Luther: How an Unheralded Young Minister Turned His Small German Town Into a Center of Publishing, Made Himself the Most Famous Man in Europe and Started the Protestant Reformation* (New York: Penguin, 2015), pp. 260–264. But even more sophisticated devotional literature, the dialogue with God through prayers needed concrete instructions, see Thomas von Kempen, *Von der Nachfolge Christi*. Transl. and ed. by Bernhard Lang (Stuttgart: Reclam, 2022).

6　Gilbert Ryle, *The Concept of the Mind* (London: Hutchinson, 1949), chapter 2; Günter Abel: 'Knowing-How. Eine scheinbar unergründliche Wissensform', in Joachim Bromand and Georg Kreis (eds.), *Was sich nicht sagen lässt. Das Nicht-Begriffliche in Wissenschaft, Kunst und Religion*. Festschrift für Wolfram Hogrebe (Berlin: Akademie, 2010), pp. 319–340; Pamela H. Smith: *From Lived Experience to the Written Word. Reconstructing Practical Knowledge in the Early Modern World* (Chicago: The University of Chicago Press, 2022); Matteo Valleriani: 'The Epistemology of Practical Knowledge', in Matteo Valleriani (ed.), *The Structures of Practical Knowledge*, (Berlin, Springer: 2017), pp. 1–21; Jasmin Meerhoff, *'Read me!' Eine Kultur- und Mediengeschichte der Bedienungsanleitung* (Bielefeld: transcript, 2011).

apps with their algorithms apparently have their predecessor in how-to books of the Early Modern Age, in the practical approach laid down in tried and tested rules.[7] Unlike propositional knowledge 'knowing-how' is not something that can be successfully stated in response to a question. Instead, it is manifested in the successful mastery of a practice. Any instruction on how to ride a bike for instance remains essentially incomplete if the instructed person does not get on the saddle and put the theoretical knowledge into practice. Or in the words of John Ferguson, the passionate book collector in the field of early modern practical knowledge literature from Glasgow: 'No amount of reading will make a sculptor, or a gardener, or a shoemaker, or a surgeon, or a musical executant.'[8] The activities in question can only be learned by practising and performing them. In these sources from all areas of learning, knowledge apparently arises directly from 'making and knowing' (Pamela H. Smith). Such sources can be compared to scripts, dance choreographies or musical notation, text forms that refer to an activity and practice that is yet to be carried out. This is already latent with the English word 'recipe' that is in its sequence of letters identical to the Latin imperative of 'take', i.e. 'take!' or 'one takes', a formula that is used in cookbooks from the Renaissance until today.[9]

How to-literature codifies knowledge in a catchy, factual and didactic way. These books are usually brief and concise, a brevity that often finds expression in the terse imperative forms of instruction.[10] Presented in affordable treatises, written in vernacular languages these tracts of action are aimed at ever wider circles of society. How to-books enabled interested laypersons to obtain information largely independently of institutions and oral teaching. It enabled also socially less privileged groups, such as women and craftsmen who did not operate in the regulated knowledge milieus of university and academy, to acquire skills and knowledge.[11] The more comprehensive the how-to books

7   Lorraine Daston, *Rules. A Short History of What We Live by* (Princeton/Oxford: Princeton University Press, 2022).

8   John Ferguson, 'Notes on Some Books of Technical Receipts, or So-Called 'Secrets'', *Transactions of the Glasgow Archaeological Society*, 2 (1882), p. 183.

9   See Deborah L. Krohn, *Food and Knowledge in Renaissance Italy. Bartolomeo Scappi's Paper Kitchens* (Farnham: Ashgate, 2015); Elizabeth Spiller, 'Recipes for Knowledge. Makers' Knowledge Traditions, Paracelsian Recipes, and the Invention of the Cookbook, 1600–1660', in Joan Fitzpatrick (ed.), *Renaissance Food from Rabelais to Shakespeare. Culinary Readings and Culinary Histories* (Farnham: Ashgate, 2010), pp. 55–72.

10   Gianna Pomata, 'The Recipe and the Case. Epistemic Genres and the Dynamics of Cognitive Practices', in Kaspar von Greyerz, Silvia Flubacher, and Philipp Senn (eds.), *Wissenschaftsgeschichte und Geschichte des Wissens im Dialog/Connecting Science and Knowledge* (Göttingen: Vanderhoeck & Ruprecht, 2013), pp. 131–154.

11   See to gender relevance Alisha Rankin, *Panacea's Daughters. Noblewomen as Healers in Early Modern Germany* (Chicago: The University of Chicago Press, 2013); Meredith K. Ray, *Daughters of Alchemy. Women and Scientific Culture in Early Modern Italy* (Cambridge (Mass.): Harvard University Press, 2015); Helen Smith, *Grossly Material Things. Woman*

became, the more diverse the knowledge they transmitted, the more other aspects of user behaviour came to the fore, such as encyclopaedic thirst and curiosity. How-to books have always served as entertainment. Obviously, it's just fun to watch people solve everyday problems, if you do not immediately indulge in incredible recipes of pure fantasy.[12]

2   Some Notes on Initiators, Content, and Formats

The transmission of knowledge depends to a decisive degree on the medium in which it is presented. It is precisely in printed form that early modern knowledge takes on its special character. If it is said that it was only in the age of typography that the author was able to fix himself and his material and present it in a controlled manner, the question arises as to who the author of how-to treatises is and how they came about, conceptually and technologically. We still know rather little about this. Undoubtedly, the serial product of an early modern how-to book, especially if it was also illustrated, cannot be called anything other than a logistical masterpiece, as it always had to be about accommodating implementable knowledge in a limited space. With every printed source, the network of relationships between author, engraver, and publisher would have to be scrutinized. The use of the conditional already indicates that this approach often fails due to a blatant lack of sources. Only rarely does the how-to book look itself in the mirror. For long stretches of the early modern period, the printing of books was an 'ars secreta', which as a rule did not pass on its knowledge in that public medium which it itself produced.[13] But even from a position where the sources are scarce, it remains undisputed that the degree of willingness to cooperate between printer, author, artist and

---

and *Book Production in Early Modern England* (Oxford: Oxford University Press, 2012); Katherine Park: *Secrets of Women. Gender, Generation, and the Origins of Human Dissection* (New York: Zone, 2006); Britta-Juliane Kruse: '*Die Arznei ist Goldes wert*' – *Mittelalterliche Frauenrezepte* (Berlin/New York: De Gruyter, 1997).

12   One particularly apt example among many others: John White's *A Rich Cabinet, with Variety of Inventions*, first published in 1651 by Whitwood in London, contains numerous instructions on how to conduct experiments, satisfy curiosity, solve problems and much more. There are instructions on arithmetic, on legerdemain (sleight of hand), painting, 'how to help deafness and to expel wind from the head' and how to make fireworks. The book went through at least eight editions until the 18th century. By the way: A section of the cover of this treatise adorns this Brill volume. See for today's time: Randall Munroe, *How to. Absurd Scientific Advice for Common Real-World Problems* (London: Murray, 2020).

13   Archives likewise report almost nothing if one wants to find out something about the activities and coordination that are indispensable for the production of this book genre.

engraver must have been considerable, as was the permanently lurking potential for conflict.

It is worth taking a closer look at the genre of the technical-instructional book, in German 'Kunstbüchlein' that responded to the ever-increasing demand for technical information in an era of economic upheaval. From the 1530s onwards, they appear in increasing numbers.[14] As William Eamon has discovered, they often go back to a handwritten original, which was edited differently depending on the preferences of the printer.[15] Ultimately, it was the printers who, through their interventions and paratextual accentuations, cast the 'leading manuscript' into divergent versions. The genre of the text remains the same; in both we are dealing with a recipe writing, which lists instructions for action for separating, dyeing and cleaning the metals. In addition, we find illustrations of stills and kilns, as well as an index to help locate specific recipes. A list of common Latin words with their translations into German also made access more convenient. Such booklets, with the help of which the user could try his or her hand at practices of tasting and distilling, mushroomed at the time.[16]

Printers, always with an eye on sales success, could not afford to ignore useful reading material, quite the contrary![17] It should be emphasized that it was not craftsmen from the various guilds, but printers who launched such books. They directed the dissemination of technical information in the first half of

---

14 See *Rechter Gebrauch der Alchimei* (Frankfurt am Main: Egenolff, 1531), USTC 690050 and *Alchimi und bergwerck* (Straßburg: Cammerlander, 1534) USTC 610654. The world of printers was not yet so large at that time. We must assume that the two printers (Christian Egenolff and Jacob Cammerlander) knew each other.

15 William Eamon, *Science and the Secrets of Nature. Books of Secrets in Medieval and Early Modern Culture* (Princeton: Princeton University Press 1994), pp. 112–133. See also the full-text thesis available on the web: Ernst Striebel, *Das Augsburger Kunstbuechlin von 1535. Eine kunsttechnologische Quellenschrift der deutschen Renaissance* (Technische Universität Munich 2007) [https://docplayer.org/4598921-Ernst-striebel-das-augsburger-kunstbuechlin-von-1535-eine-kunsttechnologische-quellenschrift-der-deutschen-renaissance.html].

16 As William Eamon and Michael Giesecke have documented, a wave of 'how-to booklets' is flooding the still relatively young book market; Michael Giesecke, *Der Buchdruck in der frühen Neuzeit. Eine historische Fallstudie über die Durchsetzung neuer Informations- und Kommunikationstechnologien* (Frankfurt am Main: Suhrkamp, 1998, first 1991); pp. 504–548; William Eamon, 'Arcana Disclosed: The Advent of Printing, the Books of Secrets Tradition and the Development of Experimental Science in the Sixteenth Century', in *History of Science* 22 (1984), pp. 111–150.

17 The first printing workshops were only profitable because they were able to sell current mass-produced goods, e.g. by reproducing municipal ordinances, indulgence slips and other cheap print; see Andrew Pettegree, *The Book in the Renaissance* (New Haven/London: Yale University Press, 2011), pp. 31–32.

the sixteenth century. Although these works originated in the workshops of the craftsmen, the information was collected and disseminated by printers (who were craftmen too, by the way) who recognized the needs of a new readership. To the often haphazardly compiled recipes that used to circulate among craftsmen, printers added title pages, tables of contents, glossaries of technical terms, and prefaces: anything that facilitated reception. They were also the ones who rearranged the texts, deleting outdated recipes and supplementing them with new ones. Often the recipes had to be translated into common vernacular languages.

As long as the transmission of knowledge and information was directly tied to paper and ink, the format of the medium has been of great importance for reading practises. While today entire libraries can be easily downloaded from clouds onto devices whose format ranges between a cigarette pack and a chocolate bar, it made a big difference for reading practice in the Early Modern Era whether one devotes oneself to the Christian tradition with the help of a Gutenberg Bible or a so-called thumb Bible.[18] The format of the how-to book was usually handy, sometimes so small and thin that one could effortlessly slip it into one's pocket. With this genre of book, the individual user no longer had to go to the book, but the book could accompany him, so to speak, as a companion at work, on journeys or in other life situations: a vademecum, in other words.[19]

As is well known, the format is determined by the number of times the sheet is folded. The more often it is folded, the smaller the book. Thus, a folio sheet folded three times can result in an eight-page work with 16 pages in a handy octavo format. Two or four such sheets yielded handsome booklets of 32 or 64 pages, apparently the most popular size for how-to books.[20] Even if in most cases the how-to book is handy and small, it can be quite voluminous. The duodecimo treatise *Ein Nutzlichs Artzneybuechlin / wie man*

---

18   The term 'Thumb Bible' first appeared in print in a reprint of John Taylor's *Verbum Sempiternum* in 1849. Comparable minibooks had appeared since the early 17th century, see Louis Bondy, *Miniaturbücher von den Anfängen bis heute* (Munich: Pressler, 1988).

19   The term has been used since the end of the Middle Ages as a generic name and title word for first mainly theological and liturgical, then since the 16th century mainly medical compendia and manuals. Since then it has established itself as a common title word for manuals, guides and advice literature of all kinds and even for dental care products (also Venimecum, Enchiridion), Gundolf Keil, 'Vademecum', in *Lexikon des Mittelalters* 8 (2003), Sp. 1363.

20   The ratio of height to width varies depending on the type of folding. For the 6°, 12° and 24° formats, the width is narrower in relation to the height than for the 2°, 4°, 8° and 16° formats. In the 'duodec', the smallest of the historical book formats, twelve sheets are obtained from one sheet.

leibliche gesundheit halten soll (Strasbourg: Bertram, 1606, HAB xb 10270) by the Paracelsist Michael Toxites runs to several hundred pages; a hand book on the profession of notary, can reach well over 1,000 pages.[21] But the complete opposite was also possible under the label 'Büchlein': thus the incunabulum 'Dies büchlin weiset die außlegung des schachzabel spils' in folio format gives instructions on chess on 39 sheets.[22] It seems that equally the small, thick as well as the large, usually thinner treatise be used for an instruction book, especially in the period of early printing. In the long run, there is a general trend towards the small format on a few dozen pages.

As the above examples show, in German-speaking countries, this type of book often bears the term 'Buchlein' as a diminutive of 'book' in its title.[23] Richard Brunckh's *Bad-Und Trinck-Chur-Büechlin* (Freiburg im Breisgau: Meyer, 1669) comprises 78 octavo pages on the correct behavior in a healing spring (HAB: Xb 12° 255). From the *Kriegs-Büchlein* (Zurich: Bodmer, 1659) by Hans Conrad Lavater to the anonymous *Rechen-Büchlein* (Ulm: [Görlin?], 1659), the 'little book' represented a passe-partout for every niche of practical knowledge. Often the title refers to 'Probir büchlein' (assaying booklet) or 'Nützlich büchlin' (useful booklet). John Ferguson whose collection is teeming with 'little octavos and duodecimos which flowed from the press in a copious stream' lists 'Berg-, Probier- bzw. Kunstbüchlein' as a Germanism because there was no English equivalent in the first half of the sixteenth century.[24] It happened more and more often that inquisitive people were equipped with a little book in their hands when they were on the move, with a compass, so to speak, that always pointed in the direction of proper practices. The title 'Nützlich Büchlin' underlines the practical character, not only in terms of the field of knowledge presented, but also the associated storage medium, small format and paperback, which could be carried everywhere.[25]

---

21   *Manuale Notariorum Bipartitum Notariat: Hand-Buechlein* (Basel: Henric Petri, 1630), HAB: Xb 10806.

22   Jacobus de Cessolis, *Dies büchlin weiset die außlegung des schachzabel spils* (Strasbourg: Knoblochzer, 1483), HAB: 11.4 Rhet. 2°.

23   See to 'Büchlein' Stefan Laube, "Wer langweilig ist, der kauffe mich'. Beiläufiges zum 'Büchlein", in: *Ephemera. Abgelegenes und Vergängliches in der Kulturgeschichte von Druck und Buch*. Festschrift für Petra Feuerstein-Herz, eds. by Hartmut Beyer and Peter Burschel (Wiesbaden: Harrassowitz, 2022), pp. 115–136.

24   Ferguson, *Books of Secrets*, pp. 10–11; see also Ernst Darmstaedter, *Berg-, Probier-, und Kunstbüchlein* (Munich: Verlag der Münchner Drucke, 1926).

25   The genre of 'Büchlein' also includes the so-called 'format büchlein' printed in the 17th century, a helpful guide in the layout of the book page for the typesetter. These treatises were less concerned with book formats such as quarto, octavo or duodec, but rather – as Gustav Milchsack, ducal librarian at Wolfenbüttel clarified at the end of the

3   Thoughts on an Exquisite Collection

'How-to Book' is the conceptual category that is used here repeatedly to capture the specifics of a text genre from different perspectives, in which theoretical insights are prepared in such a way that they can actually be put into practice: 'tracts for action' in other words.[26] There are other, more or less appropriate terms for a cross-segment book genre in which knowing-that and knowing-how converge, such as 'recipe book', 'book of secrets' or 'secrecy literature' [Secretenliteratur], 'advice book', and 'instruction manual'. In the German-speaking world, the historical term often used is 'Kunst-, Wunder- und Hausbuch' [Art, Wonder and House Book],[27] and in the community of recent research 'Historische Wissens- und Gebrauchsliteratur' [historical knowledge and utility literature].

The Ferguson Collection at Glasgow University Library is inextricably linked with the formula 'Books of Secrets'. For the book collector John Ferguson treatises acquired this label above all when they contained recipes as openers of secrets.[28] Ferguson was Regius Professor of Chemistry at the University of Glasgow between 1874 and 1916, and at the same time, as a passionate book collector, he displayed an eminent interest in cultural history.[29] Ferguson worked in the heyday of the British Empire, in the tailwind of a rapid technological development and industrialisation that was unparalleled. In this time of rescue operations, in which sources of the past were increasingly being buried, the collector handled the category of the secret; in a very specific sense:

19th century – with 'the formats which the book printer makes when he determines the spatial dimensions (height and width) of the type columns and the white bands (webs) surrounding them.' [die Formate, welche der Buchdrucker macht, wenn er die räumlichen Abmessungen (Höhe und Breite) der Schriftkolumnen und der sie umgebenden weißen Bänder (Stege) bestimmt] Gustav Milchsack, 'Die Buchformate, historisch und ästhetisch entwickelt', in *Verhandlungen der 44. Versammlung deutscher Philologen und Schulmänner in Dresden*, 30.9.1897, pp. 177–181, here p. 177. See also: Martin Boghardt, 'Formatbücher und Buchformat. Georg Wolffgers *Format-Büchlein*, Graz 1672/1673', in Martin Borghardt, *Archäologie des gedruckten Buches*, ed. by Paul Needham and Julie Boghardt (Wiesbaden: Harrassowitz, 1988), pp. 77–103.

26   Tillmann Taape brought me to 'tracts of action' when he speaks of 'texts of action' in his contribution to this volume.

27   Not art in the sense of fine art, of course, but in the sense of skill and ability, which always had an inherent magic of mystery.

28   John Ferguson, *Books of Secrets. A Paper read before the Bibliographical Society*, April 21, 1913 (London: Blades East & Blades, 1914), pp. 5–33.

29   David Weston, 'A Magus of the North? Professor John Ferguson and his Library', in *The Meanings of Magic. From the Bible to Buffalo Bill*, ed. by Amy Wygant (New York/Oxford: Berghahn, 2006), pp. 161–177.

under this label, Ferguson understood knowledge above all as a practice that uncovered what had previously been hidden. With him, the transformation of knowledge as a thesaurus of secrets and miracles into a fund of phenomena that man can use celebrates its resurrection – 'Secret' as a concept that dissolves itself through disclosure.[30]

Ferguson collected many early printed works, which dealt with a technological-practical approach in the world of knowledge. Ferguson's neologism 'Books of Secrets' may look like an ex post facto term, but at the same time it is elastic enough to do justice to the specificity of the epoch, since in the 16th and 17th centuries the wording of the titles of the relevant books often speaks of 'secreti' or 'heymlichkeit'. Ferguson's original interest was in the history of technology. He had in mind something that had long existed in German lands. Ferguson explicitly referred to the five-volume *Beyträge zur Geschichte der Erfindungen* [Contributions to a History of Inventions] by Johann Beckmann, published in Leipzig at the end of the eighteenth century. As is the way with the passion of collecting, it is difficult to control. In 1882, John Ferguson was to divide his ever-growing book collection into five thematic groups: (1) secrets of nature (general natural history, cosmogony), (2) natural magic (optics, acoustics, magnetism), (3) chemical, pharmaceutical, and medical secrets, (4) tracts on life and generation, physiological secrets, (5) treatises on technical and art secrets. In the last section, actually the starting point of his collecting interest, Ferguson still made the following distinction: 'general collections containing receipts relating to a variety of arts, and special collections containing receipts of use in one art or handicraft only.'[31]

As soon as one takes a look at the printed inventory of the Ferguson collection, one is indeed struck by the broad range of areas of knowledge:[32] chemistry alone, with its important subsections of metallurgy, distillation, fireworks, cosmetics, colour production and the dyeing of certain materials, opens up a magnificent forum of diverse knowledge: the treatises on body care lead over to fields of activity such as household, agriculture, gardening, which are far less represented overall, but nevertheless occur again and again. What is also striking, however, is how strongly Ferguson has collected so called

30 Eamon, *Science and the Secrets of Nature*; see also Elizabeth Spiller, 'Introductory Note', in *Essential Works for the Study of Early Modern Women: Part 3*. Selected and Introduced by Elizabeth Spiller (Aldershot: Ashgate, 2008), pp. xi–xvi.

31 John Ferguson, 'Notes on Some Books of Technical Receipts, or So-Called 'Secrets'', *Transactions of the Glasgow Archaeological Society*, 2 (1882), pp. 180–197, here p. 183.

32 John K. Ferguson, *Catalogue of the Ferguson Collection of Books mainly Relating to Alchemy, Chemistry, Witchcraft and Gipsies in the University of Glasgow* (2 vols, Glasgow: Maclehose, 1943).

irrational books, on magic and alchemy. In addition, there are numerous compilation works that unite numerous areas of knowledge between two covers
in a fascinating potpourri. Ferguson's original focus on the history of technology has thus expanded considerably, to the extent that the category of the
secret should also become increasingly iridescent in his work. 'Secret', then, no
longer in the status of its uncovering, but in some sense of a perpetuation of
the occult as well.[33]

4   Research Status and Starting Point

For several decades, Ferguson's approach to early modern knowledge was for-
gotten. It was not until William Eamon's groundbreaking study *Science and
the Secrets of Nature. Books of Secrets in Medieval and Early Modern Culture*
(Princeton University Press, 1994), the Books of Secrets came to the fore again.
At the same time, a fruitful thematic narrowing took place: From now on,
Books of Secrets had to be concrete, transparent guides, instructions and recipe
books, 'The Age of How-to', that is what Eamon called the sixteenth century.[34]
Accordingly, the term 'how to' primarily refers to clearly and concretely formulated instructions and advice on how to cope with everyday life, from removing
stains to operating a complex appliance to preparing a healthy meal.[35] In this
way Eamon was able to create an awareness emerged of the relevance of these
writings for the establishment of the modern scientific paradigm: no wonder
that a flourishing line of research has since been established in this area.[36] In
the last years postcolonial and philosophical accents have enriched this topic.
Recent research has argued that the genre of the recipe has been suitable for

---

33   How else can it be explained that Ferguson also includes 25 treatises by Michael Maier,
       the Paracelsist and personal physician of Emperor Rudolf II., who conveys his know-
       ledge of nature in coded emblems and mythological allusions: Ferguson, *Catalogue*, vol.
       2, pp. 438–441.
34   Eamon, *Science and the Secrets of Nature*, p. 126.
35   The fact that the how-to book, which can hardly be surpassed in transparency and didac-
       ticism, are by no means completely free of secrets results solely from the fact that they
       usually transport a good portion of implicit knowledge, knowledge that is not formulated,
       although this knowledge would be necessary if one wanted to actually implement what
       is described.
36   See Elaine Leong, *Recipes and Everyday Knowledge. Medicine, Science, and the Household
       in Early Modern England* (Chicago/London: The University of Chicago Press, 2018); Alison
       Kavey, *Books of Secrets. Natural Philosophy in England, 1550–1600* (Urbana: University of
       Illinois Press 2007); Karel Davids, 'Craft Secrecy in Europe in the Early Modern Period: A
       Comparative View', in *Early Science and Medicine* 10 (2005), pp. 341–348.

translating knowledge from one culture to another on a global scale.[37] Then how-to knowledge is quite significantly intertwined with tacit and procedural knowledge. The gap between 'knowing-how' and 'knowing-that' has been increasingly recognised as research problem in philosophy.[38] Current research shows some deficits, for example when it comes to systematically accessing details. Each individual recipe would have to be classified as precisely as possible according to ingredients, procedures, use and modes of action.[39] Digital Humanities methodologies have the potential to help uncover unidentified patterns, trends, and developments through quantitative approaches and data visualisations.

To this day, it is mainly handwritten recipes that have attracted scientific interest, and their transformation into print is analyzed much less frequently.[40] Yet it was this change of media that enabled the widespread dissemination of practical information. Relevant are above all overlooked but ubiquitous, thematically oriented small formats, but also compilations in which recipes or instructions are united encyclopaedically.[41] Special attention should be paid to cheap printed books which mostly in a few dozens of pages convey practical advice from all possible fields of knowledge.[42]

The spectrum of early modern knowledge literature is wide and varied: from the groundbreaking single study that was hardly read, such as that of Copernicus in 1542 and procedures accompanying manuals and handbooks to encyclopedic reference works and compilatory florilegias ('Buntschriftstellerei')

---

37 Marta Hanson and Gianna Pomata: 'Medicinal Formulas and Experimental Knowledge in the Seventeenth-Century Epistemic Exchange between China and Europe', in *Isis*, 108 (2017), pp. 1–25; Amanda E. Herbert and Jack B. Bouchard: 'One British Thing: A Manuscript Recipe Book, ca. 1690–1730', in *Journal of British Studies*, 59 (2020), pp. 396–399.

38 Following Gilbert Ryle's *Concept of the Mind*, our ability to act, determined by application-related skills, seems to resist being conceptually defined precisely; John Bengson and Marc A. Moffett (eds.), *Knowing How. Essays on Knowledge, Mind, and Action* (Oxford: Oxford University Press, 2012).

39 William Eamon, 'How to Read a Book of Secrets', in Elaine Leong and Alisha Rankin (eds.), *Secrets and Knowledge in Medicine and Science, 1500–1800* (Farnham: Ashgate, 2011), pp. 23–46, here p. 41.

40 See the web portals *The Recipes Project. Food, Magic, Art, Science, and Medicine* [https://recipes.hypotheses.org/] and *Netzwerk. Historische Wissens- und Gebrauchsliteratur* [https://hwgl.hypotheses.org/], which both are based on handwritten sources.

41 Laura Balbiani, *La magia naturalis di Giovan Battista della Porta. Lingua, cultura e scienza in Europa all'inizo dell'età moderna* (Bern: Lang, 2001); Simone Zweifel, *Aus Büchern Bücher machen. Zur Produktion und Multiplikation von Wissen in frühneuzeitlichen Kompilationen* (Berlin/Boston: de Gruyter, 2022).

42 Margaret Spufford, *Small Books and Pleasant Histories. Popular Fiction and its Readership in Seventeenth Century England* (Cambridge: Cambridge University Press, 1981).

that indulged in wild cut-and-paste.[43] Although all of these textual genres feed into the book genre we are interested in, how-to books have very particular characteristics: the knowledge in these books is less science than everyday coping, and the knowledge speaks directly to the user by way of performative acts. Slogans like 'The proof of the pudding is in the eating', 'Try and see' or 'There is nothing good unless you do it' come to mind for this kind of lore. The aim of this volume is to characterise this type of source. Current research lacks a typological approach. Up to now, advice literature has been analysed within specific fields of knowledge instead of analysing their commonalities as a text genre.[44] The following overarching key points, common to all how-to books, suggest themselves: Books are taken in the hand and leave traces of use. Books are subject to a change of media, from manuscript to printed work to digitization. In illustrated books, the question of visual translation is relevant. In terms of content, the written instructions are about practical implementation, whether they are followed consistently or encourage improvisation. These four focal points of the conference volume may serve as the instruction manual, so to speak, a guide to how research should best deal with this type of book.

In his introductory contribution, Stefan Laube (Berlin) discusses the volume concept using the example of plague treatises, a genre of printed instruction that was already documented in numerous copies in the last decades of the 15th century, in the age of incunabula. If the introduction of printing coincided with a plague epidemic in certain regions, we can assume that printing began

---

43   Henry E. Lowood/Robin E. Rider, 'The Scientific Book as a Cultural and Bibliographical Object', in *Thornton&Tully's Scientific Books. A Study of Bibliography and the Book Trade in Relation to the History of Science* (Aldershot: Ashgate, 2000), pp. 1–26; Tara Nummedal and Paula Findlen, 'Word of Nature: Scientific Books in the Seventeenth Century', in *Thornton&Tully's Scientific Books. A Study of Bibliography and the Book Trade in Relation to the History of Science* (Aldershot: Ashgate, 2000), pp. 164–216; Margaret Bingham Stillwell, *The Awakening Interest in Science During the First Century of Printing, 1450–1550* (New York: Bibliographical Society of America, 1970); Owen Gingerich, *The Book Nobody Read. In Pursuit of the Revolutions of Nicolaus Copernicus* (London: Heinemann, 2004); Angela N.H. Creager, Mathias Grote and Elaine Leong, 'Learning by the Book: Manuals and Handbooks in the History of Science', *The British Journal for the History of Science*, Themes, 5 (2020), pp. 1–13; Flemming Schock, 'Wissensliteratur und 'Buntschriftstellerei' in der Frühen Neuzeit: Unordnung, Zeitkürzung, Konversation, Einführung', in Flemming Schock (ed.), *Polyhistorismus und Buntschriftstellerei. Wissenskultur und Wissensvermittlung in der Frühen Neuzeit* (Berlin: de Gruyter, 2012), S. 1–20.

44   So far it has rather been the case that 'such books of recipes and secrets have not been studied as a genre, but rather have generally been treated separately in terms of their subject matter', Pamela H. Smith: 'What is a Secret? Secrets and Craft Knowledge in Early Modern Europe', in Elaine Leong and Alisha Rankin (eds.), *Secrets and Knowledge in Medicine and Science, 1500–1800,* (Farnham: Ashgate, 2011), pp. 47–66, here p. 52.

with a publication on how best to behave in times of fatal diseases.[45] The motto of these texts was to be concise, comprehensible and easy to remember, which is already striking with the title. Whether *Kurtze Berichte* or *Kurtze Unterweisungen*, nearly 100 relevant titles with the adjective 'short' can be found in the index of printed works published in the German language area (VD16, VD17).[46] Most of the nostrums presented in the plague tracts were of little medical benefit. The authority to order anything at all creates trust and welds society together; a mechanism that has also been the norm in the hard times of Covid-19. In rules of conduct, the plague guidebooks were not all that wrong in terms of content, even if no one really knew at the time how the plague develops and spreads. It was important to avoid crowds and everything with which the plague sufferer came into contact. Plague tracts show how 'modern' the contemporaries of the sixteenth century already were or how 'archaic' we still (have to) act in the twenty-first century when nature challenges us.

5   Materiality and Traces of Use

This volume does not focus on books that primarily have representative and decorative functions. Instead, we investigate tracts that have not only been read, but actually used.[47] Like any printed book, the handy how-to book is made of an interplay of materials, paper, thread, glue and ink., and is subject to physical processes of adaptation and change that reflect specific user experiences, preferences and interests.[48] Handwritten comments in the margins

---

45   The southern German city of Ulm is apparently a good example to confirm this claim.

46   Verzeichnis der im deutschen Sprachraum erschienenen Drucke des 16. Jahrhunderts (http://www.vd16.de/). Verzeichnis der im deutschen Sprachraum erschienenen Drucke des 17. Jahrhunderts (http://www.vd17.de/).

47   See Bradin Cormack and Carla Mazzio, *Book Use, Book Theory: 1500–1700* (University of Chicago Library, 2005). Most of the sources we are dealing with here were never created with a view to conservation. As a rule, they existed only as long as they were needed. At best, they were carelessly put aside, if not thrown away. The estimated number of irretrievably lost treatises must be considerable; see Andrew Pettegree, 'The Legion of the Lost. Recovering the Lost Books of Early Modern Europe', in Flavia Bruni and Andrew Pettegree (eds.), *Lost Books. Reconstructing the Print World of the Pre-Industrial Europe* (Leiden/Boston: Brill, 2016), pp. 1–27.

48   Ann Blair, 'Annotating and Indexing Natural Philosophy', in Marina Frasca-Spada and Nick Jardine (eds.), *Books and the Sciences in History* (Cambridge: Cambridge University Press, 2000), pp. 69–89; William H. Sherman, *Used Books. Marking Readers in Renaissance England* (Philadelphia: University of Pennsylvania Press, 2008); Petra Feuerstein-Herz, "Von heimlichkeit der natur'. Benutzungsspuren in alchemischen Anleitungsbüchern', in *Medium Buch* 1 (2019), pp. 45–67; Tobias Winnerling, 'Das Kräuterbuch als

show that recipes were altered by readers. Some contain underlining, corrections and additional recipes, sometimes personal and copied from other texts including corrections, or reader judgements such as 'very good'.

On the basis of copies from the holdings at the Herzog August Library Petra Feuerstein-Herz (Wolfenbüttel) makes it clear that books can be much more than a mere reading medium, as they still contain a lively discourse that is often expressed in imperatives, as 'take' (Nimb) and 'do' (Thu) in printed texts are becoming 'check' (Prüff) and 'note' (Merckh) among the handwritten annotations left by readers in the margins of surviving copies. Whether for field measurement, distillation or alchemy: the printed copy always included something like a notebook. Procedures and recipes from other books or created by the user himself wander onto the empty spaces of printed pages, the inside covers, endpapers, or even on blank flyleaves bound into the books. Such books, consumables, working tools and reception media all in one, were certainly aimed at a professionally informed audience; pure laymen could do little with such books.

No fewer than 27 copies of Gregor Reisch's *Margarita Philosophica* written in the 1490s by Gregor Reisch and first published in 1503 are kept in the University of Glasgow Library, 21 of them from the Ferguson collection. For Robert MacLean (Glasgow) this is a welcome opportuniuty to go in search of clues, not least to find out how how-to thought also found expression in this encyclopedic handbook for students. The *Margarita*, richly decorated with striking woodcuts on the seven liberal arts, offered young people practical insights in techniques required in various professions. Annotations in every second copy, then recurring navigation aids such as bookmarks still testify today to how intensively this treatise has been used. The know-how of astrology conveyed through the frontal view of a naked zodiac man was to be counteracted by massive interventionby official censors or some users, who felt offended.

6   Entanglements of Jotted, Printed and Digital Steps

The issue of media change, whether from orality to writing or from handwriting to printing, always means that the different media continue to exist side

---

frühneuzeitliches Gebrauchs-Objekt', in Friederike Elias, Albrecht Franz, Henning Murmann, and Ulrich Wilhelm Weiser (eds.), *Praxeologie. Beiträge zur interdisziplinären Reichweite praxistheoretischer Ansätze in den Geistes- und Sozialwissenschaften* (Berlin: de Gruyter, 2014), pp. 165–199.

by side in manifold connections.[49] It is obvious that the invention of writing, paper as well as printing, did not lead to people no longer communicating orally with each other any more than the emergence of radio and television led to the disappearance of the book or newspapers. Old media incorporate new ones, process them further, change them, but hardly superceded them, a process that presents itself in a completely new way in the digital age.[50]

How this overlap, the interplay of oral, handwritten and printed components can be studied in more detail was the subject of Sven Limbeck (Wolfenbüttel). He raised the question of what recipes are, what their codification means, and how they relate to books. In doing so, he found that the actual medium of the recipe is not so much the book as the loose leaf of indeterminate format, the handwritten notes. This pragmatic form of the recipe with indication, ingredients and instructions is hardly to be found in the Wolfenbüttel collections. Rather, one encounters printed recipe collections or recipe booklets, in which text and medium correspond, since the print dispositif presupposes the conceptual reproduction of texts. On the other hand, in manuscript mixtures typical of the late Middle Ages, discrepancies in recipe records are conspicuous, especially when the recipes or recipe collections do not form a recognizable thematic connection with the rest of the manuscript's contents.

Tillmann Taape (Berlin), former member of the *Making and Knowing Project* at Columbia University, traces a broad medial arc from an anonymous sixteenth century instructional manuscript (BnF Ms. Fr. 640) to its comprehensive analysis with the digital tools available to us today. This dense and vivid instruction book from France on the production of fancy objects for the Kunstkammer, documents the material practices of an ongoing work-in-progress, including numerous additions and corrections based on trial and error ('texts of action'). First, Taape focuses on the how-to of digital translation. The digital medium is predestined to present the materiality and genesis of the manuscript, from composition to later additions and subsequent material interventions, much more comprehensively and clearly than a traditional print edition. But there is

---

49   See by proxy many other studies Asa Briggs and Peter Burke (with Espen Ytreberg), *A Social History of the Media. From Gutenberg to Facebook.* Fourth Edition (Cambridge: Polity, 2020).

50   The printed book in particular becomes the stage for media change: Jan-Dirk Müller, 'Der Körper des Buches. Zum Medienwechsel zwischen Handschrift und Druck', in Hans Ulrich Gumbrecht and Karl Ludwig Pfeiffer (eds.), *Materialität der Kommunikation* (Frankfurt a. M.: Suhrkamp, 1988), pp. 203–217. See to the relationship of text and hypertext Eva Martha Eckkrammer, *Medizin für den Laien: Vom Pesttraktat zum digitalen Ratgebertext* (Berlin: Frank&Timme, 2016), pp. 1074–1080.

also great potential on the opposite side. In the tailwind of a burgeoning cultural studies, responsible for everything that has to do with the transformation and refinement of materials, recipes from the sixteenth century can always actually be tried out by researchers of our time which generates surprising insights into the early modern understanding of nature and matter.

Simone Zweifel (Sankt Gallen) takes a close look at encyclopaedically oriented recipe books and their conditions of production. Collaboration was essential for the making of books. This 'how-to' of the how-to books includes, among other things, the correspondence procuring texts, the transport of these books to the printer, the reading and the decision about which text passages should be copied, the ordering of these passages, the decision about the addressee of a dedication letter, the negotiations with a printer about price and actual printing, the printing itself and finally the sale of a book. These processes become particularly clear in Johann Jacob Wecker's *De Secretis libri XVII* (Basel 1582), which contains text fragments from different epochs, regions and knowledge traditions. Various actors as well as material constraints and external factors were involved in this heterogeneous text production. They formed, Zweifel argues, 'compilation networks', without which these kinds of books would never have come into being.

7   Text and Image Simultaneity

Particular attention has been paid to the importance of the visual in these sources.[51] Among these are above all graphic figures often in the style of technical drawings and diagrams at the interface between seeing and knowing, image and text.[52] A variety of graphic designs helps the reader and viewer to

---

51   Ernst H. Gombrich, 'Bildliche Anleitungen', in Martin Schuster and Bernard Woschek (eds.), *Nonverbale Kommunikation durch Bilder* (Stuttgart: Verlag für Angewandte Psychologie, 1989), pp. 123–142; Laurence Grove: 'Emblems and Impact', in Ingrid Hoepel and Simon McKeown (eds.), *Emblems and Impact. Volume I: Von Zentrum und Peripherie der Emblematik* (Newcastle upon Tyne: Cambridge Scholars Publishing, 2017), pp. 1–23; Birgit Emich, 'Bildlichkeit und Intermedialität in der Frühen Neuzeit. Eine interdisziplinäre Spurensuche', *Zeitschrift für historische Forschung*, 35 (2008), pp. 31–56.

52   Steffen Bogen and Felix Thürlimann, 'Jenseits der Opposition von Text und Bild. Überlegungen zu einer Theorie des Diagramms und des Diagrammatischen', in Alexander Patschovsky (ed.), *Die Bildwelt der Diagramme Joachims von Fiore. Zur Medialität religiös-politischer Programme im Mittelalter* (Ostfildern: Thorbecke, 2003), pp. 1–22; Sybille Krämer, 'Zwischen Anschauung und Denken. Zur epistemologischen Bedeutung des Graphismus', in Joachim Bromad and Guido Kreis (eds.), *Was sich nicht sagen lässt. Das Nicht-Begriffliche in Wissenschaft, Kunst und Religion* (Berlin: De Gruyter, 2010),

form a picture of complex technical processes.[53] Infographic approaches in particular were to become increasingly popular. As soon as the illustration was linked to explanatory texts by markings, by letter and number references, the image message could be didactically controlled, just as the author and publisher intended. Schematic pictures of ovens and equipment in the style of technical drawings invited the reader to copy them. Sometimes 'directing instructions' in how-to books rely on pictorialised sequences of action, reminiscent of comics or storyboards.[54]

Laurence Grove (Glasgow) (and his co-author Stefan Laube (Berlin) who is responsible for many a relevant find in the libraries) analogized emblematic illustrations from the Baroque era with the cutaways that became popular after 1945, especially in Great Britain but also in France, almost always linked to the text via a caption key, a visual trick that was already used with virtuosity by Georg Agricola in his main work *De re metallica* (Basel 1556). Grove's leading question is a how-to question that has become the signature of modernity. How can people become birds, how can we manage to keep people in the air and move them around? These are questions that only the twentieth century solved satisfactorily. In the Early Modern Era, flying was always a spiritual matter of reaching heavenly realms with the help of a vehicle. Three centuries later, the English weekly *Eagle*, published from 1950 to 1969, became famous for showing the inner workings of aeroplanes and rockets. For all the differences between aerial illustrations in the early modern period and after 1945, both types of images were about a transcending journey of discovery: both times the invisible is made visible through diagrammatic processes. Jesuit printed books and comics of knowledge shake hands.

To view recipes exclusively from the perspective of practicality would ignore other relevant motivations in this genre, according to the thesis of Andrea van Leerdam (Utrecht). In *Den sack der consten*, a collection of recipes

---

pp. 172–193; Marcus Popplow, 'Why Draw Pictures of Machines? The Social Context of Early Modern Machine Drawings', in Wolfgang Lefèvre (ed.), *Picturing Machines 1400–1700* (Cambridge, Mass.: MIT Press, 2004), pp. 17–50.

53 Clemens Schwender, 'Abbildungen zu Instruktionszwecken', in Clemens Schwender, Jakob Dittmar and Hans Prengel (eds), *Abbild – Modell – Simulation*, Technical Writing vol. 6 (Frankfurt am Main: Lang, 2005), pp. 9–37; Gottfried Boehm, 'Bildbeschreibung. Über die Grenzen von Bild und Sprache', in Gottfried Boehm and Helmut Pfotenhauer, *Beschreibungskunst – Kunstbeschreibung* (Munich: Fink, 1995), pp. 23–40.

54 Laurence Grove, 'Jesuit Emblems and Catholic Comics', in G. Richard Dimler, Pedro F. Campa, and Peter M. Daly (eds.), *Emblematic Images and Religious Texts: Studies in Honor of G. Richard Dimler, s.j.* (Philadelphia: St. Joseph's University Press, 2010), pp. 253–273; Lilli Fischel, *Bilderfolgen im frühen Buchdruck. Studien zur Inkunabel-Illustration in Ulm und Straßburg* (Stuttgart: Thorbecke, 1963).

and instructions printed in Dutch in the years 1528 and 1537, she makes it clear that pedagogical objectives are linked with entertaining elements, making the numerous woodcuts far more than mere decorations. Using research approaches to social conventions, she is able to show how much certain recipes can deviate from the conventional standard. On the one hand, the script adheres to various 'books of secrets' conventions through its presentation as a collection of individual recipes (each marked by an indented first line and a paragraph mark, with no visual distinction between serious and joking recipes); on the other hand, it playfully breaks these conventions through the presence of mocking recipes as well as quirky recipes that aim for the impossible. The reuse of pictorial motifs (or even the physical wooden blocks) that also appear in other works can be interpreted as a play with conventions as well. Like the recipes themselves, the pictures are a hodgepodge, with no clear coherence in their arrangement, a colourful mixture of texts and pictures, perhaps reminiscent of today's lifestyle magazines.

8   Prescription and Improvisation

In the last section of the conference, we addressed a theme that is located beyond written and also visual descriptions, the area of actual implementation, as difficult to grasp as it is necessary to deal with.[55] Following the motto 'We know more than we can say' (Michael Polanyi) the associated publications were usually never so detailed, never so concretely formulated, that they could actually have been implemented, which is especially true with unfamiliar practices and new complex technical procedures.[56] With the written genre of the advice manual on the one hand one obviously follows rules, but on the other hand it opens up space for improvisation by entering the realm of silent

---

55   In the meantime, the research field of 'historical praxeology' has emerged in Germany, see Dagmar Freist, 'Diskurse – Körper – Artefakte. Historische Praxeologie in der Frühneuzeitforschung – eine Annäherung', in Dagmar Freist (ed.), *Diskurse – Körper – Artefakte. Historische Praxeologie in der Frühneuzeitforschung* (Bielefeld: transcript, 2015), pp. 9–33; Lucas Haasis and Constantin Rieske, 'Historische Praxeologie. Eine Einführung', in *Historische Praxeologie. Dimensionen vergangenen Handelns* (Paderborn: Schöningh, 2015), S. 7–55.

56   Annie Gray, "A Practical Art': An Archeological Perspective on the Use of Recipe Books', in Michelle DiMeo and Sara Pennell (eds.), *Reading and writing recipe books 1550–1800*, (Manchester: Manchester University Press 2013), pp. 47–67; Reinhold Reith, 'Know-how, Technologietransfer und die Arcana Artis im Mitteleuropa der Frühen Neuzeit', *Early Science and Medicine*,10 (2005), pp. 349–377; Carlo M. Cipolla, 'The Diffusion of Innovations in Early Modern Europe', *Comparative Studies in Society and History*, 14 (1972), pp. 46–52.

knowledge.[57] If their reading is performatively oriented and can be completely detached from the source, as current research states, then the still largely unanswered question of where exactly the tipping points might be where practices become independent of the source.

A linguistic semiotic point of view can bring light into this elusive field. Laura Balbiani (Milan) examined recipes from this perspective using the example of two representative printed compilations by Giovan Battista Della Porta (Naples 1558, extended version: 1589) and Isabella Cortese (Venice 1561). In doing so, Balbiani distinguished two levels: the level of more passive reading (where an author and a reader interact), and the level of execution. For the passive reader, the added value of the recipe would be that it is placed in a broader narrative program fuelled by curiosity and the desire for pleasure. On the level of performance, the expectation would be attached to a cognitive effort (deciphering the secrets of the recipe: a 'knowing-wanting'), but which manifests itself entirely in performance, in the acquisition of certain skills (a 'doing-ability'). In this performative respect, it must always be taken into account that the cognitive gap cannot be completely overcome. This shows, for example, the not easy problem of dosage (which early modern recipes often leave to the performer). Again and again, it can be seen that important information is missing from the texts, so that the question arose as to whether the imperative in 'recipe' is to be understood literally or whether a genre of entertainment literature was created here, which always also conveys diverse general knowledge.

No recipe without wish fulfilment, without magic, so to speak. The article of Sergei Zotov (Warwick) deals with spell books (grimoires) that in contrast to the more theoretical-philosophical occult literature are practical ritual texts, how-to texts, that give very specific instructions on how the magician can harness spiritual and demonic powers for himself. Zotov explores the use of incense, perfumes, and other fragrances since the practice of suffumigation was a common element of many grimoires, scents and smells as subtle substances rising up towards the sky, to the abode of the gods and demons. One could say that grimoires implied a kind of olfactory communication between the magician and demons or angels. Grimoires not only contained magical invocations; they were magical objects themselves, which is often highlighted in long enumerations of the sorcerer's tools, among which there is always a book. In some books, there were special empty spaces where the owner of the

---

57   Neil Gascoigne and Tim Thornton, *Tacit Knowledge* (Preston: University of Central Lancashire 2013); Harry M. Collins: *Tacit and Explicit Knowledge* (Chicago: The Chicago University Press, 2010).

manuscript or the printed book should put their signature. Most of the magic books were in pocket size, which made it easier to carry the book during rituals.

The contribution by Britta-Julian Kruse (Wolfenbüttel) shows that the sheet of paper with instructions was usually integrated into a material-performative setting. The focus is on a 'home, travel and field pharmacy' of a Guelph duchess, in which several how-to dimensions can be read: the operation of a medicine chest with its various compartments and drawers had to be mastered as well as the identification of the ingredients stored in vessels. Here was a handy framework set to implement the prescriptions handwritten by the doctor. The author of the action-oriented explanations was Caspar Neefe (1514–1579), professor of medicine in Leipzig and Saxon personal physician. It was not only the duchess who was to receive medical care, but also the sick in her court. The performative act of applying the prescriptions could take place without a doctor being present or as a short-term measure for first aid before a doctor arrived.

Are there is something like a typology hidden in the four focal points of the workshop, which help us to get a better grip on the topic of the how-to books? We assume so, but further, systematic research will be necessary.[58] At the very least, the elastic expressiveness inherent in the how-to category is more than merely hinted at by the various perspectives from which how-to books are examined in the eleven contributions of this volume: thus, cheap tracts come into view as products of existential crises (S. Laube). Tracts can serve as a handwritten recording medium that is far removed from the original content (P. Feuerstein-Herz). The how-to idea can also be hidden in classical works that have not been classified under this genre so far (R. MacLean). No medium is more appropriate to know-how than a piece of paper on which a recipe is spontaneously written down (S. Limbeck). Nowadays it is possible to extract added value from such texts through digital indexing and performative reconstruction (T. Taape). The implementation, the trial and error, is increasingly in the background the more extensive and encyclopaedic the how-to books became; rather, in their book production, the know-how consists of having text modules at one's disposal and skilfully putting them together (S. Zweifel). In richly illustrated treatises, pictures with their explanations have the function of making the concealed visible (L. Grove), if they do not immediately thwart

---

58   A joint proposal based on the holdings of the University of Glasgow Library and the Herzog August Bibliothek Wolfenbüttel was submitted in February 2023 and approved in early November 2023 as part of the *UK-Gerrman funding initiative for the humanities* by the DFG and the AHRC; the applicants are Laurence Grove (Glasgow) and Stefan Laube (Berlin).

expectations and serve to entertain and amuse (A. van Leerdam). Books can be like little living creatures, from how-to tracts that address the reader directly the message goes out: 'Take me and Make It Happen!' In this dazzling realm of wishful realisation, it is always a matter of keeping the gap to 'tacit knowledge' as small as possible (L. Balbiani). In this respect, it is anything but surprising that grimoires are bursting with how-to formulas (S. Zotov), and written advice in a handy medical cabinet can even make a trained doctor superfluous (B. Kruse). While it is not possible to cover the full range of instructions manuals in this publication, tracts on plague and medical arts, distillation, metalworking techniques, flying machines, games and entertainment, and magic can be taken as telling examples. In addition, there are insights of technological know-how in encyclopaedic textbooks as well as how-to hints in the creation of book compilations.

How to-knowledge has obviously a 'problem-solving potential',[59] composed of sequenced procedures, often conveyed with intermediality in an inviting tone. This publication has set out to reflect on how-to books only theoretically, the actual (multi-sensual) testing of recipes is reserved for further research efforts. For the analytical philosopher Gilbert Ryle, 'how-to' is the fundamental knowledge even for theoretical approaches, because rational thinking only works well if you have practised it, if you have mastered the 'how-to' of thinking.

---

59 Jürgen Renn, *The Evolution of Knowledge. A Rethinking of Sciene for the Anthropocene* (Princeton/Oxford: Princeton University Press, 2020), p. 64.

CHAPTER 1

Can There Ever Be Clueless Advice Books? Remarks on Plague Tracts

Stefan Laube

1   500 Years Ago: an Example from the Middle of Germany

'Eine Unterweisung wie man sich zu der Zeit der Pestilentz verhalten soll' [Instruction how to behave at the time of the plague] is the title of an anonymous tract that left the press of a Leipzig printing workshop at the beginning of April 1521.[1] There is now no doubt about the authorship of Ulrich Rülein von Calw. With him, we have before us an all-round personality such as only the Renaissance could produce. Rülein was a physician, mathematician, mining engineer and mayor.[2] As a town planner, he played a major role in the founding of Annaberg in the Ore Mountains [Erzgebirge]. As author of the *Bergbüchlein* he is well known for the world's first non-fiction book on mining, which first appeared around 1505.[3] Sixteen years later, Rülein is active as the author of a pestilential treatise.

The plague is a modern epidemic, its spread the result of extensive trade relations in the Eurasian region. What today are Far Eastern business travelers in Europe were then sailors returning from the Crimea on Genoese merchant ships. The transmission route was millions of times from the rat via the flea to

---

1 Facsimile of this document at Wilhelm Pieper, *Ulrich Rülein von Calw und sein Bergbüchlein* (Berlin: Akademie, 1955), pp. 55–61.

2 Gundolf Keil, "ein kleiner Leonardo'. Ulrich Rülein von Kalbe als Humanist, Mathmatiker, Montanwissenschaftler und Arzt', in Gundolf Keil (ed.), *Würzburger Fachprosa-Studien. Beiträge zur mittelalterlichen Medizin-, Pharmazie- und Standesgeschichte aus dem Würzburger medizinhistorischen Institut* (Würzburg: Königshausen&Neumann, 1995), pp. 228–247; see also Carlo Cipolla, *Public Health and the Medical Profession in the Renaissance* (Cambridge: Cambridge University Press, 1976).

3 It was still attested 'a great literary interest' by mining engineer Herbert Hoover – who was to be elected the 31st president of the USA in 1929 – when he translated and commented on Georg Agricola's *De re metallica* together with his wife, the accomplished geologist Lou Henry. Herbert C. Hoover and Lou H. Hoover (eds. and transl.), *Georgius Agricola, De re metallica* (London: Salisbury House, 1912), p. 60.

FIGURE 1.1   [Ulrich Rülein van Calw], Ein Unterwysung wie man sich tzu der Tzeit der
Pestilentz halten sol Allen einwoneren der stat Freybergk tzu gut yn einn kurtze
summe gebracht (Leipzig: Schumann, 1521), Wolfenbüttel, Herzog August
Bibliothek, N 96.40 Helmst. (5)
PHOTO: AUTHOR

the human being.[4] After the pandemic in the mid-fourteenth century, which,
according to estimates, claimed the lives of a third of the European population, the Black Death became endemic. In local epidemics, the plague broke
out at almost regular intervals over the next three centuries. In 1521, it reached
Freiberg at the foot of the Ore Mountains.[5]

There was no therapy, but there were rules of conduct.[6] The advice given in
Rülein von Calw's plague treatise shows the helplessness of the medical pro-
fession, which adhered to the four-fluid doctrine, in the face of the plague.
Since Hippocrates, diseases were considered as disturbances in the mixing

---

4   It was not until 1894 that the Swiss physician Alexandre Yersin succeeded in isolating the
    plague bacterium and identifying the route of transmission.
5   Stefan Monecke, Hannelore Monecke and Jochen Monecke, 'Die Pest in Freiberg 1613–1614',
    Mitteilungen des Freiberger Altertumsvereins, 100 (2007), pp. 139–169.
6   Gerhard F. Strasser, "Niemals nüchter und niemals voll tut in Sterbens-Läufften wohl'. Der
    Stellenwert der Affekte in der Pest-Prophylaxe nach 1348' in Johann Anselm Steiger (ed.),
    Passion, Affekt und Leidenschaft in der frühen Neuzeit, vol. 2 (Wiesbaden: Harrassowitz, 2005),
    pp. 1079–1089.

ratio of the humors (blood, phlegm, green and black bile). This concept was maintained for over 2,000 years, so that even in the eighteenth century scabies was still interpreted as a disorder of the body juices, even though its causative agent, a mite, could be seen with the naked eye. Other theories pointing to the future, such as that of the Italian physician Girolamo Fracastoro of the small, contagious pathogens (1546), failed to gain acceptance, which made it difficult for a long time to introduce defense strategies against infectious diseases.[7] In accordance with the tradition going back to Hippocrates and Galen, Rülein gives a series of dietary recommendations and lifestyle advice (A good clear beer is more useful to drink than a strong wine. He who sleeps at night should not sleep during the day), which are supposed to restore the balance of the juices, but which are completely ineffective in the face of the plague. For therapy, bloodletting (the vein closest to the ulcer) and then a little juice from a pomegranate are given. Apple juice, theriac (a universal antidote) or 'mercurium precipitatum' can also be administered. In addition, there were plague barbers who also cut plague bumps. Until the introduction of antibiotics, this was the only possibility of therapy, had a pain-relieving effect and could actually lead to a cure, if the pathogen did not spread in the blood as a result of the procedure.

According to the mayor of Freiberg 'temporal flight' was the best remedy in the event of an outbreak of the plague. For all those who do not want to leave their stores, Rülein recommends moderate eating and drinking. In particular, it is important to avoid bloody food. The fact that food should be made a little sour with vinegar is certainly still a sensible measure for reducing infection today. It seems like today's anti-COVID appeals when Rülein urges people to avoid large gatherings of people. In addition, dwellings should be kept free of any stench, preferably with the help of frankincense, myrrh and juniper. In places where large numbers of people congregate, such as churches and bathhouses, incense should be burned. In general, open fires help against putrefaction in the air. Everything that comes from the sick person, such as breath, sweat, excrement and urine is harmful, as well as the clothes of the sick person, his bedding and other intimate things. Probably without this good

---

7   Karl-Heinz Leven, *Die Geschichte der Infektionskrankheiten. Von der Antike bis zum 20. Jahrhundert*, (Landsberg: ecomed, 1997), pp. 33–39; Benjamin Wallura, 'About what is Right in Times of Plague. Contagious Debates in Philosophy, Medicine, Law, and Theology at the University of Helmstedt, 1681–83' in Peter Hess (ed.), Managing Pandemics in Early Modern Germany, Spektrum. Publications of the German Studies Association (New York: Bergahn Books [to be published in 2024]).

advice, more than 2,000 plague victims would have died in Freiberg.[8] In the appendix, Rülein does not fail to point out that mercy should be shown to the sick, even if they lose their senses. Stinginess in the crisis was not his thing: the authorities should reward the nurses ' abundantly', because: 'One does not have to kiss the penny so often in the hard times as the money fools tend to do at other times'.[9]

2 Then and Nowadays

Today, our understanding of the plague and other contagious diseases has since been shaped by the explanatory model of bacteriology.[10] Crucial to this is the idea that there is a very specific cause of this plague that can be determined with certainty, defined by precisely this pathogen.[11] If it is not detectable, then it is not that disease. In the media, this has been visualised in the COVID period by the omnipresent image of the model of a spiky virus. Whether or not the virus looks anything like that under an electron microscope is secondary. Rather, it is always about satisfying the thirst for knowledge and imagination, which is directed at something that is not visible at all.[12]

The plague of the pre-modern era was miasma, the result of negative planetary constellations, it was dyscrasia, poison, supposedly thrown into the wells by Jews, the work of evil in the world and divine punishment. Physicians mostly followed the ancient teachings of Galen and Hippocrates and thus a humoral pathology that was not very appropriate. In the case of the plague in particular, it was assumed that there was contamination of the air by

---

8   The high death toll prompted the Saxon Duke Henry the Pious to designate the 'Donatskirchhof', located outside the city walls, as the general cemetery in his 'Plague Ordinance' instead of numerous burial sites within the city.

9   'Wann mus in der schwere tzeyt un grosse Noth den pfennigk nicht als offt kussenn als die gelt narren tzuandern Tzeyten pflegen tzu thun.' Ulrich Rülein von Calw, *Eine Unterweisung wie man sich zu der Zeit der Pestilentz verhalten soll* (Leipzig: Schumann, 1521), nach Pieper, *Ulrich Rülein von Calw*, p. 61.

10   Flea bites transmitted the classic bubonic plague, which had an incubation period of up to six days, after which the lymph nodes quickly swelled to form the typical bumps.

11   Katharina Wolff, *Die Theorie der Seuche. Krankheitskonzepte und Pestbewältigung im Mittelalter* (Stuttgart: Steiner, 2021); Martin Dinges, 'Neue Wege in der Seuchengeschichte? Einleitung' in Marten Dinges and Thomas Schlich (eds.), *Neue Wege in der Seuchengeschichte* (Stuttgart: Steiner, 1995), pp. 7–24.

12   The bacteriologist Robert Koch also had such great success with the scientific community and later with the general public because he was able to make pathogens visible.

certain pathological vapors, pathogenic 'miasms'.[13] Explanatory models from
the history of medicine, which could not be more different, lead to comparable conclusions in the behavior of society: 'what cannot be cured must be
endured.' We found ourselves in this awkward situation as members of highly
technological societies for many months until research succeeded in producing effective vaccines. What a time, and with consequences for the history of
media and knowledge that we can hardly foresee today, as Nils Minkmar from
the *Süddeutsche Zeitung* put out:

> What was unique about the past few months was the global practice of
> scientific education. There had often been talk of an information revo-
> lution, but now it could be experienced in everyday life. Almost in sync
> with research, the public learned everything about pathogens, preven-
> tion, therapy, and finally vaccines. Aerosol models were studied, the paths
> of the virus were explained in cartoons, documentaries showed the suf-
> fering of the sick, the news reported the various waves and stages, and
> scientists became stars.[14]

In a new emergency situation, the consequences of which cannot be estimated, it is of course extremely important to be able to formulate and convey
reasonably comprehensible advice, because this is the only way to create the
impression of a community capable of taking action. The authority of being
able to instruct something at all creates trust and brings society together. One
side orders and recommends, the other side follows, complies with the advice
as best it can, especially since simple measures such as wearing a mask, keeping
a distance and washing hands were immediately understood by most people
and were reasonably effective. The alternative would be apathetic indifference
or reckless disregard.

While the implementation of instructions in itself acts like a cure in a crisis that suddenly erupts, one question does not seem to arise at all. How far

---

13   Gerd Schwerhoff, *Die Pest in der Frühen Neuzeit – Ein ferner Spiegel. Oder: Was lehrt uns
      der Blick in die Geschichte* [https://tu-dresden.de/gsw/phil/powi/dpb/studium/lehrveran
      staltungen/die-pest-in-der-fruehen-neuzeit-ein-ferner-spiegel] (accessed 8 May 2022).

14   'Das Einzigartige an den vergangenen Monaten war die globale Praxis der wissen-
      schaftlichen Weiterbildung. Oft war schon von einer Informationsrevolution die Rede
      gewesen, nun konnte man sie im Alltag erleben. Nahezu synchron mit der Forschung
      erfuhr die Öffentlichkeit alles über Erreger, Prävention, Therapie, schließlich über die
      Impfstoffe. Aerosolmodelle wurden studiert, die Wege des Virus in Trickfilmen erklärt,
      Dokumentationen zeigten das Leid der Kranken, die Nachrichten meldeten die ver-
      schiedenen Wellen und Stadien, und Wissenschaftler und Wissenschaftlerinnen wurden
      zu Stars.' Nils Minkmar, 'Beibt alles anders', *Süddeutsche Zeitung*, 19 June 2021.

should the new instructions go, how long should they last? That is why people dutifully wore masks even in rather deserted pedestrian zones, like the one in Wolfenbüttel in these times, or rolled bulky shopping carts into the supermarket, even if they do not want to buy more than a bottle of milk. Or, as practiced in the Herzog August Library: books that have been borrowed are first sent into quarantine for several days! Books seem to be something like living beings after all.[15] And at conferences here, there are coffee breaks without coffee. Why, you may perhaps ask? This is due to the push button of the thermos, which every coffee drinker has to touch. A bon mot by cultural historian Keith Thomas may come to mind: 'If magic is to be defined as the employment of ineffective techniques to allay anxiety when effective ones are not available, then we must recognize that no society will ever be free from it.'[16]

'Those who don't study history are doomed to repeat it. Yet those who *do* study history are doomed to stand by helplessly while everyone else repeats it.'[17] Although, when it comes to lessons from history, I actually tend to follow the wisdom of a wise historian in an armchair from a cartoon in *The New Yorker*, a look at the past does not seem devoid of meaning. Such a retrospective can be motivated in different ways: we can emphasise the differences, such as wrong reactions at the time and a lack of knowledge on the part of contemporaries, in order to highlight our comparatively privileged situation.[18] Or we can look for familiar patterns in the past, according to the motto: That is how it was back then, that is how it always is in times of epidemics!

A comparison of the stock of images across the epochs alone brings surprising analogies to light. The FFP2 masks, sometimes pointed, may recall naturalistic beak masks with which doctors in Italy tried to protect themselves in plague times. The spiky COVID-19 virus is reminiscent of the arrows by which the plague saint St. Sebastian was pricked, iconographically immortalized a thousand times over. Both arrow and virus are prickly creatures that trigger defense in the viewer: please spare me, please do not touch me! The digital

---

15 The quarantining of books was a major feature of times of epidemics in the early years of public libraries in the late nineteenth century: see Gerald S. Greenberg, 'Books as Disease Carriers, 1880–1920', *Libraries & Culture*, 23 (1988), pp. 281–294. The rules of the *Coats' Public Library, Stenness, 1905* included: Books may be refused to parties dwelling in houses where infectious disease exists. I thank Andrew Pettegree for this reference.

16 Keith Thomas, *Religion and the Decline of Magic* (London: Penguin, 1973,) p. 800.

17 Cartoon by Tom Toro, *The New Yorker*, 13 March 2017.

18 Schwerhoff, *Die Pest in der Frühen Neuzeit*; Etienne François: 'Eine Krise ohne Beispiel?' in *Corona Stories. Pandemische Entwürfe* (Darmstadt: Wissenschaftliche Buchgesellschaft, 2020), pp. 92–122.

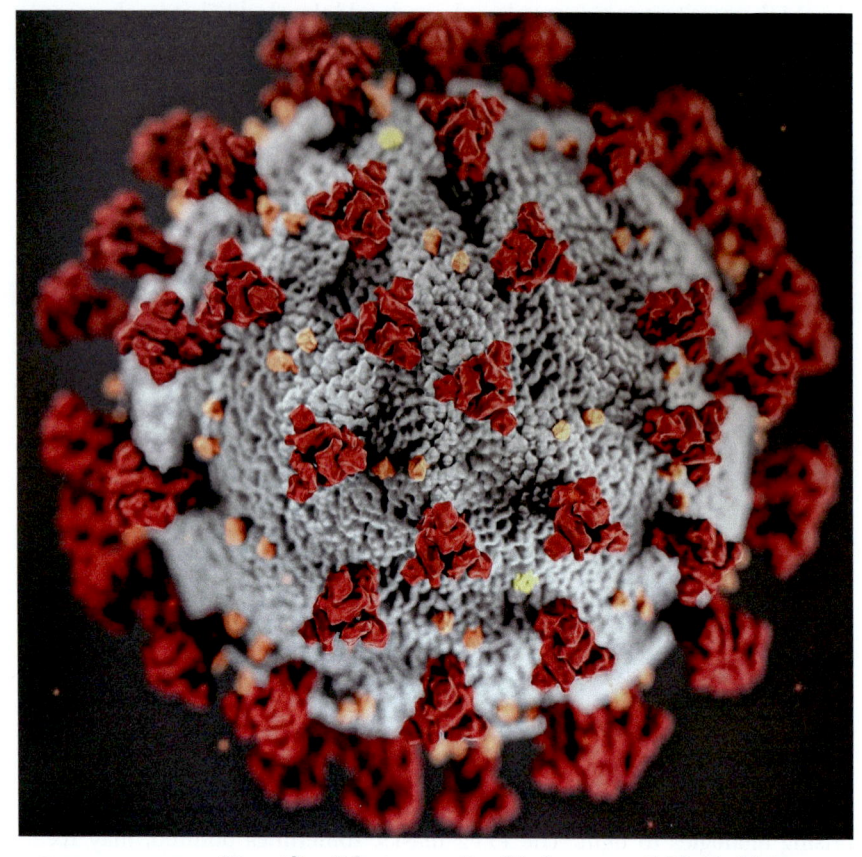

FIGURE 1.2   COVID 19-Virus, Alissa Eckert, MSMI; Dan Higgins, MAMS; Public Health Image
                     Library, Centers for Disease Control and Prevention, U.S. Government, 2020,
                     Wellcome Collection, Anna Esvcardó and Julius Wiedemann (eds.), Science
                     Illustration. A History of Visual Knowledge from the 15th Century to Today (Köln:
                     Taschen, 2023), p. 313

image as developed from the U.S. Center for Disease Control (CDC) by Allissa
Eckert and Dan Higgins became the icon of the virus: gray with red antennae.

The red S proteins of the virus have been deliberately highlighted in the
image, although the M proteins are more numerous. The S proteins are
responsible for the spread of the virus. The visualization of bullet monsters
was intended to accentuate the danger of the infection.[19] At the interface of
popular knowledge and professional knowledge, clarity and certainty have a
special significance. Fictitious pictorial constructions emerge that are not so
different from illustrations the immunologist and sociologist of knowledge

---

19   Birgit Ulrike Münch, 'Die Macht der Krankheits-Bilder. Seuchen in der Kunst', in
        Forschung&Lehre 4/21, pp. 282–284.

FIGURE 1.3 Plague in Lucches, *c.*1400, manuscript illumination, in Giovanni Sercambi, *Croniche*, Lucca, Archivio di Stato, MS 107, fol. 340r

Ludwik Fleck came across almost a hundred years ago.[20] Anyway, is it not more 'delightful' to receive an arrow from heavenly putti,[21] than to be taken away by army trucks queuing up because the local cemeteries are overcrowded?![22]

20   The following scene was depicted on a poster: In the immediate vicinity of a child, evil germs in the form of little devils fly out of the open mouth of a coughing person, Ludwik Fleck, *Entstehung und Entwicklung einer wissenschaftlichen Tatsache* [1935], eds. with an introduction by Lothar Schäfer and Thomas Schnelle (Frankfurt am Main: Suhrkamp, 1980), p. 154. See also Brigitte Weinzierl, 'Viren visualisieren: Bildgebung und Popularisierung', in Ruth Mayer and Brigitte Weinzierl (eds.), *Virus! Mutation einer Metapher* (Bielefeld: transcript, 2004), pp. 97–131.

21   Around 1400, as an illustration of the report on the plague of 1348, a mass death appears in the chronicle of Giovanni Sercambi, an apothecary from Lucca. The dying people collapsing are hit by arrows shot by two winged demons. The disease appears as punishment, but at the same time symbolizes evil in general, see Louise Marshall, 'God's Executioners: Angels, Devils and the Plague in Giovanni Sercambi's Illustrated *Chronicle* (1400)', in Jennifer Spinks and Charles Zika (eds.), *Disaster, Death and the Emotions in the Shadow of the Apocalypse, 1400–1700* (Basingstoke: Palgrave Macmillan, 2016), pp. 177–200.

22   See the iconic photo from Bergamo in March 2020: 'Diese schrecklichen Bilder – wie ein junger Italiener unsere Sicht auf das Coronavirus verändert hat' in *Neue Zürcher Zeitung*, 30 May 2020; see also https://www.zispotlight.de/frank-fehrenbach-ueber-das-bild-aus -bergamo-oder-the-common-bond-is-the-movie-theatre/ (accessed 2 May 2021); Karen Fromm, 'Leeres Zentrum – periphere Bilder. Die visuelle Berichterstattung zur Corona-epidemie', in Felix Koltermann (ed.), *Corona und die journalisitische Bildkommunikation. Praktiken und Diskurse des Visuellen* (Baden-Baden: Nomos, 2021), pp. 55–80.

FIGURE 1.4 Army trucks remove the COVID dead in Bergamo because the local cemeteries are
          overcrowded
          PHOTO: SCREENSHOT, MARCH 2020, FOTO: EMANUELE DI TERLIZZI VIA EPA

It is not the place to overdo this comparison. As a prelude to our conference volume, I would like to take a casual look at plague tracts of the early modern period, which I hope will kill two birds with one stone. On the one hand, this provides us with an extremely suitable case study for our topic of 'how-to tracts' [Rezepte-Büchlein] and on the other hand, we can use the multifaceted nature of this exemplary genre to provide systematic clues as to what this volume of essays is about.

3   Books – Small and Short

With about one thousand printed texts from the fifteenth to the eighteenth century, the Wolfenbüttel library holds a representative portion of early modern epidemic literature.[23] In addition to medical advice literature, pamphlets and calendars, theological epidemic literature, we can include regulations and decrees from towns and courts. On the title page, the authors advertise promising announcements of rapid and effective help against the deadly threat. Many plague pamphlets are characterized by their brevity, which is already strikingly apparent in the title.

'Kurz' and 'klein' for 'brief' and 'little' – these adjectives mark the wording of titles of pest tracts. Whether *Kurtze Berichte* or *Kurtze Unterweisungen*, nearly 100 relevant titles with the word 'kurz' can be found in the index of printed works published in the German-speaking world, the VD16 and VD17. The physician Philipp Imsser's *PestilentzBüchlein/ Für die armen Handwercks- und Baurs-Leuthe* [Little Book of Pestilence for the Poor Craftsmen and farmer people] from 1680 with the title addendum 'Aufs kürzeste beschrieben' [Described in the briefest possible way]' was a reprint. This simple book had first appeared in 1582. 'Jetzt in Gegenwärtiger Gefährligkeit' [Now in Present Danger], during the great European plague epidemic around 1680, the 'poor people' who found themselves outside 'auf Feldt und Strassen' [in the fields and streets] could be given a simple aid.[24] The motto of these texts was to be comprehensible. Often the contents were arranged in such a way that they could be easily remembered.

This conference volume presents many examples of such inconspicuous, small-format treatises that often convey practical tips from individual fields of knowledge in a few dozen pages. The title often refers to 'Nützlich büchlin' [Useful booklet]. The term 'Büchlein', the German diminutive of the book seems an interesting, frequently occuring category that has not yet been seriously investigated.[25] By the way, what is called 'brevety' is relatively: the size of

23   Petra Feuerstein-Herz, 'Im Druck der Seuchen – Seuchen und Buchdruck in der Frühen Neuzeit am Beispiel der Bestände der Herzog August Bibliothek', in *Gotts verhengnis und seine straffe – Zur Geschichte der Seuchen in der Frühen Neuzeit*, ed. by Petra Feuerstein-Herz, (Wiesbaden: Harrassowitz, 2005), pp. 27–36.

24   Philipp Imsser: Pestilentz Büchlein/ Für die armen Handwercks- und Baurs Leuthe. [without place] 1680.

25   Stefan Laube, 'Wer langweilig ist der kauffe mich'. Beiläufiges zum Büchlein, in *Ephemera. Abgelegenes und Vergängliches in der Kulturgeschichte von Druck und Buch*. Festschrift für Petra Feuerstein-Herz, eds. by Hartmut Beyer and Peter Burschel (Wiesbaden: Harrassowitz, 2022), pp. 115–136.

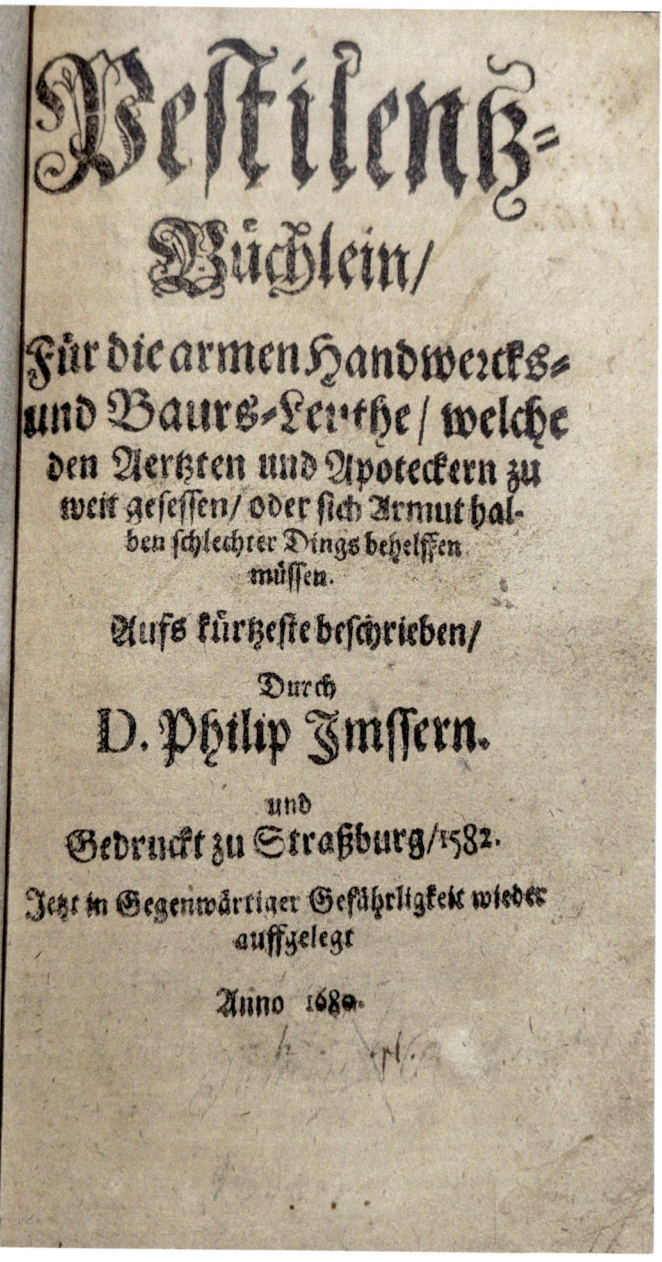

FIGURE 1.5   Philipp Imsser, Pestilentz Büchlein/ Für die armen
             Handwercks- und Baurs Leuthe. [without place] 1680,
             Wolfenbüttel, Herzog August Bibliothek, Xb 265
             PHOTO: AUTHOR

the 75 first editions of the 'Kurtzen Berichte' on plague can vary greatly, ranging from a single sheet to 200 pages.

The plague treatise can be traced back to the 'Plague Consilium' in the fourteenth century, which incorporated the expertise of a second doctor. Almost all European plague literature was influenced by the so-called Plague Consultation, which was prepared by the Medical Faculty of Paris on behalf of Philip VI and completed in October 1348, and which commented on various epidemiological, preventive and therapeutic options for the plague. It consists of two parts. The first part deals with causes and prognoses, whereby the constellation of the planets is seen as the cause and is used for further prognosis. The second part gives therapeutic advice, especially on prophylaxis according to the scheme 'sex res non naturales', and describes surgical therapies.[26] In plague tracts of the printing era their authors presented themselves as experts to a non-specific audience. Plague tracts had an appealing character, they wanted to steer people's behaviour in the right direction. Sometimes the advice is given in rhyming verse so that it can be better remembered.[27] Even in the twenty-first century during the pandemic, there are comparable procedures with pictograms, placards, slogans and also acronyms (like the AHA rules in Germany) related to hygiene measures.[28] Again and again, it is about reminding people simply and quickly of the right behaviour.

Plague tracts: what is it all about?[29] From the last decades of the fifteenth century onwards, these kinds of tracts often replaced medical care, which was increasingly unavailable even in the big cities and was in any case for many unaffordable.[30] The recurring outbreak of plague and the expected sales

---

26   With the plague consilium, a new specialist literature developed in Europe in 1348, which is closely related to the plague regimina. Plague regimina are dietary instructions for doctors and lay people. The two forms of literature intermingle; Klaus Bergdolt, *Der schwarze Tod in Europa. Die große Pest und das Ende des Mittelalters* (Munich: Beck, 1994), pp. 27–30; on the typology of these text genres dealing with the plague Eva Martha Eckkrammer, *Medizin für den Laien: Vom Pesttraktat zum digitalen Ratgebertext*, (Berlin: Frank&Timme, 2016), pp. 135–150.

27   Rhyming speech is an indicator of the continuing relevance of oral channels of communication, especially in the case of instructions on how to behave during the plague, which were read out in public places, Bernhard Dietrich Haage, 'Handschriftenfunde und Nachträge zum Pestgedicht von Hans Andree', *Sudhoffs Archiv*, 63 (1979), pp. 392–406; Georg Sticker, *Die Pest als Seuche und als Plage*, Abhandlungen aus der Seuchengeschichte und Seuchenlehre, vol. II (Gießen: Tölpelmann, 1910), pp. 300–310.

28   A = Abstand (distance), H = Hygiene, A = Alltag mit Maske (daily life with mask).

29   Karl Sudhoff, 'Pestschriften aus den ersten 150 Jahren nach der Epidemie des 'Schwarzen Todes' 1348', *Archiv für Geschichte der Medizin* 5 (1911); Heft 1 and 2.

30   Jean Delumeau, *La peur en Occident: Une cité assiégée* (Paris: Fayard, 1978); Peter Dinzelbacher, *Angst im Mittelalter. Teufels-, Todes- und Gotteserfahrung.*

success encouraged authors, printers and publishers to produce such works already in the age of early book printing, in the age of incunabula. Arnold C. Klebs and Karl Sudhoff showed in the 1920s how strongly plague writings influenced early book printing: they found 25 different plague writings in the 1470s alone, and a rapid increase in the last decades of the sixteenth century, not only in Germany, but also in Italy and France, almost all of them written in the vernacular language.[31] Whenever the plague epidemic overlapped with the technical innovation of printing, it was quite possible that the history of printing began locally with a publication on the proper behaviour in times of plague, as was apparently the case in Ulm.[32] The first printed plague treatise in German Steinhöwel's *Ordnung der Pestilenz* was published in this largely independent city (Reichsstadt) by the first local book printer Johann Zainer at the beginning of 1473, January 11, on 'Montag nach Einhardi'.[33] To date, no Ulm tract from 1472 has turned up, which does not mean that none existed. The list of incunabula published in Ulm also shows that Steinhöwel's plague tract was apparently indeed the first printed manuscript brought to market.[34]

Such sources represent an attempt to take the terror out of the unpredictable plague by explaining its causes, and to alleviate the feeling of powerlessness in view of such deadly despotism. This includes helpful recommendations to all practising colleagues from men of high authority. These classical tracts followed the same pattern: the account of the causes, course of disease, then of the prevention and remedies. Although the thesis of historians such as Jean Delumeau that attitudes toward fear, pessimism, and apocalyptic doom were

---

Mentalitätsgeschichte und Ikonographie (Paderborn: Schöningh, 1996). According to Cohn the most significant change in the reporting of plague, however, came with the plague of 1575–1578, when the threat of plague triggered an explosion of plague publications in Italy. This plague also created a more significant break in mentality and plague literature than any other later plague, Samuel K. Cohn, *Cultures of Plague. Medical Thinking at the End of the Renaissance* (Oxford: Oxford University Press, 2011).

31   Arnold C. Klebs and Karl Sudhoff, *Die ersten gedruckten Pestschriften* (Munich: Verlag der Münchner Drucke, 1926); see also Joseph P. Byrne, 'Printing', in *Encyclopedia of the Black Death*, ed. by Joseph P. Byrne (Santa Barbara/Denver/Oxford: ABC-Clio, 2012), pp. 293–294.

32   See Karl Sudhoff: 'Der Ulmer Stadarzt und Schriftsteller Heinrich Steinhöwel', in *Die ersten gedruckten Pestschriften*, eds. by Klebs/Sudhoff (Munich: Verlag der Münchner Drucke, 1926), pp. 171–213.

33   See https://www.ustc.ac.uk/editions/749219 and https://mrfh.online.uni-marburg.de /21440.

34   Bernd Breitenbruch, *Die Inkunabeln der Stadtbibliothek Ulm. Besitzgeschichte und Katalog* (Weißenhorn: Konrad, 1987), pp. 335–336. Conveniently, Zainer provided his publications with precise dates, so the first print listed in this catalogue is Steinhöwel's *Deutsche Chronik*, published on February 10, 1473, a month after the latter's *Ordnung der Pestilenz*, which the Ulm library does not have.

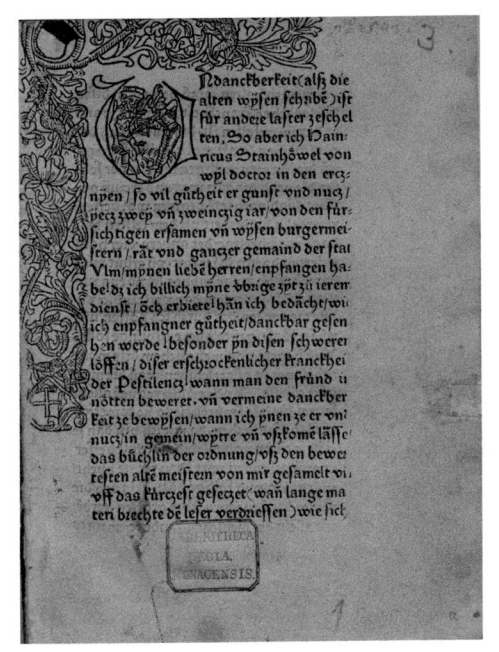 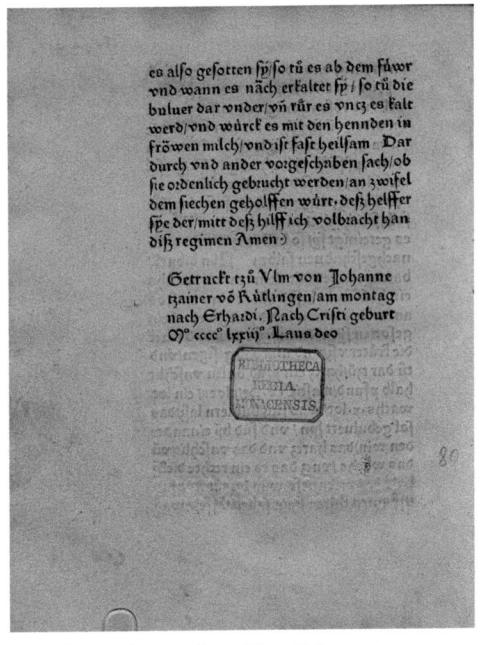

FIGURES 1.6 AND 1.7　Heinrich Steinhöwel, Büchlein der Ordnung der Pestilenz, Ulm: Zainer, 1473. Munich, Bayerische Staatsbibliothek, Rar. 307 [https://www.digitale-sammlungen .de/de/view/bsb00031805?page=7, https://www.digitale-sammlungen.de/de/view /bsb00031805?page=86]

largely unchanging in wide circles of society until the Enlightenment has since been put into perspective, with good reasons, it remains striking how little the plague tracts have changed structurally over a long period of time.

Prototype of all plague treatises at least in the German-speaking world is Heinrich Steinhöwel's *Buchlein der Ordnung der Pestilenz* [Small book of the order of pestilence]. As can be seen from the colophon, the 40-page manu-script was first printed by Johann Zainer in Ulm in 1473. This is one of the first printed medical texts in the vernacular.[35] This tract has also two parts: in the first part, Steinhöwel informs about the symptoms and causes of the plague, he gives hygienic and dietary instructions as well as recipes for disease prevention. The second part is devoted to the therapy of the disease and is aimed more at a medically trained audience. More or less effective countermeasures such as plasters with tinctures for the ulcers are mentioned, as was the all-purpose

---

35　See also an early English example: *Here begynneth a litil boke the whiche traytied many gode thinges for the pestilence* (London: Machlinia, 1485), probably mistakenly attributed to Benedikt Canutus [Bengt Knutsson].

weapon 'bloodletting' which proved, as so often, to be blunt. The contents of plague tracts show how 'modern' already the contemporaries of the sixteenth century were set or how 'archaic' we must still act in the twenty-first century, if nature in the anthropocene challenges us. What was already striking with Rülein: it seems like today's anti-COVID appeals when Steinhöwel urges us to avoid large gatherings of people and everything that comes directly from the sick person.

Accordingly, Steinhöwel considers both prevention and care for those who are already ill to be important. He wants his book to be used for both cases. At the same time, he is well aware of the limits of the human healing art of the time, when he notes in the preface that the 'rod of God' is the best medicine, since there is no better remedy than true confession, true repentance and perfect penance. For support, Steinhöwel also recommends invoking Saint Sebastian as an intercessor. Basically, however, this writing is permeated with pragmatism: Steinhöwel repeatedly refers to a way of life that is characterised by moderation. This applies not only to the satisfaction of basic needs such as food or drink; grief and joy in particular also come into focus when he states that fear make a people susceptible to illness: 'In addition, one should distract the sick person as much as possible from thoughts of death and pestilence. And one should always encourage him and keep him in joy with singing, telling stories, playing the lute and everything that brings joy.'[36] Steinhöwel thus, in a quite modern manner, emphasizes the psychological effects of positive thinking.[37]

As already indicated, the four focal points of the present volume of essays can be presented on the basis of plague tracts. Perhaps already the wording of the section headings can serve as some sort of instruction manual for our volume.

4   Books in Use and Their Traces

As the product of a complex crafting process, the handy guidebook is an artifact, or as Ursula Rautenberg has put it 'a hybrid of writing (and other symbolic signs or images), design, and matter' that generates specific information from

---

36   'Außerdem sollte man den Kranken so weit wie möglich von Gedanken an Tod und Pest ablenken. Und man sollte ihn immer wieder aufmuntern und mit Singen, Erzählen, Lautenspielen und allem, was Freude macht, bei Laune halten.' Heinrich Steinhöwel's *Buchlein der Ordnung der Pestilenz* (Ulm: Zainer, 1473), unpag.

37   Gerhard Eis, *Medizinische Fachprosa des späten Mittelalters und der frühen Neuzeit* (Amsterdam: Rodopi, 1982), p. 110. Such references to the importance of positive thinking can be found in epidemic literature up to the present day.

given formats.[38] The instruction manual is exposed to an extraordinary extent to physical processes of adaptation and change that express specific user experiences, preferences and interests: subsequent text corrections, erasures or deletions, annotations, glossing, drawings, additions of further procedures: all these changes can be made to the how-to book. These small format, unadorned books were simple in typographical terms. Many contain contemporary handwritten annotations.[39] A telling example is the already mentioned *PestilentzBüchlein/ Für die armen Handwercks- und Baurs-Leuthe* that shows inconspicuous but evident markings in the form of a cross where the text says something about prophylaxis for pregnant women. Often you find extensive recipe notes and underlining: the 1482-edition of Steinhöwel's *Pestbüchlein*, located in Wolfenbüttel, contains pages of handwritten recipe notes with a reference to the year 1525, but no mention of names.[40] It is obvious that plague tracts, mostly written in the vernacular for the general public, were eagerly used. Throughout the early modern period, we encounter the problem of a severe shortage of medical care for wide sections of the population in Germany and Europe. The advent of printing offered a fundamentally new possibility for medical assistance: unlike handwritten texts, it was possible to pass on medical knowledge to many people at the same time. Information about individual diseases, knowledge about the production of medicine, and the application of appropriate therapeutic measures could be acquired.

5   Change and Combination of Media

Once the recipes are printed in a book, it is possible to compare them, examine them, and see what they have in common. The idea of 'standard practices', as opposed to those taught by a particular master, emerged.[41] On the other hand, the numerous annotations in recipe books indicate that the elementary

---

38   Ursula Rautenberg, 'Das Buch als Artefakt und kommunikatives Angebot. Die Exemplargeschichte des 'Herbarius latinus' (Mainz: Peter Schöffer, 1484) aus der Bibliothek des Christoph Jacob Trew' in Ulrike Gleixner, Constanze Baum, Jörn Münkner and Hole Rößler (eds.), *Biographien des Buches* (Göttingen: Wallstein, 2017), pp. 39–88, here p. 47.

39   I can rely here on the research results that Petra Feuerstein-Herz brought to light for a Wolfenbüttel exhibition *Gotts verhengnis und seine straffe* [God's Fate and Punishment] on early-modern epidemics. *Gotts verhengnis und seine straffe – Zur Geschichte der Seuchen in der Frühen Neuzeit.*

40   Heinrich Steinhöwel: *Ordnung der Pestilenz* ([Nürnberg]: [Drucker der Rochuslegende] [ca. 1482–84]), [28] Bl.; 4°. [HAB 27.1 Astron. (6)].

41   Michael Giesecke, *Der Buchdruck in der frühen Neuzeit. Eine historische Fallstudie über die Durchsetzung neuer Informations- und Kommunikationstechnologien* (Frankfurt am Main: Suhrkamp, 1998), pp. 505–560.

medium of the recipe is the notebook.[42] There is certainly no printed recipe that was not previously exchanged orally and then written down. Steinhöwel's Plague tract, written as early as 1446, when Steinhöwel was a physician in Weil am Rhein and witnessed the outbreak of the plague there, circulated for decades as a manuscript, even beyond 1473, when it was to be printed for the first time.

To this must always be added the oral buzz that the treatise triggered. It was only through printing and reproduction that even the short treatise on the plague was to receive an exactly designed reading surface as well as a degree of uniformity in structure and substance that is not evident in manuscripts.[43] Although the first printed works are very similar on a formal level to the manuscripts of the period, one only has to look at the first page of Steinhöwel's book, which does without a conventional title page, a refinement of the presentation is emerging in the tailwind of technological-typographical development, which is primarily aimed at saving costs for the producer as well as time for the recipient to absorb the information. Reader-friendly elements are used early on, such as indexes, title keywords in the margin, visual paragraph marks, pagination by Arabic numerals, red markings still inserted by hand, sometimes footnotes, diagrams. The tendency towards stringent ordering schemes, already evident in medieval manuscripts,[44] is significantly expanded and strengthened by printing.

---

42 Elizabeth M. Merrill, 'Pocket-Size Architectural Notebooks and the Codification of Practical Knowledge', in Matteo Valleriani (ed.), *The Structures of Practical Knowledge*, (Berlin, Springer: 2017), pp. 21–54; Jan-Dirk Müller, 'Der Körper des Buches. Zum Medienwechsel zwischen Handschrift und Buch', in Hans-Ulrich Gumbrecht and Karl Ludwig Pfeiffer (eds.), *Materialität der Kommunikation*, (Frankfurt am Main: Suhrkamp, 1988), pp. 203–217; Norman F. Blake, 'From Manuscript to Print', in Jeremy Griffith and Derek Pearsall (eds.), *Book Production and Publishing in Britain 1375–1475* (Cambridge: Cambridge University Press, 1989), pp. 403–432.

43 Walter J. Ong, *Orality and Literacy. The Technologizing of the Word* (London: Routledge, 1995), p. 126.

44 See the classic study for the structuring of the book page in the Middle Ages Ivan Illich, *Im Weinberg des Textes. Als das Schriftbild der Moderne entstand* (Frankfurt am Main: Luchterhand, 1991).

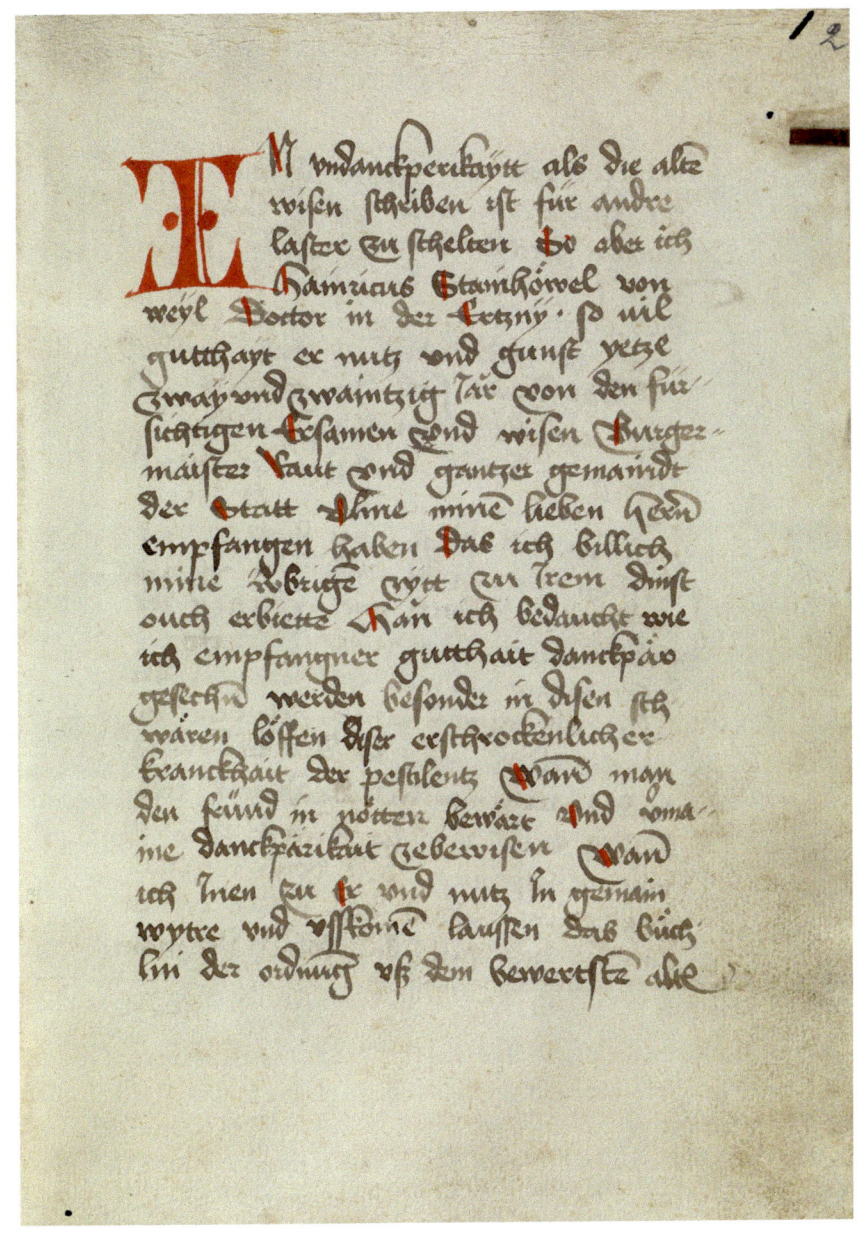

FIGURE 1.8   Heinrich Steinhöwel, Büchlein der Ordnung der Pestilenz, um 1470, Schaffhausen, Stadtbibliothek, Gen.26, fol. 2r, fol. 4v. [https://www.e-codices.ch/en/sbs /gen0026/2r/0/]

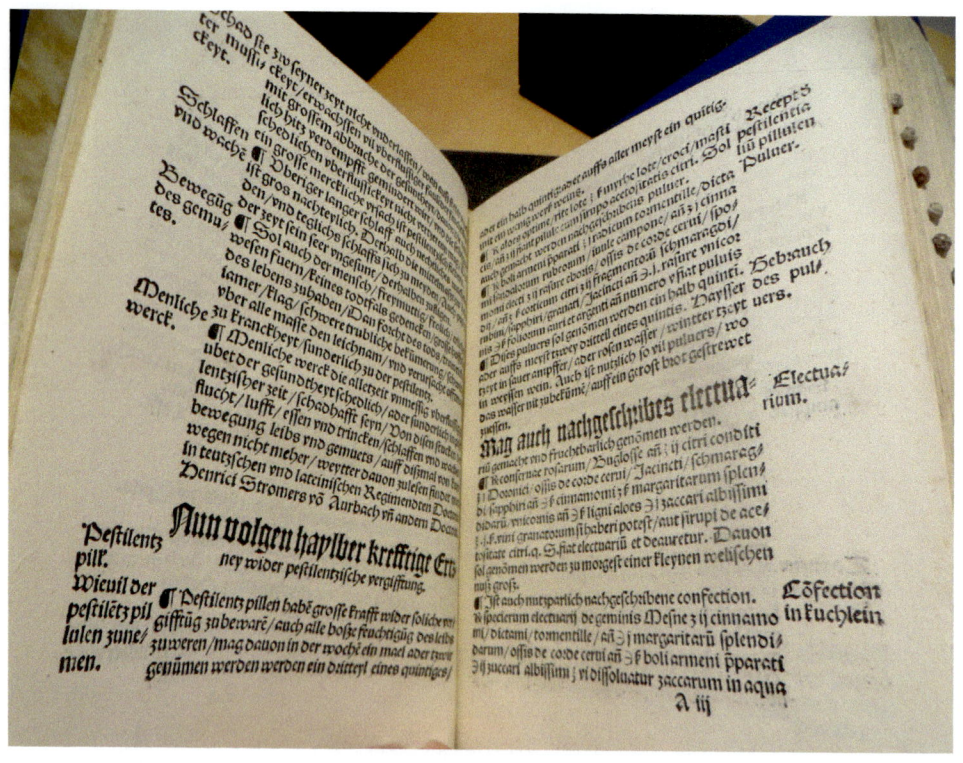

FIGURE 1.9   Ein kurtze Underrichtung heilbarer krefftiger ertzeney, mit welchem sich der Mensch wider
die pestilentz bewaren, Leipzig: Lotther, 1515. Wolfenbüttel, Herzog August Bibliothek, 76.2.
Quodlibetica
PHOTO: AUTHOR

6   Visual Translation and Intermediality

An early picture on the plague. In Hans Folz' *Ein fast köstlicher spruch von der
pestilencz* (Nürnberg 1482) a surgeon cuts open a plague wound. The draftsman
must have been there.

What role do images and graphic figures play in these treatises? They often
belong to the genre of 'technical drawing' and 'diagram'.[45] An advice treatise
rarely consists of text or images alone. Picture titles, captions, tables or speech
bubbles as well as pictograms, diagrams or arrows give reason to assume that
description and picture are only the conceptual poles of a spectrum in which
numerous mixed ratios of verbal and iconic expressions are scaled. Despite

---

45   See to the types of images Eckkrammer, *Medizin für den Laien*, pp. 1074–1080.

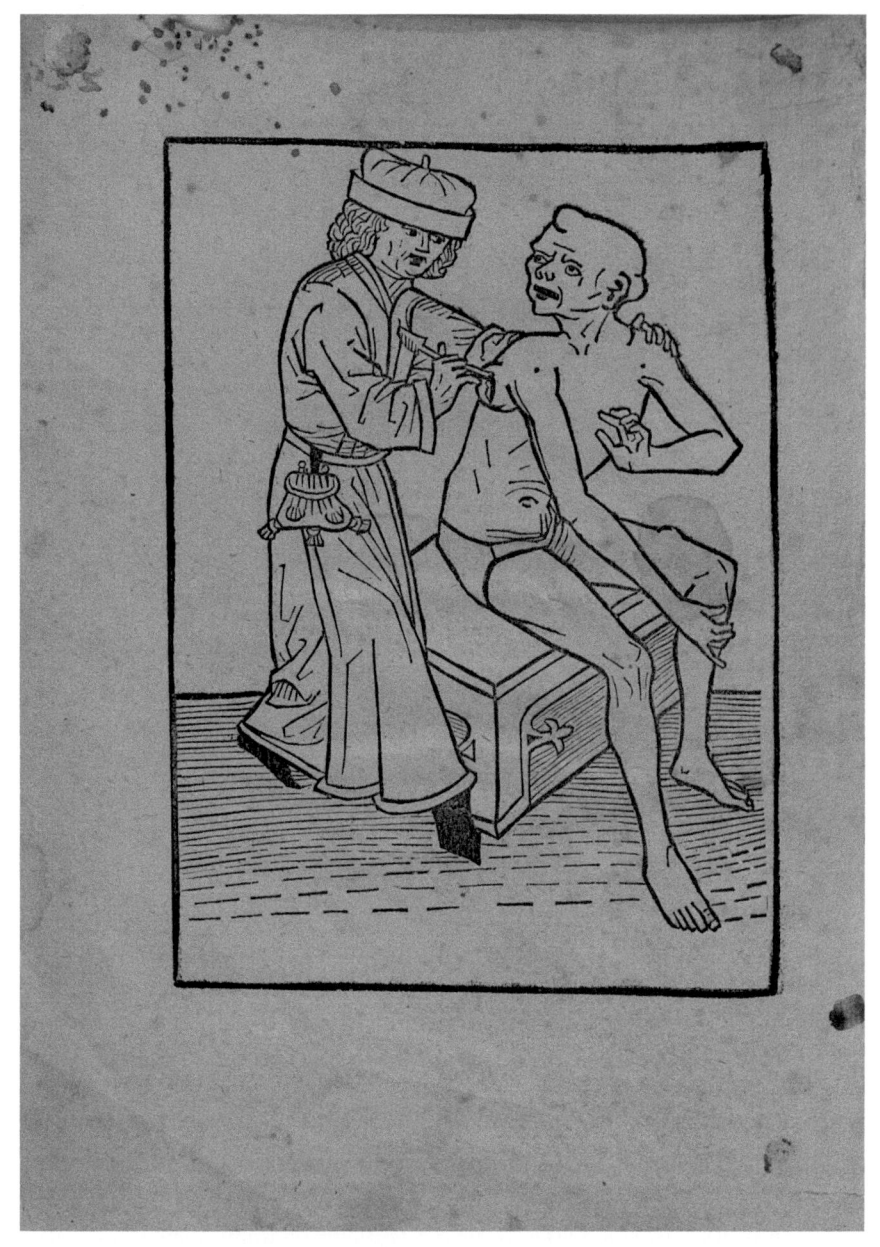

FIGURE 1.10   Hans Folz, Ein fast köstlicher spruch von der pestilencz, Nürnberg 1482.
Munich, Bayerische Staatsbibliothek, Rar. 185 [https://www.digitale
-sammlungen.de/de/view/bsb00027051?page=6]

FIGURE 1.11   Heinrich Steinhöwel, Büchlein der Ordnung der Pestilenz,
                Ulm: Zainer 1473, Bl. 3, Munich, Bayerische Staatsbibliothek,
                Rar. 307 [https://www.digitale-sammlungen.de/de/view
                /bsb00031805?page=7 (detail)]

significant exceptions, as seen here, plague advice tracts are sparsely illustrated. It is not so easy to put a contagious disease, like the plague, into the
picture.[46] It is striking that technical-referential pictorial elements, which
often appear in surgical writings, are mostly absent in the plague tracts. How
should one visually represent explanatory models of the plague, such as the
miasma theory, that is, the idea that toxic vapor or mist filled with particles
of decomposed matter caused the diseases and which was very widespread at
the time?

Steinhöwel's *Büchlein der Ordnung der Pestilenz* contains a speaking initial
as the only illustration. In the inner space of the letter 'U' we see two people:
a warrior armed with a crossbow and a barely clothed young man tormented

---

46   Robert Herrlinger, *Geschichte der medizinischen Abbildung. Von der Antike bis um 1600*
       (Munich: Moos, 1967), pp. 57–62.

by arrows. The latter is not recognizable by medical signs of illness, such as the characteristic plague bumps; rather, arrows that have struck him and are still being fired at him represent his martyrdom as St. Sebastian.[47] Arrows mirrow the fateful visitation of a deadly plague that has taken the form of disease projectiles that can strike everyone.[48] According to the scheme 'similia similibus', the depiction Sebastian refers to the religious subject matter of divine projectiles of disease, in which spears and arrows always dominate.[49] Although the roots of the cult of St. Sebastian were ancient, the depiction of this Saint became popular only in the fifteenth century. Since his martyrdom is reminiscent of that of the individuals affected by the plague, he has been considered the most important plague saint since the late Middle Ages.

Obviously, the most consistent metaphor for pestilence has been the arrow.[50] The disease itself can 'attack', 'invade', 'defeat' or 'retreat'. It is a kind of enemy waging war against our health and even our lives.[51] In battle, arrows fell from the sky, the supposed source of the plague, and struck victims indiscriminately. Skilled archers could hit targets at long distances with great accuracy, silently and without warning. Just as arrow wounds were not always fatal, neither was plague. Whether God's plague struck indiscriminately or specifically picked someone out, the arrow metaphor worked brilliantly. Crossed arrows also appeared as talismans to ward off the plague and were painted on houses in Luxembourg until the beginning of the twentieth century.

---

47   Often the 'black death' was depicted as a skeleton sitting on a galloping horse throwing arrows. On the multifaceted nature of the arrow as a pictorial symbol in old and new media Angelika Storrer and Eva Lia Wyss, 'Pfeilzeichen: Formen und Funktion in alten und neuen Medien' in Ulrich Schmitz and Horst Wenzel (eds.), *Wissen und neue Medien. Bilder und Zeichen von 800 bis 2000* (Berlin: Erich Schmidt, 2003), pp. 159–195.

48   What the arrows represented then, nowadays in COVID times the spiky viral bullet staged by the media seems to embody as an omnipresent symbol of aversion. Only the good sting of the injection syringe with the vaccine seems to neutralise the spikes, which are actually elastic feelers.

49   Dinzelbacher, *Angst im Mittelalter*, p. 211.

50   Joseph P. Byrne, 'Arrows', in *Encyclopedia of the Black Death*, ed. by Joseph P. Byrne (Santa Barbara/Denver/Oxford: ABC-Clio, 2012), pp. 22–23. Paracelsus said that the plague strikes man like a whip. Many Christians considered it a whip, a tool of divine punishment. The metaphor of plague arrows developed even before the Black Death. Famously, Homer Achilles unleashes an epidemic in the form of a barrage of arrows on the Greek camp outside Troy. The angry Yahweh declares in Deuteronomy (32:23–4), 'I will shoot all my arrows against them: consuming hunger and wasting fever and bitter pestilence', which makes those who oppose him smile.

51   Recently Emmanuel Macron, French president, has argued the same way in the face of the COVID challenge in March 2020.

In the interaction of text and image, one must always ask whether there is a more or less equal relationship between image and text, how much the conveyance of information can be replaced by the other without loss, i.e. the text information is replicated, reinforced, one can also say illustrated by the image. But it can also be that between in the relation of image and text the image factor is the dominant one, that is the image transports content that goes beyond the text. The image is more on the defensive when it works as ornamental addition. How problematic these distinctions ultimately are, however, is shown by Steinhöwel's initial, which clearly goes beyond pure decoration.

7   Practical Implementation

How-to books differ from other treatises because they address the reader directly. Verbalized explanations in an advice book have the function of prompting action. Their reading is performatively oriented. It can detach from the source, creating a space for improvisation that needs to be explored. It was not until the microscopic discoveries of Robert Koch and Louis Pasteur that a fundamental advance in knowledge was achieved. Prior to that, faith in God, humoral-pathological or dietary medicines and behavioral recommendations, magical practices and escape had long been the means of choice, all of which oscillate between prescription and improvisation always carrying a praxeological component.

The variety of medicines used was large, numerous medicinal plants were found among them, which were assigned to certain recipes, which can hardly be reconstructed. There were probably no two people in the healing business who made the miracle remedy theriac in one and the same way.[52] As a rule, 60 herbs or herbal ingredients, including opium, were mixed with three separately produced remedies. Theriac was considered particularly effective and valuable if it bore the 'Venice' brand as sign of origin. Not only there, but also in cities like Nuremberg or Strasbourg, the production of theriac resembled a public ceremony. It would, of course, be an interesting question to what extent the pharmacists and physicians operating in marketplaces made use of the abundant advice literature. In the search for a panacea, alchemical methods were also used, precious stones were placed over the heart of the plague sufferer or

---

52   Theriac as mother of all drugs, Cohn, *Cultures of Plague*, pp. 160–163.

ground into powder to sprinkle over food.[53] Ben Jonson's popular comedy *The Alchemist* (1610) is set in plague-ridden London.[54]

And last but not least, the great controversy of flight, which only works if it is implemented. Escape was considered the recipe for success par excellence: Steinhöwel says about this: 'Flee quickly, flee far, return late, for truly, these are three more useful herbs than a whole apothecary.'[55] This was a simple way out, immortalized in literature by Giovanni Boccaccio from the point of view of the well-heeled, and expressly ruled out by Martin Luther in 1527 at least for priests and other people in positions of responsibility.[56] What is to be made of this from a practioner's point of view? On the endpage of a handsome volume with a compilation of papal indulgences for the Jubilee Year, published in 1502 by the humanist Nikolaus Marschalk in Erfurt, who was known for his first printed Greek textbooks, are pasted passages cut from a Low German version (Magdeburg: Brandis) of Steinhöwel's Plague Book. Was there an apotropaic

---

53 Chiara Crisciani, Michela Pereira, 'Black Death and Golden Remedies. Some Remarks on Alchemy and the Plague' in Agostino Paravicini Bagliani, Francesco Santi (eds.), *The Regulation of Evil. Social and Cultural Attitudes to Epidemics in the Late Middle Ages* (Firenze: Sismel, 1998), pp. 7–39; Sabine Doering-Manteuffel, 'Der Stein der Weisen und die Pest. Heil und Heilung im Mittelalter und in der Frühen Neuzeit', in Sabine Doering-Manteuffel, *Das Okkulte. Eine Erfolgsgeschichte im Schatten der Aufklärung. Von Gutenberg bis zum World Wide Web* (Munich: Siedler, 2008), pp. 35–70.

54 The owner of a house has fled to escape the plague, leaving his house in the hands of servants. These lend it to a pair of rogues who 'concoct' the alchemical philosopher's stone, the panacea that promises untold wealth; Mathew Martin, 'Play and Plague in Ben Jonson's *The Alchemist*', *English Studies in Canada* 26 (2000), pp. 393–408; Cheryl L. Ross, 'The Plague of the Alchemist', *Renaissance Quarterly* 41 (1988), pp. 439–458.

55 'Flieht schnell, flieht weit, kehrt spät zurück, denn wahrlich, diese drei Kräuter sind nützlicher als eine ganze Apotheke.' Heinrich Steinhöwel: Büchlein der Ordnung Der Pestilenz (Ulm: Zainer, 1473), unpag; see also Heinz-Peter Schmiedebach and Mariacarla Gadebusch Bondio, "Fleuch pald, fleuch ferr, kum wider spat ...' Entfremdung, Flucht und Aggression im Angesicht der Pestilenz (1347–1350)', in Irene Erven and Karl-Heinz Spieß (eds.), *Fremdheit und Reisen im Mittelalter* (Stuttgart: Steiner, 1997), pp. 217–234.

56 Martin Luther, *Ob man vor dem Sterbn fliegen muge* (Wittenberg: Lufft, 1527) USTC 679040. Speaking of Luther: The forbidden 'fuga corporalis' is contrasted with a commanded, even necessary 'fuga spiritualis', through which one escapes the power of the devil and finds refuge in God, who has the necessary antidotes ready. Those affected should make use of the available bodily medicines, take measures to restore hygiene, and not expose themselves unnecessarily to the danger of infection that plague sufferers pose: "Take to you what can help you, smoke house yard and alleys, avoid also person" [nym zu dir was dich helffen kan, reuchere haus, hoff und gassen, meyde auch person ...] WA 23, 365, 24–25, see Johann Anselm Steiger, *Medizinische Theologie. Christus Medicus und Theologia Medicinalis bei Martin Luther und im Luthertum der Barockzeit* (Leiden/Boston: Brill, 2005), p. 11–12.

FIGURE 1.12   [Peraudi], Resolutiones Certorum Dubiorum, Erfurt: Marschalk, 1502, Wolfenbüttel, Herzog
             August Bibliothek, 448.1 Theol
             PHOTO: AUTHOR

motivation behind this practice? Was it to protect oneself from the plague? We
do not know.[57]

8   Books Are not Contagious – Books Are Contagious

Advice books in plague times were bestsellers, especially in the early phase of
printing but also in the decades that followed. Due to the numerous epidemics,

---

57   The plague tracts and the plague blessings are two sides of the same coin: Annica
      Schumann, 'Chronik, Pestrigimen und Pestsegen. Schriftliche Zeugnisse der Auseinander-
      setzung mit der Pest', *Pest! Eine Spurensuche*, ed. by LWL-Museum für Archäologie,
      Westfälisches Landesmuseum Herne, Stefan Leenen, Alexander Berner, Sandra Maus,
      Doreen Molders (Darmstadt: Wissenschaftliche Buchgesellschaft, 2019), pp. 190–197;
      see also Michael Schilling, 'Pest und Flugblatt', in *Gotts verhengnis und seine straffe – Zur
      Geschichte der Seuchen in der Frühen Neuzeit*, ed. by Petra Feuerstein-Herz, (Wiesbaden:
      Harrassowitz, 2005), pp. 93–99.

a climate of permanent fear prevailed, that cried out for advice in order to be processed in a halfway constructive manner. Such tracts followed the same pattern: causes, course of disease, prevention and remedies. Why such writings were written for lay persons in the first place is interpreted in different ways. Some argue that in plague times, the number of published plague tracts and books for lay people is evidence of the ethical responsibility of physicians.[58] In contrast, others see this phenomenon of the proliferation of plague texts with a prophylactic character as a sign of the impotence of the medical profession.[59]

The modern era in Europe did not begin with the Reformation, but with the plague (Egon Friedell).[60] Since the Middle Ages, Europe has regularly experienced epidemics, from plague to cholera. The associated economic crises accelerated innovations such as the canalization and supply of drinking water and in the fifteenth century printing.[61] In the longer term, the late medieval world did begin to dissolve; massive population losses led to the abandonment of poor and unprofitable farmland, so that entire villages were abandoned and swathes of land became desolate. In the cities, on the other hand, wages rose, as did the general standard of living. At the same time, higher labor costs encouraged technical innovations such as printing to mechanise cost-intensive manual labour. The plague and epidemic pamphlets had a noticeable influence on the book trade. The printing press, together with the abundant provision of paper as a carrier of information, which began as early as the fourteenth century subsequently allowed a more accurate, faster and cheaper reproduction of texts and books and thus a penetration of written form into social domains that had previously been reserved for orality.[62]

Books are not contagious! One was far less likely to contract the plague from a printed document than from a consultation with a doctor, who could hardly avoid plague sufferers. The spread of paper on which information could be stored, first by handwriting, then in the second half of the fifteenth century

---

58 Darrel W. Amundsen, *Medicine, Society, and Faith in the Ancient and Medieval Worlds* (Baltimore: John Hopkins University Press, 1996).

59 Philip Ziegler, *The Black Death* (New York: Harper & Row, 1969).

60 The *Kulturgeschichte der Neuzeit* (1927–1931) is the main work of the Austrian writer Egon Friedell. At the beginning of great turning points in time there is always a great trauma. The boundary between the Middle Ages and modern times is marked by the Black Death, which destroys the unified world view of the Middle Ages and dissolves old certainties. For Friedell, the cultural triumph of the early Renaissance was also a consequence of the Black Death.

61 Jörg Vögele, 'Cholera, Pest und Innovation', *Die Volkswirtschaft* 6/2020, pp. 22–25.

62 Giesecke, *Der Buchdruck in der frühen Neuzeit*; Elizabeth Eisenstein, *The Printing Press as an Agent of Change. Communications and Cultural Transformations in Early Modern Europe* (2 vols., Cambridge: Cambridge University Press, 1979); Rudolf Hirsch, *Printing, Selling and Reading, 1450–1550* (Wiesbaden: Harrassowitz, 1974).

increasingly by printing, guaranteed distance between people. It was no longer absolutely necessary to enter into an oral exchange with the specialist. The avoidance of the loss of human life as well as the collective fears surrounding epidemics virtually forced the emergence of text genres that opened up a preventive-therapeutic intermediate level and spoke the language of the layman. If one is not protected from the disease by the outside, by the medical profession, the medicalized society, the state, then one must protect oneself individually, with the help of a printed medium.

Books are contagious! Only with the printing press can content go viral, when hundreds, even thousands of copies from the same treatise can have their effect in different places. Perception could be readjusted. The users of printed advice literature in particular were faced with entirely new possibilities where they could adjust their behavior, try out new practices. It was only because the multiplication of literature through the printing press reached completely new dimensions that a storehouse of knowledge was created that could always be drawn upon should the need arise.

Whatever the motives of the authors, the impact of the texts must be evaluated positively; and this not only because they sometimes give sensible instructions for the avoidance of infection. Above all, the psycho-hygienic reassurance provided by the advised measures, which are always presented as tried and tested and coming from the greatest authorities, must be put on the scale. The instructions open the possibility of active intervention and thus preventive and therapeutic alternatives to the individual who is anxiously facing the epidemic. Medicines are recommended, as well as behaviours and attitudes that can be implemented without the presence or consultation of a physician.

So, can there be any clueless advice books at all? Hardly. Certainly, there can be guide books that spread nonsense, that make claims that go astray.[63] But even then, one has to deal with a setting that rather inspires confidence than causes disorientation. As wrong as the miasma theory is from today's perspective, it nevertheless represented a plausible explanation in the wake of which reasonable measures, such as avoiding crowds and improving the air, were implemented.

---

63   See a thought-provoking example from today: Rundall Munroe, *How-to. Absurd scientific advice for common real-world problems* (London: Murray, 2019).

PART 1

Materiality and Traces of Use

∴

'Take', 'Do', 'Check': Readers and Uses of Early Modern How-to Books in the Collection of the Herzog August Bibliothek

Petra Feuerstein-Herz

The article deals with the relationship between the instructive purpose of books and their actual use.[1] Specifically, it considers how printed instructional literature was used explicitly for practical application in the early modern period. Imperatives such as 'take' (Nimb) and 'do' (Thu) are examples of calls to action in the printed texts, whereas 'check' (Prüff) and 'note' (Merckh) are among the handwritten annotations left by readers in the margins of surviving copies.[2] These imperatives speak to the intentions of published books as well as to the work that was done with them. Within this volume's wider questions about material culture and praxeological aspects, I explore to what extent the traces of use in specific copies from the historical collections of the Herzog August Bibliothek Wolfenbüttel can provide answers.

1 Recipes and How-to Books: Sources at the Herzog August Bibliothek

The terms 'recipe', 'recipe book', and 'how-to text,' chosen for the conference and this volume, do not represent well-defined genres in the early modern period. Recipe books as well as guidebooks belong to the broad and amorphous sub-field of non-fictional literature known as practical or 'how-to' literature, which includes books of secrets, *Kunstbüchlein*, medical *practicae*, and other

---

1   I would like to thank Tillmann Taape for valuable advices on the content and for the translation into English.

2   See copy HAB: 35.1 Phys. 2° (1), USTC 622866; see Petra Feuerstein-Herz, 'Von *heimlichkeit der natur*. Benutzungsspuren in alchemischen Anleitungsbüchern', *Medium Buch*, 1 (2019), pp. 45–67, here p. 60; and copy HAB: 47.1 Phys. 2°, see also: 'Merckht auff ihr Lieben fillj. Zur Materialität von Alchemiebüchern in der Frühen Neuzeit', in Petra Feuerstein-Herz and Ute Frietsch (eds.): *Alchemie – Genealogie und Terminologie, Bilder, Techniken und Artefakte* (Wiesbaden: Harrassowitz 2021), pp. 259–286.

technical texts.[3] These terms for written genres (and their German equiva-
lents), are not clearly defined in reference works on media or book studies, if
they are mentioned at all, nor do they yield systematic results as search terms in
the library's online catalogue.[4] Against this background, the article will use the
term 'how-to guide' for the sources under discussion, in the sense of a didactic
and practical guide to action, in particular manual, artisanal practice.[5] This
is to be understood as a recipe-like and action-oriented concept of the text,
reflected not only in the brevity and conciseness of its presentation, but also in
the brief imperative forms of instruction familiar from the recipe. A majority
of these texts are in the vernacular, which does not exclude an academic readership per se, but this is likely not the primary audience. The last criterion for
sources selected for this study is the presence of clear traces of use.

If it may seem surprising to look for these kinds of sources in a princely book
collection founded 450 years ago, they are in fact represented here in significant quantity. This can be explained in part by the history of the collection.
Duke August the Younger of Brunswick and Lüneburg (1579–1666), who shaped
the collecting profile of the Wolfenbüttel library, acquired a comprehensive
range of subjects and genres as they appeared on the European book market.
Equally keen to complete his holdings of older works printed in the fifteenth
and sixteenth centuries, he purchased items from other collections, often in
the form of collected volumes or 'Sammelbände' of independently-published
works that had been bound together by a previous owner. Alongside individual works that filled a gap on the princely shelves, the library thus regularly
acquired works on the periphery of its collection profile, including ones not
intended for elite audiences.

Since 1990, the collection profile of the Herzog August Bibliothek has
also been shaped by its contribution to the 'Arbeitsgemeinschaft Sammlung
Deutscher Drucke,' an initiative coordinating the systematic collection of

---

3 William Eamon, *Science and the Secrets of Nature: Books of Secrets in Medieval and Early
   Modern Culture* (Princeton: Princeton University Press 1994); Elain Leong, and Alisha Rankin
   (eds.), *Secrets and Knowledge in Medicine and Science, 1500–1800* (Farnham: Ashgate, 2011).

4 Corresponding terms are missing or only provide very general references, for example in
   Severin Corsten et al. (eds.), *Lexikon des gesamten Buchwesens* (LGB), second revised edition (Stuttgart: Hiersemann 1987–2016); Ursula Rautenberg (ed.), *Sachlexikon des Buches*,
   3rd ed. (Stuttgart: Hiersemann 2015) or Thomas Keiderling (ed.), *Lexikon der Medien- und
   Buchwissenschaft: analog, digital* (Stuttgart: Hiersemann 2016ff.). Title searches in the online
   catalogue reveal either the low use of corresponding terms as title keywords or unspecific hit
   quantities that indicate a very general application of the terms. See also the contribution by
   Sven Limbeck in this volume.

5 See also Taape's essay in this volume, proposing the category 'texts of action'.

books printed in German.[6] Within this framework, the HAB focuses primarily on acquiring seventeenth-century German-language regional and small-scale printed works that are missing in its collections, mainly from antiquarian bookshops and book auctions.

There are indications that the initiative for printing how-to literature sometimes came from within courtly contexts. In the following section I examine individual copies to explore these questions about audiences and the intentions of authors, editors, publishers, and printers.

2   Authors and Addressees

The area of vernacular how-to literature delineated for the purposes of this study raises questions about intentions and audiences that speak to the socio-economic history of early print and the complexities of the relationship between expertise and lay knowledge.[7] This perspective reveals the fluid transitions between Latin technical literature, vernacular how-to books, and school textbooks. These phenomena emerged a few decades after the invention of printing and re-shaped the media landscape. Traditional concepts of medieval written culture were joined by new goals of communication on the part of authors, publishers, and printers. Intending to address a broader audience on the basis of the new technological possibilities, they more or less deliberately

---

6 Within the framework of this working group, the Herzog August Bibliothek is responsible for the antiquarian acquisition of German prints of the 17th century in order to complete its historical holdings, see on the AG Sammlung Deutscher Drucke in general: www.sdd.de.

7 The term 'expert' is to be understood in this paper in a general sense as a 'Sachverständiger, Fachmann, Kenner' (Duden) who has acquired in-depth knowledge in a subject area on the basis of both a longer wealth of experience and theoretical knowledge. It is not possible here to go into the intensive discussions of recent research and the fundamental accusation of an anachronistic use of the term for pre-modern knowledge cultures, see on this Marian Füssel, Frank Rexroth, Inga Schürmann, 'Experten in vormodernen und modernen Kulturen', in dies. (eds.), *Praktiken und Räume des Wissens. Expertenkulturen in Geschichte und Gegenwart* (Göttingen: Universitätsverlag, 2019), pp. 7–16. On the history of the term, see also Jürgen Sarnowsky, '*Expertus – experientia – experimentum*. Neue Wege der wissenschaftlichen Erkenntnis im Spätmittelalter', in Hedwig Röckelein and Udo Friedrich (eds.), *Experten der Vormoderne zwischen Wissen und Erfahrung* (Berlin: Akademie, 2012), pp. 47–59. At the same time, it should be noted that expertism today is also understood in a specific sense in individual subject areas and disciplines, see on this Brigitte Huber, 'Experten als Untersuchungsgegenstand: Definitionen und Forschungsperspektiven', in Brigitte Huber (ed.): *Öffentliche Experten. Über die Medienpräsenz von Fachleuten* (Wiesbaden: Springer 2014), pp. 23–39.

developed 'a program guiding action and orientation'.[8] Whereas before the media revolution practical and craft knowledge was primarily conveyed orally, for example from master to apprentice, or in handwritten formats for a smaller circle of readers, the printing of books offered the possibility to convey a wide range of technical knowledge to a buying public that was broad but ill-defined, especially with regard to education and literacy.[9]

The authors of practical literature came from a wide range of disciplines, including scholars as well as a variety of practitioners. Early modern courts played an important role in governing the practice of a range of subjects – including law, astrology, medicine, surveying, and technology – and produced literature aimed at practical application.[10] The *Hochnötige* [...] *Reformation/ etlicher/ in gemeinem üblichen Feldmessen/* [...] *eingeschliechener schädlicher Irrthumbe* [Highly necessary [...] reformation of some of the harmful errors that have crept into common field measurements] was printed by an anonymous land surveyor in 1625 in Giessen at the behest of Landgrave Philip of Hessia, in which he 'briefly and comprehensibly declares, explains, and describes certain and firmly established valid rules of measurement, along with an easy instrument thereto belonging',[11] so that, as the unknown author already announced on the title page, 'without error and with slight effort [...] all fields can be correctly and easily measured *ad sensum*'.[12] The small manual presented such measurements and calculations in a didactic manner by means of practical examples, clearly in order to reach an audience beyond the professional art of surveying (see below).

Within a similar context of governance, the barber Bartholomäus Vogtherr wrote a short *Regiment* in 1531 for 'ewer F[ürstlich] G[naden]' [your Grace the Duke] in Augsburg with recipes and instructions on how to behave on journeys that might take the traveller 'durch vergift luft' [through poisoned air],

---

8   Michael Giesecke, *Der Buchdruck in der frühen Neuzeit, Eine historische Fallstudie über die Durchsetzung neuer Informations- und Kommunikationstechnologien* (Frankfurt am Main: Suhrkamp 1991), p. 353 ('ein handlungs- und orientierungsanleitendes Programm').

9   Giesecke, *Buchdruck in der frühen Neuzeit*, pp. 295–296.

10   Udo Friedrich, 'Einleitung: Transfer von Expertenwissen', in Udo Friedrich, Eva Schumann (eds.), *Transfer von Expertenwissen in der Frühen Neuzeit. Gelehrte Diskurse in der volkssprachigen Praxis* (Göttingen: Universitätsverlag, 2018), p. 13.

11   'gewisse und festgegründte [...] gültige Regul zumessen/ kurtz und verständlich declarire, darthue und beschreibe/ neben einem darzu gehörigen leichten Instrument', in *Des* [...] *Fürsten* [...] *Philippi Landgraffen zu Hessen* [...] *Hochnöthige unnd Gründliche Reformation/ etlicher/ in gemeinem üblichen Feldmessen/ nach und nach eingeschliechener schädlicher Irrthumbe* (Gießen: Hampel, 1625) USTC 2059035, HAB: Xb 7222, p. 5.

12   'ohne Fehl mit leichter Mühe [...] alle Felder richtig und ad sensum müglich auß zumessen seynd', in *Des* [...] *Philippi* [...] *Gründliche Reformation*, title page.

in regions plagued by one of the many infectious diseases rampant in the early modern period.[13] Even though Vogtherr states that he personally tailored this medical guidebook to the Augsburg bishop Christoph von Stadion 'aus Dankbarkeit' [out of gratitude], the prescriptions and instructions, and above all the decision to publish them in a printed book, indicate that this was one of the local pamphlets on epidemics that were common in the sixteenth and seventeenth centuries. Often prompted or encouraged by the authorities, such publications were intended as self-help tools for the vast sections of the population that were medically underserved.

The ambiguities and transitions within this process of differentiation into relevant genres of writing can be traced in the titles and prefaces. The fixed repertoire of vernacular instructions included references to usefulness and the invocation of ancient writings. In his 'Distillierbuch [...] Wie man die Wasser [...] Brennen/ Distillieren/ halten und gebrauchen sol/ für alle Gebrechen des gantzen menschlichen Cörpers' [Distilling book [...] How to distil, keep, and use the waters for all diseases of the whole human body],[14] one of the earliest and best-known printed distillation books in the German-speaking world, the Strasbourg surgeon Hieronymus Brunschwig (1450–1512) claimed to have learned the corresponding procedures 'von manchem Gelerten unnd Layen/ Mann unnd Frawen durch Experiment erfaren hab' [through experience, from many a scholar and laypeople, men and women].[15] As a craftsman without university training, he felt it necessary to point out that he had also consulted books, 'groß unnd klein die ich gesehen hab/ in etlichen alten Liberien' [large and small, which I have seen in several old libraries], providing additional legitimation by referencing traditional knowledge.

Apart from the usefulness of these mostly small-format instruction books, the authors also frequently emphasised their efforts to keep the presentation simple and easy to understand for the general public,[16] even in the case of

---

13   Bartholomäus Vogtherr, *Ordnung und Regiment/ für die so uber land/ Meer und Wasser/ auch durch vergift lüft ferre und lange rayß thun sollen* (Augsburg: Steiner 1531) USTC 681501, HAB: 138.6 Med. (1), title page.

14   Hieronymus Brunschwig, *Distillierbuch* (Frankfurt am Main: Gülfferich 1551) USTC 640834, HAB: 35.1 Phys. 2° (2), title page; see on this Tillman Taape, 'Distilling Reliable Remedies. Hieronymus Brunschwig's 'Liber de arte distillandi (1600)' between alchemical learning and craft practice', in *Ambix*, 61 (2014), pp. 256–277, and Feuerstein-Herz, 'Von *heimlichkeit der natur*', pp. 52–67.

15   Brunschwig, *Distillierbuch* (Frankfurt am Main: Gülfferich 1551) USTC 640834, HAB: 35.1 Phys. 2° (2), fol. Aii v (VD 16 B 8702).

16   The preface to a late edition of Philipp Ulsted's distilling book, which was based on Brunschwig's editions, stated, 'das wir diß Buch [...] mit einfeltiger ongezierter rede geschriben haben [...]. Eines theyls/ das die Kunst den irrenden Arbeitern nicht lenger

decidedly specialist knowledge, such as the Giessen surveying manual or the numerous alchemical how-to books which conveyed, in popular form but in strictly coded language, ancient knowledge that could only be gleaned by the initiated adept. The well-known physician and alchemist Andreas Libavius (1555–1616), author of a sophisticated, large-format alchemical manual in Latin in 1597, published a handy German-language *Alchymistische Practic* under his name only a few years later. In the preface to the reader, he posed not as the author, but as a benefactor who wished to publish two alchemical 'litte treatises' that 'good friends had sent' to him. Libavius professed that he intended for 'solche Deutsche werck den ungelehrten die kunst gemein machen' [such German works to make the art available to the unlearned].[17] Although he had previously been of the opinion that this would amount to 'den Sewen [Säuen] die Perllen vor[zu]werfen' [casting pearls before swine], in the meantime he had understood 'daß die gelehrten mehren theils der kunst nichts achten' [that the learned increasingly do not respect the art] and that they want to prevent 'gemein Deutsche' [common Germans] from understanding it through translations. This touched on debates that were especially contentious in the sixteenth century: did expert knowledge belong in laymen's hands, or did this amount to malpractice? In medicine in particular, the dangers of incorrect treatments and applications was often invoked.[18] This resistance came primarily from the ranks of experts who feared professional disadvantages. Corresponding reservations still existed in the seventeenth century and were not without significance for the development of bona fide technical and textbook literature.[19]

3   Traces of Use: How Did People Work with How-to Books?

These brief insights into the early days of German-language how-to literature hardly serve to delineate the social groups who actually read or owned such writings. Above all, it has not yet been clarified in detail to what extent

---

verhalten wirdt/ Darnach auch/ das es die anfahend unerfarnen dester baß verstehen möchten,' Philipp Ulsted, *Coelum philosophorum* (Frankfurt am Main: Gülfferich, 1551) USTC 622866, Preface to the Reader.

17   Andreas Libavius, *Alchymistische Practic* (Frankfurt am Main: Kopff, Saur 1603), HAB: Xb 4819, p. 3.

18   Joachim Telle, 'Arzneikunst und der 'gemeine Mann''. Zum deutsch-lateinischen Sprachenstreit in der frühneuzeitlichen Medizin', in *Pharmazie und der gemeine Mann. Hausarznei und Apotheke in deutschen Schriften* der frühen *Neuzeit* (Ausstellungskataloge der Herzog August Bibliothek, 36) (Wolfenbüttel: Herzog August Bibliothek 1982), pp. 43–48.

19   Giesecke, *Buchdruck in der frühen Neuzeit*, pp. 683–688.

there was a broader interest among laypersons beyond the circle of subject experts.[20] One can assume that grey areas and fluid transitions also exist among user groups. This will be analysed in the following, based on sources of medical, natural, and technical knowledge, of which there are a number of copies with historical traces of use in the holdings of the Wolfenbüttel library. Until well into the nineteenth century, access to academically-trained physicians was by no means universal.[21] The most important healthcare providers were surgeons, barbers, apothecaries, and other artisanal practitioners who had completed apprenticeships of several years, along with informally trained men and women, such as midwives, distillers, uroscopists, lithotomists, and cataract-couchers, as well as a wide range of lay healers or pragmatic reasons alone, because of expensive fees and long distances, large sections of the population were forced to rely on well-known recipes for home remedies and folk treatments mainly transmitted by word of mouth. An interest in publications providing relevant instructions was to be expected, but due to the low reading ability of the lower classes of the population, it can be assumed that even vernacular works had only a limited circulation.

Traces of use in old books are naturally of particular interest when they provide biographical clues about previous owners. In most cases, this includes inscriptions of names and bookplates. One should not assume that evidence of use such as handwritten annotations or underlining were the work of the named owner. Manuscripts and printed books usually go through many hands during their existence. The large majority of the annotations in the printed tracts of Duke August's rich collection, for example, were not made by him, but by one or more other readers, collectors, and users whose books ended up in the Augustean Library.[22] Another surveying manual will serve as example for our purposes.[23] The name of the organist and composer J[ohann] C[aspar]

---

20   Among the available studies see, for example, Elaine Leong and Alisha Rankin (eds.), *Secrets*; Thijs Hagendijk, Márcia Vilarigues and Sven Dupré, 'Materials, Furnaces, and Texts: How to Write About Making Glass Colours in the Seventeenth Century', in *Ambix*, 67 (2020), pp. 323–345.

21   See Michael Stolberg, *Gelehrte und ärztlicher Alltag in Renaissance* (Berlin/Boston: De Gruyter/Oldenbourg 2021), pp. 486–506.

22   Exceptions are entries of short titles, for example on the spines of books, or similar, or the frequent entries in August's hand, which indicate that his works were recorded in the so-called 'Bücherradkatalog', which was also largely kept by him in handwriting. He usually noted the shelfmark he assigned to each volume and the page number of the catalogue entry, see Maria von Katte, 'August und die Kataloge in seiner Bibliothek', in *Wolfenbütteler Beiträge*, 1 (1972), pp. 168–199.

23   Jacob Köbel, *Geometrey Von künstlichem Feldmessen* (Frankfurt am Main: Egenolph 1584) USTC 659345, HAB: N 53.4° Helmst.

Trost (d. 1678) is inscribed on the title page. Even though it is known that Trost was interested in the geometrical contents, it has been shown that the extensive markings in the printed text and the sample calculations in the margins of this copy were not made by his hand.[24]

Since the book appeared in print as early as 1584 and contains contemporary entries, it can probably be assumed that Johann Trost took over the book from a previous owner whose identity cannot be confirmed. The annotations provide hints about the latter's biographical background. He focused on calculations of areas, using units of measurement known as 'Creutzruten' and 'Creutzschuhe' that were common in a number of German regions.[25] This user wrote down simple calculations based on the geometric rules explained in the text, all in German, without sketches or complex arithmetic. Rather than a professionally trained surveyor, we are likely dealing with a layman who wanted to calculate a specific area of arable land or verify a prior estimate. Before it was acquired by Trost, the volume was clearly used simply as a practical tool, as is suggested by the hasty execution of the handwritten notes as well as other material traces such as stains, holes, and tears. Nor did the previous owner bother to sign their name in the book, as Trost later did.

On the other hand, the unknown reader who consulted the Giessen surveying manual to bolster his training seems to have been more closely involved with the subject, and was perhaps himself a surveyor. Like the annotations in the Trost volume, his calculations and sometimes lengthy commentary are written in the vernacular and with a distinct practical bent, but they are more complex in content.

The reader engaged closely with the woodcuts depicting trigonometric rules. Like literacy, numeracy was not very widespread among the less educated classes in the early modern period, but it increased steadily, not least due to the spread of printed books on arithmetic. These examples suggest an audience in which the lines between formally (and even academically) trained practitioners and educated laymen were blurred.

---

24   I would like to thank Dietrich Hakelberg (Gotha) for verifying the handwritten notes as not originating from J.C. Trost and his hint that Trost, as an organ builder, must have had good geometrical knowledge. Thus Trost's work with a literary genre closely related to the guidebooks, the calculating books, can also be proven by the traces in a Wolfenbüttel copy. It contains extensive arithmetic exercises by Trost's hand, Passchier Goessens: Arithmetica oder *Rechenbuch/* [...] *mit gründtlicher Außführung der Species, schönen nützlichen* [...] *Exempeln* (Hamburg: Ohr 1601) USTC 2000004, HAB: N 38.4° Helmst.

25   Köbel, *Geometrey*, fol. 5 v; for Kreuzrute and Kreuzschuh see *Deutsches Wörterbuch von Jacob und Wilhelm Grimm*, vol. 11, sp. 2197 f. [https://drw-www.adw.uni-heidelberg.de].

Von Feldmeſſen.   10

In Feld geſtalt eines rechten Triangels/der auff allen drey ſeitten gleicher leng vnd maß Ruten hat / alſo daß keine ſeitt lenger dann die ander iſt/ Daſſelbige Feldt ſoltu alſo meſſen: nimb das maß einer ſeitten deß dreyeckichten Felds eigentlich mit deiner Meßruten/ Das behalt. Darnach nim̃ das halbtheil der ſelben ſeitten einer/ vnd manigfaltig/ mehr oder multiplicir die zal der Meßruten der gantzen ſeitten durch die zal der meßruten der halben ſeitten. Was auß ſolchem Manigfaltigen entſpringet / theil durch 28. Creußruten / ſo haſtus.

Exempel diſer Regel.

Es iſt ein dreyeckicht Feldt gleicher ſeitten/ vnnd winckel/ vnnd jede ſeitt ſechßig Ruten lang. Nun nimb von ſechßigen das halbtheil/ das iſt dreiſſig/ vnd manigfaltige die ſelben dreiſſig durch ſechßig/ ſo kommen dir tauſent achthundert / ſo viel Ruten hat das dreyeckichte Felde in jhm. So du aber die tauſent achthundert durch hundert vnnd acht vnd zwentzig theyleſt / ſo erfereſt du daß dein gemeſſen Feldt vierzehen Morgen vnd acht Ruten in jm begreifft/in folgender geſtalt.

Diß nachfolgend Feldt helt geſiert in ihm vierzehen Morgen vnd acht Creußruten.

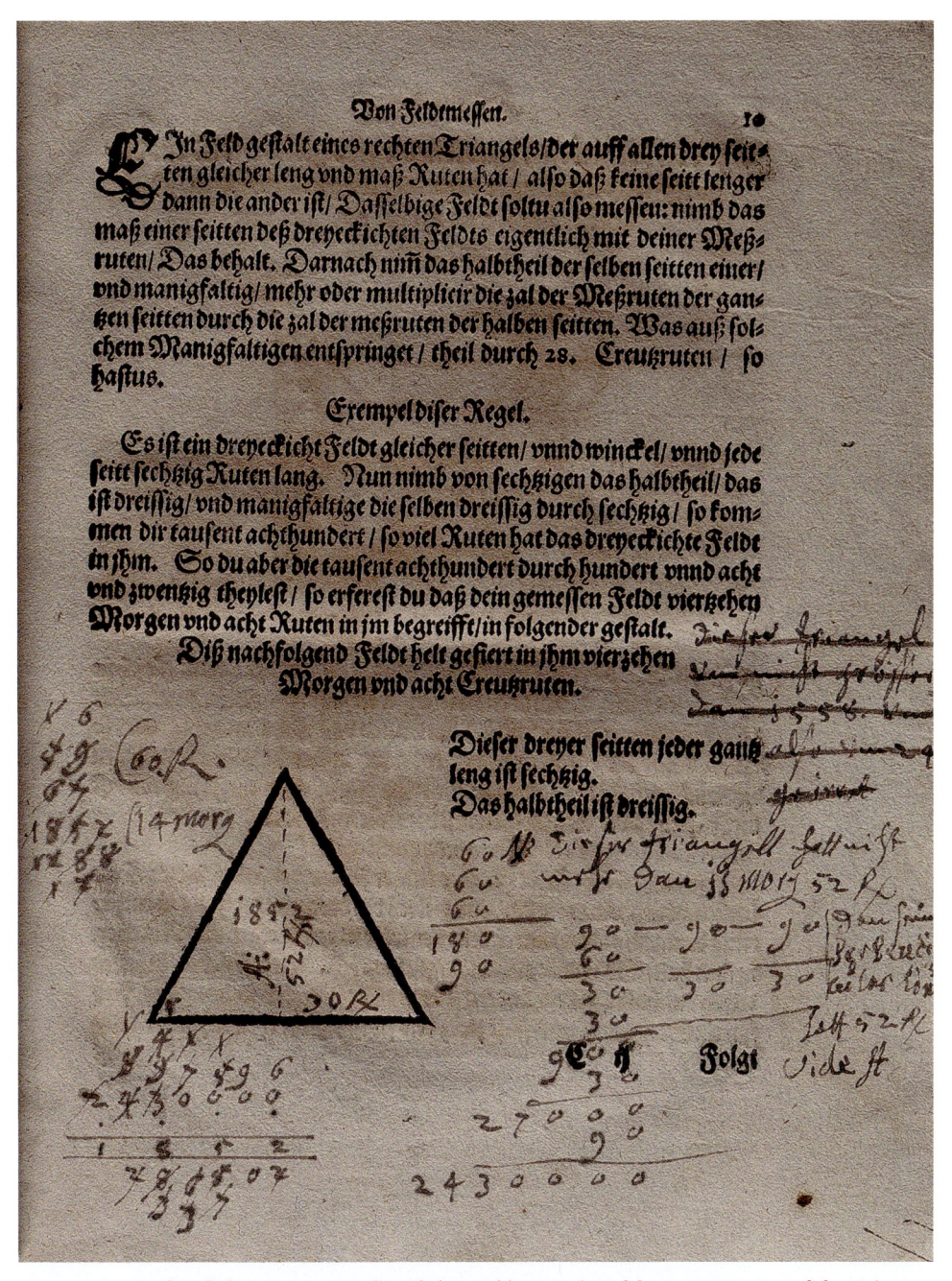

Dieſer dreyer ſeitten jeder gantz leng iſt ſechßig.
Das halbtheil iſt dreiſſig.

FIGURE 2.1 Jacob Köbel, *Geometrey Von künstlichem Feldmessen* (Frankfurt am Main: Egenolph 1584) USTC 659345, Wolfenbüttel, Herzog Auguist Bibliothek: N 53.4° Helmst., p. 10 r

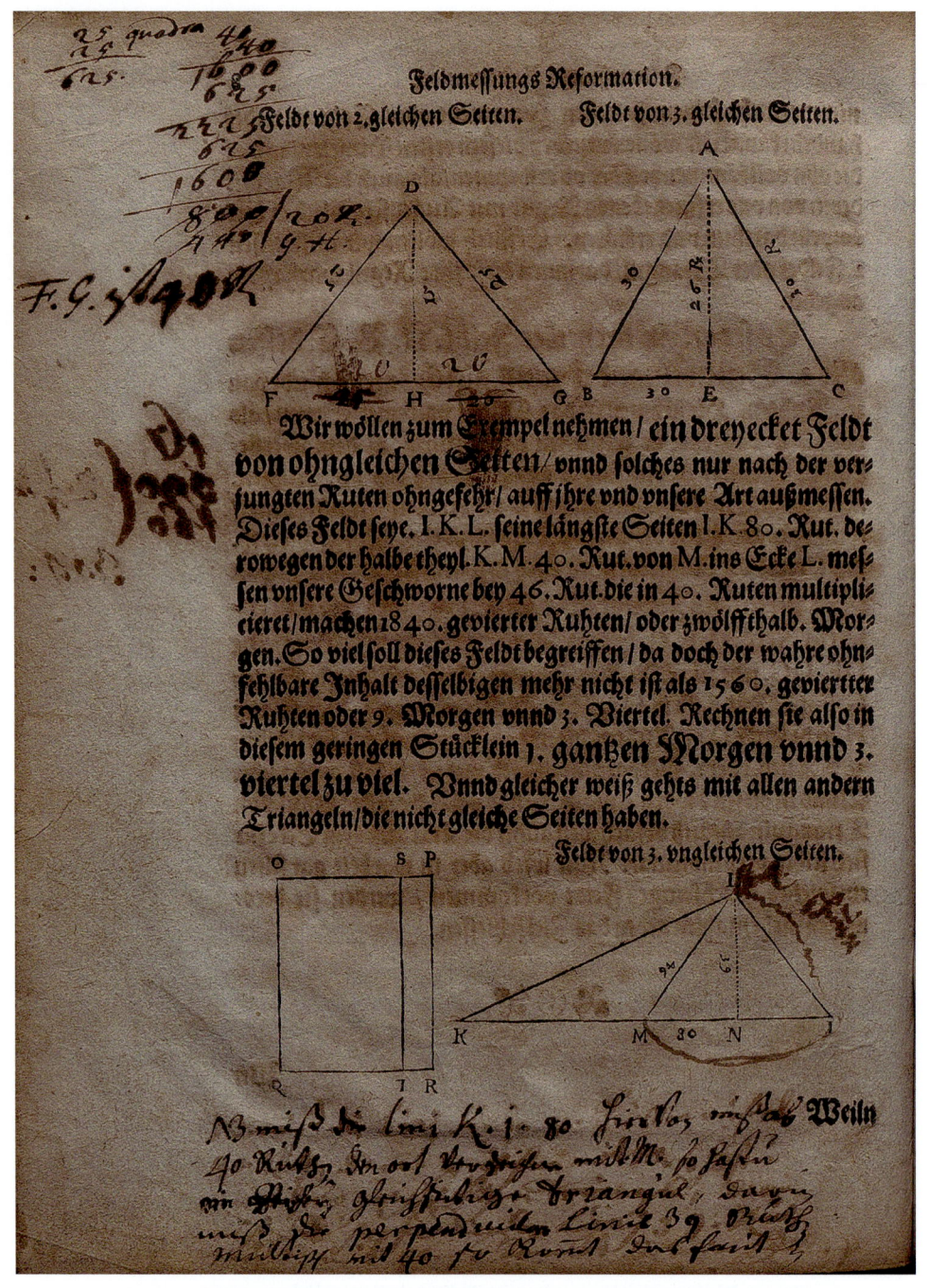

Felðmeſſungs Reformation.

Felðt von 2. gleichen Seiten.   Felðt von 3. gleichen Seiten.

Wir wöllen zum Exempel nehmen / ein dreyecket Felðt von ohngleichen Seiten / unnd ſolches nur nach der verjungten Ruten ohngefehr / auff ihre und unſere Art außmeſſen. Dieſes Felðt ſeye. I. K. L. ſeine längſte Seiten I. K. 80. Rut. derowegen der halbe theyl. K. M. 40. Rut. von M. ins Ecke L. meſſen unſere Geſchworne bey 46. Rut. die in 40. Ruten multipliciret / machen 1840. gevierter Ruhten / oder zwölffthalb. Morgen. So viel ſoll dieſes Felðt begreiffen / da doch der wahre ohnfehlbare Inhalt deſſelbigen mehr nicht iſt als 1560. gevierter Ruhten oder 9. Morgen unnd 3. Viertel. Rechnen ſie alſo in dieſem geringen Stücklein 1. gantzen Morgen unnd 3. viertel zu viel. Unnd gleicher weiß gehts mit allen andern Triangeln / die nicht gleiche Seiten haben.

Felðt von 3. ungleichen Seiten.

FIGURE 2.2   *Des Durchleuchtigen / Hochgebornen Fürsten* [...] *Philippi Landgraffen zu Hessen* [...]
*Hochnöthige unnd Gründliche Reformation / etlicher / in gemeinem üblichen Feldmessen / nach
und nach eingeschliechener schädlicher Irrthumbe* (Gießen: Hampel 1625) USTC 2059035,
Wolfenbüttel, Herzog August Bibliothek: Xb 7222, p. 8

Latin annotations in German how-to books suggest different kinds of users. One example is found in a lavishly bound half-parchment volume with blind embossing and metal clasps, containing twelve short how-to texts printed between 1529 and 1530, mainly in Nuremberg and Strasbourg, on topics including medicine for horses, distillation, epidemic diseases, and a *pharmacy for the common man*.[26] There are also two works by Paracelsus (1493/94–1531), who played a decisive role in formulating a 'new' medicine in the German vernacular, even though he was perhaps more fervent in his opposition to the Hippocratic-Galenic medical establishment than he was in his advocacy of a new medical audience of laypeople. One can surmise from the choice of works in the volume that it was deliberately compiled and used as a small how-to collection covering a range of medical topics. This is again indicated by material wear and tear, and by the abbreviated titles of the works on the fore-edge of the book, possibly intended to help navigate the volume. The annotations, which are not present in all works, include underlinings and occasional handwritten marginal notes, predominantly in Latin. Individual terms of the German printed text were glossed in Latin in the margins, and under a title woodcut depicting ancient scholars, a knowledgeable reader wrote in their names.[27] The user was particularly interested in passages on plague and other epidemic diseases: here, the page layout was visually structured by coloured markings in the text, in the manner of rubrications in manuscripts and incunabula, especially in passages with recipe-like instructions.[28] This type of annotation and the presentation of the volume suggest an educated readership and perhaps a courtly context.

The material traces of readers' textual work can be seen more clearly in another volume of publications collected around a theme. It is located in Duke August's library under the shelfmark 128.13 Med. (1–3). The three works bound together by an unknown previous owner were published between 1610 and 1617 by Johann Popp (born 1577), the 'Fürst[lich] Säch[sischen] Destillators zu Coburgk' [prince of Saxony's distiller at Coburg]. From around 1623, Popp styled himself 'Fürst:[lich] Säch:[sisch] und Brandenburgischer bestalter Chymicus'

---

26   [Hieronymus Brunschwig]; *Apoteck für den gemainen man* (Nuremberg: Stuchs 1529) USTC 612596, HAB: 23.1 Med. (9).

27   Brunschwig, *Apoteck für den gemainen man*, title woodcut, HAB: 23.1 Med. (9). The names 'Pytagoras' and 'Morienus' are inscribed by hand.

28   For instance a recipe by Brunschwig for the treatment of 'pestilential fever' using rhubarb: 'Nim Reubarbari [...] anderhalb quintlein [...],' fol. Biii r. Recipes were often more copiously annotated than other passages in early modern books; see e.g. Andrea van Leerdam, 'Popularising and Personalising an Illustrated Herbal in Dutch', in *Nuncius* 36,2 (2021), pp. 356–393.

[*Chymicus* of Saxony and Brandenburg by princely appointment].[29] Popp is known for a number of predominantly German-language works that convey chemiatric methods and recipes. Chemiatry or iatrochemistry is the technical term for a form of medicine oriented towards alchemy. One of its central procedures was distillation, which was already theoretically anchored in medieval alchemy. Largely outside this theoretical framework, small distilleries or even larger operations were quite common across social levels, for example for the production of brandy. According to Joachim Telle, the art of distilling in the sixteenth century was still almost entirely not in the hands of pharmacists or orthodox physicians.[30] Instead, it was practised by lay pharmacists and non-academic practitioners such as surgeons, barbers, or midwives, as well as the urban patriciate, landed gentry, clergy, and especially female members of the courtly nobility, who were often engaged in pharmacy.[31] Johann Popp practised as a doctor in the service of princes; whether he was also a municipal physician could not be determined.

Underlining and annotations have been made in each of the three chemiatric works in the volume. The first two works by Popp can be characterised as manuals with a broad scope.[32] The final work in the volume shows traces of particularly intensive engagement by a previous owner. This *Tractat von dem Diaphoretischen Praeparirten Antimonio* [Treatise on the diaphoretic preparation of antimony], published in 1610 in Coburg, the author's place of work, corresponds in a broader sense to the category of 'how-to guide' as defined

29   Johann Popp, *Von der Wassersucht und dero zufällen* (Leipzig: Schürer 1623) USTC 2045539.

30   Joachim Telle, 'Destillierbücher', in *Pharmazie und der gemeine Mann. Hausarznei und Apotheke in deutschen Schriften* der frühen *Neuzeit* (Ausstellungskataloge der Herzog August Bibliothek, 36) (Wolfenbüttel: Herzog August Bibliothek, 1982), pp. 91–95, here p. 92.

31   See, for example Alisha Rankin, *Panaceia's Daughters: Noblewomen as Healers in Early Modern Germany* (Chicago: The University of Chicago Press 2013); Gabriele Wacker, *Arznei und Confect. Medikale Kultur am Wolfenbütteler Hof im 16. und 17. Jahrhundert* (Wiesbaden: Harrassowitz 2013), pp. 62–64, 378–432; Jill Bepler, 'Perlen gegen Schulden', in Petra Feuerstein-Herz and Stefan Laube (eds.), *Goldenes Wissen. Die Alchemie – Substanzen, Synthesen, Symbolik* (Wiesbaden: Harrassowitz 2014), pp. 155–159.

32   Johann Popp, *Chymische Medicin Von dem nutz und gebrauch der destillierten Wasser* (Frankfurt am Main: Schamberger 1617) USTC 2043464, in which Popp compiled the observations and results of his 'Fewer-Arbeit [...] den Kunstliebenden [...] zu schaffung grosses Nutzes und Frucht' on more than 500 pages and brought them to print, as well as the *Handbüchlein und Experiment vieler Arzneien*, also published in Frankfurt am Main in the same year, in which Popp gives an overview of all the materials suitable from the three kingdoms of nature for the production of medicines by distillation.

above.[33] In only fifteen pages, the short text concentrates on alchemical preparations of antimony and their use as remedies. The text is not written throughout in the concise manner and terse prompts typically associated with recipe-like instructions. Preparations of the metalloid antimonyhave been used in medicine since antiquity for external application in eye ointments and for wound care.[34] The internal use of antimony preparations, as propagated by Paracelsus, was highly controversial in the sixteenth and seventeenth centuries. They were mainly used as emetics and purgatives.[35]

The handwritten traces left behind in the copy reveal the reader's particular interests and distinct processes of working with the text. He divided text passages into individual sections by means of numbering and other markings in the margins.[36] One of the aims was to characterise different physical states of antimony during its alchemical preparation. In Popp's description of the procedure, single and double underlining marks sensory cues such as discolouration, odour, and taste, that made it possible to recognise the key stages of the process. In alchemy, with its long tradition of communication in symbols, metaphors, and other codes, the instructions in how-to literature often left room for interpretation, even to the initiated. Where substance names and dosage instructions could be ambiguous, recognising individual stages of the lengthy transmutation processes was not an easy task even for experienced practitioners. One of the passages marked by the reader describes how the distillation of 'raw antimony' produces an *aqua* that was called 'Glüend Aquilae [...] und nachher brennend wie ein Fewer auf der zungen' [glowing *Aquilae* [...] and afterwards burned like fire on the tongue]. The text cautions the reader, 'habe achtung daß man ihm [...] nicht zu groß Fewer gebe / dann diß Weisse Saltz [...] / fehet (fängt) von sich selbsten an Schwartz zu werden / wie ein Dinten' [one should take care that one does not give it [...] too much fire, for this white salt [...] of its own accord begins to turn black like ink].

The annotations and markings in Popp's instructions for making medicinal antimony suggest that the reader might have worked with antimony in the laboratory. The identity of the book's owner cannot be established, since there is no named inscription or bookplate, and the initials 'IP' on the front endpaper provide far too unspecific a clue. It is unlikely that he was a practitioner of limited education or even a 'layman'. His annotations extend to the occasional

---

33   Johann Popp, *Tractat von dem Diaphoretischen Praeparirten Antimonio* (Coburg: Hauck 1610) USTC 2041499, HAB: 128.13 Med. (3).

34   Antimony occurs in nature mainly as antimony sulphide, also called stibnite.

35   Gerhard Brey, 'Antimony', in Claus Priesner and Karin Figala (eds.), *Alchemie. Lexikon einer hermetischen Kunst* (Munich: Beck, 1998), pp. 48–50.

36   Popp, *Von dem Diaphoretischen* [...] *Antimonio*, fol. Aii v.

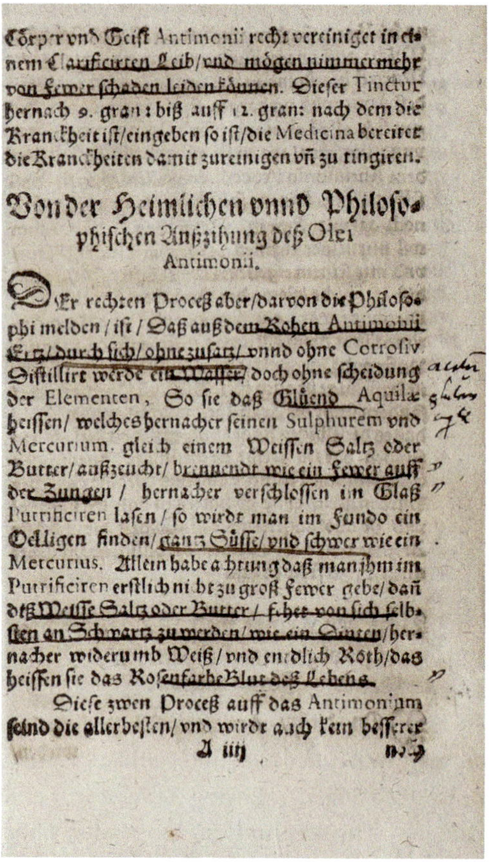

FIGURE 2.3

Johann Popp, *Tractat von dem Diaphoretischen Praepariten Antimonio* (Coburg: Hauck 1610) USTC 2041499, Wolfenbüttel, Herzog August Bibliothek: 128.13 Med. (3), fol. Aiiii r

passage in Latin, suggesting that he was proficient in this language. He was clearly interested in bolstering his antimony experimentations with a relevant work, to verify his experiences or improve his techniques. A Latin recipe for a purgative that was added to the back endpaper suggests that the book might even have been in the hands of an academically trained doctor seeking to educate himself in iatrochemistry.[37]

Handwritten recipes for the preparation of remedies can be found again and again in the large collection of printed books on medicine and natural history in the Wolfenbüttel library. It is often evident that they are not copied from the printed text of the work, but rather originate from other books, the reader's own experiences, or their exchanges with other healers. Recipes were written

---

37   On this recipe, see 'Magisterium Scammoni', in Johann Heinrich Zedler, *Großes vollständiges Universal-Lexicon aller Wissenschaften und Künste*, vol. 19 (Leipzig: Zedler 1738), p. 208.

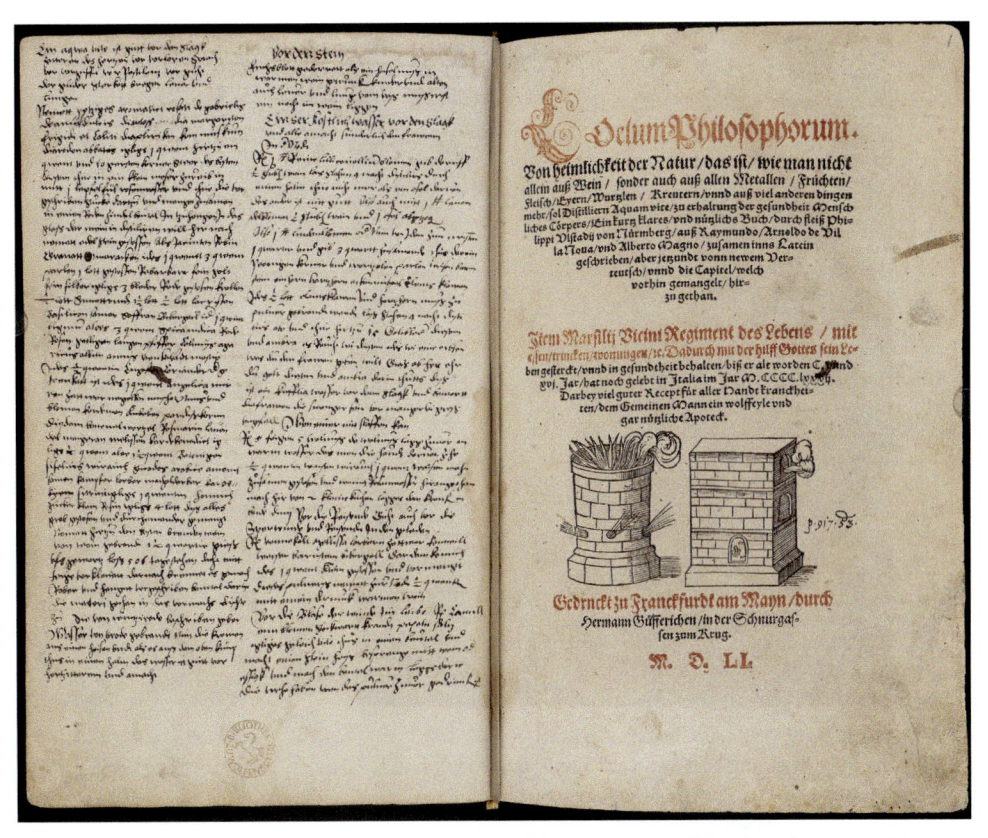

FIGURE 2.4   Philipp Ulsted, *Coelum philosophorum* (Frankfurt am Main: Gülfferich 1551) USTC 622866,
Wolfenbüttel, Herzog August Bibliothek: 35.1 Phys. 2° (1), title page and, on the left, the last
verso side of 15 blank leaves with handwritten notes bound in at the beginning of the volume

down in empty spaces on printed pages, the inside covers, endpapers, or even
on blank flyleaves bound into the books. A particularly striking example is an
extensive collection of recipes, applications, and diagnoses that were noted
by hand on numerous blank leaves bound in a hard cover with the distillation
books by Hieronymus Brunschwig and Philipp Ulsted, which were particularly
popular in the sixteenth century.[38]

What is striking about this volume is that it otherwise contains relatively
few annotations or underlining of the printed texts. These include, for example, the note 'Prüff' [check] on individual sections of text, obviously for
laboratory use. Similar kinds of book use are suggested by other alchemical,
botanical, and medical volumes preserved in the library: they were not used

---

38   [HAB: 35.1 Phys. 2°] see Feuerstein-Herz, 'Von *heimlichkeit der natur*', pp. 52–67.

FIGURE 2.5   Andreas Libavius, *Alchymistische Practic*
(Frankfurt am Main: Kopff, Saur 1603),
Wolfenbüttel, Herzog August Bibliothek:
Xb 4819, front cover

solely as instructional texts for the production of remedies or for alchemical experiments; rather, the copies served as records documenting the practitioners' own work.

The Wolfenbüttel copy of Andreas Libavius' *Alchymistische Practic* also contains virtually no annotations or markings in the printed text, although the volume has certainly been used in the laboratory, in close proximity to fire and liquids. This is clearly reflected in its state of preservation.

The entire book block is ravaged by burn marks, tears, liquid stains. The plain binding is very worn, with traces of mechanical damage that suggest intensive use during practical work outside the scholar's study or library. This distance to the usual spaces of book use is also indicated by the unusual mark of ownership, the name 'Johannes W B' and the year '1660' are carved into the front cover.[39] Apart from two short handwritten entries on the title page and in the index, longer notes are again found only on the inside front cover.

---

39   This possibly spontaneous unusual ownership marking probably corresponds with a name written in ink on the title page that is difficult to read, which must be pointed out for the sake of correctness.

In Brunschwig's and Libavius' works, the publishers or printers used a ploy that became an established strategy in sixteenth-century how-to books: the textual information and action-oriented instructions were accompanied by woodcuts depicting laboratory equipment, distilling apparatus, and furnaces, providing a quick overview to the reader, and a general idea of the topic to those who could not read. The visual detail of a complex set-up for distillation- could be directly juxtaposed with a corresponding text passage,

FIGURE 2.6 Andreas Libavius, *Alchymistische Practic* (Frankfurt am Main: Kopff, Saur 1603), Wolfenbüttel, Herzog August Bibliothek: Xb 4819, p. 10

such that the image could replace a, potentially wordy, textual description. Text and image thus alternate in close succession.[40]

In contrast to the Giessen surveying manual, however, neither the wood-cuts in the distillation books nor those in Libavius' *Practic* were annotated with

---

40 On the relationship of text and image in early print, see Brigitte Baumann and Helmut Baumann, *Die Mainzer Kräuterbuch-Inkunabeln 'Herbarius Moguntinus' (1484), 'Gart Der Gesundheit' (1485), 'Hortus Sanitatis' (1491). Wissenschaftshistorische Untersuchung Der Drei Prototypen Botanisch-Medizinischer Literatur Des Spätmittelalters* (Stuttgart: Hiersemann 2010); on the use of images in Brunschwig's distillation book, see Tillmann Taape, 'Distilling Reliable Remedies', pp. 236–256.

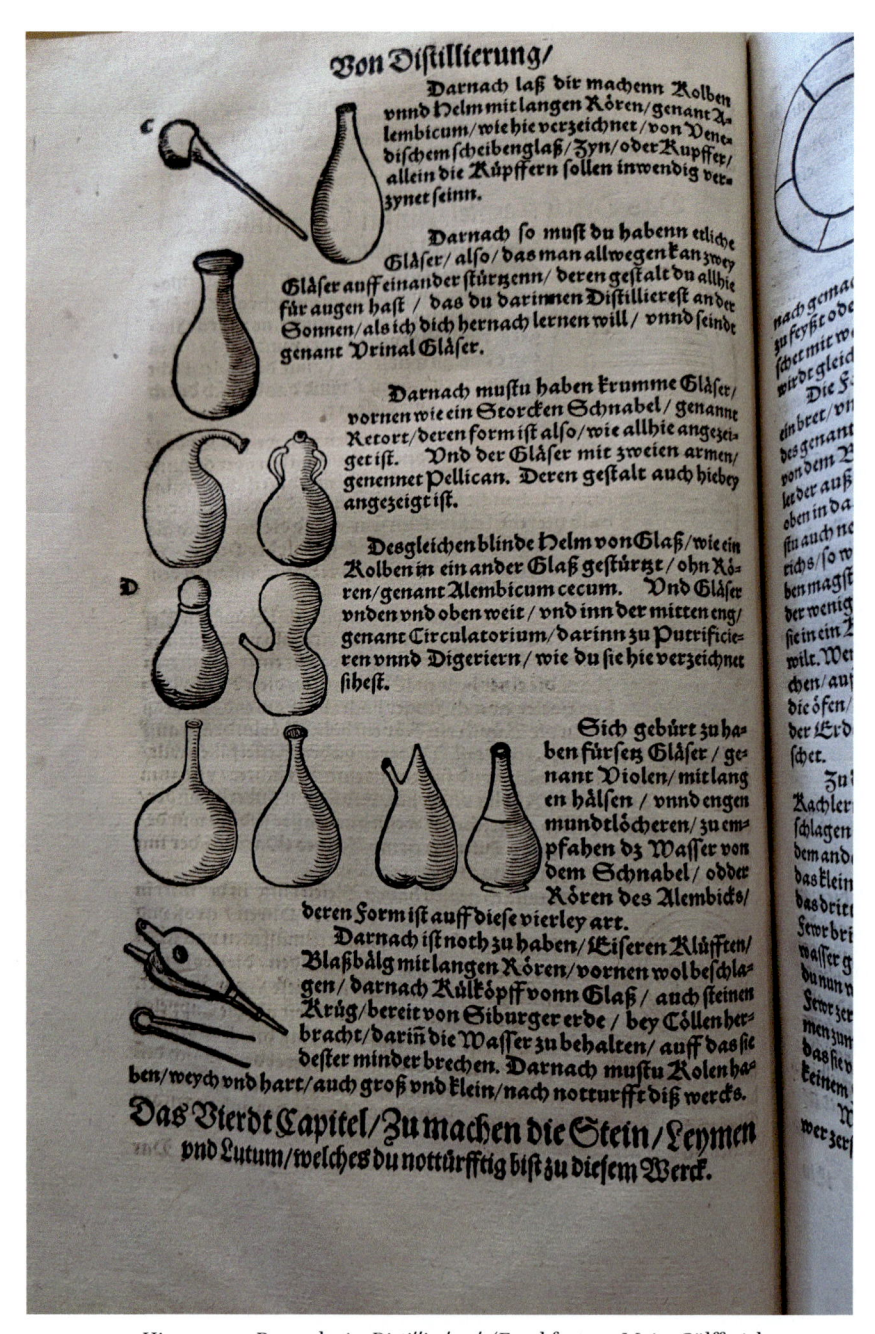

FIGURE 2.7 Hieronymus Brunschwig, *Distillierbuch* (Frankfurt am Main: Gülfferich 1551
USTC 640834, VD 16 B 8702), Wolfenbüttel, Herzog August Bibliothek: 35.1
Phys. 2° (2), fol. Cv v.k

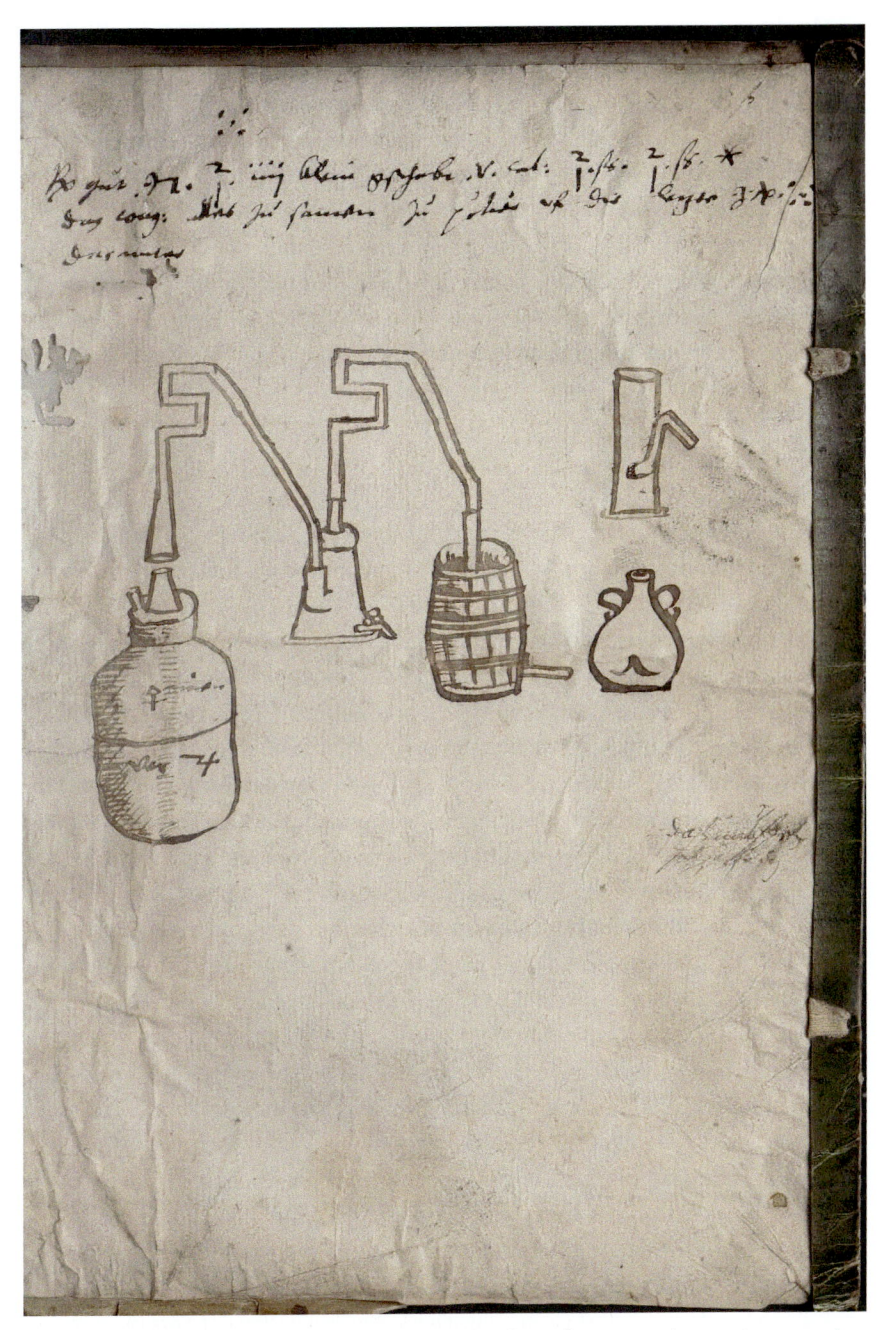

FIGURE 2.8 Paracelsus, *Medici libelli* (Köln: Virendunck, Birckmann 1567) USTC 675439, and
ders, *Büchlin von der Tinctura Physica* (Basel: Apiarius, Perna 1570) USTC 604964,
Wolfenbüttel, Herzog August Bibliothek: 46.2 Med. (1–2), back inside cover with
sketch of distillation apparatus

handwritten text or sketches that would indicate an engagement with these images. There are traces of a contemporary reception of this visual material. A chance find in the Wolfenbüttel collection reveals, on the back inside cover of the volume containing the two Paracelsian works,[41] a sketch of the distillation apparatus that closely corresponds to a woodcut on page ten of Libavius' *Practic*, where it is succinctly labelled as a 'Figur der distillation durchs Instrumentum' [figure of distillation by means of the *instrumentum*].[42]

While the image could have been copied for a number of different reasons, it is tempting to speculate that it might have served as a blueprint for the construction of complex distillation apparatus.

4   Conclusion

With the advent of print, there were fundamental changes in practices of knowledge communication, which soon contributed to the emergence of a new understanding of education: 'from now on it is not only the *magister* who teaches, but also the technical medium of the book', as Michael Giesecke sums up the formation of non-fiction and technical literature, which also includes how-to books for broad sections of the population.[43] In a small case study of copies from the holdings of the Herzog August Bibliothek, this article has explored some of the actors who wrote and used German-language literature for practical instruction in technical, medical, and alchemical contexts, by way of surviving volumes whose material traces testify to concrete use. As only a small number of copies could be examined within the framework of this article, the results should not be read as conclusive, but as a starting point.

Overall, it should be noted that all of the examples were written and published by practitioners, including some with academic training. They aimed for a practical, application-oriented presentation of technical content, explicitly addressed to lay readers. In their instructions for surveying land, preparing remedies, or conducting alchemical experiments, the authors employed more or less clearly recognisable didactic approaches. This included 'einfeltige ongezierte rede' [simple, unadorned speech] in the vernacular (Ulsted (1551), Preface), i.e. descriptions that were far removed from theory and less complex in their terminology. Ownership and use of instructional literature are

---

41   Paracelsus, *Medici libelli* (Cologne: Virendunck, Birckmann 1567) USTC 675439, HAB: 46.2
      Med. (1) and ders, *Büchlin von der Tinctura Physica* (Basel: Apiarius, Perna 1570) USTC
      604964, HAB: 46.2 Med. (2).

42   The copy kept in the HAB cannot have served as a model, as it was acquired antiquarily
      only a few years ago within the framework of the SDD.

43   Giesecke, *Buchdruck in der frühen Neuzeit*, p. 295.

reflected in handwritten entries, inscriptions of owners' names, annotations and underlining, and in the material wear-and-tear of the book block and binding.

The exploration of actual readers revealed little evidence to suggest a lay audience with limited technical knowledge. Only the short surveying manual could, at a stretch, be used by a layperson. The medical and alchemical guides under investigation clearly point towards readers with previous training, or even experienced practitioners. It is important to remember that the copies considered here originate not only from the historical collections of the Herzog August Bibliothek, but also from the antiquarian trade. They can thus come from a completely different context of previous ownership.

These books were apparently understood as consumables, since inscriptions of ownership or bookplates are rarely present. Even if the works were extensively annotated, as in the volume of writings by Johann Popp, which seems to have been in frequent use as a working tool, it was apparently not a priority for the owner to identify the book as his personal property.

Concerning medical how-to books, a number of volumes stand out that suggest a specific form of use beyond an engagement with the printed texts: if the recipes were no doubt read and perhaps also executed, the book served primarily as a medium for writing down other recipes, perhaps variations of those in the printed text, or altogether different recipes from other books or the readers' own practice. Where distillation books and other how-to works were available in the laboratory, they were apparently often used for notes from one's own practical work, regarding quantities, substances, ingredients, observations on processes, and so forth. The appeal of such recording practices is evident: they fixed practical in books with relevant printed content and allowed it to be passed on to other practitioners and across generations.

Translation: Tillmann Taape

CHAPTER 3

Who Owned the *Margarita Philosophica* and How Was It Read?

A Survey of the Sixteenth-Century Copies in the University of Glasgow Archives & Special Collections

Robert MacLean

Margarita Philosophica, The philosophical pearl, is an educational handbook written in the 1490s by Gregor Reisch and first published in 1503. While Reisch was prior of the charterhouse in Freiburg at the time of publication, the text was completed when he was at the University of Ingolstadt, likely employed as a tutor to Franz Wolfgang, Duke of Zollern and Waldburg, a young nobleman student. Composition of the *Margarita* started well before his engagement as a tutor, but it was young scholars like Zollern for whom Reisch intended the work, stating in the opening address that it was for 'adolescentes', for young men, and was intended to be an epitome or compendium of all of philosophy: in essence a handbook on 'how-to-do' philosophy.[1]

The *Margarita* was very popular during the sixteenth century with examples surviving from thirteen editions published before 1601.[2]

While the contents grew over time, with piracies and later editions interpolating new text not authored by Reisch, the subject matter and sequencing remained the same: twelve 'books', the first seven on rational philosophy (the seven liberal arts of grammar, logic, rhetoric, arithmetic, music, geometry, and astronomy), the next four on natural philosophy (on the principles of natural things, on the origin of natural things, on the soul and its power, on the nature, origin and immortality of the rational soul), and the final book on moral philosophy, all presented in the form of a dialogue between teacher and

---

1 Andrew Cunningham and Sachiko Kusukawa (tr & eds.), *Natural philosophy epitomized: a translation of books 8–11 of Gregor Reisch's Philosophical pearl (1503)* (London: Routledge, 2016), pp. x–xviii. Also see Peter G. Bietenholz and Thomas B. Deutscher, *Contemporaries of Erasmus: a biographical register of the Renaissance and Reformation* (Toronto: Toronto University Press, 2003), vol. 3, p. 137.

2 All editions were in Latin except for the final three which were published in Italian. See *Universal Short Title Catalogue (i.e., USTC)*: https://www.ustc.ac.uk/ (consulted 27 September 2021). Also see Cunningham and Kusukawa, *Natural philosophy epitomized*, pp. xxviii–xxx, where it is contended as many as sixteen sixteenth-century editions may have been published.

TABLE 3.1   Sixteenth-century editions of the *Margarita* with USTC number

Title	Date	Imprint	USTC number
Margarita philosophica	1503	[Freiburg im Breisgau, Johann Schott]	675099
Aepitoma omnis phyloso-phiae. Alias Margarita phylosophica	1504	[Strasbourg, per Johann Grüninger, 1504]	609451 & 609452 (variant)
Margarita philosophica	1504	[Strasbourg], Johann Schott	748439
Margarita philosophica	1508	Basel, [tertio industria cimplicu Michael Furter et Johann Schott]	605010
Margarita philosophica nova	1508	[Strasbourg, Johann Grüninger]	675100
Margarita philosophica nova	1512	[Strasbourg, Johann Grüninger]	675097
Margarita philosophica nova	1515	[Strasbourg, Johann Grüninger]	675098
Margarita philosophica	1517	[Basel, Michael Furter]	605011
Margarita philosophica	1535	Basel, [excudebat Heinrich aus Basel Petri ac Konrad Resch]	605012
Margarita philosophica	1583	Basel, per Sebastian Henricpetri	605013
Margarita filosofica	1599	Venezia, appresso Giacomo Antonio Somasco	852315
Margarita filosofica	1599	Venezia, presso Barezzo Barezzi & C.	852316
Margarita filosofica	1600	Venezia, appresso Giacomo Antonio Somasco	852317

pupil.[3] This sequence reflected the contemporary university philosophy curriculum and we know that it was widely used in universities across Europe.

---

3 On the publishing history see Cunningham and Kusukawa, *Natural philosophy epitomized*, pp. xxviii–xxx; and, John Ferguson, 'The Margarita Philosophica of Gregorius Reisch: a bibliography', *The Library*, s4-X, (2), (1929), pp. 194–216.

In their translation of the natural philosophy books (eight to eleven), Andrew Cunningham and Sachiko Kusukawa suggest the *Margarita* was:

> probably the most widely used resource for educating young men in northern Europe for more than a generation .... [and] probably as central a work as we are ever going to find to understand the education and mind-set of sixteenth-century university-level, Latin-reading, men.[4]

Yet, as significant as it might have been, can we really lay claim to the *Margarita* as a how-to text? I would argue that we can, or we can at least, in part. While some of the books are clearly intended to instruct the internal life and offer little by way of practical advice, others give detailed and illustrated advice on various practical topics and methods. In book four on arithmetic, for example, the text instructs the reader how to perform calculations via written notation and with a counting board, all illustrated with copious marginal woodcuts. Annotations in surviving copies witness readers practising calculations in the margins.[5] Books six and seven, on geometry and astronomy respectively, are similarly practical. In each case illustrations are arguably key in transforming the work from something theoretical into a how-to text.[6]

The *Margarita* is richly decorated with striking woodcut images. In his art-historical analysis Frank Büttner groups the images into different 'types' moving on a spectrum from the allegorical and figurative to the more descriptive and diagrammatic.[7] The *Margarita*'s 'how to do' credentials can be traced across the spectrum. A full-page woodcut opens each of the liberal arts books.[8] These allegorical woodcuts take the form of a female personification of each liberal art interacting with the major historical figures associated with the field's development. They perform a dual role summarising or encapsulating the content to come on the one hand, while establishing the text's authority, on the other. From a 'how to do' perspective the depicted figures

4 Cunningham and Kusukawa, *Natural philosophy epitomized*, pp. xii–xiii.
5 See for example, Ferguson Af-a.26, USTC 748439; Ferguson Af-b.40, USTC 605010; and Ferguson Af-a.35, USTC 675098.
6 This obtains for the first eight extant editions up to 1535. From Henricpetri's 1583 Basel edition, USTC 605013, onwards illustrations were considerably reduced.
7 See Frank Büttner, 'Die Illustrationen der Margarita Philosophica des Gregor Reisch. Zur Typologie der Illustration in gedruckten enzyklopädischen Werken der Frühen Neuzeit', in Frank Büttner, Markus Friedrich, Helmut Zedelmaier (eds.), *Sammeln, Ordnen, Veranschaulichen* (Münster: Lit, 2003), pp. 269–299.
8 For a more book-historical appraisal of the illustrations see Barbara C. Halporn, 'The 'Margarita Philosophica': a case study in early modern book design', *Journal of the Early Book Society*, 3 (2000), pp. 152–166.

are often shown performing the sorts of skilled practical activities in which the text offers training. Take for example the full-page woodcut opening book seven: 'Astronomy' is seen instructing Ptolemy in the use of the quadrant. Similarly, the opening woodcut of book four sees 'Arithmetic' in the background with Pythagoras and Boethius sitting in the foreground manipulating counting tables.[9] While missing from the first edition, from the second edition of 1504, the opening full-page woodcut of book six shows a seated 'Geometry' using a compass while other figures use an astrolabe and surveying equipment (see figure 3.2).[10] Book six is one of the most heavily illustrated. In the 1504 Schott edition, in the thirty-six pages of book six, over 180 separate woodcut images are inserted illustrating shapes, solids, geometrical diagrams etc.[11] Many of these, Büttner describes as 'explicative diagrams', used to define terms and explain the text: a genre with an ancient tradition in geometry treatises.[12] Yet, a key focus is practical geometry, with the text describing and illustrating the tools and methods required to put theory into practice in the fields of navigation and engineering. To better serve this end, what Büttner describes as 'demonstrative illustrations' are also employed.[13]

Take for example the woodcut demonstrating how to use the 'Jacob's staff', a device for measuring angles and heights in surveying (see figure 3.1). The image shows a man holding the staff up in front of his face, pointing it at a tower to measure the tower's height. This category of practical demonstrative illustration is found in various books of the *Margarita* and testifies to the how-to nature of the text.[14] The 'Jacob's staff' illustration is particularly interesting because, as Büttner notes, it contains an error: the measuring angle should lie in the eyeline of the observer, hence the staff is being held too high in the illustration, a mistake repeated in later editions.[15] This repeated error might lend

---

9   Büttner, 'Die Illustrationen der Margarita Philosophica des Gregor Reisch', p. 276.

10   Büttner, 'Die Illustrationen der Margarita Philosophica des Gregor Reisch', p. 278. This illustration first appears in USTC 748439.

11   While Schott was the first to publish the *Margarita*, Reisch had initially engaged the Basel printer Johannes Amerbach. The correspondence between Amberbach and one of the illustrators, Alban Graf, survives, specifically discussing the design of the geometry woodcuts. See Barbara C. Halporn, *The correspondence of Johann Amerbach: early printing in its social context* (Ann Arbor: University of Michigan Press, 2000), pp. 48–4 9.

12   Büttner, 'Die Illustrationen der Margarita Philosophica des Gregor Reisch', pp. 286–287.

13   Büttner, 'Die Illustrationen der Margarita Philosophica des Gregor Reisch', pp. 296–297.

14   For another example see the illustration demonstrating the 'oculus superior' and 'oculus inferior' method for empirically proving the curvature of the Earth's surface in book seven on Astronomy; see Büttner, 'Die Illustrationen der Margarita Philosophica des Gregor Reisch', p. 294.

15   Büttner, 'Die Illustrationen der Margarita Philosophica des Gregor Reisch', p. 295.

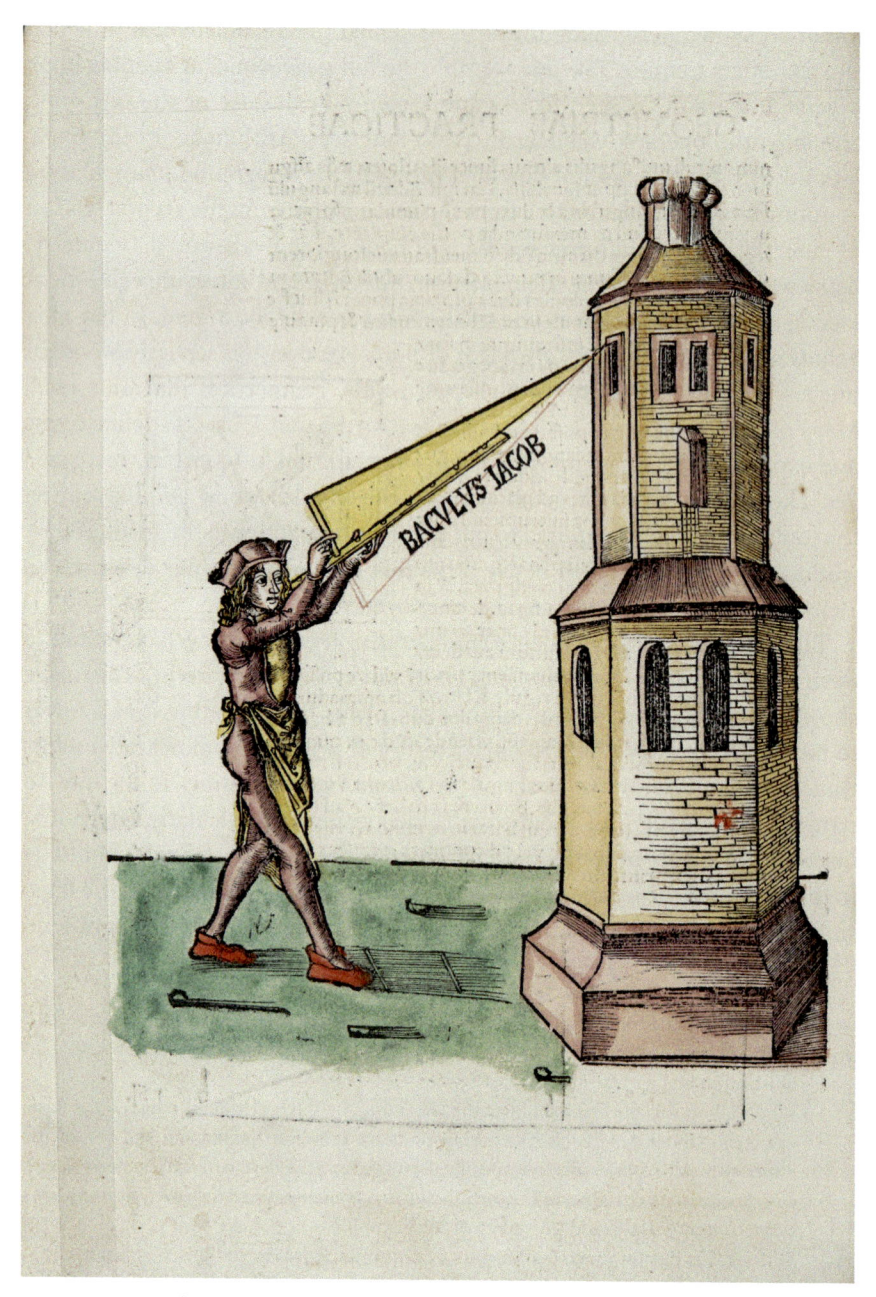

FIGURE 3.1 Woodcut illustration from book six, showing the correct use of the 'Baculus Jacob' (Jacob's staff) in surveying. Note the red line added by an early user or rubricator to correct the positioning of the staff. A hand-coloured copy from Ferguson Ag-a.30, USTC 748439

credence to an argument against the *Margarita*'s practical credentials; yet, if we look again at figure 3.2, we can see that in this particular copy (owned by the Carthusians in Freiburg, see later in the chapter for more details), an early user or rubricator has corrected the mistake by adding in new lines to rectify the angle at which the staff should be held. This seems to be clear evidence of contemporaries recognising the importance of accurate illustration in such how-to texts.

As the sixteenth century progressed, the *Margarita* arguably became even more practical with new material (not authored by Reisch) interpolated. Illustrated texts on reading Greek and Hebrew, a treatise on architectural tools and methods, instructions on drawing using perspective, and texts on the workings of the astrolabe and torquetum were all added initially within existing books and then, from 1512, annexed as an appendix. *Margarita Philosophica* was no mere series of thought experiments; it offered young people practical and illustrated introductions to the activities and techniques required in various professions.

1   The Margarita Philosophica and the University of Glasgow Library

Universal Short Title Catalogue (USTC) locates 373 surviving copies of the thirteen sixteenth-century editions, held by 166 libraries worldwide.[16] The total number of copies of the *Margarita* printed during the sixteenth century is unknown.[17] The University of Glasgow Archives & Special Collections (ASC) holds a staggering twenty-seven of them (7.2% of those located by USTC). The Glasgow holdings seem to be, by some margin, the largest collection of early-printed copies of the *Margarita* extant, with nearly double the number of copies located in any other institutional library.[18] Twenty-one of the copies

---

16   Figures from USTC (Consulted 27 September 2021).

17   Court records tell us the 1517 edition, USTC 605011, ran to 480 copies (see Cunningham and Kusukawa, *Natural philosophy epitomized*, p. xxxi). While print runs likely varied between editions of the *Margarita* a run of ca. 480 copies was not unusual for early printed works, which were commonly issued in runs of 500–2,000 copies (see Philip Gaskell, *A new introduction to bibliography* (Oxford: Clarendon Press, 1972), pp. 160–162). We could estimate the total number of sixteenth-century copies of the *Margarita* by multiplying 480 by the number of surviving editions to give us a notional total of 6,240. This is likely an underestimate since some edition print runs may have been larger, while other editions may have been printed, of which no copies survive.

18   Bayerische Staatsbibliothek, Munich = 15 copies; Staatsbibliothek Preußischer Kulturbesitz, Berlin = 12; New York Public Library = 10; Universitäts- und Stadtbibliothek, Cologne, and Österreichische Nationalbibliothek, Vienna = 9 each; Herzog August

were collected by John Ferguson, a noted book collector, bibliographer, and Professor of Chemistry at the University of Glasgow, where the bulk of his book collection remains. Although not now well-known, Ferguson was significant in the development of the history of science. His detailed study of the alchemical roots of modern chemistry was firmly based in descriptive bibliography fuelled by book collecting. A distinctive feature of his collecting was his propensity, when interested in a text, to seek out an example of every edition he could locate, often in multiple copies.[19] Ferguson collected more than twenty editions of the hermetic texts of Jābir ibn Ḥayyān, twenty-one incunable and post-incunable editions alone, of Pseudo-Albertus Magnus's books of secrets, thirty editions of Basilius Valentinus, and an incredible seventy-two editions of the occult philosopher Heinrich Cornelius Agrippa von Nettesheim.[20] Ferguson acquired his first copy of the *Margarita* in October of 1887, going on to collect a further sixteen copies over the next decade, and five more before the end of the century (twenty-one sixteenth-century copies collected in just thirteen years). He used them to compile a detailed and still very useful bibliography of the work, presenting a lecture on the topic to The Bibliographical Society in 1900.[21]

We can often tell when and from whom Ferguson acquired his copies (and what he considered significant about them) from short pencil notes he added to the pastedowns. From this we can tell that he purchased three of his copies from the booksellers Rosenthal Antiquarian (Ludwig and Jacques Rosenthal) in Munich, two from bookseller Anatole Claudin in Paris, and other copies from booksellers in London and Edinburgh. Now, for the first time, we are examining and cataloguing this significant collection in detail, looking at Ferguson's notes but also all earlier copy-specific evidence including early provenance and annotation. While the findings from this analysis fall some way short of what might be uncovered by a full census of all the surviving sixteenth-century copies, a closer look at the Glasgow corpus can nevertheless offer some indications on who owned the *Margarita Philosophica* and how it was read.

Bibliothek, Wolfenbüttel = 8; British Library, London, and Bibliothèque Mazarine, Paris = 7. Figures from USTC.

19   See David Weston, 'A Magus of the North? Professor John Ferguson and his Library', in Amy Wygant (ed.), *The Meanings of Magic: from the Bible to Buffalo Bill* (New York/Oxford: Berghahn Books, 2006), p. 169.

20   For more on Ferguson's collecting see Weston, 'A Magus of the North? Professor John Ferguson and his Library', pp. 161–177; and Anke Timmerman, 'Alchemy in Britain IV: John 'Soda' Ferguson and the Creation of a Great Chymical Library', in *The Book Collector*, (2019), pp. 665–683.

21   Ferguson, 'The Margarita Philosophica of Gregorius Reisch: a bibliography', pp. 194–216.

2   Ownership

Sixty separate provenances have been identified across the twenty-seven Glasgow copies. This chapter will concentrate on earlier provenance and material evidence, describing some of those owners living before 1700, of which there are twenty. Before turning to specific examples, it might be instructive to look at them as a group.

'Where were they from?' It has been possible to identify the likely nationality or residency in fourteen of the twenty provenances. The largest number, eight, are identifiably German.[22] This is perhaps not surprising given all but three of the known sixteenth-century editions were published in German-speaking states of the Holy Roman Empire or German-speaking Switzerland. Indeed, of the six unlocated provenances, the names of three – Hardt, Faber, Buttner – may also suggest a German language or cultural background but no conclusive evidence has been located to confirm.[23] The remaining owners are found dotted around Europe: Belgium, Poland, France, Spain, and a couple in Italy.[24]

'Who were they and what did they do?' In thirteen of the twenty provenances, it has been possible to determine something about the status or occupation of the owner. The largest group, eight in total, are religious institutional provenances from various orders: two from Augustinian houses, one from the Capuchin order, another from the Cistercians, one Jesuit College, one from an Italian house of the Patres Fillipini order, and one from Gregor Reisch's own Carthusian order, indeed from the very charterhouse in Freiburg of which he was prior.[25] Other occupations or backgrounds represented include: two medics, a cleric, a minor noble, an early Munich collector, and tantalisingly one

---

22   Antonius de Columbergia (i.e. Colmar, Alsace) – Ferguson Af-a.28; Augustinian Canons of Blessed Virgin Mary, Gaesdonck, North Rhine Westphalia – Ferguson Ag-a.36; Capuchins, Weissenhorn, Baden-Württemberg – BD9-e.7; Carthusians, Freiburg-im-Bresgau, Baden-Württemberg – Ferguson Ag-a.30; Cistercians, Schöntal, Baden-Württemberg – Ferguson Ag-a.38; Augustinian Canons, Passau, Bavaria – Sp Coll E.d.20; Georg Lindaur, Munich, Bavaria – Ferguson Ag-a.38; Johann Georg Werdenstein, Eichstatt/Augsburg, Bavaria – Ferguson Ag-a.35.

23   'Joannij Hardj' – Ferguson Af-a.37; 'J.H. Fabrj' – BD9-e.7; 'Friderici Buttner' – Ferguson Af-a.33.

24   Francisci Mayeri Alostani (i.e., Aalst, Belgium) – Sp Coll 978; Christoph Wentzel, Grav von Nostitz, Jawor, Poland – Ferguson Ag-a.33; J. Visorius, Johannes Vignius, Petrus Scala, and Stephanus Machus, Paris – Ferguson Af-b.66; Laurentius Vascus(?), Cartagena(?), Spain; and Cosimo Granitus, Naples/Cassano, Italy – Mu54-c.10; Patres Fillipini order [unidentified Italian monastery] – Ferguson Ag-a.34.

25   Augustinians: Canons of BVM, Gaesdonck, North Rhine Westphalia – Ferguson Ag-a.36, and Canons, Passau, Bavaria – Sp Coll E.d.20; Capuchins: Weissenhorn, Baden-Württemberg – BD9-e.7; Cistercians: Schöntal, Baden-Württemberg – Ferguson Ag-a.38;

inscription connecting a copy with possible student ownership.[26] In discussing some of these owners in a little more detail, it is here that we will begin.

There is a handwritten contract between three students and their teacher on the rear of the final blank leaf of a copy of the first Grüninger edition, published in Strasbourg, 1504.[27] It states that Johannes Vignius, Petrus Scala, and Stephanus Machus, on 22 August, have concluded a contract for 'lectiones', lessons, with a tutor called J. Visorius, for the sum of 5 solidi.[28] Beyond their names, the students remain unidentified; however, Johannes Visorius is possibly to be identified as Jean Le Voyer, a philosophy teacher active during the 1530s at the Collège de Bourgogne, part of the University of Paris.[29] We know that the work was conceived by Reisch for students and we know it was used elsewhere as a university textbook; this copy seems to be providing further material evidence of the *Margarita* being used in such a university setting, though it is unclear whether it belonged to Le Voyer, one of the three students, or a third party.[30]

An interesting seventeenth-century medical provenance, indeed a 'radical' provenance, is associated with a copy of the 1583 edition published in Basel by Sebastian Henricpetri.[31] It is one of the handful of copies from the Glasgow corpus not once owned by John Ferguson.[32] At the foot of the titlepage is penned the name 'Cosmas Granitus', very likely the signature of the Italian physician Cosimo Granito. Granito played a minor but noteworthy role in the revolt

---

Jesuits: [unidentified house] – Ferguson Af-a.1; Patres Fillipini order [unidentified Italian house] – Ferguson Ag-a.34.

26   Medics: Cosimo Granito and Laurentius Vascus, Iatrophysicus – Mu54-c.10; cleric: Johann Georg von Werdenstein, Canon of Eichstatt and Augsburg – Ferguson Ag-a.35; noble: Christoph Wentzel, Grav von Nostitz; early Munich collector: Georg Lindauer – Ferguson Ag-a.38.

27   Ferguson Af-b.66, USTC 609452.

28   Many thanks to Jack Baldwin, principal researcher on the Glasgow Incunabula Project, for helping decipher this inscription and for his advice on several of the other provenances.

29   See 'Visorius, Iohannes' [record cnp01241159], *CERL Thesaurus*: https://data.cerl.org/thesaurus/cnp01241159 (Consulted 11 May 2022).

30   For biographical details and a description of some of Le Voyer's teaching methods see Barthélemy Haréau (ed.) *Histoire Littérarire du Maine* (Paris: Du Moulin, 1874), Vol. 7. pp. 235–238.

31   Mu54-c.10, USTC 605013.

32   In this case coming from the sizeable collection of nineteenth-century Glasgow lawyer David Murray. For more on Murray see, 'Murray Collection' *University of Glasgow Library Archives & Special Collections* https://www.gla.ac.uk/myglasgow/archivespecial collections/discover/specialcollectionsa-z/murraycollection/ (consulted 30 June 2022).

against Spanish rule in Naples and Calabria in the late 1640s.[33] He was from a medical family, with both his grandfather and father before him respected physicians. After studying medicine and philosophy at the University of Naples, he opened a medical surgery in his hometown of Cassano in which he treated the town's neediest free of charge. In 1647, when parts of the Calabrian populace rose to protest unfair taxation and heavy-handed Spanish rule, Granito led the Cassano revolt, successfully besieging the town's castle before distributing the feudal lands amongst the people. But this romantic tale did not have a happy ending. Though initially pardoned and protected by powerful friends (including the Bishop of Cassano), Granito continued fighting. A new revolt ended in defeat with the rebels barricading themselves into the same castle they had previously taken. Granito was arrested, summarily hanged, and then beheaded, his head prominently displayed on a spike.[34] The unpopularity of his execution can be inferred by a folk tale reporting that the moment of his hanging was disrupted by a huge storm, with lightning crashing down, dispersing the assembled onlookers.[35]

The next example for discussion is a religious institutional provenance, found in a copy of the second of Johannes Schott's editions, published in Strasbourg, 1504.[36] An inscription asserts ownership by the Carthusians of the Mount of Saint John the Baptist in Freiburg, the charterhouse of which Gregor Reisch was prior. While not a first edition, it is a copy of the authorised second edition; indeed, it is a rather deluxe copy. The book has flourished initial letters, rubrication professionally added throughout, and beautifully hand-coloured woodcut illustrations. This professional decoration and colouring may well have been commissioned by Reisch or the charterhouse, or perhaps the copy was presented to the author or institution by the publisher.[37]

While modern researchers and collectors enthuse over copies like this, hand-colouring has not always been appreciated. John Ferguson, for example, was not a fan. On the front pastedown Ferguson has penciled, 'spoiled with colouring', which seems a harsh judgment given the excellent quality of execution.

---

33   For more on the revolt see Rosario Villari, *The revolt of Naples* (Cambridge: Polity Press, 1993), especially chapter 6.

34   All biographical details here from Leonardo R. Alario, *Crontassi dei vescovi di Cassano: diocesi calabro-lucana dei due mari. XVII secolo* (Cosenza: Luigi Pellegrini editore, 2019), pp. 200–201 (see especially n. 14).

35   Domenico Arena, 'Istoria delli disturbi e Revolutioni acceduti nella Citta di Cosenza', *Archivio storico per le province napoletane* (Anno quarto; fasiculo 1) (1879), p. 18.

36   Ferguson Ag-a.30, USTC 748439.

37   For more on presentation copies see Richard Ovenden, 'Presentation copy', in Michael F. Suarez and H.R. Woudhuysen (eds.), *The Oxford Companion to the Book* (Oxford: Oxford University Press, 2010), p. 1049.

FIGURE 3.2   The opening hand-coloured woodcut of book six, on Geometry, with hand-flourished initials
in the *Margarita* owned by the Carthusians of the Mount of Saint John the Baptist in Freiburg,
Ferguson Ag-a.30, USTC 748439.

Similarly, in other copies he remarks, 'spoiled by colouring', 'not coloured', and
perhaps most revealingly, 'has not been spoiled by sham illuminator'.[38]

Susan Dackerman has written about the often-misplaced skepticism towards
hand-colouring expressed by collectors of the recent past.[39] This distaste manifested itself in different ways. It was a common assertion in art history literature
that, 'to colour prints is to spoil prints' first stated in this way by Willem Goeree
in the late seventeenth century (coming from the rhyming Dutch, 'printen bev-
erven is printen bederven').[40] In large part Dackerman lays the blame for this
idea at Erasmus's door since in a 1528 tribute to Dürer, Erasmus praised his ability to master, 'light, shade, splendor, eminences and depressions', in black and
white alone. Erasmus dismissed the addition of colour to such accomplished
monochrome print work as straightforward 'injury'. Dackerman suggests

---

38   In Ferguson Af-a.37, Ferguson Ag-a.36, and Ferguson Af-y.74, respectively. All are USTC
675099.

39   See Susan Dackerman, *Painted prints: the revelation of color* (University Park: Penn State
University Press, [2002]).

40   Dackerman, *Painted prints: the revelation of color*, p. 1, 6 (n. 1).

Erasmus was simply employing a rhetorical flourish, arguing for Dürer's legacy as an independent genius with no need of hand-colourists. Yet, in so doing he inadvertently, 'prejudiced the reception of hand-coloured prints ever since'.[41]

Another reason past collectors and art historians disliked hand-coloured prints was an assumption that colouring was inauthentic, added long after printing.[42] On the contrary, we now know that hand-colouring of printed illustration was popular, was desirable, and was often an integral part of print production right through the seventeenth century.[43] We now have the benefits of scientific analysis which, through techniques like X-ray fluorescence, can identify minerals within pigments and indicate which are synthetic and later.[44] Without scientific analysis it is not possible to say definitively whether colouring is contemporary or later; yet, given the Freiburg Carthusian copy's unique provenance, we would now be far less likely to dismiss it out of hand as the work of a later or 'sham' illuminator.

In summary, surviving provenance evidence points to copies of the *Margarita* being owned during the early-modern period by a range of professional men and religious institutions. Yet, even where such evidence is located, it offers just a snapshot of a single copy's ownership history, making it difficult to draw any wider conclusions on the motivation for acquisition or how/if the copy was used. The problem is well illustrated by a final example, another copy of the second of Johannes Schott's editions, Strasbourg, 1504.[45] It is known to have been owned by Georg Lindauer, a book collector active in Munich around 1600. But when and why did Lindauer buy it? Was it acquired in middle or later life, to add to his burgeoning book collection? Or was it bought earlier? As a young man he is known to have studied jurisprudence in Bologna, Sienna, Rome, and Pisa, so it is perhaps more likely he bought his *Margarita* as a textbook during his student days.[46] After Lindauer's death the copy passed into the institutional library of the Cistercians at Schöntal in Baden-Württemberg. Was

---

41   Dackerman, *Painted prints: the revelation of color*, pp. 11–12. Citing e.g., USTC 631329.
42   Dackerman, *Painted prints: the revelation of color*, p. 3.
43   Dackerman, *Painted prints: the revelation of color*, p. 11.
44   See Thomas Primeau, 'The materials and technology of Renaissance and Baroque hand-colored prints', in Dackerman, *Painted prints: the revelation of color*, pp. 49–75; also see Shelley Fletcher, Lisha Glinsman and Doris Oltrogge, 'The pigments on hand-coloured fifteenth-century relief prints from collections of the National Gallery of Art and the Germanisches Nationalmuseum', in Peter Parshall, *The Woodcut in fifteenth-century Europe* (Washington DC, National Gallery of Art, 2009), pp. 277–291.
45   Ferguson Ag-a.38, USTC 748439.
46   For more on Lindauer and his book collection see Paul Ruf, *Säkularisation und Bayerische Staatsbibliothek. 1: Die Bibliotheken der Mendikanten und Theatiner, 1799–1802* (Wiesbaden: Harrassowitz, 1962), p. 464.

it acquired by them because someone thought it would be particularly useful? We just do not know; yet, given a sizeable collection of Lindauer's books ended up in Schöntal, the *Margarita* probably formed part of a larger acquisition and this text was not sought by the Cistercians specifically. But we are fortunate to have these two connected provenances in this copy, allowing us to think more deeply about ownership. In most cases this sort of context is lacking meaning provenance evidence is difficult to interpret. We know, for example, that eight copies from the Glasgow corpus were owned pre-1700 by religious houses but what does this really mean? Is it because they were actively being used in monasteries? Or is it simply that monasteries were the final resting place for many professional men's private book collections, often including those texts they bought in adolescence? It is difficult to know, and provenance evidence often cannot answer these questions satisfactorily.

3   Evidence of Reading: Annotations

How was the *Margarita* read? As discussed earlier, it could certainly be read in places as a practical manual or 'how to do' book. But did readers approach it as a work to be read through, starting on the first page? Or was it read more discontinuously or sporadically, with readers dipping in and out of different books? This is an important question to address; as Cunningham and Kusukawa have noted, the *Margarita* has often been described as an encyclopedia, implying purposeful, just-in-time use but in their view:

> The philosophical pearl was certainly intended to be read through, rather than dipped into as the continuing line of argument of the text indicates. It thus puts into a more accessible and attractive format all the materials that a university student would become acquainted with through lectures.[47]

Can a study of the Glasgow corpus provide evidence of how the *Margarita* was actually read? We might attempt to explore this by applying a quantitative method recently employed by Daniel Margócsy, Mark Somos and Stephen N. Joffe in their 2018 descriptive census of surviving copies of the first two editions of Vesalius's *Fabrica*.[48] This approach focuses on material evidence of reading: annotations. Study after study has confirmed that reader

---

47   Cunningham and Kusukawa, *Natural philosophy epitomized*, p. xi.
48   See Daniel Margócsy, Mark Somos and Stephen N. Joffe, *The Fabrica of Andreas Vesalius: a worldwide descriptive census, ownership, and annotations of the 1543 and 1555 editions* (Leiden: Brill, [2018]). A worldwide census of USTC 606035 and USTC 606036.

annotations are extremely commonly found in early-printed works. While Margócsy et al. acknowledge that a reader may have read a volume cover to cover and thought deeply about the contents, the pages they stopped to annotate might suggest the areas in which they were most interested. While it is an imperfect metric, mapping the pattern of annotation can be used as a proxy for mapping reader engagement.[49]

Margócsy et al. separately mapped out annotation data for the two editions of the *Fabrica*, page by page. The corpus of Glasgow copies of the *Margarita* is somewhat different, with multiple editions included, therefore the methodology has been adapted. Rather than looking at which pages within a copy have been annotated, this study instead considers which books have received annotation to give a proxy for broad areas of reader engagement.[50]

Sixteen of the twenty-seven Glasgow copies are annotated (59%). More specifically, ninety-two books in total are annotated (28.5%). The distribution of annotations between books can be plotted to crudely visualise which received the most attention from readers.

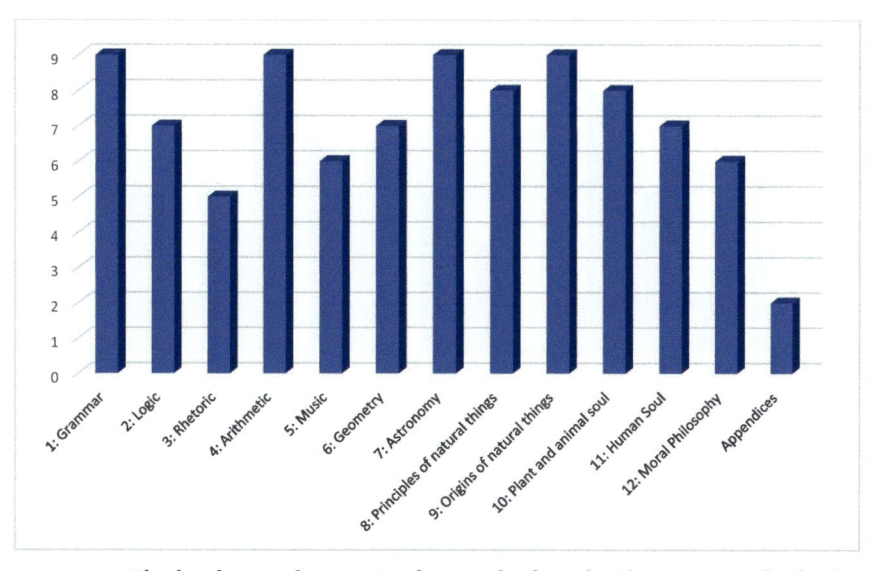

FIGURE 3.3 The distribution of annotations between books in the Glasgow corpus (book title on the x-axis and number of copies on y-axis)

---

49 Margócsy, Somos and Joffe, *The Fabrica of Andreas Vesalius*, pp. 58, 61.

50 Book- and hence subject-sequence within the *Margarita* remained consistent over the century. Given multiple editions are included in the corpus, to permit equivalence in comparison it was necessary to convert the overall number of annotated pages in a book into a percentage of the book's total pages. A book within a copy has been considered annotated if even a single reader annotation (marginal comment, underlining, manicule etc) has been added to one of the pages.

This distribution seems reasonably even, though the books on Grammar, Arithmetic, Astronomy, and the Origins of Natural Things are most frequently annotated (in nine copies), and the book on Rhetoric, comparatively slightly less frequently annotated (five copies). Least frequently annotated is the appendix (two copies). The appendix was a publishing innovation first appearing in 1512 but even accounting for this it is annotated in just 18% of the copies where present. Appendix aside though, annotations are reasonably well distributed, arguably indicating no single book was markedly of more interest to readers than another. This evidence may support Cunningham and Kusukawa's characterisation of the *Margarita* as an epitome and university textbook, read through sequentially rather than sporadically.[51]

While Figure 3.3 provides some insight on the distribution of annotations between books in the corpus, it does not tell us where annotation is most concentrated. We can plot the number of copies where 10% or more of the pages of a book have been annotated, and those where 25% or more pages are annotated to get a better sense of the parts of the *Margarita* in which readers were most focused (see figure 3.4).

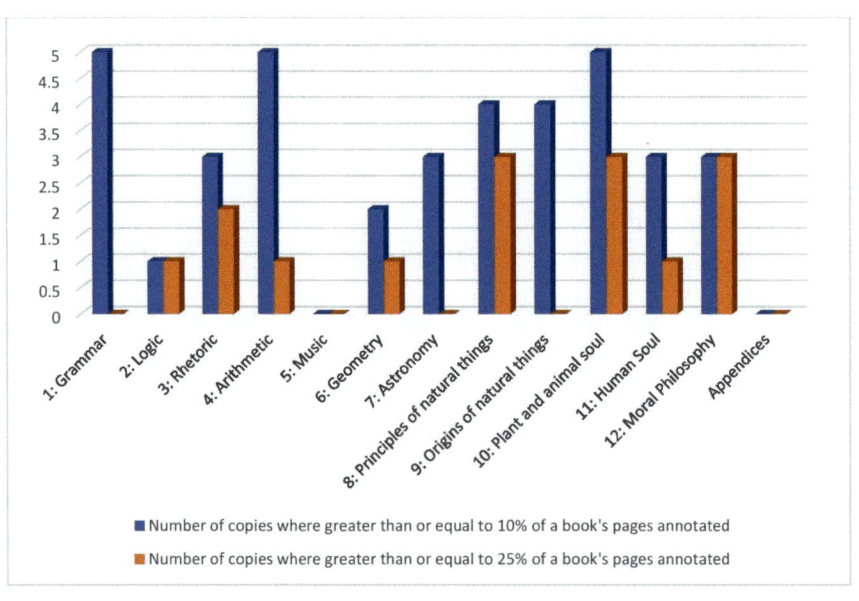

FIGURE 3.4 Number of copies where greater than or equal to 10% and 25% of a book's pages are annotated (book title on x-axis and number of copies on y-axis)

51   Cunningham and Kusukawa, *Natural philosophy epitomized*, p. x–xi.

If we consider the number of copies where 10% or more of the pages of a book have been annotated, distribution appears reasonably even apart from book five, on music. There are nineteen instances of greater than or equal to 10% of pages annotated in the first seven books (on the liberal arts) and nineteen instances for the remaining five books (the more advanced natural and moral philosophy). So again, this might be interpreted as evidence supporting a systematic approach to reading and engagement, where the text is being read through and readers are paying close attention to most parts.

A smaller number of copies demonstrate more than or equal to 25% of the pages of a book annotated. The small number of instances in which this is taking place indicate such concentrated annotation is uncommon.[52] It is difficult to draw any safe conclusions. It might be interpreted as the more advanced natural or moral philosophical sections are those where a reader is most likely to become very engaged with a book, since these last five books are twice as likely as the first seven to receive such treatment.[53]

A final caveat for this sort of analysis: while twenty-seven copies is a substantial corpus for study, it is small for a quantitative approach so these findings are only indicative of what a wider survey might consider.[54]

4   Evidence of Reading: Navigation Aids

In common with many early-printed works, the earlier editions of the *Margarita* (prior to the 1535 Basel edition) were printed without page or folio numbers.[55] The text was divided into twelve books, each book subdivided into chapters with an index added to help readers locate different sections, chapter by chapter. Readers often tried to make such unpaginated books easier to use and these copy-specific alterations can provide clues on how the book was read.

One approach was to add pagination or foliation by hand and then to amend the index. If we consider just the pre-1535 portion of the Glasgow corpus (twenty copies), handwritten pagination/foliation is found in just a single copy of the Grüninger edition, Strasbourg, 1515.[56] Yet, given the style of handwriting, and that the copy has been completely rebound in the nineteenth-century,

52   Just fifteen instances in total.

53   Ten instances of 25% or more of pages annotated in books 8–12 compared with five instances in books 1–7.

54   Margócsy et al. included 630 copies in their corpus. See Margócsy, Somos and Joffe, *The Fabrica of Andreas Vesalius*, p. 9.

55   USTC 605012.

56   Ferguson Af-a.35, USTC 675098.

it seems very likely that this pagination is later perhaps added by the owner who commissioned the new binding, Belgian collector and aristocrat Anselm vanden Bogaerde.

Navigation might also be improved through the addition of leaf tab markers. These tabs were affixed to, and protruded beyond the edge of, leaves of the book the reader wished to easily locate. This sort of adaptation to a book's fore-edge would commonly be lost if the copy were later rebound (since usually the edges would need to be ploughed after the gatherings were resewn). Only six of the twenty pre-1535 Glasgow copies survive with early bindings intact. Two of these (both the Johannes Schott edition of Strasbourg, 1504), display leaf tab markers.[57]

In the first example, the tabs are formed from pink-stained, alum-tawed leather. They comprise thirteen in total, affixed to leaves allowing quick navigation to the start of each of the twelve books and to the index. This copy (as previously discussed) was owned by Gregor Reisch's own Carthusian charterhouse in Freiburg. The pattern of the leaf tab markers seems sensible and unremarkable, but it nevertheless indicates the copy was sufficiently valued for someone to go to the trouble of making it easier to use.

The second example has leaf tab markers of knotted parchment manuscript waste, with each knot covered in red wax. Again, they comprise thirteen in total and are affixed in a very similar pattern to the first example, allowing easy access to the start of each book and to the index. This second example displays one noticeable difference: the knotted leaf tab marker affixed to the start of book eight, on the principles of natural things, is much larger and more elaborate than the others, and is not covered in red wax.

This might indicate that the tab creator wished to mark out book eight, seeing it as particularly important. Or perhaps more likely, the marker is being used to divide the text into two sections. If so, this could be material evidence confirming the reader conceived the first seven books on the liberal arts differently from the subsequent five on natural and moral philosophy. The copy is bound in blind-stamped tawed pigskin over wooden boards of the type commonly used in Germany; yet, unfortunately, we have no surviving early provenance evidence in this copy which might allow us to speculate further about owner or motivation for this leaf tab marker choice.

---

57   Ferguson Ag-a.30 and Ferguson Ag-a.22, USTC 748439.

FIGURE 3.5 Three images of leaf tab markers from Ferguson Ag-a.22, USTC 748439. On left: fore-edge. Centre: large knotted marker for book eight. On right: knotted wax-covered markers

5 Evidence of Reading: Expurgation and Modification[58]

While there has been no attempt to analyse the contents of handwritten annotations in individual copies for this brief survey, some noteworthy patterns of copy-specific intervention should be highlighted. Two copies of the *Margarita* contain expurgated woodcut illustrations obliterated in pen. One modified woodcut is the zodiac man located in book seven, the other is the anatomical cut showing human organ distribution located in book nine. The former depicts a full-frontal nude man, with the signs of the zodiac arranged around the body.[59] The latter is a three-quarter-length nude man dissected to reveal the body cavity and supposed placement of the internal organs. While the figure is truncated at the thighs, a partial hint of genitalia is included. In one copy both images have been censored blacking out the genitals in pen.[60]

---

58   With thanks to Suzanne Karr Schmidt whose thoughts I have benefitted from for this section.

59   Different parts of the body were thought to be 'ruled' by different signs of the zodiac and hence medical interventions on each body part was believed to be most propitiously carried out during certain times of year. See Charles Clark, 'The Zodiac Man in Medieval Medical Astrology' *Quidditas* 3, (1982), p. 13.

60   Ferguson Ag-a.30, USTC 748439.

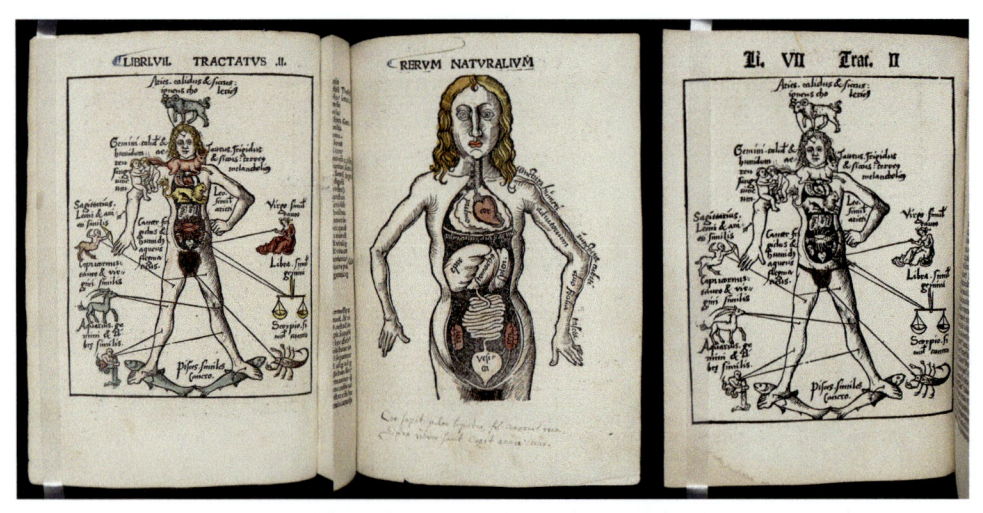

FIGURE 3.6   Three expurgated images. On left and centre: the zodiac man and organ man illustrations
            from Ferguson Ag-a.30, USTC 748439. On right: zodiac man from Sp Coll E.d.20, USTC 605010

In the other, the zodiac man alone has been censored with what looks like underwear overdrawn to protect his modesty.[61]

Encountering copies of early printed books with illustrations altered in this way is not uncommon and is found in various contexts.[62] In each case expurgation might be a private and personal intervention by a modest or censorious reader, or a more public act of censorship mandated by an institution and often applying to multiple copies of a text. Alteration might be motivated by moral and religious objections. When examining copies of books with expurgated images, it can be difficult to know who was responsible for the intervention, their motivation, or when it occurred.

Landau and Parshall mention several early sixteenth-century examples of civic authorities attempting to control the publication of illustrated erotic literature. Nuremberg Town Council banned one such book in 1535 explaining that, 'lustful images alone can provoke great scandal and incite the youth to sinful vices'.[63] It is perhaps not surprising that there were institutional attempts

---

61   Sp Coll E.d.20, USTC 605010.
62   The US Association of College and Research Libraries (ACRL) Rare Books and Manuscripts Section (RBMS) controlled vocabulary – intended to harmonise descriptive metadata between libraries – has even listed an entry to describe the practice, see 'Expurgated copies' in *RBMS Controlled Vocabularies: Provenance Evidence Terms*: https://rbms .info/vocabularies/provenance/tr108.htm (consulted 30 June 2022).
63   David Landau and Peter Parshall, *The Renaissance Print: 1470–1550* (New Haven, Yale University Press, 1994) pp. 225–226.

to control public access to pornography; yet, other types of literature have also been attacked by civic authorities where images of nudity are present.[64] The 1497 first edition of Giovanni Bonsignori's illustrated *Metamorphoses* of Ovid is one example.[65] Under threat of excommunication the publisher and printer were forced by the Venetian patriarch to censor the already-printed sheets, obliterating in ink all woodcuts with nude figures, while also modifying the woodcut blocks for the subsequent edition by carving out the genitalia.[66]

Medical works have also fallen foul of censors.[67] In their census of the first two editions of Vesalius's *Fabrica*, Margócsy et al. report more than twenty examples of copies with anatomical woodcuts censored to conceal genitalia, very similar to those found in the Glasgow copies of the *Margarita*.[68] They attribute it to Catholic Church censorship noting that the *Index prohibitorum librorum* did not just focus on heretical works but also those considered licentious.[69] In response to the Reformation, the Catholic Church published several indexes prohibiting certain texts or mandating expurgation before copies were permitted to be read. It was the responsibility of various agents

---

64   For the early modern view of how 'passions' were potentially inflamed when reading and the corporeal and moral dangers, see Adrian Johns, *The Nature of the Book: Print and Knowledge in the Making* (Chicago: The University of Chicago Press, 1998), pp. 380–433.

65   USTC 992722.

66   Giuseppe Capriotti, 'Eroticism under a watchful eye: censorship and alteration of woodcuts in Ovid's Metamorphoses between the Fifteenth and the Sixteenth centuries' in Grażyna Jurkowlaniec and Magdalena Herman (eds.), *The reception of the printed image in the fifteenth and sixteenth centuries: multiplied and modified* (New York: Routledge, 2021), p. 118. Similar systematic expurgation of nude woodcuts in the printing workshop is reported by George D. Painter for the first edition of *Hypnerotomachia Poliphili*, USTC 995631. See George D. Painter, 'The Hypnerotomachia Poliphili of 1499: an introduction on the dream, the dreamer, the artist, and the printer' in *Studies in fifteenth-century printing* (1984), pp. 177–178. It should be noted that Neil Harris is sceptical about this claim saying, 'censorship is only found in a small number of cases and in none of them does it appear to be contemporary'. Neil Harris (University of Udine), personal communication, 2022.

67   For additional examples see Harry Newman, "[P]rophane fidlers': medical paratexts and indecent readers in early modern England' in Hannah C. Tweed and Diane G. Scott (eds.), *Medical paratexts from medieval to modern* (Basingstoke: Palgrave Macmillan, 2018), pp. 15–41. For evidence of copy-specific reader censorship of individual medical images see Suzanne Karr Schmidt with Kimberly Nichols, *Altered and Adorned: using Renaissance prints in daily life* (The Art Institute of Chicago, 2011), pp. 13–14, 87–91.

68   Margócsy, Somos and Joffe, *The Fabrica of Andreas Vesalius*, p. 121–130.

69   For the wording of 1564 Tridentine Index, USTC 804340 and others, on 'lascivious or obscene' subjects, see George Haven Putnam, *The censorship of the Church of Rome and its influence upon the production and distribution of literature: a study of the history of the prohibitory and expurgatory indexes, together with some consideration of the effects of Protestant censorship and of censorship by the state* (vol. 1, New York: Benjamin Blom, 1967), p. 185.

(including book owners, book sellers, bishops, and local inquisitors) to interpret the demands of the indexes and to expurgate copies to comply, something
that they achieved by obliterating with pen, excising with a blade, or covering
text using paper and glue or wax.[70] But were anatomical or natural philosophy
woodcuts really considered by those would-be expurgators as licentious and
contravening the *Index*? Perhaps, according to scholar of early modern scientific works, Hannah Marcus:

> Whether a work was anatomical or titillating lay in part in the eye of
> the beholder or in the reader's interpretation of censorship laws ....
> Anatomical images of genitalia were not automatically licentious, though
> some readers of Vesalius, especially of copies held in monastic libraries,
> have obliterated or removed images of genitalia.[71]

While thousands of such church-censored examples survive, Marcus notes
that, '[b]ooks that spent the sixteenth and seventeenth centuries in Northern
Europe are rarely expurgated [to comply with Catholic censorship], since
Northern Europe was predominantly Protestant and there was, therefore, no
need ...'.[72] There is no material evidence placing either expurgated Glasgow
Margarita outside northern Europe; however, provenance inscriptions do place
both examples in southern German religious houses, one in the Carthusian
charterhouse in Freiburg, Baden-Württemberg, the other in the possession
of the Augustinians in Passau, Bavaria. So, while the *Margarita* is not specifically named in the *Index*, it does contain anatomical images that might be
construed as licentious by a censor. Given the pattern of expurgation and the
known provenance of these copies in Catholic institutions, it seems plausible
that we are seeing here the same Catholic censorship in response to the general prohibitions of the *Index* as described by Margócsy et al.[73] Moreover, if
these copies were censored in southern German monasteries, it perhaps indicates the *Margarita* was actively being read and used in this setting rather than
merely having migrated as part of a private collection.

---

70   Hannah Marcus, 'Expurgated Books as an Archive of Practice', *The Archive Journal*
      (August 2017), online at http://www.archivejournal.net/essays/expurgated-books-as-an
      -archive-of-practice/ (Consulted 30 June 2022).
71   Hannah Marcus, *Forbidden knowledge: medicine, science, and censorship in early modern
      Italy* (Chicago: The University of Chicago Press, 2021), p. 120, (n. 102).
72   Marcus, 'Expurgated Books as an Archive of Practice', *The Archive Journal* (2017).
73   On post-Tridentine Catholic censorship in Bavaria, including the publication of a spe-
      cial edition of the *Index of Trent*, USTC 672991, to be used by Bavarian monasteries, see
      Putnam, *The censorship of the church of Rome*, Vol. 1, pp. 216–220.

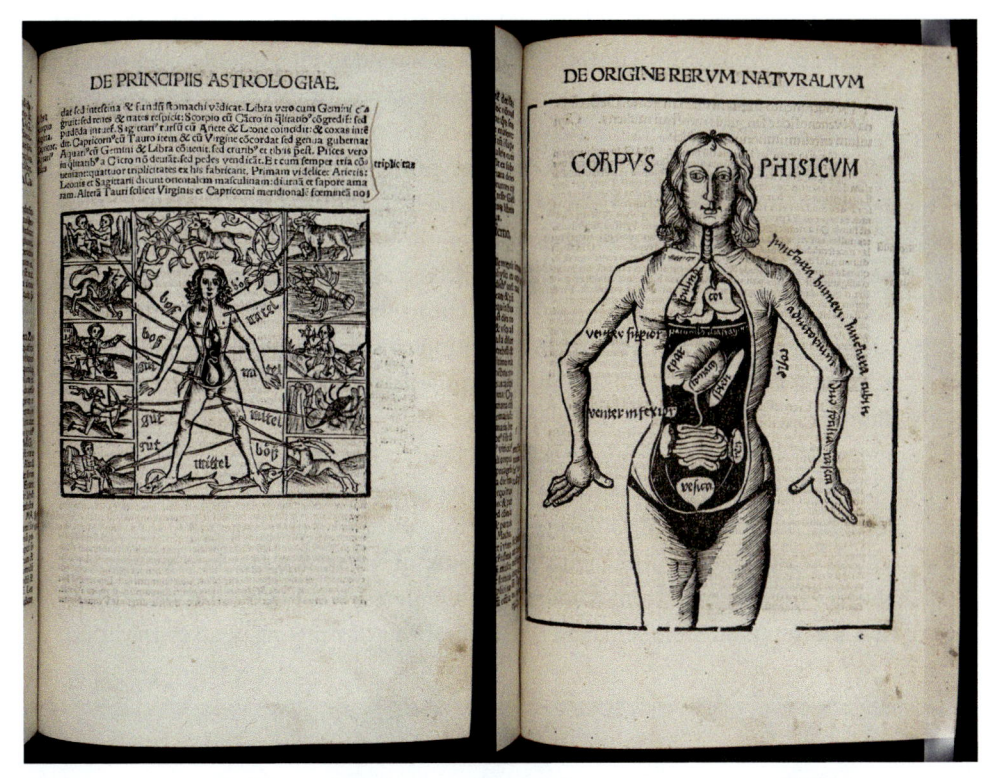

FIGURE 3.7 Pre-censored images from the first Grüninger edition, 1504 – Ferguson Af-b.66, USTC 609452. On left: zodiac man from book seven. On right: organ man from book nine

The woodcuts targeted for censorship in the Glasgow corpus appear in copies of the *Margarita* published by Johannes Schott. If we examine the comparable woodcuts in the editions published by Johannes Grüninger, first appearing in 1504, a striking difference can be seen. The woodcuts have been pre-censored, with the genitalia concealed.[74]

This perhaps suggests anxiety (on Grüninger's part at least, if not Schott's) about the propriety of these images well before the *Index* was first published. The already cited examples from Nuremberg and Venice demonstrate that

---

74 The organ man illustration found in book nine is based on those found in the Schott editions but with genitalia concealed. The lack of genitalia in the zodiac man image in book seven might be attributed to Grüninger's illustrator employing a different exemplar from Schott, since it bears a much closer resemblance to illustrations by Johannes Prüss. See 'The zodiac man' in *Medical Astrology: Science, Art, and Influence in early-modern Europe. The Zodiac Man.* Yale University Library Online Exhibition (2021): https://onlineexhibits .library.yale.edu/s/medicalastrology/page/astrological-anatomy (consulted 30 June 2022).

censorship on moral grounds was already taking place at a civic level across Europe, pre-*Index*. Since the *Margarita* was intended for students, conceivably Grüninger's choice to exclude genitalia from woodcuts can be viewed as a concern for younger readers' moral welfare, rather than a response to any specific injunction. Although the pattern of expurgation in our copies of the *Margarita* may date from the second half of the sixteenth century (after the publication of the *Index prohibitorum librorum*), given the earlier anxieties over the publication of nude images, we cannot be certain it was not earlier.

If we return to the organ man woodcut in the Schott editions, an entirely contradictory pattern of reader intervention can also be reported. Rather than censoring the hint of genitalia in book nine's organ man illustration, in three different Glasgow copies of the *Margarita*, a penis has been fully drawn in by a reader.[75]

In his examination of annotated copies of early editions of Bonsignori's *Metamorphoses* of Ovid, Giuseppe Capriotti noticed a similar contrasting pattern of reader intervention, with one reader of the 1505 edition censoring and obliterating genitalia from woodcuts, while in a second copy of the same edition another reader embellished the illustrations by drawing penises on various

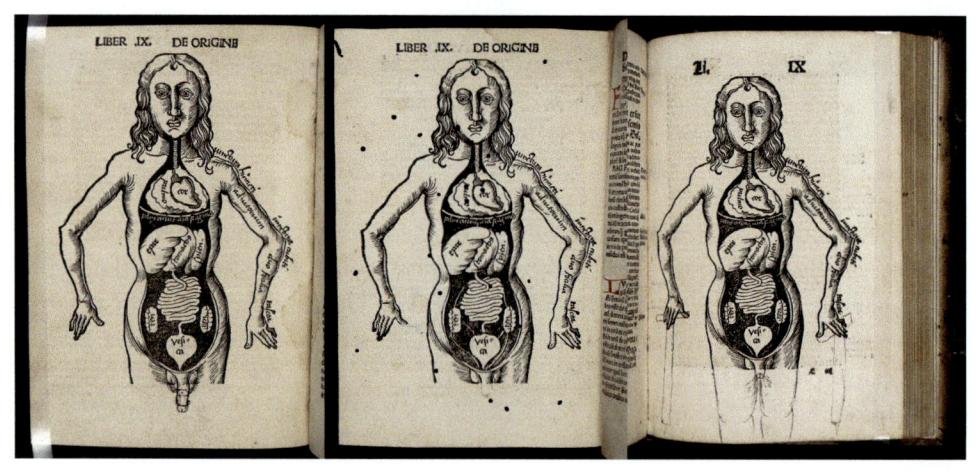

FIGURE 3.8   Three organ man illustrations with penises drawn in. On left: Ferguson Af-y.74, USTC 676099. Centre: Ferguson Ag-a.36, USTC 676099. On right: Ferguson Af-b.40, USTC 605010

75   Ferguson Af-y.74 and Ferguson Ag-a.36, USTC 676099; Ferguson Af-b.40, USTC 605010. In one further example (Ferguson Af-b.40, USTC 605010) with unknown early provenance, the annotator has gone even further and added in legs and what look like crutches in either hand. The book survives in a sixteenth-century German pigskin binding and has extensive mathematical marginalia. Noticeably the organ man woodcut has also been altered in this copy, adding by pen a line of urine from the penis.

figures.[76] As Capriotti notes, readers react differently to the same image, some with a desire to censor, some apparently ironically or humorously; however, in both instances the images are being read in an eroticised way.[77] Capriotti concludes that Ovid's *Metamorphoses* was, 'not a neutral encyclopedia of myths but an erotic device whose imagery provoked sexual arousal in the reader and the observer'.[78] But can the same really be said of the *Margarita*? It seems unlikely. With conspicuous efforts to keep sexualized images away from the lustful gaze of young people, perhaps all we are seeing with these adapted woodcuts is the humorous or rebellious reaction of young readers when they do encounter a woodcut with even a hint of genitalia.[79]

Of course, to blame this bawdy graffiti on students might be unfair: we simply do not know who was responsible. In two cases we have no early provenance clues but interestingly, we do know that the third example was owned in 1541 by the Augustinians at Gaesdonck in North Rhine-Westphalia.[80] Whether it was a naughty or subversive Augustinian responsible it is just not possible to say. And while there remains the amusing possibility of a censorship arms race in sixteenth-century monastic libraries (with some monks zealously scoring out licentious penises while others mischievously added them in), perhaps more likely the graffiti points to earlier use of these copies of the *Margarita* by students, with the copies later migrating to religious houses. These conflicting patterns of modification, when considered together, certainly seem to point to an ambivalence over the place of sexualised imagery within the *Margarita* probably conditioned by its student readership.

John Ferguson may have been motivated to collect multiple copies of editions and texts to better understand a work's printing history and textual variance. Yet, as this short study on his collection of copies of the *Margarita philosophica* demonstrates, his legacy, a 7,500 volume-strong collection of practical and philosophical early-printed works with texts commonly surviving in multiple editions and copies, now offers a rich resource for those investigating copy-specific evidence of ownership and use.

---

76   USTC 763696.

77   Capriotti, 'Eroticism under a watchful eye', pp. 118–124.

78   Capriotti, 'Eroticism under a watchful eye', p. 127.

79   As Capriotti notes, Michel Foucault recognised that early modern censorship indirectly intensified fascination in sexuality since attempts at repressing only increase desire. See Michel Foucault, *Histoire de la sexualité: La volonté de savoir* (Paris: Gallimard, 1978) as cited by Capriotti, 'Eroticism under a watchful eye', p. 126.

80   Ferguson Ag-a.36, USTC 676099.

PART 2

Entanglements of Jotted, Printed and Digital Steps

∴

CHAPTER 4

Text – Medium – Recording System: Recipes in Books

Sven Limbeck

In the beginning was the single sheet of paper (or parchment). The genuine medium of recipes does not seem to be the book, but a loose handwritten piece of undefined format.[1] In the fourth vision of his *Philander von Sittewald*, German Baroque writer and satirist Johann Michael Moscherosch (1601–1669) had pharmacists appear alongside physicians in his 'army of the dead':

> The gentlemen apothecaries were most often covered with cedulas of strange Chinese, *stenographic* writings .... The beginning of such cedulas was commonly marked thus: Rp. that is to say *Per decem*, because out of ten recipes only one may help, or, out of ten patients only one survives.[2]

Recipes are pieces of paper downright signifying the pharmacist's status. Thanks to their encryption, these texts are unreadable to the uninitiated. They begin with the conventional abbreviation for the Latin expression 'Recipe', which in one of several interpretations is read as a combination of the letter P with the Roman numeral x, resolving in 'Per decem' because only one in ten patients escapes with their life.[3] To the satirist, the successful practical medical application of recipes appears highly questionable.

---

1 See Georg Stanitzek, 'Zettel', in Christina Bartz, Ludwig Jäger etc. (eds.), *Handbuch der Mediologie. Signaturen des Medialen* (Munich: Fink, 2012), pp. 329–335.

2 'Die Herren Apothecker waren meiste mit Zedulen behencket/ von wunderlichen Chinesischen/ *Stenographi*schen schrifften .... Der anfang solcher Zedulen war gemeiniglichen also bezeichnet: Rp. so viel gesagt/ als *Per decem*, weil vnder zehen *Recepten* eines mag helffen; oder/ unter zehen krancken einer davon kommen.' Johann Michael Moscherosch, *Les Visiones de Don Francesco de Quevedo Villegas oder Wunderbahre Satyrische gesichte Verteutscht durch Philander von Sittewalt* (Strasbourg: Johann Philipp Mülbe, [1640]), pp. 168–169.

3 In the original, 'Rp.' is given as the conventional typographical ligature of R and p for 'Recipe': a capital R with a cauda that is crossed by a diagonal stroke. See Liselotte Buchheim, *Geschichte der Rezepteinleitung. Horusauge – Jupiterzeichen – Recipe* (Habil.schrift, Bonn, 1965), pp. 119–121.

© KONINKLIJKE BRILL BV, LEIDEN, 2024 | DOI:10.1163/9789004683389_006

The recipe's pragmatic form consisting of indications, ingredients and instructions for preparing and applying remedies, food or any other means in which text, medium and usage coincide, is hardly ever found in the sources, regardless whether its intended application is medical, technological, magical, alchemical or culinary. Recipes from antiquity, the Middle Ages and modern times are generally found in books.[4] But not every recipe found in a book makes that book a recipe book, or even a recipe booklet ('Rezeptbüchlein'); reason enough to examine the relationship between recipe and book and to reconsider the specifics of this relationship.

1   Recipes as Text and Social Practice

I would like to begin by asking a few guiding questions based on an example from the second volume of the *Theatrum Poenarum* (1697) by the jurist Jakob Döpler († 1693):

> Furthermore, it is found that cruel murderers and highwaymen are very diligent in watching out when they get pregnant women to cut them open, to open also the unborn and unchristened children at once, to pulverize and eat their little hearts, so that if they are caught they may still confess nothing even under torture.[5]

Then, the exact preparation and administration of the said powder is described, using the example of a murderous father, who, after killing his own two children,

---

4   See Simone Zweifel, *Aus Büchern Bücher machen. Zur Produktion und Multiplikation von Wissen in frühneuzeitlichen Kompilationen* (Berlin/Boston: De Gruyter, 2022), pp. 70–78. Historical study of recipes is primarily textual, as it traditionally refers not to the recipes themselves, but to recipe collections, their tradition, literary form and sources; exemplary for this philological approach to recipe literature is Henry E. Sigerist, *Studien und Texte zur frühmittelalterlichen Rezeptliteratur* (Leipzig: Barth, 1923).

5   'Ferner findet man daß grausame Mörder und Strassenräuber sehr fleissig aufgepasset wenn sie schwangere Weiber bekommen können/ solche aufzuschneiden/ die ungebohrne und ungetauffte Kinder gleichfals zu öffnen ihre Hertzlein zu *pulverisi*ren und zu fressen/ daß wenn sie etwan gefangen würden/ dennoch auf der Volter nichts bekennen möchten.' Jakob Döpler, *Theatri Poenarum, Supplicium et Executionum Criminalium, Oder Schau-Platzes Derer Leibes- und Lebens-Strafen Anderer Theil* (Leipzig: Friedrich Lanckische Erben, 1697), p. 311. See Hole Rößler, 'Jacob Döpler, Theatrum Poenarum', in *Theatrum-Literatur der Frühen Neuzeit. Repertorium* (Wolfenbüttel: Herzog August Bibliothek, 2012), http://diglib.hab.de /edoc/ed000062/start.htm [3 November 2022].

cut them open at the back, tore their hearts out of their bodies, cut them up on sticks and put them in the oven, powdered them and put them in soup, and toasted with it to his comrades.[6]

The description of a remedy causing a criminal not to confess even under torture does not begin with the word 'Recipe', nor is its text distinguished from the narrative by a marker of any kind. But, based on indications of purpose, ingredients, preparation and administration, a magical recipe may be extrapolated from this narrative, presenting the idea that childlike innocence may be acquired with the help of a drug.[7] Every element that constitutes a recipe is present.[8] Whether the pulverisation of children's hearts ever actually played a role in the arcane knowledge of the early modern professional criminal or merely in a jurist's imagination is of secondary importance.[9] The writing down provides meaning and validity to this knowledge, be it passed down or invented. In his use of detailed description, Döpler's intention was more likely to satisfy the reader's desire for cruelty rather than to provide instructions for imitation.

This example may serve to ask questions of what a recipe is, what it means to write down a recipe, and how it relates to the book. They concern textuality, pragmatics and mediality: What textual boundaries and markers define a recipe text? What knowledge is recorded in recipes and what use do they serve? Does the recording of recipes aim for imitative action? What are the relations between recipe texts and recipe media and in what way does the medium determine the meaning and use of each text?

Recipes and recipe literature form a core area in a field of literature we call the literature of knowledge and use ('Wissens- und Gebrauchsliteratur'), because they seem to aim at transferring available knowledge into current

---

6 'dieselbe an den Rücken aufgeschnitten/ ihre Hertzlein aus dem Leibe gerissen/ auf Stücken zerschnitten in Backofen gedörret/ gepulvert in eine Suppen gestreuet/ und dieser seinen andern Cammeraden davon zugetruncken.' Döpler, *Theatri Poenarum*, p. 311.

7 As a magical practice, it is a sympathy spell, see Karl Beth, 'Sympathie', in Hanns Bächtold-Stäubli (ed.), *Handwörterbuch des deutschen Aberglaubens* (vol. 8, Berlin: De Gruyter, 1937), cols. 619–628.

8 See Joachim Telle, 'Das Rezept als literarische Form. Zum multifunktionalen Gebrauch des Rezepts in der deutschen Literatur', *Berichte zur Wissenschaftsgeschichte* 26 (2003), pp. 251–274, here p. 252; Peter Dilg, 'Rezept, Rezeptliteratur', in Werner E. Gerabek, Bernhard D. Haage, Gundolf Keil etc. (eds.), *Enzyklopädie Medizingeschichte* (Berlin/New York: De Gruyter, 2005), pp. 1246–1247.

9 See very briefly on the so-called 'Gaunerliteratur', but with further references Bernhard D. Haage and Wolfgang Wegner, *Deutsche Fachliteratur der Artes in Mittelalter und Früher Neuzeit* (Berlin: Schmidt, 2007), pp. 126–129.

use.[10] In a recent attempt to define its genre, the recipe has also been described as the 'primary epistemic genre', less as a literary genre than one that is related to knowledge, whereby genres are no longer understood exclusively as structural or aesthetic phenomena, but rather as social practices.[11] These insights lead me to the following considerations: the literature of knowledge and use can be defined by the encounter of knowledge and use and their conceptual connection, rather than their mutual exclusivity. The literature of knowledge and use records both theory (systematics, methodology and content of a particular discourse) as well as practice, the action that is actually, intentionally or allegedly derived from theory. The recording of knowledge follows the intention of assurance and archiving of tradition, whereas its use aims for its operationalisation, the retrieval of the archived knowledge for the sake of application. The literary field extends from authority and tradition on the one hand to practice on the other: theory is fed by tradition and knowledge is based on authorisation, whereas practice aims to guide action. The poles spanning this literary field, however, are themselves exterior: neither is tradition identical with the text, nor is the text the application of its content.[12]

---

10   See Jerry Stannard, 'Rezeptliteratur as Fachliteratur', in William Eamon (ed.), *Studies on Medieval Fachliteratur* (Brussels: Omirel, 1982), pp. 59–73; for medical recipe literature Haage/Wegner, *Fachliteratur*, pp. 194–209.

11   Gianna Pomata, 'The Recipe and the Case: Epistemic Genres and the Dynamics of Cognitive Practices', in Kaspar von Greyerz, Silvia Flubacher and Philipp Senn (eds.), *Wissenschaftsgeschichte und Geschichte des Wissens im Dialog – Connecting Science and Knowledge* (Göttingen: V&R Unipress, 2013), pp. 131–154, here p. 136.

12   My reflections on the literature of knowledge and use follow on from specialist literature research since Eis, but attempt to break down its bias in a canon of subjects (such as the Artes series) by an approach based on media theory. On German-language 'Fachliteratur' of the Middle Ages and early modern period see Gerhard Eis, *Mittelalterliche Fachliteratur* (2nd ed., Stuttgart: Metzler, 1967); Peter Assion, *Altdeutsche Fachliteratur* (Berlin: Schmidt, 1973); William Crossgrove, *Die deutsche Sachliteratur des Mittelalters* (Bern: Lang 1994); Haage/Wegner, *Fachliteratur*. On the concept of the literary field see Pierre Bourdieu, *The Rules of Art: Genesis and Structure of the Literary Field* (Cambridge: Polity Press, 1996). On cultural studies of knowledge in the Middle Ages and early modern period see Martin Kintzinger and Sita Steckel (eds.), *Akademische Wissenskulturen. Praktiken des Lehrens und Forschens vom Mittelalter bis zur Moderne* (Basel: Schwabe, 2015); Marian Füssel (ed.), *Höfe und Experten. Relationen von Macht und Wissen in Mittelalter und Früher Neuzeit* (Göttingen: Vandenhoeck & Ruprecht, 2018); Frank Rexroth, *Fröhliche Scholastik. Die Wissenschaftsrevolution des Mittelalters* (Munich: Beck, 2018); Frank Rexroth and Teresa Schröder-Stapper (eds.), *Experten, Wissen, Symbole. Performanz und Medialität vormoderner Wissenskulturen* (Berlin/Boston: De Gruyter Oldenbourg, 2018); Marian Füssel, Frank Rexroth and Inga Schürmann (eds.), *Praktiken und Räume des Wissens. Expertenkulturen in Geschichte und Gegenwart* (Göttingen: Vandenhoeck & Ruprecht, 2019). This perspective is extended by the approaches of historical praxeology,

In this respect, the literature of knowledge and use differs essentially from other literary fields or areas and forms of writing (fictional/aesthetic literature, knowledge literature, spiritual literature, pragmatic writing, etc.) as it adds use to knowledge. The practice of applying this knowledge lies outside the literary field, if it is traceable at all. One way to capture the distinctive characteristics of the literature of knowledge and use is media theory. Examples for its particular media practices include inscribed use (intended or conceptually anticipated) within the text, or the particular physical form of the text transmission.[13]

2 Recipes and Books: Types of Relation

In the following, I will apply the latter approach to some concrete examples from the holdings of the Herzog August Bibliothek Wolfenbüttel (HAB) and examine the recipes' media forms, particularly as they appear in manuscripts and printed books, mainly, but not exclusively concentrating on the alchemical tradition for pragmatic reasons. To do so, the copying and reproduction of already existing and transmitted recipe collections as well as the planned collection of recipes must be distinguished from recordings of single recipes.[14]

---

see Andreas Reckwitz, 'Grundelemente einer Theorie sozialer Praktiken. Eine sozialtheoretische Perspektive', *Zeitschrift für Soziologie* 32 (2003), pp. 282–301; more recently Arndt Brendecke (ed.), *Praktiken der Frühen Neuzeit. Akteure, Handlungen, Artefakte* (Cologne/Weimar/Vienna: Böhlau, 2015); Dagmar Freist (ed.), *Diskurse – Körper – Artefakte. Historische Praxeologie in der Frühneuzeitforschung* (Bielefeld: transcript, 2015); Lucas Haasis and Constantin Rieske, 'Historische Praxeologie. Zur Einführung', in Lucas Haasis and Constantin Rieske (eds.), *Historische Praxeologie. Dimensionen vergangenen Handelns* (Paderborn: Schöningh, 2015), pp. 7–54.

13 The concept of affordance, which has been adopted in linguistics, appears to be a fruitful approach to a definition of the literature of knowledge and use, see Nicole Zillien, 'Die (Wieder-)Entdeckung der Medien. Das Affordanzkonzept in der Mediensoziologie', *Sociologia Internationalis* 46 (2008), pp. 161–181. On the structure and function of recipes see Elvira Glaser, 'Die textuelle Struktur handschriftlicher und gedruckter Kochrezepte im Wandel. Zur Sprachgeschichte einer Textsorte', in Rudolf Große and Hans Wellmann (eds.), *Textarten im Sprachwandel – nach Erfindung des Buchdrucks* (Heidelberg: Winter, 1996), pp. 225–249; Thomas Gloning, 'Textgebrauch und sprachliche Gestalt älterer deutscher Kochrezepte (1350–1800). Ergebnisse und Aufgaben', in Franz Simmler (ed.), *Textsorten deutscher Prosa vom 12./13. bis 18. Jahrhundert und ihre Merkmale*. Akten zum Internationalen Kongress in Berlin 20. bis 22. September 1999 (Bern: Lang, 2002), pp. 517–550.

14 See Gundolf Keil, 'Rezept, Rezeptliteratur', in *Lexikon des Mittelalters* (vol. 7, Munich: Artemis, 1995), col. 778–779; on the practice and intention of collecting see Kathrin Pfister and Ulrike Schofer, "Allen Hausvattern entsprüngender nutz'. Das Heidelberger 'Artzney Buch' des Apothekers Christoph Wirsung (1500–1571)', in Christoph Friedrich

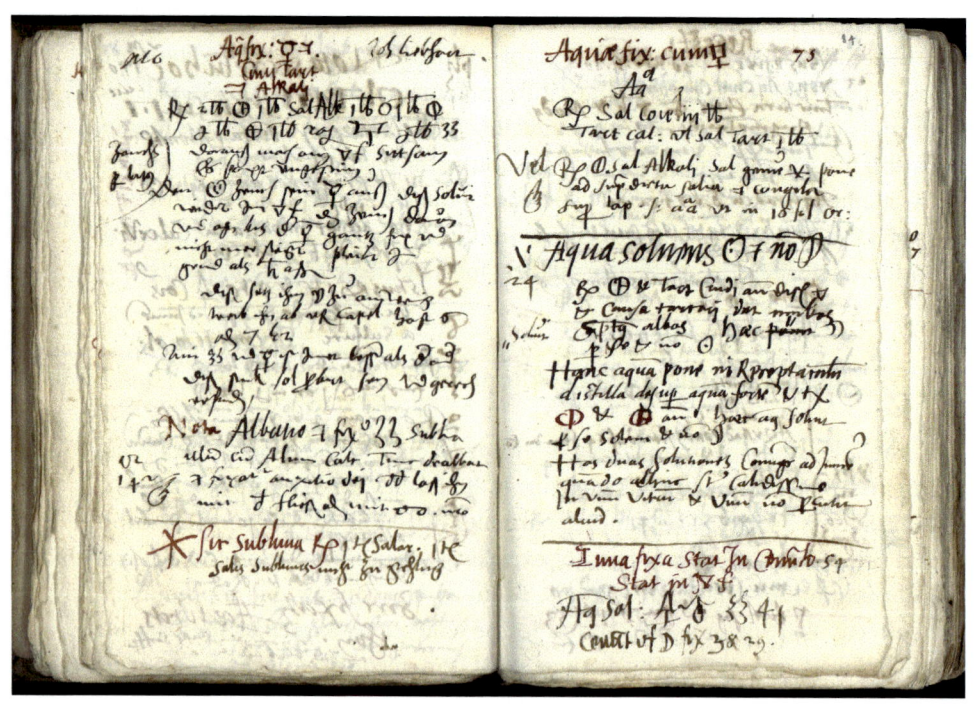

FIGURE 4.1   Cod. Guelf. 60.5 Aug. 8°, fols. 83v–84r. Wolfenbüttel, Herrzog August Bibliothek

Manuscript 60.5 Aug. 8° of the HAB, a small-format paper manuscript from around 1600, exclusively holds a collection of Latin and German alchemical recipes.[15] The continuous recording and layout reveal the scribe's planned design of the manuscript as a recipe booklet. It shows a complete congruence of text and medium, in which the conceived collection of recipes (text) forms the book (medium). This congruence is characteristic of most printed transmission of recipes. Whereas the manuscript's function may oscillate between production medium and publication, the printed book is basically a conceptual reproduction of texts.[16]

and Joachim Telle (eds.), *Pharmazie in Geschichte und Gegenwart. Festgabe für Wolf-Dieter Müller-Jahncke* (Stuttgart: Wissenschaftliche Verlags-Gesellschaft, 2009), pp. 345–361.

15   See the – inadequate – description by Otto von Heinemann, *Die Handschriften der Herzog-lichen Bibliothek zu Wolfenbüttel*, 2. Abt.: *Die Augusteischen Handschrift v* (Wolfenbüttel: Zwissler, 1903), p. 95 (no. 3640).

16   On letterpress printing as text processing see Michael Giesecke, *Der Buchdruck in der frühen Neuzeit. Eine historische Fallstudie über die Durchsetzung neuer Informations- und Kommunikationstechnologien* (Frankfurt a. M.: Suhrkamp, 1991), pp. 86–123; on the functions of manuscripts (based on the alchemical tradition) see Sven Limbeck,

Nevertheless, recipes appear in printed books in quite diverse forms, namely when they represent neither individual texts nor planned collections, but form parts of a continuous text. In an edition of the *Triumphwagen Antimonii* by Basilius Valentinus, recipes appear within the text alongside theoretical explanations.[17] Here, the text boundary of the recipe is indicated by a paragraph beginning with 'Nimb' and additionally marked by a marginal note indicating its content ('Calcinatio Antimonij').[18]

In an edition of *Chemia rationalis*, a handbook of chemistry from 1696, the recipes are also part of a textual continuum, but are typographically separated through a specific layout (headings marked by a larger font size and indentation, list of ingredients introduced by 'R.' and marked by a smaller font size and indentation).[19]

The textual continuum can also consist solely of a sequence of recipes. This form of presentation resembles the recipe booklet ('Rezeptbüchlein') or the conceived collection of recipes, such as the supplementary text in a German edition of Geber's *Summa perfectio* of 1625.[20] Here, the body of the text is structured with headings and specific introductory phrases ('Nehmet' or 'Nimm').

As frequent as the congruence of text and medium, a discrepancy becomes apparent, especially in the miscellaneous or composite manuscripts typical of the late Middle Ages.[21] These recipes or recipe collections often have

'Alchemische Literatur zwischen Handschrift und Buchdruck. Mediengeschichtliche Beobachtungen zur Überlieferung der Alchemie', in Petra Feuerstein-Herz and Stefan Laube (eds.), *Goldenes Wissen. Die Alchemie – Substanzen, Synthesen, Symbolik* (Wolfenbüttel: Harrassowitz, 2014), pp. 43–54; id., 'Alchemische Überlieferung in Kodex und Manuskript. Mediologische Aspekte ihrer Erschließung', in Petra Feuerstein-Herz and Ute Frietsch (eds.), *Alchemie – Genealogie und Terminologie, Bilder, Techniken und Artefakte. Forschungen aus der Herzog August Bibliothek* (Wolfenbüttel: Herzog August Bibliothek, 2021), pp. 27–48.

17   Basilius Valentinus, *Triumph-Wagen Antimonii*, ed. by Johann Thölde (Nuremberg: Johann Christoph Lochner and Johann Hoffmann, 1676) [HAB: Xb 4277].

18   On the typographical structuring of the text body by paragraphs see Frans A. Janssen, 'The Rise of the Typographical Paragraph', in Karl A.E. Enenkel and Wolfgang Neuber (eds.), *Cognition and the Book. Typologies of Formal Organisation of Knowledge in the Printed Book of the Early Modern Period* (Leiden/Boston: Brill, 2005), pp. 9–32.

19   *Chemia Rationalis, das ist Vernunfftmäßige Anweisung/ wie vermittelst der Spagyrischen Kunst/ aus den drey Reichen der Natur die itziger Zeit gebräuchlisten Artzeney-Mittel vorbereitet werden sollen* (Frankfurt/Leipzig: Johann Justus Erythropel, 1696) [HAB: Xb 8896 (1)].

20   'Ein ander Tractätlein von *lapide philosophorum*', in Geber, *Summa Perfectio. Das ist/ Deß Königlichen/ weitberühmbten/ Arabischen Philosophi/ Geber Büchlin/ von der Gebenedeyten/ vnd aller höchsten Vollkommenheit/ der Allgemainen Artzeney* (Strasbourg: Heirs of Lazarus Zetzner, 1625), pp. 283–288 [HAB: Xb 2325 (1)].

21   Both miscellaneous manuscripts and composite manuscripts have a function as hinge in the media history of the late Middle Ages and early modern period. For this reason, the

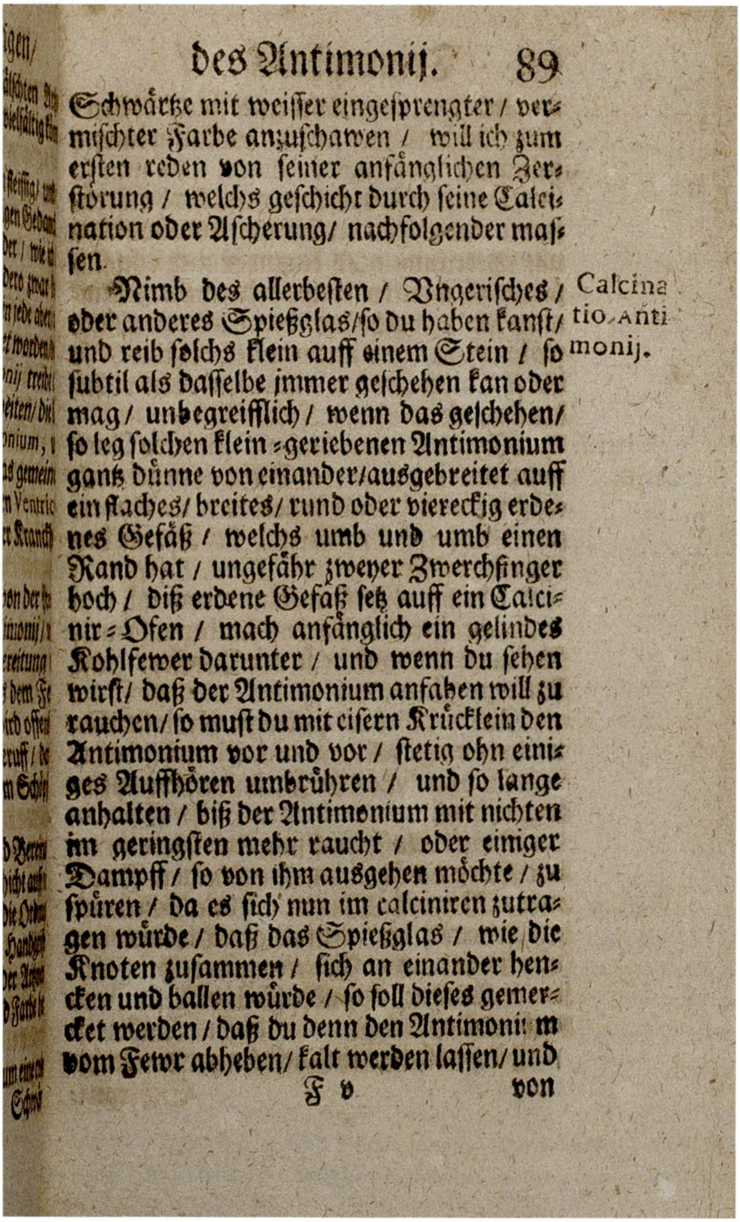

des Antimonij. 89

Schwärtze mit weisser eingesprengter / vermischter Farbe anzuschawen / wil ich zum ersten reden von seiner anfänglichen Zerstörung / welchs geschicht durch seine Calcination oder Ascherung/ nachfolgender massen.

Nimb des allerbesten / Vngerisches / oder anderes Spießglas/so du haben kanst/ und reib solchs klein auff einem Stein / so subtil als dasselbe immer geschehen kan oder mag/ unbegreifflich / wenn das geschehen/ so leg solchen klein =geriebenen Antimonium gantz dünne von einander/ausgebreitet auff ein flaches/ breites/ rund oder viereckig erdenes Gefäß / welchs umb und umb einen Rand hat / ungefähr zweyer Zwerchfinger hoch / diß erdene Gefaß setz auff ein Calcinir = Ofen / mach anfänglich ein gelindes Kohlfewer darunter / und wenn du sehen wirst/ daß der Antimonium anfahen will zu rauchen/ so must du mit eisern Krücklein den Antimonium vor und vor / stetig ohn einiges Auffhören umbrühren / und so lange anhalten / biß der Antimonium mit nichten im geringsten mehr raucht / oder einiger Dampff / so von ihm ausgehen möchte / zu spüren / da es sich nun im calciniren zutragen würde / daß das Spießglas / wie die Knoten zusammen / sich an einander hencken und ballen würde / so soll dieses gemercket werden / daß du denn den Antimoni: m vom Fewr abheben/ kalt werden lassen/ und

F v von

Calcinatio Antimonij. [marginal note]

FIGURE 4.2 Basilius Valentinus, *Triumph-Wagen Antimonii*, ed. by Johann Thölde (Nuremberg: Johann Christoph Lochner and Johann Hoffmann, 1676), p. 89. Wolfenbüttel, Herzog August Bibliothek: Xb 4277

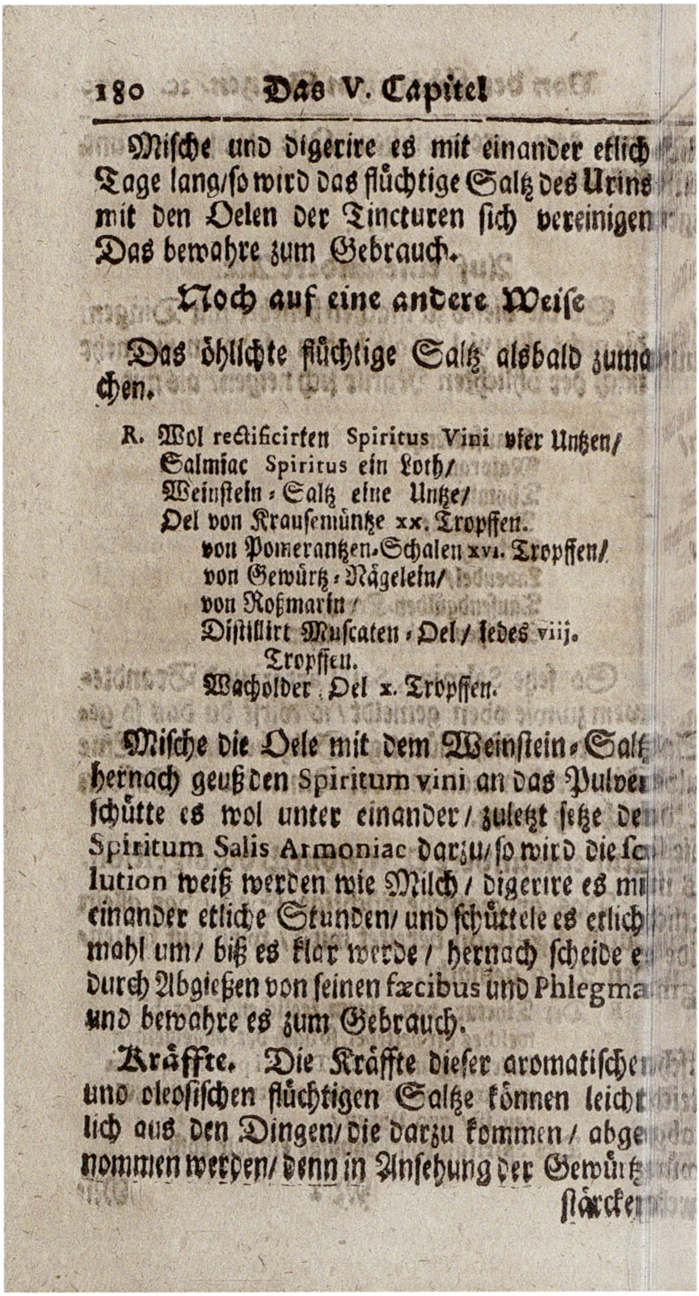

180 **Das V. Capitel**

Mische und digerire es mit einander etlich
Tage lang/so wird das flüchtige Saltz des Urins
mit den Oelen der Tincturen sich vereinigen
Das bewahre zum Gebrauch.

Noch auf eine andere Weise

Das öhllchte flüchtige Saltz alsbald zuma
chen.

> R. Wol rectificirten Spiritus Vini vier Untzen/
> Salmiac Spiritus ein Loth/
> Weinstein = Saltz eine Untze/
> Oel von Krausemüntze xx. Tropffen.
> von Pomerantzen-Schalen xvi. Tropffen/
> von Gewürtz = Nägelein/
> von Roßmarin /
> Distillirt Muscaten = Oel / iedes viij.
> Tropffen.
> Wacholder Oel x. Tropffen.

Mische die Oele mit dem Weinstein = Saltz
hernach geuß den Spiritum vini an das Pulver
schütte es wol unter einander/ zuletzt setze de
Spiritum Salis Armoniac darzu/so wird die so
lution weiß werden wie Milch/ digerire es mi
einander etliche Stunden/ und schüttele es etlich
mahl um/ biß es klar werde/ hernach scheide e
durch Abgießen von seinen fæcibus und Phlegma
und bewahre es zum Gebrauch.

Kräffte. Die Kräffte dieser aromatische
und oleosischen flüchtigen Saltze können leicht
lich aus den Dingen/ die darzu kommen/ abge
nommen werden/ denn in Ansehung der Gewürtz
stärcke

FIGURE 4.3 *Chemia Rationalis* (Frankfurt/Leipzig: Johann Justus Erythropel,
1696), p. 180. Wolfenbüttel, Herzog August Bibliothek: Xb 8896 (1)

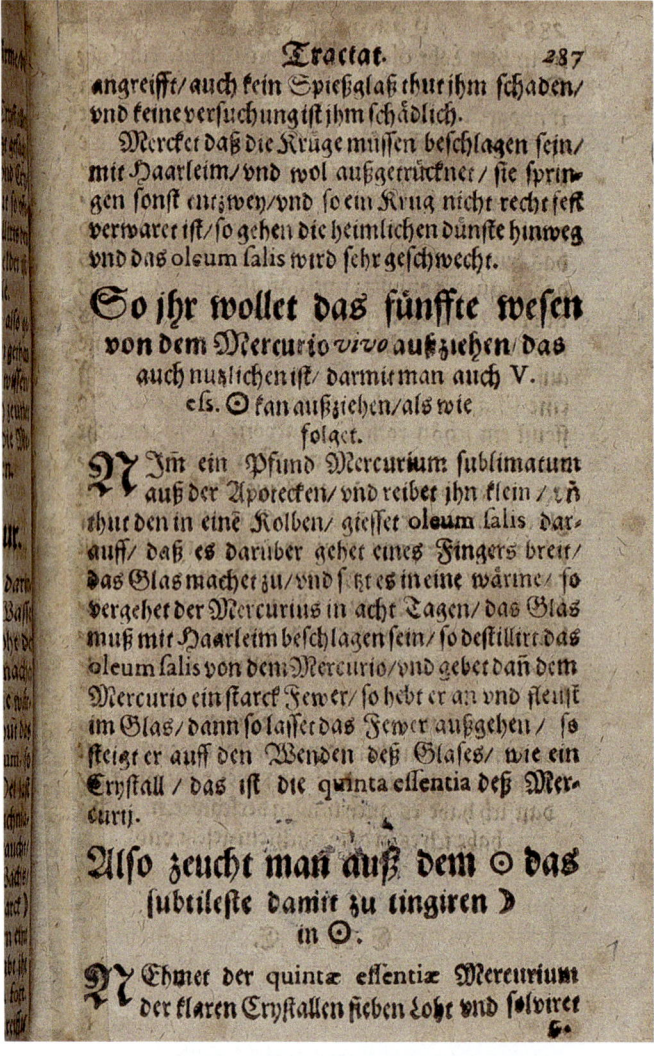

FIGURE 4.4 Geber, *Summa Perfectio* (Strasbourg: Lazarus Zetzners
Erben, 1625), p. 287. Wolfenbüttel, Herzog August
Bibliothek: Xb 2325 (1)

precise distinction between miscellaneous manuscripts (collection of several texts in one
codex) and composite manuscripts (bookbinder's syntheses of several originally independent fascicles, sometimes with prints) is of great importance for understanding the
text. See J. Peter Gumbert, 'Codicological Units. Towards a Terminology for the Stratigraphy
of the Non-Homogeneous Codex', *Segno e testo* 2 (2004), pp. 17–42; id., 'Zur Kodikologie
und Katalographie der zusammengesetzten Handschrift', in Edoardo Crisci, Marilena
Maniaci and Pasquale Orsini (eds.), *La descrizione dei manoscritti. Esperienze a confronto*
(Cassino: Università degli Studi di Cassino, 2010), pp. 1–18; Karin Kranich-Hofbauer,

no recognisable connection with the rest of the manuscript's content. The Wolfenbüttel composite manuscript 771 Helmst., parts of which were written around 1400 and which formerly belonged to the library of the Benedictine monastery of Clus, contains several alchemical texts, a collection of seventy-eight recipes (fol. 177v–186r), and a *Liber maiorum operum in alchemia* by Magister Saphirus (fol. 194r–195v). They appear out of place within this collection of ecclesiastical texts most likely in the hands of a priest: the volume primarily consists of sermons, catechetical and moral theological texts, and the pastoral treatise *Stella clericorum*. In addition to the aforementioned alchemica, the codex also contains three discontinuous entries of *Elixir domini Johannis episcopi ad solem* (fol. 170v–171v, 186r and 195v), suggesting amendments, as pages previously left blank were used for this purpose. The sections of the text thus distributed are connected by several references ('Residuum quere …').[22]

The continuous copy of a collection of alchemical recipes on fols. 177v–186r in the vicinity of the *Elixir* text is arranged differently. Textually, it is related to the alchemical treatise *De perfecto magisterio* occasionally attributed to Aristotle or Rhazes (ar-Rāzī).[23] While the recipes in *Elixir* are part of a continuous text that also contains descriptive and theoretical sections, this text consists of a mere sequence of recipes without passages connecting them, reducing the source text to its pragmatic parts. The authorship of this text can hardly be attributed to the scribe of the Helmstedt codex, but is likely based on a preceding version. In any case, the compilation of spiritual and alchemical texts is not the result of an original conception, and it is impossible to trace the specific interest in this compilation.

An arbitrary nature or lack of concept may also be attributed to another miscellaneous manuscript in the Wolfenbüttel collection. The small-format paper manuscript 62.4 Aug. 8°, written in the late fifteenth or early sixteenth

'Zusammengesetzte Handschriften – Sammelhandschriften. Materialität – Kodikologie – Editorik', in Martin Schubert (ed.), *Materialität in der Editionswissenschaft* (Berlin/New York: De Gruyter, 2010), pp. 309–321; Jürgen Wolf, 'Sammelhandschriften – mehr als die Summe der Einzelteile', in Dorothea Klein etc. (eds.), *Überlieferungsgeschichte transdisziplinär. Neue Perspektiven auf ein germanistisches Forschungsparadigma* (Wiesbaden: Reichert, 2016), pp. 69–81.

22   See Bertram Lesser, *Die mittelalterlichen Helmstedter Handschriften der Herzog August Bibliothek*, Teil V: Cod. Guelf. 616 to 927 Helmst.; online: https://diglib.hab.de/?db=mss &list=ms&id=771-helmst&catalog=Lesser [4 November 2022].

23   See [Pseudo-]Aristotle, 'De Perfecto Magisterio', in *Theatrum Chemicum, Praecipuos Selectorum Auctorum Tractatus de Chemiae et Lapidis Philosophici Antiquitate, veritate, iure, praestantia et operationibus, continens* (vol. 3, Strasbourg: Lazarus Zetzner, 1602), pp. 56–118; Guillaume Delmeulle, 'At the Origins of the *De Perfecto Magisterio*. A Translation from Arabic or a Latin Composition?', *Ambix*, 68 (2021), pp. 431–441.

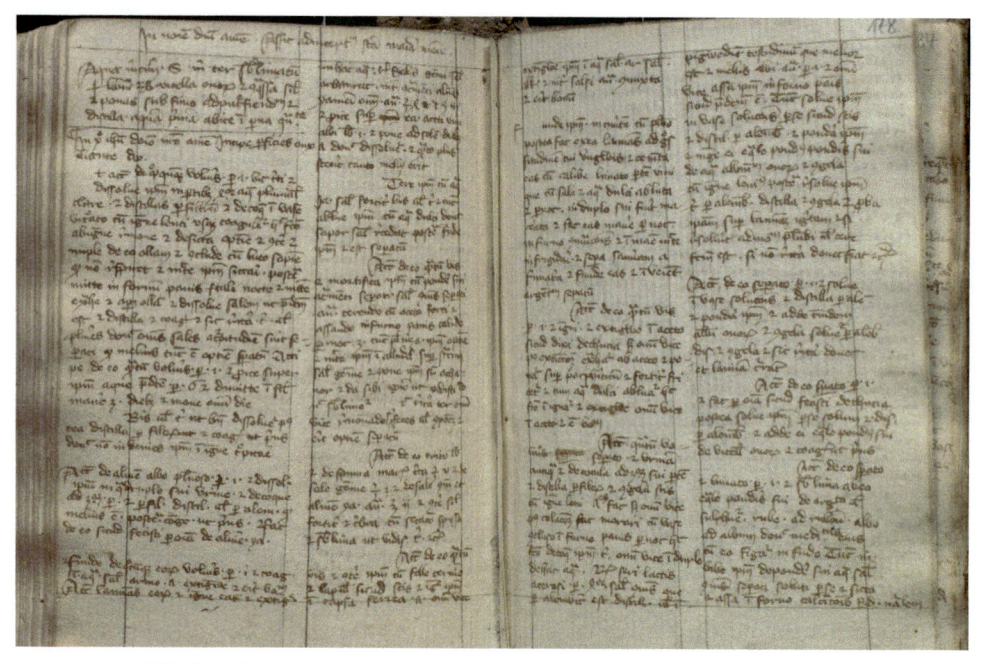

FIGURE 4.5   Wolfenbüttel, Herzog August Bibliothek: Cod. Guelf. 771 Helmst., fols. 177v–178r

century, contains Latin and Low German alchemical recipes on only one page (fol. 117v). Otherwise, the collected texts deal with astronomy, animals, plants, and other natural history, medicine, grammar, ecclesiastical topics such as a short explanation of the Mass, and canon law.[24] At the end an incomplete printed version of the Windesheim breviary is bound in. The compilation of this manuscript seems pointless if viewed as a traditional medium of archiving and transmission. Its broad range of contents, from *artes,* natural history to spiritual texts, makes sense if understood as an individually compiled vade mecum of useful knowledge in a handy format for a religious cleric. The significance of recipes passed down by chance obviously differs from that of recipes recorded to serve archiving and publication purposes from the outset.

A fundamental change in the function of the manuscript in the late Middle Ages, as is evident here, can also be seen in the new type of the so-called household book ('Hausbuch').[25] The Nuremberg household book 16.3 Aug. 4°

---

24   See Heinemann, *Die Augusteischen Handschriften v*, pp. 113–114 (no. 3683).

25   On the type of household book see Dieter H. Meyer, *Literarische Hausbücher des 16. Jahrhunderts. Die Sammlungen des Ulrich Mostl, des Valentin Holl und des Simprecht Kröll* (2 vols., Würzburg: Königshausen & Neumann, 1989); Barbara Schmid, 'Das Hausbuch

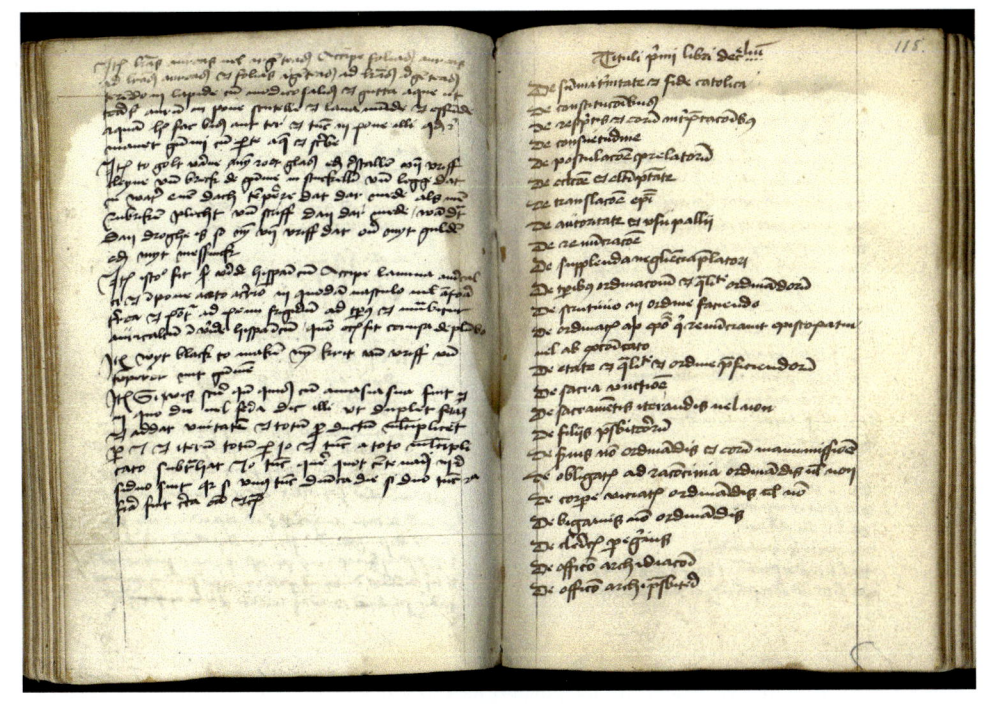

FIGURE 4.6   Wolfenbüttel, Herzog August Bibliothek: Cod. Guelf. 62.4 Aug. 8°, fols. 117v–118r

of the HAB is a codex composed of several fascicles that were initially created independently of one another, dating from the late fifteenth to early sixteenth century, and holds several works independent of each other. These include a gunsmith's book (fol. 366r–415v), a treatise on fragrant waters by the Nuremberg arithmetician Hans Neudörffer (fol. 182r–186r) and three different cookery books (fol. 188r–205v, 206r–217v and 281r–296r).[26] In addition to the variety of scribal hands and papers, other features indicate that the fascicles of this composite volume were created entirely independently of each other, leading previous lives before being bound together, as is evident thanks to the

als literarische Gattung. Die Aufzeichnungen Johann Heinrich Wasers (1600–1669) und die Zürcher Hausbuchüberlieferung', *Daphnis* 34 (2005), pp. 603–656; Frank Fürbeth, 'Wissensorganisierende Komposithandschriften. Materiale Indizien eines spätmittelalterlichen Handschriftentyps am Beispiel des sog. 'Hausbuchs' von Michael de Leone', in Schubert (ed.), *Materialität in der Editionswissenschaft*, pp. 293–308.

26   See Otto von Heinemann, *Die Handschriften der Herzoglichen Bibliothek zu Wolfenbüttel*, 2. Abt.: Die Augusteischen Handschrift IV (Wolfenbüttel: Zwissler, 1900), pp. 195–196 (No. 3074).

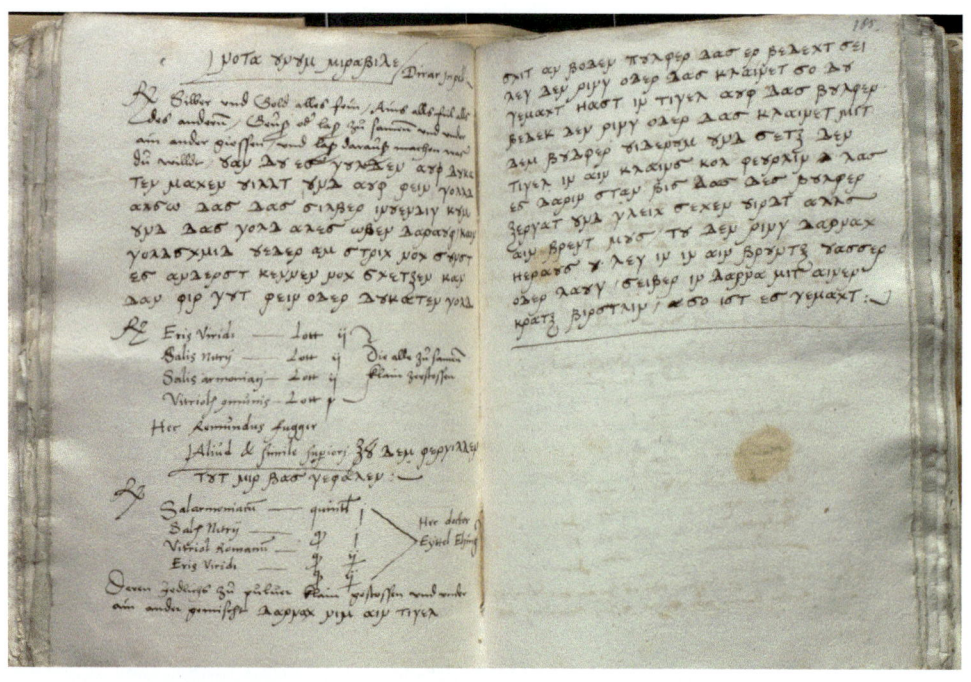

FIGURE 4.7   Wolfenbüttel, Herzog August Bibliothek: Cod. Guelf. 16.3 Aug. 4°, fols. 164v–165r

heavily soiled first and last pages of its first cookery book.[27] These sections
are connected by rather miscellaneous recipes, many of which are medical,
veterinary, technological or alchemical. A significant portion contains advice
on how to arrange one's love life and might be called an early modern *Joy of
Sex* ('Concumbendi modus facilimus …', fol. 13r–17r, 'Sequuntur medicinae
quaedam excerpta libidinem mirabiliter incitantes, penemque erigentes', fol.
17v–22r). As a codification of useful, while also entertaining, knowledge for an
urban civic household, this repertoire represents a transition from standardised traditions to manuscript recordings with a degree of individual openness.
Its range of applied knowledge also includes metallurgical and transmuta-
tional alchemy. Instructions on how to 'make gold' (fol. 159v) are found within
a series of metallurgical recipes (fol. 159r–160r), which follows a mining treatise ('Ain bewartte kunst alle arzt zu arbaittn vnnd das Silber herauß zupringen
an fewer', 157r–158v). Transmutatory alchemical recipes recorded on two
pages (fol. 164v–165r) seem to have fallen into the collection by chance. The
fact that passages of these were written phonetically in Greek letters shows

27   See the codicological description by Barbara Denicolò (2021), in Helmut W. Klug, Astrid
        Böhm and Christian Steiner (eds.) *CoReMA – Cooking Recipes of the Middle Ages. Corpus –
        Analysis – Visualisation*, http://hdl.handle.net/11471/562.10.4518 [6 November 2022].

that the recording of such texts was more an end in itself and did not serve application, indicating a playful approach to the tradition rather than a professional interest.

Even where recipes are written on single sheets, we are not dealing with the original medium of the recipe. The volume of over 500 pages that today forms the Wolfenbüttel manuscript 9 Noviss. 2°, contains records for archival purposes, possibly also working material, either as a book insert or for a slip box ('Zettelkasten').[28]

Beyond the types of recipe records as books or in books described so far, typical forms of recipe transmission include entries in and addenda to a conceptually self-contained handwritten or printed book. The back endpaper of the HAB copy of Andreas Libavius' *Commentationes metallicae* continues with a recipe ('Rp. den Safft ...').[29] By enriching the print with a factually connected text, reading matter merges into writing. The accumulation of knowledge represents a specific form of use that differs from the practical application of knowledge, as can be illustrated by a very similar example: like the Libavius volume, a HAB copy of the *Bref Discours des Admirables Vertus de l'Orpotable* by Alexandre de La Tourrette contains a handwritten recipe text on the back endpaper. This is a parody recipe taking aim at 'alchimistarey' – alchemy is the evil to be cured: a composite of ashes, sweat, sighs, deceit, shame and disgrace promising recovery ('keep all this before the eyes of the mind, until it becomes clear and well pure, then you will soon be well, if you are not otherwise foolish, mad and insane').[30] Not only is this a parody of the conventional recipe, it is also a familiar way of recording recipes on the blank pages of a book: it is easy to misread it as a serious recipe at first glance.

The process of textual enrichment is particularly vivid in the Wolfenbüttel manuscript 306.1 Extrav. This is a collection of German-language alchemical texts, all written by the same hand.[31] In several places it is supplemented by recipes on inserted slips of paper: between fols. 65v and 66r there is a recipe headed 'Vniuersal', in front of fol. 1r is a strip of paper introducing the recipe with the words: 'another powder g [?] have I found thus' ('ain ander

---

28 See Renate Giermann, *Die neueren Handschriften der Gruppe Novissimi* (Frankfurt a. M.: Klostermann, 1992), pp. 8–9.

29 Addition on the back endpaper of Andreas Libavius, *Commentationum Metallicarum Libri Quatuor* (Frankfurt a. M.: Johannes Saur and Peter Kopf, 1597) [HAB: 17.2 Phys. (2)].

30 'halt diß alleß vor den augen deß verstandts, biß er lauter vnd wol rein wird, so wirstu bald genösen, wann du anderst nit gar Närrisch, toll, vnnd vnsinnig bist.' Addition on the back endpaper of Alexandre de La Tourrette, *Bref Discours des Admirables Vertus de l'Orpotable* (Paris: Jean de l'Astre, 1575) [HAB: 152.3 Phys. (1)].

31 See Hans Butzmann, *Die mittelalterlichen Handschriften der Gruppen Extravagantes, Novi und Novissimi* (Frankfurt a. M.: Klostermann, 1972), p. 167.

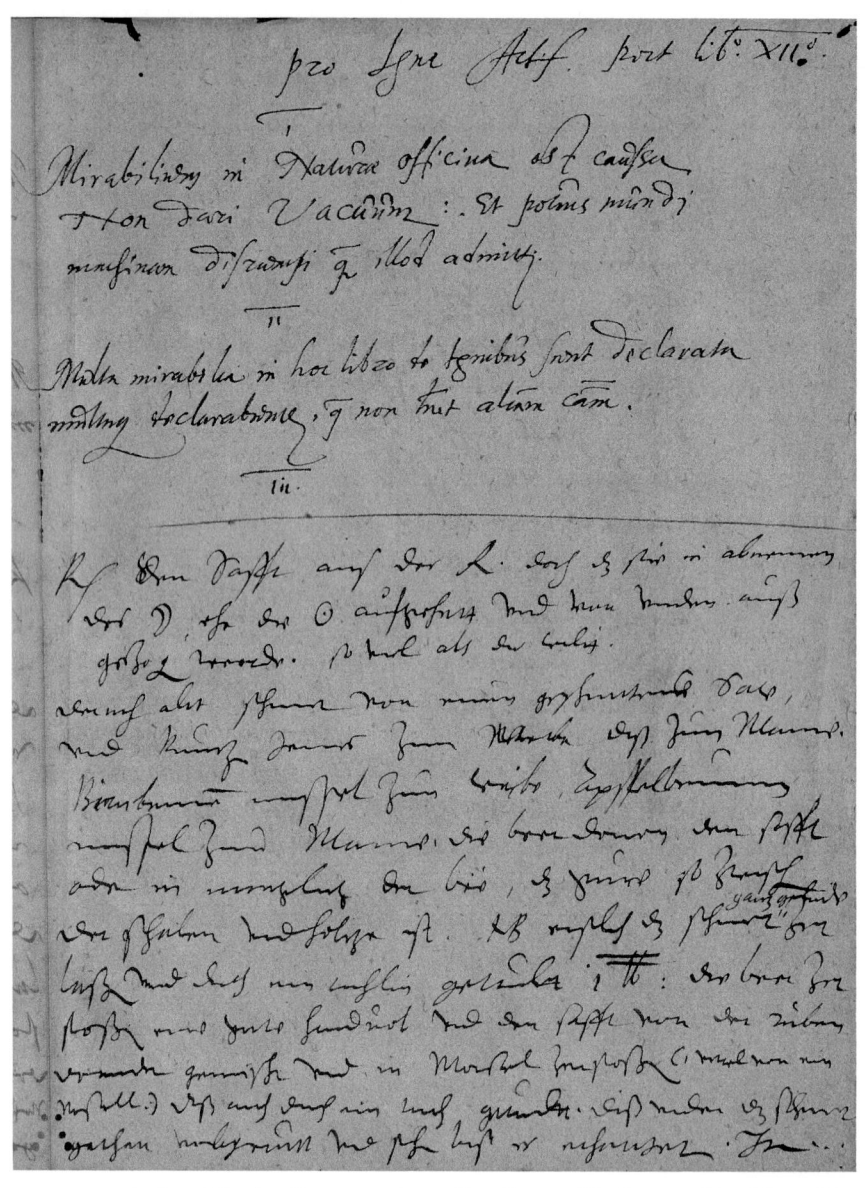

FIGURE 4.8 Andreas Libavius, *Commentationum Metallicarum Libri Quatuor* (Frankfurt a. M.:
Johannes Saur and Peter Kopf, 1597), back endpaper. Wolfenbüttel, Herzog August
Bibliothek: 17.2 Phys. (2)

puluer g [?] hab ich funden also'). This autobiographical introduction depicts
the process of text production itself by stating that the writer has notated his
exploratory findings. The entire volume represents a type of manuscript that,
in its production and function, differs fundamentally from conventional text

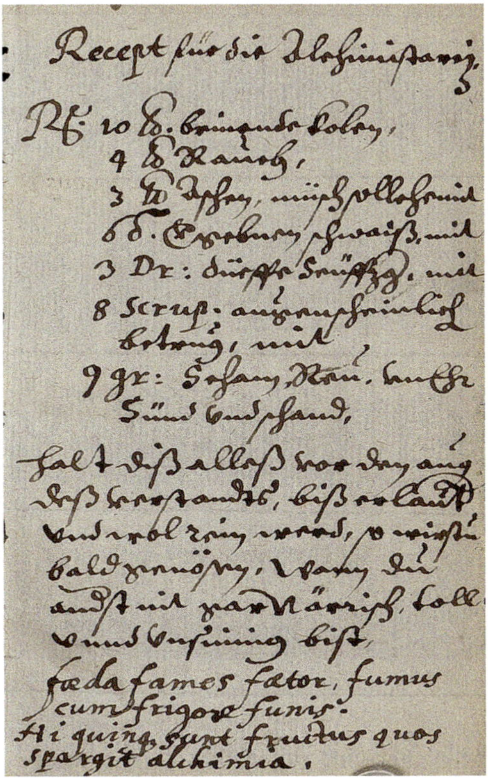

FIGURE 4.9
Alexandre de La Tourrette, *Bref Discours des Admirables Vertus de l'Orpotable* (Paris: Jean de l'Astre, 1575), back endpaper. Wolfenbüttel, Herzog August Bibliothek: 152.3 Phys. (1)

copies for archiving and publication purposes. Although this manuscript also reproduces existing texts, it is unique in its composition and its intended use is tailored to the one person who wrote it. The recording serves the purpose of appropriation, but not the transmission of knowledge. It is the product of a new recording system that differs from the monastic scriptorium, the chancery, the urban writing workshop or the printing workshop.

Additional recipes may be interpreted as traces of individual reading, working and writing processes, that is, they can be explained plausibly as evidence of a professional interest and use. This cannot be said for entries in books that are in no way connected with the added recipes' content.

In many cases, the seemingly random of recipe transmission can easily be linked to the materiality of book-binding work. The upper margin of the back mirror from a Wolfenbüttel incunabulum with the *Corpus iuris civilis* shows a Low German recipe for a sleeping aid.[32] The page consists of parchment leaf inscribed on one side, while the written side is glued onto the wooden cover.

Bookbinder's unit of two separate incunabula: (1) *Corpus iuris civilis. Iustiniani Institutiones,* with the Glossa ordinaria of Franciscus Accursius (Basel: Michael Wenssler, 1481.

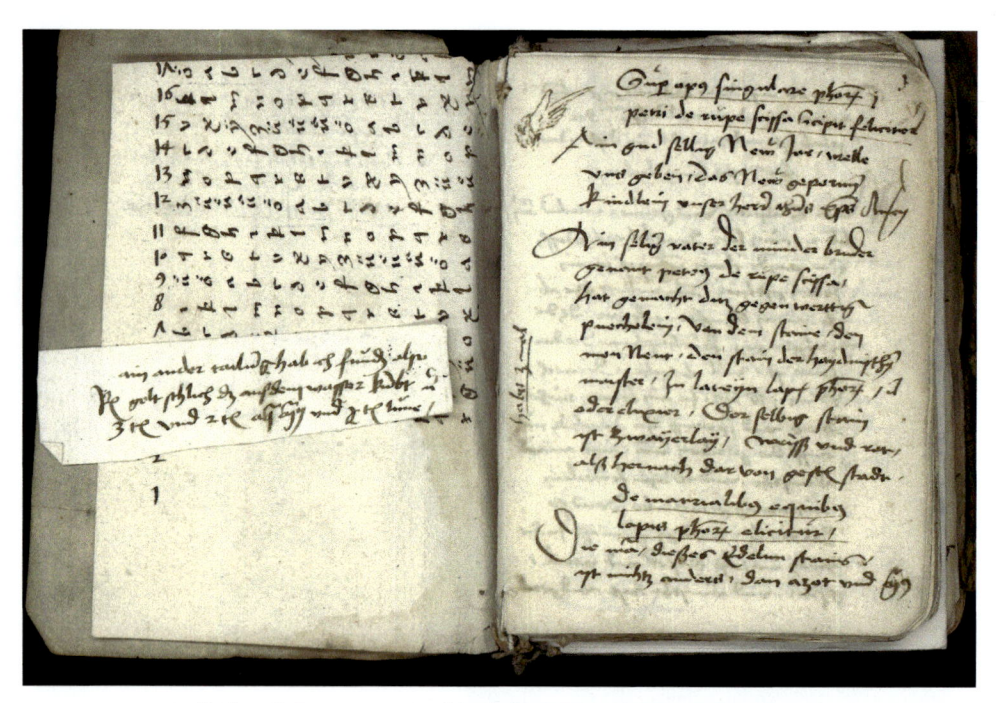

FIGURE 4.10   Wolfenbüttel, Herzog August Bibliothek: Cod. Guelf. 306.1 Extrav., fol. 1r

As the contemporary writing on the visible outer side makes clear, it is a copy
of a charter ('Instrumentum concordie …'), which was only subsequently used
for the recipe. The use of binding material is thus a third application that took
place only after the recipe had been written down, because the mounting of
the chain eyelet on the upper edge of the cover partially conceals the text. The
leaf, its layers of inscriptions and its use as binding material have no connection to the contents of the volume.

Examples of recipe entries on free pages, especially endpapers and flyleaves
of bound prints – and composite volumes of several prints – are numerous, but
it is difficult to identify them systematically, since the entries are contingent
phenomena that are only found when historic holdings in libraries are indexed
with their individual traits. Here are some randomly selected examples:

A Low German recipe for loss of appetite ('If you don't feel like eating, make a
[deleted: salad] salsa with garlic') can be found in a composite volume of five
separate prints with exegetical and homiletical writings of the Reformation

GW 7605); (2) *Corpus iuris civilis. Novellae etc.* [here only: *Consuetudines feudorum*] (Basel:
Michael Wenssler, 1478. GW 7752) [HAB: 29.19.1 Jur. 2°].

FIGURE 4.11 *Corpus iuris civilis* (Basel: Michael Wenssler, 1481. GW 7605), back mirror page. Wolfenbüttel, Herzog August Bibliothek: 29.19.1 Jur. 2°

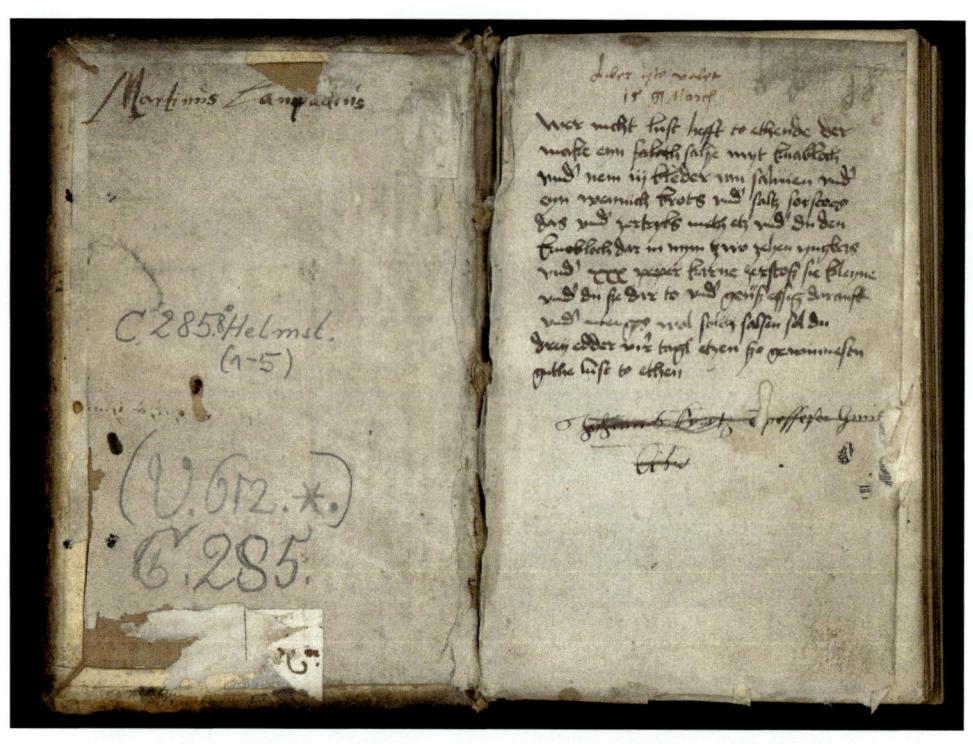

FIGURE 4.12   Philipp Melanchthon, *Annotationes … in Euangelium Matthaei* (Nuremberg: Johann
Petreius, 1523), front mirror and flyleaf. Wolfenbüttel, Herzog August Bibliothek:
C 285.8° Helmst

(Theobald Billicanus, Johannes Bugenhagen, Erasmus of Rotterdam, Philipp
Melanchthon).[33] The recipe is written between other entries by different
hands (purchase price, ownership note) on the front flyleaf, which, as part of
the binding, has no connection with the prints.

The back flyleaf of a copy of Melanchthon's *Heubtartikel Christlicher Lere*
reveals a recipe for horse ointment.[34] Reference should also be made to a composite volume of five separate printed works from the years 1605 and 1612–14,
bringing together writings by Latin and Greek authors (Cicero, Cornelius
Nepos, Basil the Great, Justus Lipsius) probably used in academic (rhetorical)

---

33   'Wer nicht lust hefft to ethende der make ein [deleted: salath] salße mit knabloch.' Philipp
Melanchthon, *Annotationes … in Euangelium Matthaei* (Nuremberg: Johann Petreius,
1523) together with four further small-format prints from the years 1524 and 1525 [HAB: C
285.8° Helmst.].

34   'Ein gutte Salbe für den grint So die perde haben.' Philipp Melanchthon, *Die Heubtartikel
Christlicher Lere / … Im latin genant / Loci communes Theologici*, translated by Justus Jonas
(Wittenberg: Veit Kreutzer, 1544) [HAB: J 526.4° Helmst.].

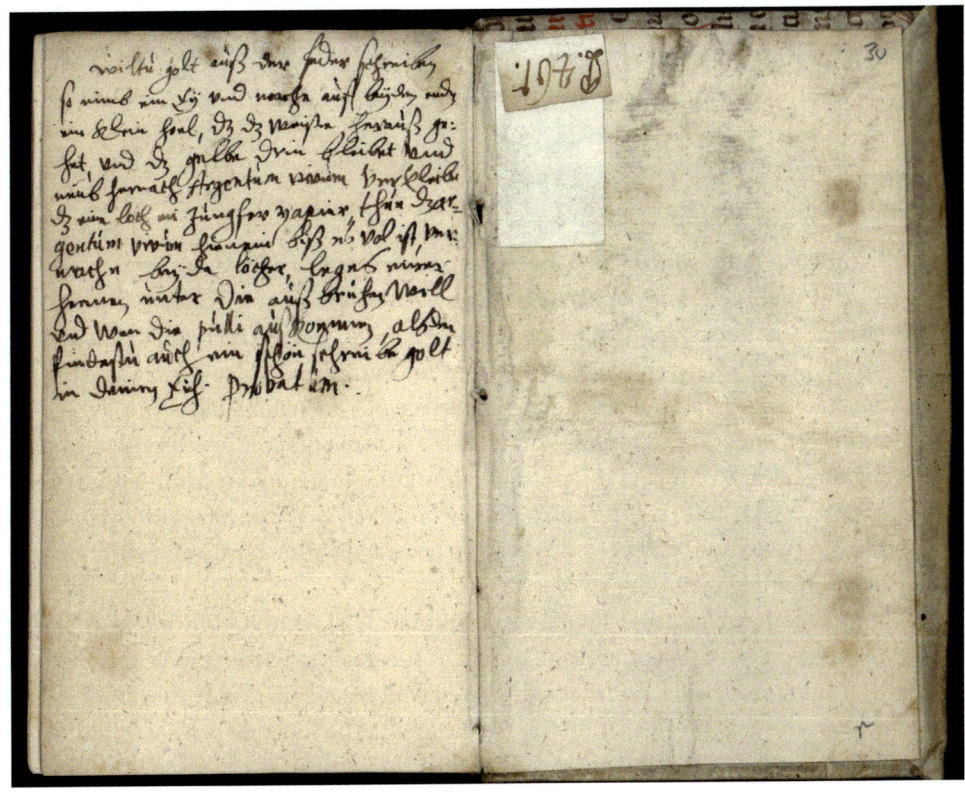

FIGURE 4.13   Cicero, *Pro A. Licinio Archia Poeta & M. Marcello Orationes*, ed. by Daniel Vechner (Leipzig: Thomas Schürer, 1612), last page and back mirror. Wolfenbüttel, Herzog August Bibliothek: QuH 142

teaching.[35] The volume ends in a manuscript section related to the printed works regarding their content and function (*Tropi verborum* with definitions of rhetorical figures, fol. 1r–9v, *Elementa apud Hebraeos sunt 22*, explanation of the Hebrew alphabet, fol. 10r–13v), corresponding with the neat humanistic cursive of the first text. After thirty-one blank pages, there is a recipe for gold ink ('If you want to write with gold from a feather, take an egg and make a small opening at both ends', fol. 29v), which has a less technological than alchemical character.[36] As a German-language text written in German script ('Kurrent'), the recipe forms no formal connection or spatial proximity with the preceding text.

3   Recording Systems of Recipes

In order to draw conclusions from these observations, it is necessary to apply several parameters for analysis of each case of recipe recording and reproduction in books. A distinction must be made between manuscript and printed text, whereby hybridity is frequent. Furthermore, we need to distinguish between the transmission of single recipes and such collections, which form transmission filiations. Standardised transmission contexts with a higher stability of text and repertoire differ from individual records with non-standard texts and repertoire. Within a book, recipes can have a functional proximity to other texts or otherwise be recorded contingently and without a corresponding context.

It becomes clear that the concept and terms of 'text' and 'work' in traditional literary criticism are not sufficient for dealing with recipes and their transmission. Friedrich Kittler confronted with his media theory the blindness of conventional literary studies to the realm that lies outside textual notation, which is a specific problem for the literature of knowledge and use:

> The traditional study of literature ... has examined everything about books other than their data processing. Meaning as the basic concept of hermeneutics and work as the basic concept of the sociology of literature both skip over the information channel of writing and those institutions that, like school or university, interconnect books with people.[37]

---

36   'wiltu golt auß der feder schreiben so nimb ein Ey vnd mache auff beyden enden ein klein hoel ...' No similar source has been recorded by Vera Trost, *Gold- und Silbertinten. Technologische Untersuchungen zur abendländischen Chrysographie und Argyrographie von der Spätantike bis zum hohen Mittelalter* (Wiesbaden: Harrassowitz, 1991).

37   '[D]ie hergebrachte Literaturwissenschaft ... hat an Büchern alles andere als ihre Datenverarbeitung untersucht. Sinn als Grundbegriff der Hermeneutik und Arbeit als Grundbegriff der Literatursoziologie überspringen beide den Informationskanal Schrift und jene Institutionen, die wie Schule oder Universität die Bücher mit den Leuten verschalten.' Friedrich A. Kittler, *Aufschreibesysteme 1800–1900* (3rd ed., Munich: Fink 1995), pp. 519–520.

Kittler's focus lies on the threshold periods around 1800 and 1900. Neverthe-less, several consequences may be drawn for the premodern period from his theoretical and sociological expansion of literary criticism: Following Kittler, a recording system is a 'condition of possibility' of the literary field of knowl-edge and use. The term recording system refers to 'the network of techniques and institutions ... that allow a given culture to address, store and process rel-evant data'.[38] The diverse types of the transmission of recipes in books are the effects of the diverse recording systems that existed side by side in the late Middle Ages and early modern period and which produce different meanings of recipes. In general, we assume that recipes are pragmatic texts and that consequently recipes in books, books with recipes, recipe books and booklets are media that aim at practice and convey knowledge of application, because the more recipes that are accumulated and systematised in a book, the more practical application should be gained from it.[39] This is precisely what is to be questioned in its general validity – both as a historical experience and as the indisputable intention of recording.

The single sheet of paper as the genuine medium of recipe actually forms the object of a practical process since, as a record for a particular occa-sion, it detaches knowledge from the totality of the medical, pharmaceutical, alchemical, culinary or other tradition, updates it and operationalises it in the concrete production of a remedy or in the performance of a procedure. With the production of the remedy, arcanum etc., however, the note loses its imme-diate practical function. Moreover, we could ask why an apothecary, alchemist or other professional would have to study for years, specialise, professionalise

---

38 'das Netzwerk von Techniken und Institutionen ..., die einer gegebenen Kultur die Adressierung, Speicherung und Verarbeitung relevanter Daten erlauben', Kittler, *Auf-schreibesysteme*, p. 519.

39 Giesecke has already fundamentally questioned the premise that specialist literature is recording of experiential and operationalisable knowledge, and instead emphasised its social and symbolic functions; see Michael Giesecke, 'Überlegungen zur sozialen Funktion und zur Struktur handschriftlicher Rezepte im Mittelalter', *Zeitschrift für Literaturwissenschaft und Linguistik*, 51/52 (1983), pp. 167–184. It is a problem that Giesecke – despite the title – does not base his considerations on the medieval medi-eval manuscript tradition of recipes (but on printed herbal books of the early modern period). Moreover, it is questionable whether the change in media around 1500 actually brought about the decisive paradigm shift that is the prerequisite for 'Fachliteratur', or, instead, it was the urbanisation of late medieval society with its professionalisation of the 'arts'. Apart from all this, a differentiation of recipes according to its various areas of application would make sense. For cookery recipes and cookery books, for example, Gloning, 'Textgebrauch', p. 522, has distinguished between three recording functions: Recipe records serve (1) collection purposes, (2) instruction and transmission, (3) mem-ory support and documentation of one's own practice.

and gain experience if the art they practised could be accomplished with a piece of paper alone. For actions, the recipes are usually not necessary: specialists have mastered their profession, experienced users know what to do and how. In certain cases they can even be illiterate without this affecting their competence.

The recipe is neither the exclusive medium of pragmatics nor of episteme, but rather of symbolic communication, mostly among specialists. On the one hand, it serves to assure that the right means is chosen for a purpose and that its execution is handled correctly, and, if necessary, to ensure that the execution can be repeated with the same result.[40] On the other hand, the recipe secures the knowledge and practice of specialists and thus is a social practice that delimits the ingroup from the lay or uninitiated. In order to describe adequately the functions of recipes, it is not enough to consider text, structure and content alone; rather, we have to consider recipes as a social and cultural practice. It is only from this perspective that the inscription of recipes in books can be properly understood. In the cultural practice of the recipe, the ostensible pragmatic function is surrounded by less ostensible, but equally important socio-practical functions. But the inscription of recipes in books removes them from application, recording does not increase pragmatics. Recipes in books are withdrawn from action, not transformed into action.[41]

Practising from books represents merely one of several possibilities of use. Physical traces of use are often thought to authenticate the factual historical use of pragmatic literature. But unanswered questions remain: which traces attest to what kind of use? In any case, we have to distinguish traces of reading (marks, notes, entries) as literary use, which is not specific to pragmatic literature, from the application of the recorded knowledge.[42] The search for traces

---

40   See Ulrich Seidel, *Rezept und Apotheke. Zur Geschichte der Arzneiverordnung vom 13. bis zum 16. Jahrhundert* (dissertation, Marburg a. d. Lahn, 1977).

41   Gerd Boßhammer, *Technologische und Farbrezepte des Kasseler Codex medicus 4° 10. Untersuchungen zur Berufssoziologie des mittelalterlichen Laienarztes* (Pattensen: Wellm, 1977), pp. 7–14, has made it clear, on the basis of the frequent coexistence of medical, technological and other recipes in handwritten collections of the late Middle Ages, that these records are precisely not practices of demarcation of an expert class, but 'social indicators' (p. 10) of the fact that knowledge is to be made available here beyond social and professional confinement.

42   William H. Sherman, *Used Books. Marking Readers in Renaissance England* (Philadelphia: University of Pennsylvania Press, 2008); Sabine Häußermann, 'Von Eselsohren und Zeigehändchen. Überlegungen zu Gebrauchsspuren in Büchern', in Annette Hoffmann, Frank Martin and Gerhard Wolf (eds.), *BücherGänge. Miszellen zu Buchkunst, Leselust und Bibliotheksgeschichte. Hommage an Dieter Klein* (Heidelberg: Manutius, 2006), pp. 19–28; Magnus Wieland, 'Materialität des Lesens. Zur Topographie von Annotationsspuren

of use generally leaves open the significance of the much more frequent case, the absence of any traces indicating the non-use of pragmatic literature.

It seems necessary to ask which recording system produced which books with recipes. The change in media history from the late Middle Ages to the early modern period brought with it a diversification of the functions of manuscript and printed tradition. Against the backdrop of changing cultures of knowledge, the modernisation tendencies in written culture and the transformation of media from manuscript to print, the function of manuscripts changed from a medium of publication, archiving and transmission to a medium of text production, communication and self-understanding.[43] The types of late medieval and early modern miscellaneous or composite manuscripts form the main textual milieu for the recording of recipes alongside the conceived recipe collections: household books, manuals of professional practice, academic or spiritual miscellanies and notebooks all demonstrate an increasing tendency towards individualisation. This development led from the standardised codex to the individually designed manuscript, while standardisation of texts and media fell in the area of printed books.

The various forms of recipe tradition, in particular the manuscript recipe books common until modern times, show that wide areas of written culture (including arcane disciplines such as alchemy) remained independent from the printed book beyond the media revolution. We do not face the total replacement of manuscript transmission by print, nor the mutual exclusivity of handwritten and printed tradition, but rather, the continuity of media characterised by complex exchange processes between prints and manuscripts. The provided examples of handwritten portions in printed books are only one of several forms of this hybridisation of media.

---

in Autorenbibliotheken', in Michael Knoche (ed.), *Autorenbibliotheken. Erschließung, Rekonstruktion, Wissensordnung* (Wiesbaden: Harrassowitz, 2015), pp. 147–173; exemplary in the differentiation of reading and usage traces is Petra Feuerstein-Herz, 'Von heimlichkeit der Natur. Benutzungsspuren in alchemischen Anleitungsbüchern', *Medium Buch*, 1 (2019), pp. 47–67.

43 As early as the 12th century, a profound change in Latin writing can be observed, which can be described in simple terms as a change in the book from a medium for reading aloud to a medium for reading silently. This permanently changes the conditions of text and book production because, on the one hand, the medial form of books (word division, writing style, layout, etc.) adapts to these changes and the writers themselves gain authority and autonomy. This is accompanied by a new practice of authorship, since the authors of texts under these new conditions increasingly write themselves instead of dictating. See Ivan Illich, *In the Vineyard of the Text: A Commentary to Hugh's Didascalicon* (Chicago: The University of Chicago Press, 1993); Paul Saenger, *Space Between Words: The Origins of Silent Reading* (Stanford: Stanford University Press, 1997), pp. 243–276.

4   Conclusion

By interpreting written recorded recipes in books from a perspective of social practices and media history, several conclusions may be drawn:

Writing down recipes provides them with validity including tradition, legitimacy and authority, underscored by the quality of the decoration in certain recipe manuscripts (as well as printed recipe books).[44] The collection, systematisation and presentation of recipes is an accumulation of symbolic capital from which the power and exclusivity of a professional, specialised, arcane knowledge or social status can be derived.

Much like the writing of books itself, recording recipes in books increasingly becomes a process of individual appropriation. What is recorded is not necessarily knowledge to be passed on or even to be used; instead, what is documented in writing is the acquisition of knowledge itself. The inscription of recipes in books may thus be considered a technique of the self.[45]

In one form or another, recipe usage seems to point to reading or other social practices rather than the application of recorded knowledge. As a ubiquitous phenomenon, the recipe is open to cultural imagination and lends itself, like comparably familiar phenomena such as songs or liturgy, to parody and other forms of playful adaptation. In this respect, recorded recipes' playful and entertaining values should not be underestimated.[46]

---

44   An example from the Library in Wolfenbüttel would be the large-format and highly illuminated alchemical recipe codex 340 Helmst. (around 1600; presumably in the possession of Duke Heinrich Julius of Brunswick-Lüneburg). See Petra Feuerstein-Herz, 'Kristalle und Korallen', in Feuerstein-Herz and Laube (eds.), *Goldenes Wissen,* pp. 308–309. Christoph Wirsung, *Artzney Buch/ Darinn werden fast alle eusserliche vnd innerliche Glieder des Menschlichen leibs/ mit jhrer gestalt/ aigenschafft vnd würckung beschriben* (Heidelberg: Johannes Mayer, 1568) [HAB: Ma 4° 90] due to its format alone, also has the claim of being representative and authoritative. See Pfister/Schofer, 'Das Heidelberger 'Artzney Buch".

45   The insertion of small and individual texts into an individually designed codex can also serve to give them validity, as Griese has shown with examples from the 15th century, see Sabine Griese, 'Exklusion und Inklusion. Formen der Überlieferung des Gebrauchs von Literatur im 15. Jahrhundert', in Felix Heinzer and Hans-Peter Schmit (eds.), *Codex und Geltung* (Wiesbaden: Harrassowitz, 2015), pp. 175–190.

46   See Rudolf Schenda, *Volk ohne Buch. Studien zur Sozialgeschichte der populären Lesestoffe 1770–1910* (Munich: dtv 1977), pp. 253, 285 and 329–330; Sonja Kerth, 'Das schmeckt lecker und tut gut. Scherzrezepte in der deutschen Literatur des Mittelalters', in Hans Wolf Jäger, Holger Böning and Gert Sautermeister (eds.), *Genußmittel und Literatur* (Bremen: Edition Lumière, 2003), pp. 101–110; Telle, 'Das Rezept'; Hiram Kümper, 'Von Ameiseneiern und Fledermausblut. Ein spätmittelalterliches Rezept für ein kurzweiliges Badevergnügen', in Iris Kwiatkowski and Michael Oberweis (eds.), *Recht, Religion, Gesellschaft und Kultur im Wandel der Geschichte. Ferculum de cibis spiritualibus. Festschrift für Dieter Scheler*

From a diachronic perspective, the explosion of printed specialist literature on the book market in the early modern period, especially from the medical, pharmaceutical and alchemical fields, shows that recipes have a market value completely independent of their usefulness. Capital can be gained thanks to the exclusivity of specialist knowledge. The dynamics of book market economy thus contribute to the popularisation of the recipe that this exclusivity was actually supposed to prevent.[47]

Revision of the translation: Elisabeth Obermeier

(Hamburg: Kovač 2008), pp. 347–350; Marco Heiles, 'Das Wunderbare in der deutschen Rezeptliteratur des 15. Jahrhunderts', in Stefanie Kreuzer and Uwe Durst (eds.), *Das Wunderbare. Dimensionen eines Phänomens in Kunst und Kultur* (Paderborn: Fink, 2018), pp. 233–250.

47 See Joachim Telle, 'Arzneikunst und der 'gemeine Mann'. Zum deutsch-lateinischen Sprachenstreit in der frühneuzeitlichen Medizin', in id. (ed.), *Pharmazie und der gemeine Mann. Hausarznei und Apotheke in der frühen Neuzeit* (2nd ed., Weinheim: VCH Acta Humaniora, 1988), pp. 43–48; Petra Feuerstein-Herz, 'Öffentliche Geheimnisse. Alchemische Drucke der frühen Neuzeit', in Feuerstein-Herz and Laube (eds.), *Goldenes Wissen*, pp. 55–65; Utz Maas, 'Lesen – Schreiben – Schrift. Die Demotisierung eines professionellen Arkanums im Spätmittelalter und in der frühen Neuzeit', *Zeitschrift für Literaturwissenschaft und Linguistik* 59 (1985), pp. 55–81.

CHAPTER 5

A Commerce of Secrets: Digital and Performative Approaches to an Early Modern How-to Manuscript at the Making and Knowing Project

Tillmann Taape

1 Introduction

This chapter discusses some of the insights of several years' research on a rich early modern how-to text: Ms. Fr. 640, an anonymous French manuscript containing recipes, technical instructions, and observations on art and craft practices from 1580s Toulouse, now held at the Bibliothèque Nationale de France. The work was carried out at the Making and Knowing Project, a research and pedagogy initiative of the Center for Science and Society at Columbia University in New York, founded by Pamela Smith. The Project's approach to this unique source is two-fold: through textual and editorial work using tools from Digital Humanities, and through a practical hands-on approach in the laboratory where we reconstruct the techniques described in the manuscript. The result of our work is a digital publication called *Secrets of Craft and Nature in Renaissance France*, which includes a critical edition and English translation of the text, as well as research essays written by scholarly collaborators and by students of our laboratory class 'Craft and Science'.[1]

BnF Ms. Fr. 640 is a unique source, providing unprecedented detail about artisanal ways of making things and understanding the material world, especially metalworking techniques such as moulding and casting as well as sword-making and firearms. At the same time, it embodies many of the characteristics and challenges typical of early modern 'how-to' literature and historians' engagement with it. It forms part of a larger history of practical genres such as cook books, Books of secrets, 'Kunstbüchlein' or 'Rezeptbüchlein'. Scholarship in history of science and cultural history has taught us to take

---

1 Making and Knowing Project, Pamela H. Smith, Naomi Rosenkranz, Tianna Helena Uchacz, Tillmann Taape, Clément Godbarge, Sophie Pitman, Jenny Boulboullé, Joel Klein, Donna Bilak, Marc Smith, and Terry Catapano, eds., *Secrets of Craft and Nature in Renaissance France. A Digital Critical Edition and English Translation of BnF Ms. Fr. 640* (New York: Making and Knowing Project, 2020), https://edition640.makingandknowing.org.

recipes, 'secrets', and other how-to writing seriously as practical forms of knowledge that were increasingly valued in the sixteenth and seventeenth centuries.[2] As Pamela Smith has shown, among the apparently jumbled jottings and musings of artisans we can often discern what she calls a 'vernacular science' of matter and its transformation.[3] But these kinds of how-to sources present a challenge to the historian. In contrast with more literary and expository texts, they are often unforthcoming as sources. They offer thin, uncircumstantiated accounts, leaving us to puzzle over the meaning of terse instructions or even the basic ingredients. However detailed the recipe, there is a lot that remains unsaid, and really cannot be said, but only known and experienced in the body.[4]

Ms. Fr. 640 is also typical in its structure: a collection of many largely independent textual units. Here the historian faces a second challenge: how can we read those fragmentary texts as a whole, as an articulation of expertise and of an underlying worldview? Elaine Leong has risen brilliantly to this challenge in her study of recipe collections, which, as she shows, could become veritable knowledge-making machines, especially in the hands of early modern women.[5] With collections like Ms. Fr. 640 consisting of miscellaneous instructions and observations on a wide variety of topics, without much of an apparent ordering principle, it remains difficult to make sense of the whole as an epistemic project, at least with traditional tools of scholarly analysis.

---

2 William Eamon, *Science and the Secrets of Nature. Books of Secrets in Medieval and Early Modern Culture* (Princeton: Princeton University Press, 1994); Vera Keller, 'Mining Tacitus: Secrets of Empire, Nature and Art in the Reason of State', *The British Journal for the History of Science* 45, (2012): 189–212; Elaine Leong and Alisha Rankin, *Secrets and Knowledge in Medicine and Science, 1500–1800* (Farnham: Ashgate, 2011).

3 Pamela H. Smith, *The Body of the Artisan: Art and Experience in the Scientific Revolution* (Chicago: The University of Chicago Press, 2004), pp. 129–153; Pamela H. Smith, 'Making as Knowing: Craft as Natural Philosophy', in *Ways of Making and Knowing*, ed. Pamela H. Smith, Harold Cook, and Amy Meyers (Ann Arbor: University of Michigan Press, 2014), pp. 17–47. See also, Pamela H. Smith, *From Lived Experience to the Written Word: Reconstructing Practical Knowledge in the Early Modern World* (Chicago: The University of Chicago Press, 2022).

4 Pamela H. Smith, 'In a Sixteenth-Century Goldsmith's Workshop', in *The Mindful Hand: Inquiry and Invention from the Late Renaissance to Early Industrialisation*, ed. Lissa Roberts and Simon Schaffer (Amsterdam: Royal Netherlands Academy of Arts and Sciences, 2007), pp. 33–57.

5 Elaine Leong, 'Collecting Knowledge for the Family: Recipes, Gender and Practical Knowledge in the Early Modern English Household', *Centaurus*, 55 (2013), pp. 81–103; Elaine Leong, *Recipes and Everyday Knowledge: Medicine, Science, and the Household in Early Modern England* (Chicago: The University of Chicago Press, 2018). On the use of recipes by German noblewomen, see Alisha Rankin, *Panacea's Daughters: Noblewomen as Healers in Early Modern Germany* (Chicago: The University of Chicago Press, 2013).

Our manuscript, then, is a rich but complex source that typifies the twin challenges of dealing with early modern how-to texts: the problem of tacit knowledge, and the problem of analysing miscellaneous collections as cohesive bodies of texts that can tell us something about the author's intentions and expertise. In this chapter, I explore how the Making and Knowing Project tackled these challenges through novel methodological approaches. Taking up one of the major themes of this volume, I begin by exploring the materiality of the manuscript and what it can tell us about its composition, use, and the intentions of the anonymous author-practitioner, as we call him. I then discuss our creation of a digital critical edition of the manuscript, and how the digital medium and computational analysis tools help us make sense of a miscellaneous how-to text. Finally, I show how we use hands-on 'reconstruction' in the laboratory as a complementary approach, an active way of reading that enables us to recover some of the tacit knowledge and material expertise hidden between the lines.

2   A Commerce of Secrets: Materiality and Genesis of Ms. Fr. 640

Ms. Fr. 640 has been preserved since the early seventeenth century in a red morocco binding with a coat of arms signalling that it was once part of the collection of Philippe de Béthune (1561–1649), count of Selles and Charost, diplomat and adviser to three consecutive kings of France. Along with some two thousand other volumes contained in the Béthune library, Ms. Fr. 640 was donated to the King's Library, which formed the core of the later Bibliothèque nationale de France, where it is still held today. Probably in the course of applying the elegant binding to make the manuscript fit in with the rest of the Béthune collection, the original gatherings were cut up into separate leaves, which were then re-margined by gluing paper strips along all edges, before sewing them back together into quires for binding. Collectors liked the volumes on their shelves to be of the same height, and such re-binding was by no means uncommon.[6]

Moving from the exterior binding of the manuscript to the inside, its pages reveal further material traces that speak to the way the text was composed

---

6   On the material construction and composition of Ms. Fr. 640, see the following essay in *Secrets of Craft and Nature in Renaissance* France: Alexis Hagadorn, 'The Physical Construction of Ms. Fr. 640', https://edition640.makingandknowing.org/#/essays/ann_328_ie_19, Pamela H. Smith, 'Introduction to Ms. Fr. 640', https://edition640.makingandknowing.org/#/essays/ann_300_ie_19, and Marc Smith, 'Making Ms. Fr. 640' (forthcoming).

by the anonymous author-practitioner. The last page of the manuscript is upside-down, and contains three short notes in a hand that does not appear anywhere else in the manuscript. They concern the management of lands belonging to the Ouvrier, an influential Toulouse family of merchants and politicians. Below this are medical and bibliographical notes in the author-practitioner's characteristic handwriting.[7] This final page suggests that the author-practitioner may have got hold of a nearly-empty accounting book of the Ouvrier family, abandoned after half a page, and recycled it for his own use. He crossed out the original entries and filled the remainder of the first page, but then decided to flip the book over and start afresh. As a physical object, the manuscript has a tangible material link to the world of trade and craft that the author-practitioner described in its pages.

That description is neither coherent nor linear; it is refracted in a motley miscellany of over 900 individual entries on a variety of topics. Notable for its detailed observations on moulding and casting from life, the manuscript also contains entries on pigments, dyes, and varnishes, instructions for planting melons and catching lizards, practical jokes, and medical recipes.[8] While there are clusters of entries dealing with similar topics, there is no discernible overall organising principle – although, as I discuss below, digital tools can uncover hidden thematic structures.

The closest the author-practitioner comes to an overall statement of purpose are two entries titled 'La Boutique', which may well be early drafts of a preface for a planned publication. They loosely string together a collection of classical topoi that relate to collecting and disseminating 'secrets of the arts'.[9] Some artisans might object to having their secrets divulged in writing, but are they really theirs to keep? After all, as the author-practitioner points out in an elegant Latin phrase borrowed from the Roman playwright Terence, 'nothing is said now that has not been said or done before'.[10] In another classical simile, he likens himself to a hen rooting around the rubbish heap of a grand house, hoping to find 'a crumb or a grain that she divides among her chicks'. In the same way, he gathers crumbs of knowledge from arts and crafts that are often considered 'vile and abject' and distributes them to 'orphans', imagining

7   Making and Knowing Project et al., *Secrets of Craft and Nature in Renaissance France. A Digital Critical Edition and English Translation of BnF Ms. Fr.*, fol. 170v. See the image in the digital edition: https://edition640.makingandknowing.org/#/folios/170v.

8   For an overview of to the manuscript's contents, see Pamela H. Smith, 'Introduction to Ms. Fr. 640', https://edition640.makingandknowing.org/#/essays/ann_300_ie_19.

9   Making and Knowing Project et al., *Secrets of Craft and Nature in Renaissance France. A Digital Critical Edition and English Translation of BnF Ms. Fr.*, fol. 166r.

10   Making and Knowing Project et al., *Secrets of Craft and Nature*, fol. 166r.

perhaps a readership of enthusiasts who did not have a master craftsman *in loco parentis* who passed on his secrets to his apprentice.[11] Whoever he thought his readers might be, the author-practitioner throws the doors of his *boutique* wide open for them:

> As small peddlers lay open small wares in order to buy richer ones & to profit more and more, so I, from a desire to learn, am exposing what little is in my workshop to receive, through a common commerce of letters, much rarer secrets from my benevolent readers.[12]

The idea of the 'boutique', of a shop or workshop, fittingly encompasses the author-practitioner's project of collecting and exchanging craft secrets, both in his writing and in his bustling workshop.

The material text of the manuscript yields important clues to what this commerce of secrets may have looked like in terms of composition and compilation. It is mainly in the author-practitioner's own handwriting, fast and regular, but not that of a professional scribe. There are, however, three other hands present in the manuscript (apart from the crossed-out notes on the inverted final page). One is an elegant italic hand that provides only two short entries on mercantile book-keeping, perhaps that of a Toulouse merchant obliging the ever-curious author-practitioner with a sample of his trade. Similarly, a second hand (distinctly French but more elaborate than the author-practitioner's) provides a single recipe for 'millas', a local delicacy. The third hand contributes more extensive passages at two points in the manuscript, spanning several folios. It is a fairly sophisticated hand, likely that of a scribe whom the author-practitioner engaged to copy a number of painting recipes, perhaps by taking dictation. Judging by the number and kind of spelling mistakes he introduced, he was certainly no expert on the subject matter. We can imagine the author-practitioner collecting contributions from others who could provide recipes, cast accounts, or simply write legibly, underscoring the varied scope and miscellaneous nature of the manuscript.

While the author-practitioner may have handed the manuscript around on occasion, it does not look like a rough book that was kept open among the smoky furnaces and pigment dust of the workshop. Indeed, it may have been intended as a fair copy for presentation or even publication. The entries are set out in a clear visual structure, with titles in a larger italic hand, and the entries themselves show consistent spacing. On the first folio there is a long

---

11   Making and Knowing Project et al., *Secrets of Craft and Nature*, fol. 166r.
12   Making and Knowing Project et al., *Secrets of Craft and Nature*, fol. 162r.

list of books, from classical authors to more recent works on history, natural history, and books of secrets, assembling what was likely a working bibliography. Together with the entries on 'La Boutique', these are plausible foundations of an intellectual and literary framework for a published work, perhaps one intended to be sold as a 'book of secrets'.

This neat structure, however, was soon abandoned. Small changes in ink colour and nib width show that the author-practitioner often added to his entries after the fact. These additions becomes more obvious when they spill into the margin and around the next entry, as they frequently do. Some entries, especially those on different sands used for moulding and casting, were perhaps begun as short sets of notes, but the author-practitioner ended up adding more and more observations and insights from repeated experiments, filling many folio pages. He frequently returns to his previous writing to cross things out or scribble in the margin to suggest alternative materials and processes – for example, he makes a note to 'try burnt oysters' in a future iteration of making a particular kind of casting sand.[13]

These traces of the manuscript's material construction document a dynamic knowledge-making process. The author-practitioner's iterative and seemingly haphazard manner of writing things down is of a piece with his workshop practice: both in what he does and what he writes, he is constantly experimenting, failing, trying again, and amending his records. It is an approach typical of early modern artisans, bound up with their understanding of the material world: they knew that materials were complex entities that resist understanding by purely intellectual means, yielding only to a concerted investigation of the mind and hand, through trial and error.[14]

With Ms. Fr. 640, then, we have a rich and eclectic source that documents an anonymous artisan's exploration of a wide range of techniques, with a material genesis that reflects its author's epistemic project of trying out, writing down, amending, and starting over. This richness of content and composition presents huge potential to the historian, but also major challenges, many of which are typical for our engagement with recipes and recipe collections. How do we read a text that presents no continuous narrative, but is fragmented into individual recipes and entries of terse and frequently enigmatic practical instructions, on a range of techniques that goes beyond the expertise of

---

13   Making and Knowing Project et al., *Secrets of Craft and Nature*, fol. 84v.

14   *Materials and Expertise in Early Modern Europe: Between Market and Laboratory* (Chicago: The University of Chicago Press, 2010); Lissa Roberts and Simon Schaffer, *The Mindful Hand: Inquiry and Invention From the Late Renaissance to Early Industrialisation* (Amsterdam: Royal Netherlands Academy of Arts and Sciences, 2007).

individual historical fields? How can we make sense of the unfamiliar materials, technical terms, and unlikely-sounding processes in individual recipes? In the remainder of this chapter, I will show how the Making and Knowing Project tackled these challenges through complementary approaches from the digital humanities and hands-on reconstruction in the laboratory.

3   Editing a How-to Manuscript for the Digital Age

To make sense of Ms. Fr. 640 and open it up to further research, we needed a critical edition and workable English translation of the Middle French text. It was clear, however, that a traditional scholarly edition would be of limited use for such a complex and fragmented text as Ms. Fr. 640. The digital medium offered new and more dynamic ways of presenting and analysing the text, as well as bringing its own challenges. In 2020, after more than six years of intensely collaborative work, the Making and Knowing published *Secrets of Craft and Nature*, an online publication that integrates a digital critical edition and translation of the manuscript text with research tools and scholarly analysis.[15]

To provide a quick introduction, there are three main elements to the edition: the source text, research essays, and a number of resources and tools. In contrast to a traditional printed edition, we are able to present the text in four different versions: a high-definition digital image of the manuscript page, a diplomatic transcription (the industry standard in Anglophone scholarship), a lightly normalised transcription with added punctuation and some diacritics (according to French editing conventions), and an English translation. The site displays two panels, in which any two versions of the text can be viewed side by side, for example the facsimile and a transcription for teaching palaeography, or a transcription alongside our translation to help English-speaking researchers navigate the Middle French source text. The research essays represent the equivalent of an extensive edited volume of scholarly research on the text, from a wide range of collaborators and graduate students. Many of the essays document our efforts of reconstruction in the laboratory; others provide background information on the manuscript and its local context or explore how it yields new insights in histories of early modern science, art, and culture. The resources include an annotated glossary of technical terms, and a list of entries

---

15   Pamela H. Smith, 'Making the Edition of Ms. Fr. 640', in *Secrets of Craft and Nature*, https:// edition640.makingandknowing.org/#/essays/ann_329_ie_19.

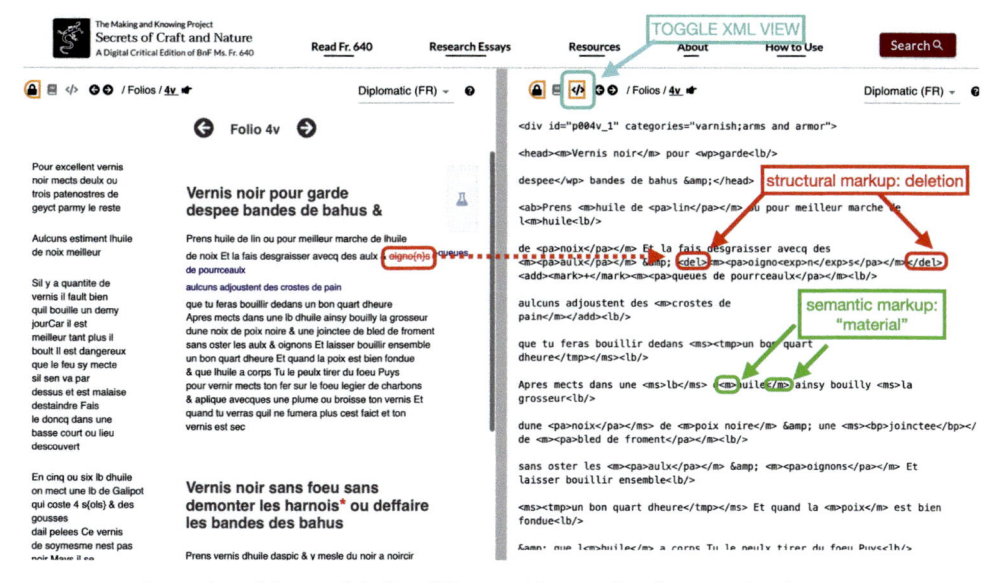

FIGURE 5.1   Screenshot of *Secrets of Craft and Nature*, with examples of structural and semantic
             markup highlighted
             (C) THE MAKING AND KNOWING PROJECT (CC BY-NC-SA)

that provides an overview over the manuscript's miscellaneous contents and
allows users to navigate through the text in dynamic ways.

The work of creating the edition began with the task of transcribing and
translating close to 1000 entries, on over 300 pages, of middle French (sometimes knotty and elliptic), in fairly challenging handwriting. This was done
in collaboration with graduate students from all over the world, in a series of
workshops held over several years, co-led by project director Pamela Smith and
Marc Smith (no relation) of the École Nationale des Chartes in Paris. Working
digitally allowed us to work collaboratively and simultaneously on the same
text and within the same file. For most of the graduate workshop phase, we
used Google Docs, but for the later stages of data management and cleanup,
we switched to Github, which takes a little effort to learn, but offers more
sophisticated version control and backups.

Another affordance of the digital medium is the ability to encode the source
text. We used xml markup, a minimally invasive and platform-independent language, to encode the text in two different ways. The first is structural markup,
using xml tags to define features such as headings, blocks of text, illustrations,
etc. This data can be used to determine the page layout and how the text is
rendered in the edition. The second type of encoding is semantic markup,
operating at the level of content and meaning of the text. Here we used xml

tags to identify specific terms or phrases as materials, tools, plants, animals, words in different languages and dialects, and so on. In the edition, there is a toggle to switch between the standard view of the text, where the xml tags are silent, and an xml view where the code is revealed. Figure 5.1 highlights examples of structural markup (for a deletion in the text) and semantic markup (identifying oil as a material).

4   Materiality and Genesis of Ms. Fr. 640 on the Screen

The digital medium and textual tools such as xml markup allow us to preserve a real sense of the manuscript's intriguing materiality and genesis as part of our edition. Our structural markup defines headings and text blocks, recording their position on the page. This means that, in the edition, the text can be rendered in a spatial pattern that is a decent approximation of the original page layout, even on more complex pages (such as fol. 3r), as seen in Figure 5.2.

Thus, even the transcribed and translated version of the text give a sense of the way the author-practitioner organised the page, where he added text at a later point or supplied additional information in the margins.

Similarly, we marked up the author-practitioner's deletions and corrections. In the edition, these are displayed in all versions of the text, struck through

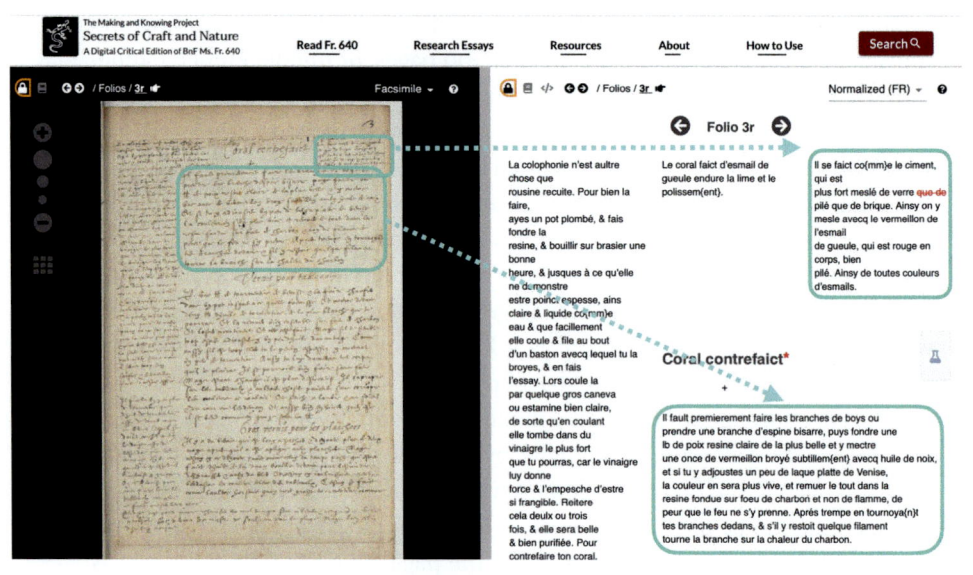

FIGURE 5.2   Screenshot of *Secrets of Craft and Nature* displaying the facsimile and normalised
transcription of fol. 3r of Ms. Fr. 640, with corresponding blocks of text highlighted.
(C) THE MAKING AND KNOWING PROJECT (CC BY-NC-SA)

in red. Where necessary, we clarified the often messy interventions with an editorial comment, marked with a red asterisk that expands into a hovering text bubble when clicked on. These explain, for example, where the author-practitioner wrote one letter on top of another to correct himself. These editorial comments are also used to indicate when the entry continues some-where else on the page, or where the writing changes to a different hand. Where the materiality of the binding interferes with the text, this too is indicated. As noted above, the manuscript was re-bound to size by gluing paper strips around the edges of the original page. In the edition, grey highlighting signals those occasional parts of the text that are obscured by these strips. Some of these passages cannot be clearly made out even in the digital image, and had to be verified by shining a light through the back of the original manuscript page at the BnF.

Although an edition can never fully replace the original material object, the digital medium has allowed us to go much further than a traditional print edition in presenting the materiality and genesis of the manuscript, from com-position to later additions and emendations to material interventions such as the Béthune binding.

5   Secrets, Jokes, and Experiments: What Is a Recipe?

Marking up the structural units of the text and presenting them visually in a digital edition forces us to think about their nature as a genre of text. In a mis-cellaneous collection like this, how can we define units of text in a meaningful way, and what are the elements that make up these units? Structurally, we defined units as 'entries' consisting of one or more blocks of text, sometimes including marginal blocks that were likely added later, but can be identified as belonging to the entry. Entries are usually preceded by a heading in a larger, italic script, although there are some without headers. We deliberately chose the neutral term 'entries' to cover their variety in terms of content and tex-tual form. While we had initially fallen into a habit of referring to entries as 'recipes', it became clear that this was in many cases not an appropriate label.

But what makes a text a recipe? Structurally, the only logically necessary element are the ingredients, although other elements – title, instructions for preparation and application, evaluation or statement of efficacy, storage, expiry date, etc. – are often present, in any order or combination.[16] Many of

---

16   Francisco Alonso-Almeida, 'Genre Conventions in English Recipes, 1600–1800', in *Reading and Writing Recipe Books, 1550–1800*, ed. Michelle DiMeo and Sara Pennell (Manchester:

the entries in Ms. Fr. 640 clearly correspond to this scheme. There are four that have the word *recepte* in the title; interestingly, they are all in the hand of the scribe who intervenes on several folios, rather than the author-practitioner's own writing. Many more entries begin with the imperative 'take' (*prends*, *prenez*, etc.), whose Latin form (*recipe*) gave the recipe genre its name.

Some entries have many of the elements, but go beyond what we would expect from a recipe. An entry entitled 'Experimented sands' spreads over several folios.[17] It begins 'I have experimented with sands from Toulouse', and then proceeds to recount in great detail and in the past tense different ways in which the author-practitioner prepared the sand he used for moulding and casting. He supplements this with additional observations in the margin, and summarises his findings under sub-headings written in the same italic script normally reserved for headings, to make them stand out. The first of these rubrics reads 'I find that ...' followed by observations on the nature and behaviour of different sands, for example when ground to a fine consistency. The second rubric is headed 'I believe that ...' and marks the beginning of the author-practitioner's conclusions (albeit preliminary and speculative) about the 'secret of casting well'.[18] Rather than a generally applicable set of instructions, this entry provides circumstantial narratives of individual instances of workshop practice, with general observations and conclusions drawn in a separate step.

Within Ms. Fr. 640, then, there are wildly different kinds of entries on a wide spectrum of what historians have termed thickness of description: from epistemically 'thin' recipes that provide only a minimal list of ingredients and actions, to more detailed and heavily edited recipes, to thickly circumstantiated entries like that on experimented sands, which looks less like a recipe and more like a precursor to the 'experimental essay' that became the epistemic genre par excellence of the 'new science' at the Royal Society and elsewhere.[19] Although we opted for structural rather than analytical units that we gave the neutral term 'entries', thinking about how to structure a digital text raises

_____

      Manchester University Press, 2013), pp. 68–90. On recipes as a genre, see also Joachim Telle, 'Das Rezept als literarische Form. Zum multifunktionalen Gebrauch des Rezepts in der Deutschen Literatur', *Berichte zur Wissenschaftsgeschichte* 26, (2003) pp. 251–274.

17   Making and Knowing Project et al., *Secrets of Craft and Nature*, fols 85v–86r.

18   Making and Knowing Project et al., *Secrets of Craft and Nature*, fol. 86r.

19   Vera Keller, '"Everything Depends Upon the Trial (*Le tout gist à l'essay*)": Four Manuscripts Between the Recipe and the Experimental Essay', in *Secrets of Craft and Nature*, https://edition640.makingandknowing.org/#/essays/ann_320_ie_19; Tillmann Taape, '"Experience Will Teach You:" Recording, Testing, Knowing, and the Language of Experience in Ms. Fr. 640', in *Secrets of Craft and Nature*, https://edition640.makingandknowing.org/#/essays/ann_303_ie_19.

useful questions about different text types and their modalities of encoding practical knowledge.

6 The Miscellany as Discourse: Reading Fragmentary Text

These epistemic questions get more complicated when we look beyond the individual entry. With such an eclectic and miscellaneous collection, how can we make sense of it as a whole, as something that has a meaning greater than the sum of its many and diverse parts? Francisco Alonso-Almeida has suggested that we can think of recipe collections as a 'discourse colony', a concept originally developed by the linguist Michael Hoey to describe encyclopaedias and other collective texts.[20] Like a colony of ants or bees, such texts are made up of individually independent units that nevertheless serve an overall purpose. That purpose or collective meaning of the text does not derive from the sequence in which the individual units appear. There often is a sequence (chronological, alphabetical, numerical, etc.), but this is a question of utility rather than meaning. Hoey notes several other properties of discourse colonies, for example that they are often anonymous or not by a single author. The most important feature is the modular nature of individual units: they can work independently without reference to any other, adjacent units do not form continuous prose, and individual units can be re-ordered, altered, or removed altogether without altering the overall meaning. Even if connections between the units are weak, the collection is held together by intention and utility, forming a textual unity that can be analysed as a whole, beyond the merely miscellaneous. Hoey and Alonso-Almeida's ideas about fragmented texts as a discourse colony point to a useful way of conceptualising the anonymous, eclectic, and apparently jumbled collection of entries that is Ms. Fr. 640 as a unified text with collective meaning.

While this gives us a framework for making sense of the author-practitioner's commerce of secrets, it does not change the fact that our fragmentary text is difficult to read and analyse. A digital edition of such a discourse colony provides practical tools for making sense of the whole by disaggregating the reading experience. Rather than following the sequence of entries in the manuscript, which tells us more about the chronology of its composition than the author-practitioner's guiding intentions, we can re-organise and re-group the entries according to different analytical questions. In our edition we

---

20   Alonso-Almeida, 'Genre Conventions in English Recipes, 1600–1800'.

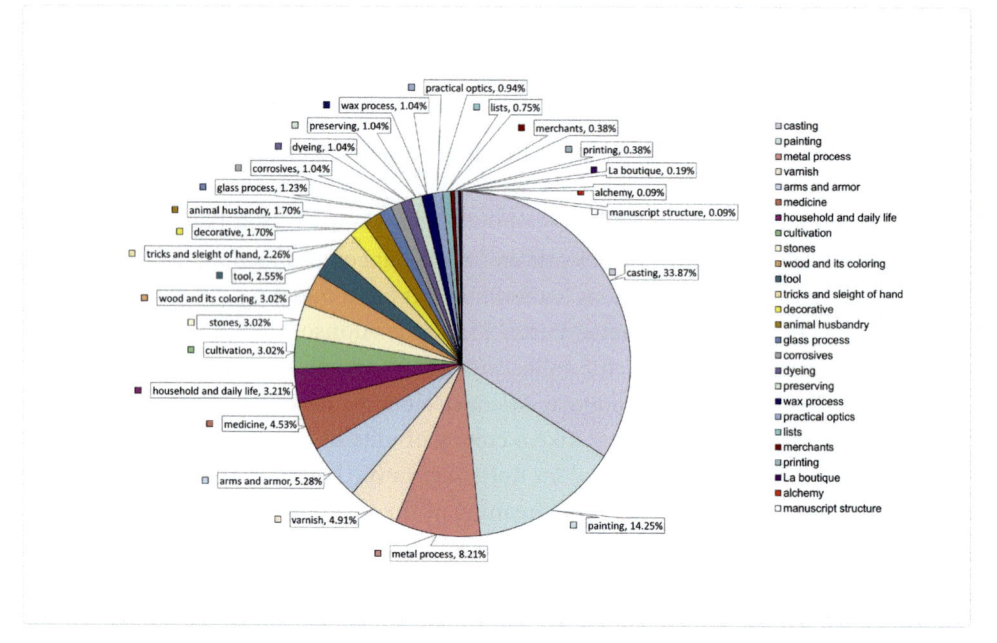

provide two ways of doing this, and we think of these as different pathways
through the manuscript.

The first digital disaggregating tool are the entry categories. We assigned
each of the 927 entries to 26 broad categories that we felt represent the main
preoccupations of the author-practitioner: for example alchemy, medicine,
casting, painting, metal processes, arms and armour, household, and daily
life.[21] Each entry was assigned at least one and up to three categories, allowing
for overlap – for example, the entry on steel mirrors has the categories casting,
metal process, and practical optics. This gives us useful data about the manuscript. We can see that there is a clear winning category: a third of the entries
deal with the casting of metal, followed by painting and other metal processes.

More importantly, the categories provide users of the edition with a path-
way into the manuscript via the list of entries. By default, it simply lists all the
entries in the order in which they appear in the manuscript, not necessarily a
meaningful sequence in a discourse colony. To create more analytical pathways
through the manuscript, there are several ways of filtering the entries. One of

---

21   For a complete list and discussion of our categories, see https://edition640.makingand
      knowing.org/#/content/resources.

them is to filter according to the entries' assigned categories. If the user selects 'casting', they will see all 358 entries on that topic listed, with a link to the corresponding folio in the edition. Another set of pathways leads through the semantic markup, that is, the xml code that we used to tag words or phrases as an animal, a tool, a material, a place, and so on. If the 'animal' filter option is selected, the list will display all 212 entries in which a word has been tagged as an animal. For each entry, there is a drop-down box showing the terms that were tagged 'animal', as well as any other tags in the same entry. A beaker icon indicates entries that have one or more research essays associated with them. We can combine multiple filtering options within and between the entry categories and xml tags: for instance one could look for words tagged as an animal in entries belonging to the category 'alchemy' or 'household and everyday life'. For a more specific approach to the text, there is also a word search function that searches across all three versions of the text, and even the research essays.

The ability to filter the manuscript's close to a thousand entries by assigned categories and semantic tags can help us grasp the collection as a whole. It provides new thematic pathways through the manuscript, and allows us to see different unities within the text. We can read it as a manual for casting or painting, a book of secrets, or a recipe collection. Of course the manuscript is all of those things; our digital tools merely help us to bring out these different aspects in more coherent ways.

7 Seeing the Whole from a Distance: Computational Approaches

In addition to these dynamic reading experiences, computational analysis of the digital text allows us to explore new relationships between the fragmented entries of the manuscript and thus make better sense of its cohesion as a whole. Scholars in the digital humanities have developed approaches for visualising statistic data from vast corpora of texts to give a synthetic picture of the whole: a perspective known as 'distant reading' or macroanalysis.[22] Clément Godbarge, Making and Knowing postdoc and member of the editorial team, has demonstrated that similar methods can be fruitful if applied to a single, complex text such as Ms. Fr. 640, what he calls 'semi-distant reading'.[23]

---

22   Franco Moretti, *Distant Reading* (London: Verso, 2013); Matthew L. Jockers, *Macroanalysis: Digital Methods and Literary History* (Urbana: University of Illinois Press, 2013).

23   Clément Godbarge, 'The Manuscript Seen from Afar: A Computational Approach to Ms. Fr. 640', in *Secrets of Craft and Nature*, https://edition640.makingandknowing.org/#/essays/ann_301_ie_19. See also https://www.clementgodbarge.com/post/visualization.

The entry category data, for example, can be visualised to show the distribution of categories throughout the manuscript.[24]

This shows that many categories, such as 'arms and armor,' form distinct clusters. Their distribution can be aligned with other structural information, entries on 'wood and its colouring', for example, are concentrated on pages that were written by the scribe rather than the author-practitioner. Incidentally, this includes the few entries that have 'recipe' (*recepte*) in the title. Another visualisation technique known as treemapping presents the entry category data in a more comparative view of the whole text.

Each category is represented as a rectangle whose size is proportional to its accumulated word count, while the colour indicates the category's average

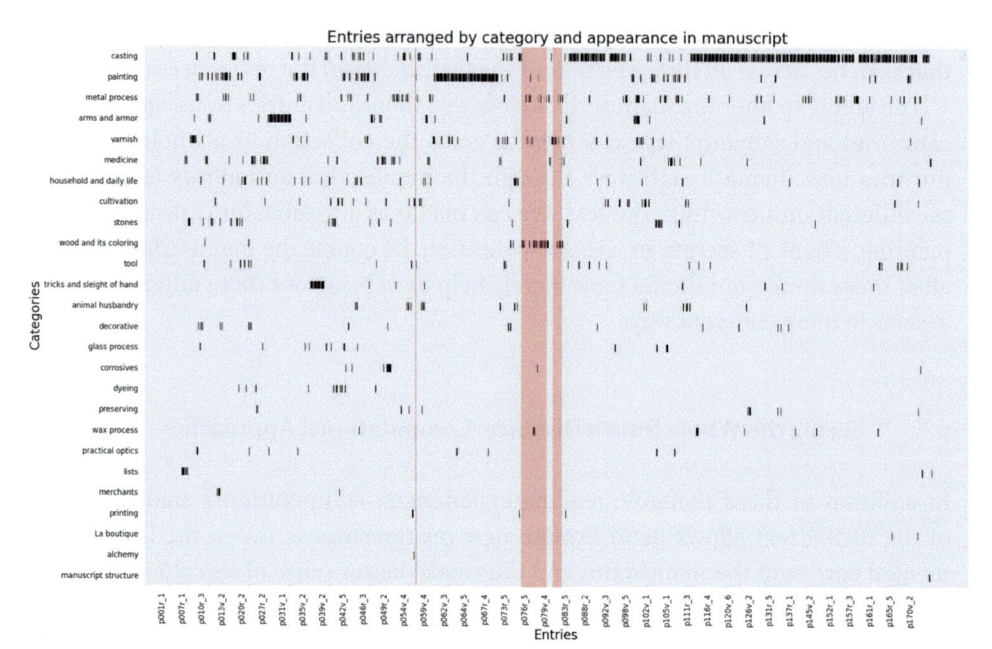

FIGURE 5.4   Graph showing the distribution of entry categories across Ms. Fr. 640, created by Naomi Rosenkranz. The entry categories are listed on the y-axis, plotted over the chronological order of manuscript entries on the x-axis. While some categories form distinct clusters (e.g. 'tricks and sleight-of-hand' on folios 33–36), others (e.g. 'cultivation' or 'stones') are more dispersed throughout the manuscript. The red highlighting corresponds to the folios written in the hand of the scribe rather than the author-practitioner

(C) THE MAKING AND KNOWING PROJECT (CC BY-NC-SA)

---

24   For this graph and further visualisations and analysis, see Naomi Rosenkranz, 'Understanding and Analyzing the Categories of the Entries in BnF Ms. Fr. 640', https://cu-mkp .github.io/sandbox/docs/categories.html.

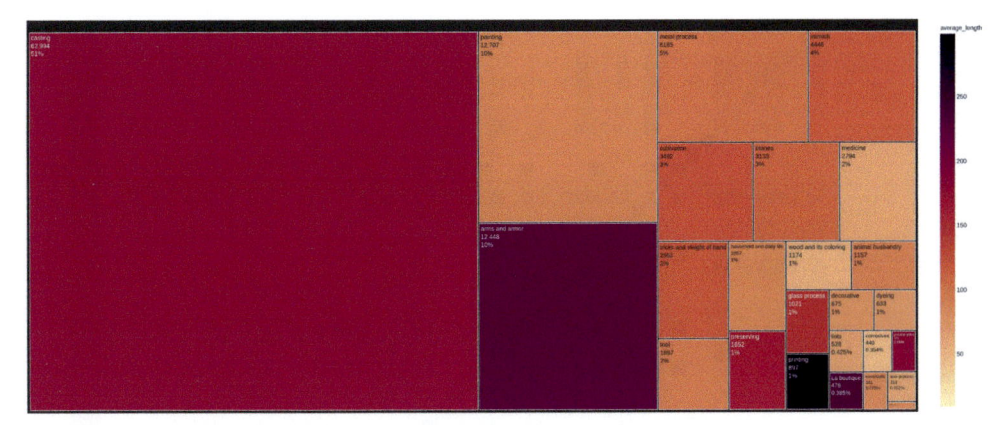

FIGURE 5.5 'Treemap' of the entry categories of Ms. Fr. 640, created by Clément Godbarge. The size of the tiles corresponds to the category's proportion of the overall word count; the colour scale indicates the average length of the entries in a category
(c) THE MAKING AND KNOWING PROJECT (CC BY-NC-SA)

word count. At a glance, this tells us that 'casting' is not only the largest category, making up over 50 per cent of the manuscript's words, but also tends to have longer entries. It was clearly the topic with which the author practitioner engaged most extensively and intensively. The treemap also tells us that 'printing' averages by far the longest entries, and that 'painting' and 'arms and armor', for all that they occupy a similar proportion of the overall word count, this is distributed over fewer and longer entries on arms and armor and more but shorter entries in the case of painting. These are insights that would be difficult to obtain by simply reading the manuscript, and they raise new questions about the author-practitioner's interests and the textual forms he uses for different topics.

The semantic markup also yields rich data that can show correlations between different semantic categories (materials, tools, animals, etc.), and between these and the entry categories. Such a correlation matrix can be visualised as a heat map.

It indicates, for example, that terms tagged as 'weapon' often correlate with terms tagged as 'measurement'. Furthermore, we can see that entries in the category 'arms and armor' show a high density of terms tagged as 'profession' and phrases identified as a 'definition' given by the author. Between this heatmap and the treemap, we can discern a specific formal and semantic profile of the entries in the category 'arms and armor': the visualised text data allows us to see their distinctive voice. This prompts new questions about the author-practitioner's purpose in recording different kinds of topics, and invites us to take a closer look at the 'arms and armor' entries. Longer and detailed

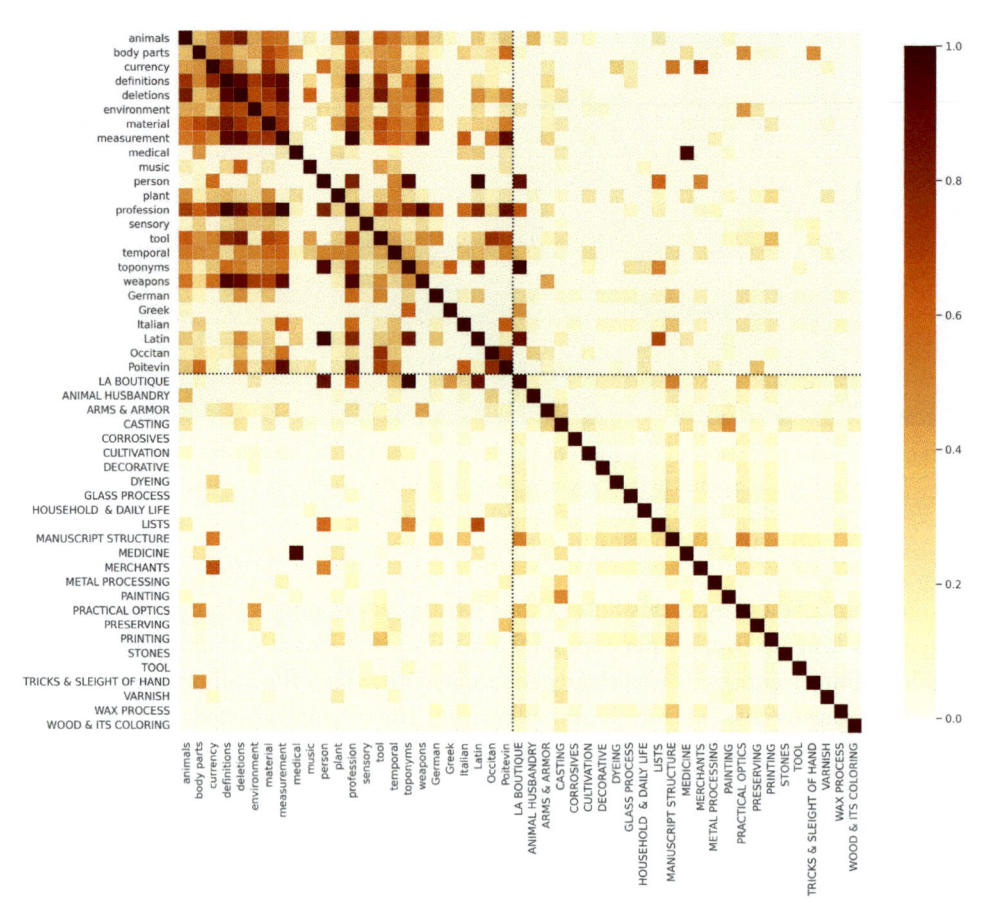

FIGURE 5.6 Heatmap showing correlations between semantic tag categories and entry categories, created
by Clément Godbarge
(C) THE MAKING AND KNOWING PROJECT (CC BY-NC-SA)

than many other entries, they report on the professional expertise of gunners, 'furbishers' or sword-makers, and others, using precise measurements and explaining large numbers of technical terms. They are more descriptive than the entries on, say, casting or painting, which contain instructions for action. It is tempting to speculate that this different mode of writing reflects a different audience, real or imagined – perhaps the illustrious administrators of the fairly autonomous city of Toulouse during a time of religious wars, or even political advisers to the king. That, in any case, may well be the purpose the manuscript served in the collection of Philippe de Béthune.[25]

25   Colin Debuiche, 'Ms. Fr. 640 and the Béthune Collection', in *Secrets of Craft and Nature*,
       https://edition640.makingandknowing.org/#/essays/ann_337_ie_19.

The manuscript data can also tell us more about the relative distribution of the author-practitioner's mode of writing. Looking at the distribution of marginal annotations, where the author-practitioner added more material at a later date, the 'casting' category once more stands out: 42 per cent of its entries are annotated, a far greater proportion than other categories. It also has the highest proportion of deletions, suggesting a very involved process of composition, with the author-practitioner going back and forth between the manuscript and the workshop, documenting his trial and error, correcting himself, and adding further observations. In contrast, the entries in the 'medicine' category are among the shortest and do not have any marginal annotations or deletions. Many of them are recipes with sparse and straightforward instructions for making medicinal remedies, perhaps already tried and tested by others (such as one Monsieur Montorsin to whom a plague remedy is attributed),[26] circulated and copied wholesale rather than endlessly experimented upon. As noted above, the manuscript contains a wide range of text types, from recipes to proto-experiments. Computational analysis and visualisation of the text data can help us understand these different modalities of making, knowing, and writing in the author-practitioner's commerce of secrets.

8   How to Translate How-to

Translating a source text for a critical edition is always an act of compromise and interpretation. Translating a digital text presents a host of new challenges and opportunities. Like most parts of the Project, the translation was a collaborative effort by researchers and graduate students. During dedicated text workshops, we worked in groups of at least one English native speaker and at least one French native speaker. Once we had devised our entry categories, we were able to assign specific categories to certain groups who then became experts in that area, and were occasionally joined by external subject experts. With a collaborative translation of a fragmented text, our major challenge was to make and implement consistent translation decision and maintain a unified voice overall.[27]

To manage consistency, we devised a translation protocol that defined the way common phrases in the French should be rendered in English, and an evolving vocabulary list where we noted our translation decisions for

26   Making and Knowing Project et al., *Secrets of Craft and Nature*, fol. 44v.

27   Soersha Dyon and Heather Wacha, 'Turning Turtle: The Process of Translating BnF Ms. Fr. 640', in *Secrets of Craft and Nature*, https://edition640.makingandknowing.org/# /essays/ann_318_ie_19.

uncommon or technical terms, and also documented our research on that term. While labour-intensive, this brought a granular level of self-reflection to the translation process. The resulting vocabulary list evolved into a rich repository of terminology from the early modern arts and crafts, and it is available in the edition in the form of a glossary.[28]

We were conscious that consistency was a high priority, well worth the investment of time and effort, because it has implications for four key aspects of the digital critical edition. First, the edition text was intended for use in laboratory reconstructions by researchers or students with varying levels of proficiency in French, so the translation had to be as precise as possible with respect to materials, tools, and processes.

Second, we wanted to preserve a sense of the sometimes knotty and inelegant syntax of the author-practitioner, and also his rich language and technical terminology. Lara Broecke's translation of Cennini's *Libro dell'Arte* provides a model for dealing with difficult early modern how-to texts, albeit in a traditional printed edition. Broecke opted for an almost brutally literal approach, preserving the awkwardness of Cennini's struggle to put practice into words, even if that resulted in 'excruciating English', as she put it.[29] We adopted this guiding principle of being as literal as possible and not making our translation more polished than the original, although in some places we made concessions to make the text more accessible. What we resolutely resisted were overly interpretive translations and the anachronistic imposition of modern categories on a sixteenth-century text. In this spirit, we did our best to render the author-practitioner's highly technical language. Contemporary dictionaries, such as Randle Cotgrave's *Dictionarie of the French and English Tongues*, are a huge help in making sense of unfamiliar French terms for materials and tools, but oftentimes the English cognates they suggest are just as unfamiliar.[30] Take, for example, the word 'mattras'. It is a type of long-necked glass vessel, 'mattelas' in French, that the author-practitioner mentions in entries on sublimating orpiment and breeding alchemically supercharged silk worms. So why use an English word that is so obscure to most modern readers? For one thing, it avoids over-interpretation, using a term that contemporary experts on both sides of the channel would have recognised as referring to the same thing. For another, it helps to paint a better picture of past cultures of expertise where

---

28   https://edition640.makingandknowing.org/#/content/resources.

29   Cennino Cennini, *Cennino Cennini's Il libro dell'arte: a new English translation and commentary with Italian transcription*, transl. Lara Broecke (London: Archetype, 2015).

30   Randle Cotgrave, *A dictionarie of the french and english tongues* (London: Adam Islip, 1611) USTC 3004892, http://www.pbm.com/~lindahl/cotgrave.

many people were indeed familiar with this kind of language and the rich material culture it described.

In the same vein, we were keen to maintain the author's voice because it reflects the way he thinks about materials and their transformations by nature or human art, what we call his 'material imaginary'. The author-practitioner often describes materials as alive and active, with a will of their own. 'Azur d'esmail' (a blue pigment), for example, 'hates more than any other to be ground, especially with water', and with good reason, since this would mean that it 'dies & loses all its color'.[31] Other examples include materials that 'drink' rather than simply 'absorb' liquid, or wet sand 'refusing' to settle in an oiled mould. This may sound anthropomorphic and quaint to modern readers, but early modern artists and artisans genuinely conceived of matter as a living agent that had to be coaxed or even subdued.[32] By preserving the agency, grammatical and semantic, of materials as well as humans and animals, our translation allows the reader to be immersed in the author-practitioner's world.

The third aspect of the digital edition where consistency and precision of translation play a key part is the text's fitness for xml markup and computational analysis. To provide a robust corpus, we ensured that the structural and semantic tags were stable across all three versions of the text; if there is a *poulet* tagged as an animal in the French, we need a corresponding 'chicken' in the translation, and this only gets more complicated with the markup of entire phrases, for example of definitions or deletions. Such painstaking consistency work is necessary, however, if computational analysis of xml-tagged terms or raw text data (such as the semi-distant reading approaches discussed above) are to yield meaningful results when applied to the translation. While serious corpus linguistics are best applied to the original text, a consistent and literal translation is a commitment to accessibility and overall robustness of digital data.

Finally, translating matters because every digital text is its own index. In the digital world, it has become second nature to run word searches rather than reading whole texts, and with a miscellaneous text such as Ms. Fr. 640 this often makes good sense. But it means that translating is always also indexing. We even have the opportunity to make the translation a better index than the original. Our translation uses unified terms where the French original might use any number of variant early modern spellings or conjugations that are difficult to locate in the text. For example, an alloy known in French as *laiton* is variously spelled *laicton*, *latton*, *leton*, or *letton*. By translating these variants

---

31   Making and Knowing Project et al., *Secrets of Craft and Nature*, fol. 58v.
32   Klein and Spary, *Materials and Expertise*, esp. 'Introduction', pp. 1–19.

with the unified term 'latten', the English version is a more robust (self-)index since all occurrences of the alloy in the manuscript can be captured in a single word search. Conversely, the translation also disaggregates polysemic terms. Our research revealed that the term *gect* usually means 'cast' or 'casting', but occasionally refers to a specific part of the casting infrastructure, the place where the metal is poured in, known in English as the gate. By making and informed decision to render *gect* as either 'cast(ing)' or 'gate', the translation indexes these meanings separately and makes it possible to locate them independently in the text.

In sum, the affordances of a digital edition – structural and semantic encoding, translation, and computational analysis – provide useful tools for reading the complex and fragmented 'discourse colony' of technical manuscripts such Ms. Fr. 640. They allow us to bring out material features of the text, hidden structures in its apparently jumbled entries, the author-practitioner's voice, and his material imaginary. This comes at the cost of rigorous encoding and translating, and with important methodological responsibilities. As editors, we have to be aware that our translation decisions, our choice of entry categories and semantic markup shape the way the text can be read through a digital lens. It amounts to nothing less than constructing a distinct digital ontology of words and things.

9   Reading Texts of Action: Historical Reconstruction

In conjunction with digital editing and analysis, the Making and Knowing Project has developed hands-on laboratory work as a key approach to technical texts such as Ms. Fr. 640. Practical or performative historical methodologies are a growing field, sometimes collectively known as 'RRR': reconstruction, replication, and re-enactment.[33] This terminology reflects a broad range of questions and approaches, outlined in a recent overview by Hjalmar Fors, Lawrence Principe, and Heinz Otto Sibum. Reproductions of historical experimental phenomena relying on complex and sensitive experimental apparatus, such

---

33   Sven Dupré, Anna Harris, Patricia Lulof, Julia Kursell, and Maartje Stols-Witlox (eds.), *Reconstruction, Replication and Re-enactment in the Humanities and Social Sciences* (Amsterdam: Amsterdam University Press, 2020). See also Marieke M.A. Hendriksen, 'Rethinking Performative Methods in the History of Science', *Berichte Zur Wissenschaftsgeschichte* 43, (2020), pp. 313–322. Other Projects using performative methods include the ARTECHNE Project at Utrecht University (https://artechne.wp.hum.uu.nl), Refashioning the Renaissance at Aalto University (https://refashioningrenaissance.eu), and Microscopic Records at Manchester University (https://sites.manchester.ac.uk/microscopic-records/).

as Joule's paddle wheel investigated by Sibum, require 'high-fidelity' replicas of the material set-up in order to function at all. Other objects of enquiry, such as chemical processes, rely on a multitude of reagents, impurities, temperatures, apparatus, and other unfathomable variables which it would be impossible to get right from the start. Here, more can be learned by starting with a workable, 'streamlined' version of the historical process, making compromises such as using modern-day chemicals and heat sources. Historical variables can then be re-introduced one by one in a controlled manner.[34]

For our project, we chose 'reconstruction' as the most apt term for what we do: it implies exploration in pedagogy and research, piecing together materials and processes of the past, and reconstructing the author-practitioner's imaginary of materials and skill. For our work, 'replication' implies too much of an exact reproduction of past practices, and similarly, 're-enactment' does not seem to sufficiently problematise our key questions about embodied skill and the caveats of deploying untrained twenty-first-century bodies in encounters with materials and techniques.

For us, like for many RRR researchers, our hands-on engagement with an early modern how-to text is underpinned by the realisation that there is much that the text by itself does not tell us. We think of recipes and other kinds of how-to as texts of action: they aim to convey information about or instructions for action, for performing particular gestures. And written words are simply an imperfect way of encoding actions, because they are known in the body, often through years of habit and training. This means that there are limits to understanding such a text by merely reading it. The written recipe is a flattened, fossilised reflection of a once-dynamic process, unfolding in real time in an interplay between skilled bodies and highly localised materials and expertise. Much of our work at the Making and Knowing Project has focused on ways of re-hydrating these kinds of fossilised instant noodles of past practice, to the point where they make a certain amount of sense to modern historians. In a way, the Project was founded around the idea that texts of action become more fully accessible when we place them back in a context of action, reading them with our hands and our whole bodies rather than just with our eyes.

In practical terms, the Project took over a 1940s chemistry laboratory on the Columbia Campus as a space for hands-on research and teaching. We taught semester-long seminars for up to twelve graduate students, starting with relatively simple 'skill-building exercises', such as moulding objects in bread and

---

34   Hjalmar Fors, Lawrence M. Principe, and H. Otto Sibum, 'From the Library to the Laboratory and Back Again: Experiment as a Tool for Historians of Science', *Ambix*, 63 (2016), pp. 85–97.

casting them in wax, according to an intriguing entry in Ms. Fr. 640. Each semester is based around a theme – casting and metalwork, natural history, or pigment-making, for example – and students develop their own research project based on entries from the manuscript. They write detailed field notes on their practical work and produce a research essay. A plethora of these essays are now published as a part of the digital edition.

This is a very open way of conducting research, because while it seemed obvious that acting out the text would tell us more than reading it, we did not know at the outset what the payoff would be. We had occasion to reflect at some length on our approach in a recent article that forms part of a special issue on 'Rethinking Performative Methods in the History of Science', and I am summarising some of our key insights here.[35]

One of the key outcomes of hands-on work is that it recalibrates our eyes and hands in a way that allows us to appreciate the material literacy artisans of the past must have possessed, and to become slightly more literate in reading historical objects and materials ourselves. One example from the early days of the Project was Pamela Smith's and Tonny Beentjes's research on lifecasting. Briefly explained, lifecasting is a technique whereby a real animal or plant is moulded in plaster and then cast in metal. There are many surviving objects from the early modern period, and it was while examining a sixteenth-century lifecast lizard that Pamela and Tonny noted knob-like protrusions on the feet of the lizard that had not been explained. Their reconstruction of lifecasting instructions in Ms. Fr. 640 revealed that these protrusions were caused by metal pins used to fix the dead lizard on its clay base before moulding.[36] This performative research produced a more informed reading not only of the text, but also of surviving lifecast objects.

Over the years, our reconstruction work has not only answered specific questions such as the knobs on lizards' feet, but also proved to be a powerful way of raising new questions that do not arise from reading alone. Two of our students decided to reconstruct a recipe for making powder used for hourglasses. This involved mixing salt with molten lead, and then washing this mixture in water. Working through the process, our students balked at these latter instructions, would this dissolve the salt and undo their work? As it turns out, it does not, but their question sparked further research into the interaction

35   Tillmann Taape, Pamela H. Smith, and Tianna Helena Uchacz, 'Schooling the Eye and Hand: Performative Methods of Research and Pedagogy in the Making and Knowing Project', *Berichte zur Wissenschaftsgeschichte*, 43 (2020), pp. 323–340.

36   Pamela H. Smith and Tonny Beentjes, 'Nature and Art, Making and Knowing: Reconstructing Sixteenth-Century Life-Casting Techniques', *Renaissance Quarterly* 63, (2010), pp. 128–179.

of hourglass sand and water, and it turned up a fascinating story: until the middle of the eighteenth century, it was impossible to blow an hourglass in one piece, and since there was always a danger of moisture entering through an improperly sealed joint between the two halves, it was crucial that hourglass sand did not react with water.[37] Their hands-on reading of the recipe led to detailed questions about materials, production, and calibration, questions that would not have been raised by a 'dry' reading of the recipe.

In addition to raising new questions, reconstruction yields surprising insights into the author-practitioner's understanding of nature and matter, his material imaginary, and its cultural and spiritual resonances. A recipe for burn salve, for example, includes instructions to wash with holy water for specific intervals, measured by the time it takes to recite the paternoster (the Lord's Prayer in Latin) nine times, then eight times, and so on. The connections to religion and timekeeping practices are obvious at first read, but the full extent of their relationship with the process and the final product only emerge when we immerse ourselves in the making process. As we add holy water while reciting prayers, we witness the dramatic transformation of the transparent yellowish mixture of wax and linseed oil into a thick, fluffy substance of an opaque white, a vivid material instantiation of the spiritual purification implicit in the use of prayers and holy water.[38]

Exciting and evocative as these reconstructions can be, there are important methodological caveats. Early modern people had diverse and completely different ways of understanding and experiencing their bodies compared to us moderns.[39] For a start, few of us trained our bodies to specific manual tasks and expertise through years of apprenticeship. And that is before we get into problems of historical authenticity surrounding the use of pure modern ingredients and reading the paternoster off a laptop screen rather than reciting it by heart from lifelong habit. Properly considered, however, these limitations of reconstruction can be turned into a virtue, especially in a pedagogic context. They force students to think carefully about the historicity of materials and embodied experience, and help them problematise terms such as 'the body'

---

37   Stephanie Pope, 'Powder for Hourglasses', in *Secrets of Craft and Nature*, https://edition640 .makingandknowing.org/#/essays/ann_021_sp_15.

38   Xiaomeng Liu, 'An Excellent Salve for Burns', in *Secrets of Craft and Nature*, https://edition 640.makingandknowing.org/#/essays/ann_080_sp_17. The transformation can be seen much more clearly in the video of the process: https://cu-mkp.github.io/sandbox/docs /burnsalve.html.

39   This is a central tenet in scholarship on the history of the body; see Barbara Duden, *The Woman Beneath the Skin: A Doctor's Patients in Eighteenth-Century Germany* (Cambridge, MA: Harvard University Press, 1991).

FIGURE 5.7 Burn salve made according to the recipe in Ms. Fr. 640 (fol. 103r). The transparent
yellow mixture of melted wax and linseed oil (left) transformed into a thick white
salve (right)

or 'nature': categories that historians take for granted at their peril. Our students leave the laboratory with a greater critical awareness of what it means to understand material processes and to know by doing rather than through text, both in the present and the past.

To make sense of texts of action such as Ms. Fr. 640, historians must get their hands dirty, however imperfect our modern ingredients and bodies may be for the job. The knowledge encoded in texts of action is emergent knowledge, to use Pamela Smith's term: it unfolds not in the reading, but in the doing. At best, reconstruction allows us glimpses into past worlds of materials and expertise; at worst, it shows us the gaps in the recipe that most early modern artisans or householders would have easily filled in, and the gaping holes in our own mastery of the requisite materials, gestures, and ideas.

10   Conclusion: Orphans and the Commerce of Secrets

If the author-practitioner thought of his potential readers as orphans without the parentage of an apprenticeship or guild, then we, his modern readers, are doubly orphaned, at home neither in the Renaissance workshop nor in the lived reality of early modern bodies, materials, gestures, or prayers. Across historical distance, we face a host of challenges in trying to make sense of his 'crumbs' of practical knowledge, scintillating though they often are, or of the way their rich but motley scattering makes up a body of words and knowledge. As I have shown in this chapter, however, novel approaches to early modern how-to writing, moving back and forth between the (digital) text and the laboratory, go a long way towards bridging that historical distance.

Our digital editorial work provides new ways of reading the text and also focuses our attention to language, processes of material making and textual composition, and their underlying ontology. In rendering the manuscript's key material features, including layout and scribal interventions, our digital critical edition shines a light on its genesis, an iterative process of trial and error reflecting early modern workshop practice. Encoding the structure of the text raises productive questions about different textual forms and their epistemic function, especially as part of a fragmented whole. The digital medium provides new pathways for reading such a 'discourse colony' by disaggregating and regrouping the miscellany according to analytic categories of entry topics and of semantic xml tags. Computational analysis tools delve deeper into the text data to reveal hidden structural and semantic unities. Our encoding and translation choices sharpen the editorial focus on representing the author-practitioner's voice and outlook and make the most of the self-indexing nature of digital text. In these ways, the digital critical edition helps us understand the modalities of writing and knowledge-making in the author-practitioner's commerce of secrets.

In synergy with digital textual work, hands-on reconstruction helps us understand how-to writing as texts of action that need to be re-immersed in a context of action if they are to reveal some of the tacit, emergent knowledge they once held. As the author-practitioner reminds his orphan readers, a theoretical, text-based education is 'idle', whereas 'the *boutique* represents all things active'. This active engagement attunes historians' eyes and hands to the material literacies of the past, raises new questions, and offers experiential glimpses into past practitioners' material imaginaries, honing our historiographical awareness along the way.

Overall, digital and practical work on early modern how-to texts combine to make us modern orphans less alienated and more at home in the workshop of the past.

CHAPTER 6

Compilation Networks: Making Early Modern Books of Secrets

Simone Zweifel

Recipe books are how-to books, that is, books which describe practices of making products. This aspect is often focused on in research and questions such as 'how did this production work' and 'who was involved in it' are discussed.[1] It is remarkable that the same research tends to disregard the practices involved in making the books themselves. The specific practices I want to focus on in this article are those that are involved in the production of recipe books. They, in turn, formed the basis for producing things such as food, beverages, medication or soaps, as the production of such things was often based on the instructions offered by recipe books. This assumption is confirmed by the high number of surviving texts.[2] It is impossible to put a figure on these books and other recipe

---

1   For this field, see a.o. Pamela H. Smith and Benjamin Schmidt (eds.), *Making Knowledge in Early Modern Europe. Practices, Objects, and Texts, 1400–1800* (The University of Chicago Press, 2007); Elaine Leong, *Recipes and Everyday Knowledge. Medicine, Science, and the Household in Early Modern England* (Chicago, London: The University of Chicago Press, 2018); Michelle DiMeo and Sara Pennell (eds.), *Reading and Writing Recipe Books, 1550–1800* (Manchester University Press, 2013); Elaine Leong and Alisha Michelle Rankin (eds.), *Secrets and Knowledge in Medicine and Science, 1500–1800* (= *The History of Medicine in Context*) (Farnham: Ashgate, 2011); Pamela H. Smith: 'What is a Secret? Secrets and Craft Knowledge in Early Modern Europe', in Elaine Leong and Alisha Michelle Rankin (eds.), *Secrets and Knowledge in Medicine and Science, 1500–1800* (Farnham: Ashgate, 2011), pp. 47–66; Michelle DiMeo: 'Authorship and Medical Networks: Reading Attributions in Early Modern Manuscript Recipe Books', in Michelle DiMeo and Sara Pennell (eds.), *Reading and Writing Recipe Books, 1550–1800* (Manchester: Manchester University Press, 2013), pp. 25–46, here pp. 37; Alisha M. Rankin, *Panaceia's Daughters. Noblewomen as Healers in Early Modern Germany* (Chicago: The University of Chicago Press, 2013); Elizabeth Tebeaux, 'Women and Technical Writing, 1475–1700: Technology, Literacy and Developement of a Genre', in Lynette Hunter, Sarah Hutton (eds), *Women, Science and Medicine, 1500–1700. Mothers and Sisters of the Royal Society* (Stroud: Sutton Publishing, 1997), pp. 29–62. I want to thank Kaspar von Greyerz, Kirstin Bentley, and Kathia Müller for their helpful comments.
2   See, for example, William Eamon, *Science and the Secrets of Nature. Books of Secrets in Medieval and Early Modern Culture* (Princeton: Princeton University Press, 1996).

© KONINKLIJKE BRILL BV, LEIDEN, 2024 | DOI:10.1163/9789004683389_008

compilations that circulated at a given time. Not only were they present in print, but some circulated also as manuscripts.[3]

How were these books produced and which actors were involved? In this article, I argue that several elements – people, things, and external factors – contributed to the making of recipe books, and that, taken together, they formed a compilation network. These networks created the books and transferred knowledge to a new public, who was enabled to turn to new books as well as products such as soaps or medicaments, thanks to the recipes.[4] It is important to consider recipe books as compilations. Compilations collect, order and recontextualise textual fragments or pictures and build new books out of them.[5] This practice of accumulating and enlarging knowledge is one of the main characteristics of recipe collections. In this way, recipes could be brought together quickly and spread widely, not only in different households, but also in different languages and regions.[6]

In this contribution, I examine Books of Secrets edited by or in the name of Johann Jacob Wecker (1528–1586). From 1559 to 1750, over a hundred books including more than eighty Books of Secrets were published in his name. This publication activity began with a translation of the *De Secretis del Reverendo donno Alessio Piemontese*, issued in 1555 in Venice by Sigismondo Bordogna. In 1559, Wecker published his first Latin translation of this book, which was the starting point for many editions, at every step enlarged with new recipes. This was also the case with his German book production, which began in 1569.[7] In 1582, Wecker issued the *De Secretis libri XVII*, which differed from the earlier versions. It contained not only recipes for producing food, beverages,

---

3   See, amongst other works, Eamon, *Science and the Secrets of Nature*; Leong, *Recipes and Everyday Knowledge*; Rankin, *Panaceia's Daughters*. Here, I focus on printed recipe books. Most of my arguments also apply to manuscript books, as well as to other recipe compilations.

4   The present contribution is based on *Simone Zweifel, Aus Büchern Bücher machen. Zur Produktion und Multiplikation von Wissen in frühneuzeitlichen Kompilationen (= Cultures and Practices of Knowledge in History, 10)* (Berlin, Boston: De Gruyter Oldenbourg, 2021). Open access on: https://doi.org/10.1515/9783110740516 [11 February 2024].

5   See Susanne Kaup, *De beatitudinibus. Gerhard von Sterngassen OP und sein Beitrag zur spätmittelalterlichen Spiritualitätsgeschichte* (Berlin: Akademie, 2012), pp. 129–30; Ann M. Blair, 'Reading Strategies for Coping with Information Overload ca.1550–1700', *Journal of the History of Ideas*, 64 (2003), pp. 11–28, at p. 12.

6   For the role of households in recipe books, see Leong, *Recipes and Everyday Knowledge*.

7   Johann Jacob Wecker, *De secretis libri sex mira quadam rerum varietate referti Alexius Pedemontanus ex Italico in latinum sermonem nunc primum translati* (Basileae: [Peter Perna], 1559) USTC 605159; Johann Jacob Wecker, *Kunstbuch Deß Wolerfaren Herren Alexij Pedemontani von mancherley nutzlichen vnnd bewerten Secreten oder Künsten / jetz neuwlich auß Welscher vnnd Lateinischer sprach in Teutsch gebracht [...]* (Basel: Peter Perna, 1569) USTC 605151.

medication, soaps, or colours, but also an immense collection of knowledge from different fields and times.[8] In this book, it is possible to find knowledge on angels and God, on illnesses and their treatment, on metals and stones, on grammar, rhetoric, mathematics, music and astrology, on how to stuff a duck as well as on winds and harps. The *De Secretis libri XVII* is an encyclopaedic collection of recipes.[9] In the sixteenth and seventeenth centuries it was translated and re-published in French and English.[10] The latest version of the *Secretis libri XVII* was issued in 1750 in Basel.[11]

The publication activities of Wecker and his successors provide us with insights into the mechanisms of the production of Books of Secrets, as they reveal the process of compiling and therefore multiplying and spreading recipes. Thanks to Wecker's correspondence part of which has survived, the mechanisms of making Books of Secrets can be brought to light and analysed. In the first section of this contribution, I will focus on recipe books. In the second section, I will introduce the concept of the compilation network, which

8 Johann Jacob Wecker, *De Secretis libri XVII. Ex varijs authoribus collecti, methodice'que digesti.* [...] (Basileæ: [s.typ.], 1582) USTC 606196. These publications, as all of the Weckerian Books of Secrets, can be found in the list of the Weckerian publications, in: Zweifel, *Aus Büchern Bücher machen*, pp. 266–272.

9 Such publications can be understood as encyclopaedic in the sense that they represent – as Rudolf Schenda put it – an 'ordered presentation of a general knowledge, which is considered useful and important for a large circle of inquisitive persons.' ('[...] Darstellung eines jeweils für wichtig erachteten und für einen größeren Kreis von Wissbegierigen brauchbaren Gesamtwissens [...]'). Rudolf Schenda, 'Hand-Wissen. Zur Vorgeschichte der grossen Enzyklopädien', in Universität Zürich (ed.), *Populäre Enzyklopädien. Von der Auswahl, Ordnung und Vermittlung des Wissens* (Zürich: Chronos, 2002), pp. 15–34, here p. 21. See also Ulrich Dierse, *Enzyklopädie. Zur Geschichte eines philosophischen und wissenschaftstheoretischen Begriffs,* (= *Archiv für Begriffsgeschichte Supplementheft,* 2) (Bonn: Bouvier, 1977), p. 339; Ruth Conrad, *Lexikonpolitik. Die erste Auflage der RGG im Horizont protestantischer Lexikographie* (Berlin: De Gruyter, 2006), p. 32. For the Weckerian publications, see the list in: Zweifel, *Aus Büchern Bücher machen*, pp. 266–272.

10 The first of 35 French editions was issued 1563: Johann Jacob Wecker, *Les secrets et merveilles de natvre* [...] *en XVII liures recueillis de divers autheurs* [...] (Lyon: Rigaud, 1563), the last ones in 1699: Johann Jacob Wecker, *Les Secrets et merveilles de nature* [...] *et divisez en 17. livres recueillis de divers auteurs* [...]. *Reveu, & corrige, augmente* (Rouen: Nicolas le Tourneur, 1699); Johann Jacob Wecker, *Les secrets et merveilles de nature* [...] *en XVII livres* [...] (Rouen: Jean-Baptiste Besongne, 1699). In English, only two editions exist: Johann Jacob Wecker, R. Read, *Eighteen Books of the Secrets of Art & Nature Being the Summe and Substance of Naturall Philosophy, Methodically Digested* (London: Simon Miller, 1660); Johann Jacob Wecker, R. Read, *Eighteen books of the secrets of art and nature* [...] (London: Simon Miller, 1661).

11 Johann Jacob Wecker, Theodor Zwinger, *De Secretis Libri XVII. Ex Variis Auctoribus Collecti, Methodice Digesti, Et Mizaldi, Alex. Pedemontani Atque Portae Secretis inprimis locupletati* [...] (Basilea: Joh. Rod. Thurneisen, 1750).

comprises people, things, and external factors, connected in order to produce recipe books. Such networks were responsible for the rapid multiplication and dissemination of recipes. The third section is dedicated to concrete practices of making Books of Secrets, as performed by actors of compilation networks.

1 Books of Secrets as Recipe Books

Books of Secrets are called recipe books due to their instructional and performative character and because they describe 'a set of ingredients of operations in more or less detail'.[12] Recipe books can furthermore be considered a 'primary epistemic genre', as Gianna Pomata has argued. This genre cannot only be found in different historical, but also in different cultural contexts.[13] Between the Middle Ages and the early modern period, as Pomata explains, it was divided into 'formula' and 'recipe'. While the 'formula' was the theoretical and universal form, the 'recipe' was individualised and practical.[14] The 'formula', for example information about basic substances of recipes, formed the 'Antidotaria', while 'recipes', such as the one for producing soaps or medicaments, formed the 'experimenta'.[15] In consequence, Pomata sees Books of Secrets as successors of the 'experimenta'. This assumption is confirmed by the example of Johann Jacob Wecker's publications. In his *Antidotariae Generale* he described the basic substances of the elements from which products can be made, whereas he explained the concrete operations of making products in his *Antidotariae Speciale* and in his *Libri de Secretis*.[16] Books of Secrets should be regarded as 'experimenta', as recipe books.

---

12 Smith, *What is a Secret?*, p. 53.

13 Gianna Pomata, 'The Recipe and the Case. Epistemic Genres and the Dynamic of Cognitive Practices', in Kaspar von Greyerz, Silvia Flubacher, Philipp Senn (eds.), *Wissenschaftsgeschichte und Geschichte des Wissens im Dialog – Connecting Science and Knowledge. Schauplätze der Forschung – Scenes of Research* (Göttingen: V&R Unipress, 2013), pp. 131–154, here p. 136. According to Pomata, 'Epistemic genres' are characterised by their keeping in step with scientific practice: Gianna Pomata, 'The Medical Case Narrative: Distant Reading of an Epistemic Genre', *Literature and Medicine*, 32 (2014), pp. 1–23, at p. 2.

14 Pomata, *The Recipe and the Case*, pp. 138–139.

15 Ibid. On the pairing of theory and practice, see Peter Dear, 'What Is the History of Science the History Of? Early Modern Roots of the Ideology of Modern Science', *Isis*, 96 (3) (2005), pp. 390–406, at p. 393.

16 Pomata, The *Recipe and the Case*, pp. 138–139. Concerning the Weckerian *Antidotariae*, see Zweifel, *Aus Büchern Bücher machen*, p. 16, and ibid, pp. 266–272, the list of Weckerian publications.

According to William Eamon, Books of Secrets form a genre of its own. For him, they contain more alchemistic recipes than 'classical' recipe books do and aim at revealing the 'secrets of nature'.[17] Another important characteristic is the development of these recipes. In contrast to the 'normal' recipes, which, according to Eamon, are based on a 'trial-and-error experimentation', secrets were tested through a pre-Baconian experimental procedure.[18] This argument, however, is not entirely convincing, as such books often contain over a thousand recipes. Testing each of these recipes would have taken many, many years. Considering the high number of Books of Secrets published in the early modern period, such a practice of verification would have been unfeasible.[19] Furthermore, the existence of the 'Accademia Secreta', which, according to Eamon, enacted such testing, cannot be proven.[20] In contrast to Eamon, I argue that the most relevant aspect of Books of Secrets is not the pre-Baconian experimentation, but their compilatory nature.[21]

This compilatory nature implies a cooperation and involvement of a lot of persons, as a considerable number of different practices resulted in the production of these books: the writing of new text, the organising of books out of which text components could be copied, correspondence, reading, translating, and compiling, writing prefaces and dedication preambles, revising and correcting, decoupling chapters to make new books out of them, and the printing. Furthermore, establishing social relationships, such as with printers, was also of importance.[22] In the case of manuscript books, the printing aspect was obviously irrelevant, but most other practices were carried out as well. What all Books of Secrets had in common was above all the fact that many people had to work together in order to perform the practices necessary for their production. Such collaboration is part of the concept of the compilation network, which will be looked at in the following section.

---

17   William Eamon, 'How to Read a Book of Secrets', in Elaine Leong and Alisha M. Rankin (eds.), *Secrets and Knowledge in Medicine and Science, 1500–1800* (Farnham: Routledge, 2011), pp. 23–46, here p. 35.

18   Eamon, *Science and the Secrets of Nature*, pp. 7, 9, 150–151, et passim.

19   See the bibliography of Ad Stijnman, *A short-title bibliography of the Secreti by Alessio Piemontese, 1992–1994*, online on: https://www.academia.edu/35914604/A_short-title_bibliography_of_the_Secreti_by_Alessio_Piemontese [accessed 11 February 2024].

20   Zweifel, *Aus Büchern Bücher machen*, p. 8.

21   Ibid.

22   Ibid., p. 37; Simone Zweifel, 'Ein Blick hinter die Produktion von Kompilationen im 16. Jahrhundert am Beispiel Johann Jacob Weckers', *Jahrbuch für Kommunikationsgeschichte*, 20 (2018), pp. 27–42, at p. 36.

2   Compilation Networks

Compilation networks include three elements: persons, things, and external factors. The collaboration they implied was the basis of organising, collecting, and connecting knowledge, followed by a re-arrangement of this information in a new order. A significant part of this cooperation was made up of correspondence; without it, books could not have been organised in order to make new books out of the old. This was especially important in the case of Johann Jacob Wecker, since he lived in Colmar, midway between Basel und Strasbourg, and not in a centre of book production. He wrote to the Basel medical professor Theodor Zwinger (1533–1588): 'I am missing several books, which D[r.] Grineus[23] should send me from Frankfurt, which one cannot find in Basel.'[24] Zwinger was the central collaborator in Wecker's book production. He assisted Wecker not only in organising books but also in correcting text passages, and in assessing the structures of compilations. He even wrote prefaces in the name of Wecker.[25] Furthermore, he initialised the relation to the Basel printer Pietro Perna (* before 1522–1582), who printed most of Wecker's books, and all of his Books of Secrets.[26] Not only these visible individuals were involved in the early modern production of compilations. Other persons too, such as carriers, were indispensable, because the letters as well as the books sent by letters had to reach the addressees, so that new books could continue to be made. This procedure did not always function smoothly. In 1574, Wecker wrote to Zwinger: 'My carrier has now been absent for 8 weeks, I don't know how it is going, whether he is alive or dead (I gave him a lot of money for the food)'.[27] A missing carrier could clearly influence the production of a compilation.

Next to persons, things also formed an important part of compilation networks. In the present context, when I refer to things, I speak especially of printed books, and other 'basic material' such as manuscripts, which influenced

---

23   Simon Grynæus (1539–1582).

24   '[...] manglen mir noch etliche büecher, so D. Grineus mir zu schicken soll von Frankfurt, welche man zu Basel nitt bekummen mag'. Johann Jacob Wecker, *Letter to Theodor Zwinger*, Basel University Library (UB), Frey-Gryn Mscr II 28:Nr.374.

25   See also Johann Jacob Wecker, *Letter to Theodor Zwinger*, Basel University Library (UB), Frey-Gryn Mscr II 23:Nr.487; Wilhelm Kühlmann and Joachim Telle (eds.), *Corpus Paracelsisticum: Band II: Der Frühparacelsismus* (Berlin: De Gruyter, 2004), pp. 729–731, 746.

26   Johann Jacob Wecker, *Letter to Theodor Zwinger*, Basel University Library (UB), Frey-Gryn Mscr II 27:Nr.245. See Zweifel, *Aus Büchern Bücher machen*, p. 108.

27   'Mein bott ist jetz bei 8 wůchen auss, weiss auch nitt wie ess stodt, ob er tod oder lebendig {hab im vil gelt geben für die zerrung}.' Johann Jacob Wecker, *Letter to Theodor Zwinger*, Basel University Library (UB), Frey-Gryn Mscr II 5:Nr. 94.

the actions carried out within these networks.[28] These things were elements of several practices of producing books, and did not actively trigger them.[29] Practices, as Elizabeth Shove argues, presuppose an active reproduction and performance acted out by people.[30] For her, as well as Mika Pantzar and Matt Watson, practices are relational and exist only as long as the elements involved are connected:[31] '[...] practices emerge, persist and disappear as links between their defining elements are made and broken.'[32] This means, that the copying of textual components in order to produce new textual compilations could only be performed if the 'basic material', e.g. a printed book or a manuscript, from which these components were taken, was present to the producers. The latter had to take the action-initiating step.

The notion of practices assumed here, implies that a compilation network existed only as long as the individual actors were connected to each other. Thus, when a book was finished, the compilation network was dissolved.[33] A new network had to be established for each new publication. For just as each individual edition varies from the others, so does the network behind it. This is why I assume that each individual edition is different. 'The 'same' work is in fact not the same when it changes its language, its text, or its punctuation', as Roger Chartier has argued.[34] In the Weckerian book production, many actors

---

28   Ian Hodder, 'Human-Thing Entanglement. Towards an Integrated Archeological Perspective', *Journal of the Royal Anthropological Institute*, 17 (2011), pp. 154–177, at p. 155. See also Karl H. Hörning and Julia Reuter, 'Doing Culture: Kultur als Praxis', in Karl H. Hörning, Julia Reuter (eds.), *Doing Culture. Neue Positionen zum Verhältnis von Kultur und sozialer Praxis* (Bielefeld: transcript, 2004), pp. 9–15, at p. 11; Andreas Reckwitz, 'Grundelemente einer Theorie sozialer Praktiken. Eine sozialtheoretische Perspektive', *Zeitschrift für Soziologie*, 32 (2003), pp. 282–301, at p. 291.

29   In contrast to Bruno Latour, I take a moderate position in regard to the agency of things, see Bruno Latour, *Reassembling the Social. An Introduction to Actor-Network-Theory* (Oxford: Oxford University Press, 2005), p. 107; Bruno Latour, 'Where are the Missing Masses, Sociology of a few Mundane Artefacts Application', in Wiebe E. Bijker, John Law (eds.), *Shaping Technology – Building Society. Studies in Sociotechnical Change* (= *Inside Technology*) (Cambridge (Mass.): MIT Press, 1992), pp. 225–259, at p. 241. For things as 'active entities', see also Alex Preda, 'The Turn to Things. Arguments for a Sociological Theory of Things', *The Sociological Quarterly*, 40 (1999), pp. 347–366.

30   Elizabeth Shove, 'Everyday Practice and the Production and Consumption of Time', in Elizabeth Shove, Frank Trentmann, Richard Wilk (eds.), *Time, Consumption and Everyday Life: Practice, Materiality and Culture* (Oxford/New York: Berg, 2009), pp. 17–33, here p. 18.

31   Elizabeth Shove, Mika Pantzar, and Matt Watson, *The Dynamics of Social Practice: Everyday Life and how it Changes* (Los Angeles: SAGE, 2012), for example pp. 14–15, p. 21, p. 40.

32   Ibid., p. 21.

33   Zweifel, *Aus Büchern Bücher machen*, passim. To the dissolvement of actors in practices, see Shove, Pantzar, Watson, *The Dynamics of Social Practice*.

34   Roger Chartier, *The Author's Hand and the Printer's Mind* (Cambridge: Polity, 2014), p. IX. In the French original, one reads: 'La 'même' œuvre, en effet, n'est plus la même quand

of the compilation networks remained identical over the years. Sometimes, actors had to be replaced, for example when someone died. This was also the case with Johann Jacob Wecker himself. After his death, at least for the publication of the *Antidotarium speciale* of 1588, his wife Anna Wecker (* before 1572–1596) took over his role.[35] She was not only directly involved in Wecker's publications, but also in the relevant correspondence.[36] Likewise, the material elements could also change from one network to the other. Whenever a text passage was added to a new book, it became part of the compilation network. Such additions were very frequent. An example is the *Eighteenth Books of the Secrets*, published in 1660.[37] This enlarged edition of the *De Secretis libri XVII* of 1582 in an English translation included no longer 'just' 129, but 159 authors whose works were exploited for compilation.[38]

Not only people and things, such as printed books or manuscripts, but also external factors influenced book productions, as Donald McKenzie emphasises:

> Almost all texts of any consequence are the product of the concurrent inter-action of ideologies and institutions, of writers, publishers, printers, binders, wholesalers, travellers, retailers, as well as of the material sources (and their makers and suppliers) of type, paper, cord, and all the appurtenances of a printing house.[39]

---

changent sa langue, sa ponctuation, son format ou sa mise en page.' Roger Chartier, *La main de l'auteur et l'esprit de l'imprimeur. XVIe–XVIIIe siècle* (Paris: Gallimard, 2015), p. 15.

35 Johann Jacob Wecker, *Antidotarium speciale. Ex opt. avthorvm tam veterum quàm recentiorum scriptis fideliter congestum, methodicè digestum, & ampliùs triente auctum* (Basileae: Episcopius, 1588). See Zweifel, *Aus Büchern Bücher machen*, p. 75.

36 This is demonstrated by Johann Jacob Wecker's correspondence. For the importance of women in the production of recipe books, see also Monica Helen Green (ed.), *Women's Healthcare in the Medieval West. Texts and Contexts* (Aldershot: Ashgate, 2000); Leong, *Recipes and Everyday Knowledge*; Rankin, *Panaceia's Daughters*.

37 Wecker, Read, *Eighteen Books of the Secrets*.

38 Wecker, *De Secretis libri XVII* (1582); Wecker, Read, *Eighteen Books of the Secrets* (1660).

39 Donald Francis McKenzie, '5. The London Book Trade in 1644', in Donald Francis McKenzie, Peter D. McDonald, and Michael F. Suarez (eds.), *Making Meaning. 'Printers of the Mind' and other Essays* (= *Studies in Print Culture and the History of the Book*) (Amherst: University of Massachusetts Press, 2002), pp. 126–143, at p. 128. Other well-known models of book production by Robert Darnton and Thomas R. Adams and Nicolas Barker also include external factors. Robert Darnton, 'What is the History of Books?', *Daedalus*, 111 (1982), pp. 65–83; Thomas R. Adams, Nicolas Barker, 'A New Model for the Study of the Book', in Nicholas Barker (ed.), *A Potencie of Life. Books in Society* (London: British Library, 1993), pp. 5–43. To the model of Darnton, see also Robert Darnton: "What is the History of Books' Revisited', *Modern Intellectual History*, 4 (2007), pp. 495–508.

All these elements affect the book production and are thus part of the compilation network. Additional external factors can be found in the book production of Johann Jacob Wecker. An important one was the Frankfurt Book Fair.[40] The extent to which it paced the book production in the Weckerian compilation network is shown by the following letter. 1573, Wecker wrote to Zwinger:

> As far as printing is concerned, it would be very dear to me if you would have it printed now for the coming spring fair and that [the book, sz] would be printed and published by the next autumn fair. There are many who have been waiting for it now for more than a whole year. If you do not have the Vesalian figures, they must be left out and [the book, sz] printed without them.[41]

I could not find any publication by Wecker with figures from works of Andreas Vesalius (1514–1564), which indirectly illustrates the great influence of the book fair. The latter, in turn, was influenced by the buyers, who were eagerly waiting for a book. Here, the economic influence becomes evident, yet another external factor, which cannot be grasped satisfactorily regarding the Weckerian book production, as sources such as account books are missing.

3   Making Books of Secrets

Persons, things and external factors thus form the compilation network. They worked together in making new Books of Secrets in order to multiply and disseminate as many recipes as possible in a fast way and, as a result, enabled the making of more products such as soaps or colours. The Weckerian book production built on either one or several books, out of which text components were copied to be added to the new book. Wecker's first publications were based on the *De Secreti del Reverendo Alessio Piemontese*, which he translated into German and Latin. Both versions grew with each new publication,

---

40   For the Frankfurt Book Fair, see a.o. David Paisey, 'Prints at the Frankfurt Book Fairs, 1568–1600', *Print Quarterly*, 23 (2006), pp. 54–71; Peter Weidhaas, *Zur Geschichte der Frankfurter Buchmesse* (Frankfurt am Main: Suhrkamp, 2003).

41   'So vil daß trucken betriffet, were mir vast lieb, daß irß noch ietz künfftiger franckfurter vasten meß ad prelum kummen liesen, vnd auff die <ander> herbst meß getruckt vnd auß kummen mechte. Eß sindt vil, die ietz mher dan ein gantz iar darauff gewartet haben. So ir <die> Vesalij figuras nitt haben megen, můß man sie bleiben lassen, vnd on die selbigen trůcken [...].' Johann Jacob Wecker, *Letter to Theodor Zwinger*, Basel University Library (UB), G² I 30 fol. 185. 186 [Apogr.: G II 36, 1]. This letter is a copy; the original has not survived.

sometimes single recipes were added, sometimes whole chapters. This is illustrated by the titles of the Latin editions: the *De Secretis libri sex* of 1559 became
in 1563 the *De Secretis libri septem*. Many recipes were added for the *De Secretis
libri XVII* published in 1582.[42] The reason why Wecker took such a big step
between the latter two editions has to do with the new character of the book
published in 1582. It comprised much more and different knowledge than the
previous ones and went beyond the 'traditional' recipes of Books of Secrets,
such as advice on making food or colours.[43] As Wecker saw it, it aimed to integrate 'as many books as possible'.[44] How broad the variety of these books was,
is illustrated by the following list of authors included:[45]

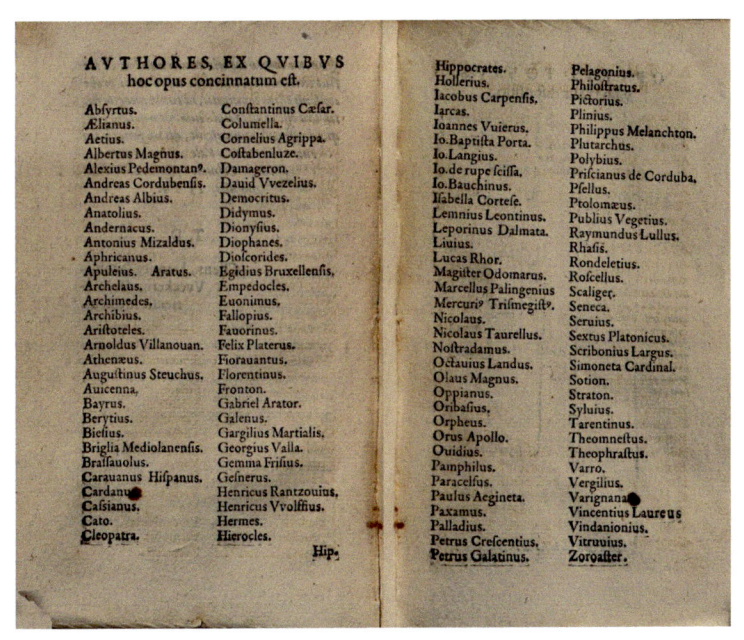

FIGURE 6.1   Johann Jacob Wecker, *De Secretis libri XVII. Ex varijs authoribus
             collecti, methodice'que digesti* (Basileae: [s.typ.], 1582). Augsburg,
             Staats- und Stadtbibliothek, Med 4773, s.p. urn:nbn:de:bvb:12-
             bsb11270075-1, s.p.

---

42   Wecker, *De secretis libri sex*, 1559; Johann Jacob Wecker, *D. Alexii Pedemontani De Secretis
     libri septem*, 1563 USTC 605161; Wecker, *De Secretis libri XVII*.

43   For these 'traditional' Books of Secrets, see a.o. Eamon, *Science and the Secrets of Nature*;
     Allison Kavey, *Books of Secrets. Natural Philosophy in England, 1550–1960* (Urbana: Univer-
     sity of Illinois Press, 2007); Smith, *What is a Secret?*.

44   Johann Jacob Wecker, *Letter to Theodor Zwinger*, Basel University Library (UB), Frey-Gryn
     Mscr II 4:Nr. 326.

45   Johann Jacob Wecker, *De Secretis libri XVII. Ex varijs authoribus collecti, methodice'que
     digesti* (Basileae: [s.typ.], 1582). Augsburg, Staats- und Stadtbibliothek, Med 4773, s.p.
     urn:nbn:de:bvb:12-bsb11270075-1.

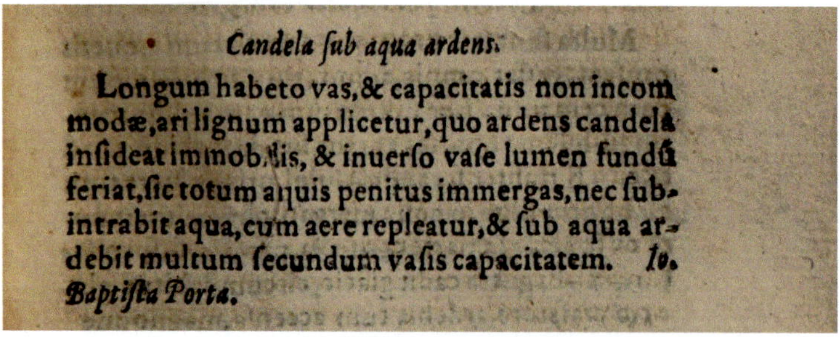

Candela sub aqua ardens.

Longum habeto vas,& capacitatis non incom
modæ,ari lignum applicetur,quo ardens candelâ
infideat immob.lis, & inuerfo vafe lumen fundû
feriat,fic totum aljuis penitus immergas,nec fub-
intrabit aqua,cum aere repleatur,& fub aqua ar-
debit multum fecundum vafis capacitatem.   *Io.*
Baptifta Porta.

FIGURE 6.2   Johann Jacob Wecker, *De Secretis libri XVII. Ex varijs authoribus
              collecti, methodice'que digesti* (Basileae: [s.typ.], 1582). Augsburg,
              Staats- und Stadtbibliothek, Med 4773, s.p. urn:nbn:de:bvb:12-
              bsb11270075-1, pp. 49

Here, one finds names from different periods and traditions of knowledge,
Galen is named as well as Paracelsus, Cleopatra as well as Nicolaus Taurellus
(1547–1606). Taurellus was a contemporary physician and philosopher, married
to Katharina Keller, the daughter from the first marriage of Anna Wecker, the
wife of Johann Jacob Wecker. This connection also points to the considerable
importance of family networks in the early modern production of compilations. As the text in question shows, even more textual passages of additional
'authors' were included. All this knowledge was extracted from existing books
or other textual collections. This practice is implied not only by the list of
authors, but also by the fact, that these authors were cited after each text passage. The recipe for 'Candela sub aqua ardens' (a candle burning under water)
illustrates this tellingly.

In this case, the recipe was copied out of the *Magiæ naturalis* [...] *Libri IIII*
of Giambattista della Porta (1535–1615).[46] Consequently, this particular book
had to be present at Wecker's working place in a printed or handwritten form.

---

46   Wecker, *De Secretis libri XVII*, p. 49. The recipe was possibly taken out of Johannes Baptista
      Della Porta, *Magiæ Naturalis, siue, De Miraculis rerum Naturalium Libri IIII* (Antverpiæ:
      Johannes Stelius, 1562) USTC 401106, pp. 58–59. The book production of Giambattista
      della Porta was also characterized by many changed, translated and expanded editions.
      His first edition of the *Magia Naturalis*, which was edited in 1558, was published in 58
      editions in five languages: Latin, French, Italian, Dutch, and German (*Magiae Natvralis,
      sive de miracolis rervm natvralium libri IIII* (Neapoli: apud Matthiam Cancer, 1558) USTC
      826301). 1586, he printed a second edition, which was expanded into twenty books, and
      published thirty times. Furthermore, English was added to the languages of translation.
      Laura Balbiani, 'La ricezione della 'Magia Naturalis' di Giovan Battista Della Porta. Cultura
      e scienza dall'Italia all'Europa', *Bruniana & Campanelliana*, 5 (2) (1999), pp. 277–303, at
      p. 280. See also Laura Balbiani, *La Magia Naturalis di Giovan Battista Della Porta. Lingua,
      cultura e scienza in Europa all'inizio dell'età moderna* (Bern: Peter Lang, 2001). It can be

Since Wecker had no capacity to purchase these books for example at the Frankfurt fair, they were mostly organised by people connected to him by correspondence. This organisation of additional works was the first step toward the preparation of a new Book of Secrets and it was followed by numerous other production steps. Some of them will be looked at in what follows.

Following the correspondence stage, books had to be transferred and read, and text passages had to be selected in order to reuse them. In this as well as in most other production steps, Theodor Zwinger was the most important co-operator.[47] He helped Wecker to obtain books, offered ideas about books Wecker could include in his new publications, corrected, gave advice on which person a dedication letter should be addressed to, wrote prefaces and so on. The question concerning possible additional books was important, as Wecker wanted some of his books to be as voluminous as possible.[48] He wrote to Zwinger: 'And if the gentleman can help me with good advice to enlarge this book, I ask him to do the best.'[49] If Zwinger knew about other books Wecker could copy from, which the latter would borrow from Zwinger, he would 'return [them, sz] with best thanks'.[50] Furthermore, Wecker and Zwinger cooperated regarding the organisation of knowledge in the books themselves. One of the collocation practices was the division of knowledge within books, another, that of dividing knowledge into different books, for example, when chapters were taken from one book in order to make a new publication or even new publications on this basis. At the level of the individual book, content had to be assigned to various components of a book. This included title page, dedication, preface, main text, and index. The most important structuring method used by Wecker was the division of knowledge into synoptic tables; these were

assumed that compilation networks were also the basis of this book production, and that Della Porta did not single-handedly produce all these editions.

47   This is revealed by the correspondence between Wecker and Zwinger. See also Kaspar von Greyerz, 'Basel im 16. und 17. Jahrhundert. Universität, Humanismus und Wissenschaft', in Martin Wallraff (ed.), *Gelehrte zwischen Humanismus und Reformation. Kontexte der Universitätsgründung in Basel 1460* (= *Litterae et Theologia*) (Berlin: De Gruyter, 2011), pp. 74–94, at p. 77.

48   Johann Jacob Wecker, *Letter to Theodor Zwinger*, Basel University Library (UB), Frey-Gryn Mscr II 4:Nr. 326.

49   'Vnd so mir der herr in diesem bůch zů mheren, kann mitt gůtem rhat behülfflich sein, bitt ich den herren, welle daß best thůn.' Johann Jacob Wecker, *Letter to Theodor Zwinger*, Basel University Library (UB), Frey-Gryn Mscr II 4:Nr.327.

50   'Die authores würt der herr ein anfang meines bůchs finden. Wüssen ir andere mher, die mir so lang mechten verlichen werden welte ichs erlich den selbigen mitt danck widerumb zů stellen.' Ibid.

integrated into the book structure just mentioned.[51] Such tables can be found in the table of contents of the *De Secretis libri XVII* of 1582:[52]

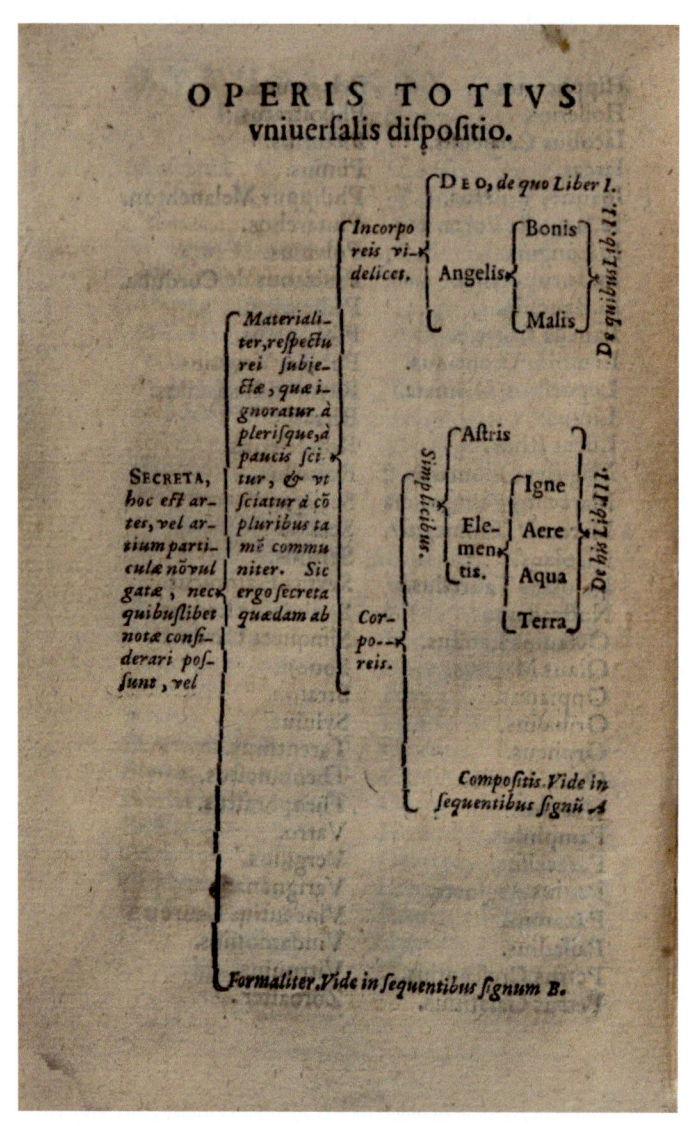

FIGURE 6.3 Johann Jacob Wecker, *De Secretis libri XVII*. Ex varijs authoribus collecti, methodice'que digesti. Basileae: [s.typ.], 1582. Augsburg, Staats- und Stadtbibliothek, Med 4773, [Titelblatt]. urn:nbn:de:bvb:12-bsb11270075-1, s.p.

51   Zweifel, *Aus Büchern Bücher machen*, p. 130.

52   Johann Jacob Wecker, *De Secretis libri XVII. Ex varijs authoribus collecti, methodice'que digesti* (Basileae: [s.typ.], 1582). Augsburg, Staats- und Stadtbibliothek, Med 4773, s.p. urn:nbn:de:bvb:12-bsb11270075-1.

This book is entirely divided into diagrammatic tables based on the 'method' championed by the French scholar Petrus Ramus (1515–1572). The Ramist approach divides a text into different subordinate dichotomous parts: 'A division takes place when the whole is divided into parts. The whole is what contains the parts. A part is a portion of the whole.'[53] Cognition is either possible in advancing from the subordinate part to the whole, or from the whole to the subordinate part. While many contemporaries such as Zwinger and Wecker used synoptic tables to illustrate these divisions, Ramus himself did not work with such diagrams.[54]

In adhering to a Ramist approach, Wecker had 'a lot of work' in 'searching [works of, SZ] many authors and putting them in an order'.[55] The production of such tables required 'much effort and trouble, and time and diligence [...]'.[56] An effort, which should be remunerated in the end, at least this was Wecker's hope. Considering this issue, Wecker again relied on Zwinger: 'In the meantime, my request is to negotiate with the printer regarding the price.'[57] Zwinger in turn negotiated with Pietro Perna who hesitated to print the *De Secretis libri XVII*. This was discussed in several letters between Wecker, Zwinger, and Perna. Even 'inappropriate words' were exchanged.[58] The connection between

---

53 'Distributio est cum totum in partem distribuitur. Totum est, quot continet partes. Pars est, quae continetur à toto.' Petrus Ramus, *Dialecticae libri duo*, ed. Sebastian Lalla (Stuttgart-Bad Cannstatt: Frommann-Holzboog, 2011), pp. 69–71.

54 For Petrus Ramus and synoptic tables, see for example Sebastian Lalla, 'Einleitung', in Petrus Ramus, *Dialecticae libri duo* (= *Editionen zur frühen Neuzeit*), ed. by Sebastian Lalla (Stuttgart-Bad Cannstatt: Frommann-Holzboog, 2011); Joseph S. Freedman, Wolfgang Rother, and Mordechai Feingold (eds.): *The Influence of Petrus Ramus. Studies in Sixteenth and Seventeenth Century Philosophy and Sciences* (Basel: Schwabe, 2001); Wilhelm Schmidt-Biggemann, *Topica universalis. Eine Modellgeschichte humanistischer und barocker Wissenschaft* (Hamburg: Meiner, 1983); Ann M. Blair, *Too Much to Know. Managing Scholarly Information before the Modern Age* (New Haven: Yale University Press, 2010), pp. 144–145; Arndt Brendecke, 'Tabellenwerke in der Praxis der frühneuzeitlichen Geschichtsvermittlung', in Theo Stammen and Wolfgang E.J. Weber (eds.): *Wissenssicherung, Wissensordnung und Wissensverarbeitung. Das europäische Modell der Enzyklopädien* (Berlin: Akademie, 2004), pp. 157–189, at pp. 164–165.

55 'Dan vil arbeit darüber ghadt, so vil aůthores důrch sůchen, vnd in ein ordnůng zů bringen [...].' Johann Jacob Wecker, *Letter to Theodor Zwinger*, Basel University Library (UB), Frey-Gryn Mscr II 5:Bl.100.

56 'Eß erfordern solche tabulæ <[unreadable]> vil müh, arbeitt, <vnd> zeitt vnd fleiß, also daß ich vil ringer vnd lieber sonst 4 bogen vertieren welte, dan ein bogen tabularum zů ordern, hoff ir werden mich <nicht> nitt im schaden ligen lassen.' Johann Jacob Wecker, *Letter to Simon Grynæus*, Basel University Library (UB), G² I 30 fol. 185. 186 [= G II 36:Bl.1].

57 'Hiezwijschen ist mein dienstlich bitt an herren, mitt den herren *Typographis* zů handlen *pretij* halben.' Johann Jacob Wecker, *Letter to Theodor Zwinger*, Basel University Library (UB), Frey-Gryn Mscr II 28:Nr.372.

58 Johann Jacob Wecker, *Letter to Theodor Zwinger*, Basel University Library (UB), Frey-Gryn Mscr II 4:Nr. 326.

Wecker and Perna could only be kept in operation thanks to Zwinger's intervention and effort. It was an indispensable requirement for the production of *De Secretis libri XVII*, probably the most successful book published by Johann Jacob Wecker.[59]

4   Conclusion

Collaboration was essential for the making of early modern Books of Secrets, which the book-production of Johann Jacob Wecker, city physician of Colmar in the late sixteenth century, exemplifies. More than eighty Books of Secrets were published in his name. They, and the surviving correspondence, provide us with a valuable insight into the mechanisms of producing early modern compilations, which were based on the production of books using existing books. This is made particularly evident by Wecker's *De Secretis libri XVII* of 1582, which comprises text fragments of different periods, regions, and traditions of knowledge. The work mentions 129 authors as 'providers of material'. This considerable number of authors included in the *De Secretis libri XVII* mirrors Wecker's aim to make this book as big as possible, which could only be achieved by working with different actors.[60] This cooperation included among other things correspondence in order to obtain books, transporting these books to the book producer, reading and deciding about which textual passages should be copied, the ordering of these passages, the decision about an addressee of a dedication letter, negotiations with a printer about price and actual printing, the printing itself and finally the selling of a book. In most of these steps, not only people, but also things and external factors were involved. The 'things' were mainly books which had to be present in material form in order to copy from them. External factors could be events such as the Frankfurt Book Fair, which could determine whether an image was included in a publication or not. All these elements were connected to compilation networks. They shaped practices, thanks to which 'recipe'-knowledge could be stored in books and passed on a wider audience of practitioners. This 'how-to' of 'how-to'-books should be considered in analyses of the practices of producing recipe books, as without them, many of the practitioners would have had no instructions for making their own products, which were based on specific recipes.

---

59   Zweifel, *Aus Büchern Bücher machen*, pp. 159–161.
60   Johann Jacob Wecker, *Letter to Theodor Zwinger*, Basel University Library (UB), Frey-Gryn Mscr II 4:Nr 326.

PART 3

Text and Image Simultaneity

∴

CHAPTER 7

How to Fly? Some Thoughts on a Windy Skill

Laurence Grove and Stefan Laube

If one deals with the know-how of flying today and back then, one is confronted with heterogeneous topics. For long stretches of the Early Modern Era, it was obviously important not to hinder the individual soul in its flight towards heaven. The bereaved family immediately opened the window wide as the dying woman drew her last breath. In this respect, every instruction book on Christian piety is also an instruction book on flying to a post-mortem, heavenly existence. In addition to this competence in flight, which is dismissed as 'imaginary' by sceptics of faith, flying always aroused very concrete technological ambitions. What do birds have that humans do not? Can inventive humans acquire protheses to compensate for their deficits compared to birds? – these were questions that not only Leonardo Da Vinci pondered. In 'Books of Secrets', in 'Kunstbüchlein', instructions for flying have also been handed down, in the intermedial sphere of text and image, usually with an uncertain outcome (breakage of the neck not excluded). In the fossil upheaval of technology and industrialisation, when flying could actually be realised for many, the 'how-to-fly' diversified into highly specialised training over many years, which is now only accessible to experts, and popular science, which was less about flying yourself than explaining how flying objects work in a catchy and entertaining way.

The following contribution offers offers material for reflection, hopefully playful inspiration for the flight of the mind. Strands that at first glance may seem only slightly allied are in fact linked together: the theme of flying is the gateway that allows us to examine an important intertwining between early modernity and modernity.[1]

---

1   I would like to express my sincere thanks to Stefan Laube, specifically for the early modern examples he has provided, but more generally without whose help this chapter could never have taken off.

1   Getting to the Heavens Using Early-Modern Manuals

Early-Modern books could use flying as a way to show you how to do other things. Best known might be Caesare Ripa's *Iconologia*, from 1593 onwards, where flight represents the rising or the setting of the sun and all that goes with that.[2]

However, if you want to learn to fly, short of having Leonardo da Vinci's help via his famous aviation machine inventions, what that generally meant at this time was getting to the heavens. Here the instructors par excellence, known for their visual didacticism, were the Jesuits. Jerome Nadal's *Adnotationes et meditations in Evangelica* of 1595, for example, explains the Bible visually, often providing narrative within a single plate, as in that of the Third Sunday of Advent, 'Mittunt Iudaei ad Ioannem' ['Jews are Sent to John'].[3] In order for us to understand, to look and learn, the images are accompanied by letters which refer to short explanatory text, including for that of the celestial flying chariot.

Possibly my favourite example to which I have referred in previous writings (see my *Emblematics and 17th-Century French Literature*) is that of Joannes David's *Duodecim specula* [*Twelve Mirrors*] of 1610, depicting a series of twelve mirrors, as the title suggests, that lead us to God. In particular, the 'Speculum creaturum' ['Mirror of Creations'], if we follow the key, will lead us to God in the Heavens, through a method of making visible that which is normally hidden, or as the text puts it, 'Invisibilium per visibilia contemplatio'.[4]

Who however actually came up with the formula 'Ars volandi'?[5] One looks in vain for the term in Leonardo da Vinci. For this, one finds something in the German provinces, at a small Protestant university in the southwest, where

---

2   The edition consulted and pictured is that of 1611 (GUL SMAdd. q 13): Cesare Ripa, *Iconologia overo descrittione d'imagini delle virtu', vitii, affetti, passioni humane, corpi celesti, mondo e sue parti* (Padua: Per Pietro Paulo Tozzi, 1611) USTC 4023040.

3   Jerome Nadal, *Adnotationes et meditationes in Evangelia* (Antwerp: Martin Nutius, 1595) USTC 413154. This work can be consulted at https://catholic-resources.org/Art/Nadal.htm. From the same site, *Biblical and Religious Art and Music*, see also *Felix Just, Nadal's Gospel Illustrations*.

4   Laurence Grove, *Emblematics and 17th-Century French Literature* (Charlottesville VA: Rookwood, 2000), in particular pages 12–14; Joannes David, *Duodecim specula* aliquando *videre desideranti concinnata* (Antwerp: Christopher Plantin, 1610) USTC 1009428. The copy consulted and pictured is GUL SM 383.

5   Wolfgang Behringer, 'Ars volandi. Gedankenspiele im Umfeld einer europäischen Debatte der Neuzeit', in Dieter R. Bauer and Wolfgang Behringer (eds.), *Fliegen und Schweben: Annäherung an eine menschliche Sensation* (Munich: Deutscher Taschenbuch Verlag, 1997), pp. 16–37. Again, I would like to thank Stefan Laube throughout, in particular for this section on early modern explorations of the 'Ars volandi'.

Di Cesare Ripa. 109

La Cortesia è virtù, che serra spesso gli occhi ne demeriti altrui, per nó serrar il passo alla propria benignità.

CREPVSCVLO DELLA MATTINA.

FANCIVLLO di carnagione bruna, c'habbia l'ali a gli omeri del medesimo colore, stando in atto di volare in alto, hauerà in cima del capo vna grande, & rilucente stella , & che con la sinistra mano tenghi vn' vrna riuolta all'ingiù versando con essa minutissime gocciole d'aqua , & con la destra vna facella accesa, riuolta da la parte di dietro, & per l'aria vna rondinella .

Crepusculo (per quello che riferisce il Boccaccio nel primo libro della Geneologia de gli Dei) viene detto da crepero che significa dubbio, cóciosia che pare si dubiti, se quello spatio di tempo sia da concedere alla notte passata , o al giorno venente , essendo ne li confini tra l'vno, & l'altro , Onde per tal cagione dipingeremo il crepusculo di color bruno.

Fanciullo alato lo rappresentiamo, come parte del tempo, e per significare

FIGURE 7.1   Cesare Ripa, *Iconologia* (Padua: Tozzi, 1611), p. 109. Glasgow University Library SMAdd. q 13

FIGURE 7.2   Jerome Nadal, *Adnotationes et meditationes in Evangelia*, (Antwerp:
Moretus, 1607), The 153 picture plates are bound together at the back, here
plate 11, Wolfenbüttel, Herzog August Library, M: Td 2° 4

FIGURE 7.3 Joannes David, *Duodecim specula* (Antwerp: Plantin, 1610), University of Glasgow
Library SM 383

a young scholar and librarian called for a public Latin debate on the topic of
'De arte volandi': the pros and cons of flying![6] Friedrich Hermann Flayder's
(1596–1640) argumentation is ambivalent. On the one hand, he believed in the
technical possibility of flight, not least with reference to a large bird skeleton
in the natural history collection of the Tübingen University Library. On the
other hand, he distanced himself from the often-ridiculous attempts at flight,
in which daredevils risked life and limb with inadequate means. The philolo-
gist saw the 'real art of flying' in rising into the sky with the 'wings of the spirit',
the 'divine vibrating feathers' are the 'tools of reason' (Flayer, pp. 32–37). 'Ars
volandi' as a spiritual art is thus more likely to belong to the Artes liberales – a
radically climate-friendly solution, in other words.

But the inventive spirit of the mechanics and later engineers was not to be
satisfied, nor was a certain Anglican clergyman: John Wilkins (1614–1672), pioneer of the 'New Philosophy' and co-founder of the Royal Society, who knew
Flayer's booklet.[7] His book, *Mathematicall Magick* (1648), about the practical
implementation of mathematical knowledge, was divided into two parts: the
first about 'Powers' was dedicated to Archimedes; the second about 'Motions'
was named 'Daedalus'. There, in three chapters, flying was unfolded: according
to Wilkins, one could fly with the help of angels and devils, with wings, bird
flying machines or flying chariots. Unfortunately, these chapters in particular
lack illustrations, as if Wilkins did not dare to provide visual evidence for these
bold ideas.

For a long time, ships on the sea were projected into the sky according to
the idea that a ship filled with fire-matter would be able to sail in the sea of air
just like an air-filled ship on water. In the case of the Jesuit Francesco Lana de
Terzi (1631–1687), large hollow spheres whose contents had to be 'lighter than
air' were to carry the ship aloft. Lana did not fail to give practical instructions
for the construction of an airship.

Try it with the help of drawings, letter indices and the explanations in the
text! Until Lana Terzi's bold design, airships served as props for allegorical

---

6   Friedrich Hermann Flayder, *De Arte Volandi* (Tübingen: Werlin, 1628).
       https://books.google.de/books?id=pQAyMwEACAAJ&printsec=frontcover&redir_esc
    =y#v=onepage&q&f=false 'Le premier [to use 'ars volandi', LG] est un professeur, un de
    ces reveurs de bibliothèques qui prosperent en pays allemand', Jules Dahem, *Histoire des
    idées aéronautiques avant Montgolfier* (Paris: Sorlot 1943), p. 104. See also Viktoria Tkaczyk,
    Himmels-Falten: Zur Theatralität des Fliegens in der Frühen Neuzeit (Paderborn: Fink, 2011),
    pp. 178–190.
7   John Wilkins, *Mathematicall Magick, or: The Wonders that may be Performed by Mechanical
    Geometry, Book II: Daedalus a Treatise on Mechanical Motions* (London: Gellibrand, 1648),
    pp. 199–223, reference on Flayder, p. 203.

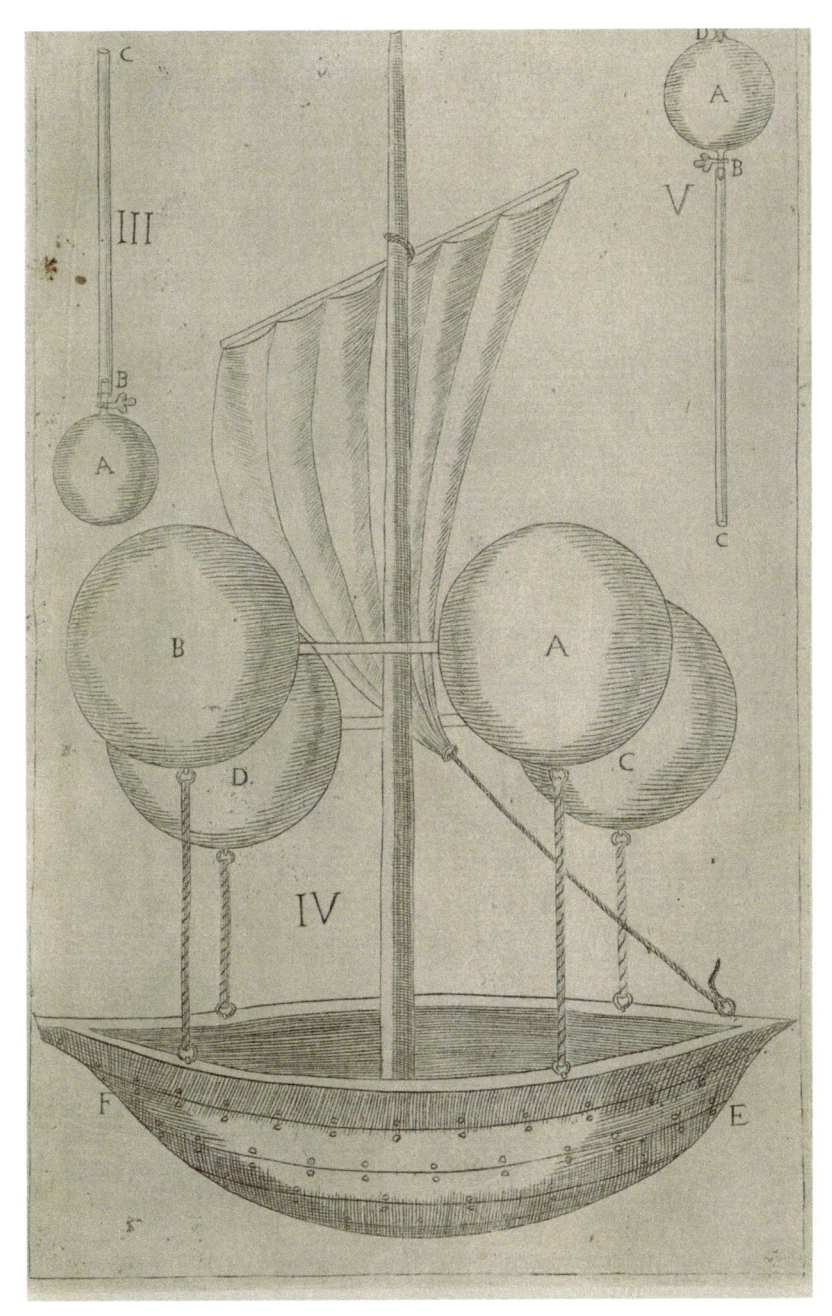

FIGURE 7.4 Francesco Lana di Terzi: *Prodromo overo saggio di alcune inventioni nuove premesso all'arte maestra* (Brescia: Rizzardi 1670), p. 50–51 (Figure bound in the back section), Wolfenbüttel, Herzog August Library, M: Nc 4° 55

FIGURE 7.5   Woodcut from Peter Attendorn, Johannes Geiler von Kaysersberg, Jacob
             Wimpfeling and Jodocus Gallus: Directoriu[m] statuu[m]. Seu verius. Tribulatio
             seculi, Strasbourg 1489 USTC 740476 (unpaginated). Kunstbibliothek, SMB-PK,
             Gris126 kl

festive decorations, as airy means of transport for members of the heavenly gods. Or they stood as vehicles of satire for the unsteady lives of 'airheads'. One of the first printed depictions of a flying 'ship of fools' can be found in the publication of a university joke speech from Heidelberg in 1489.

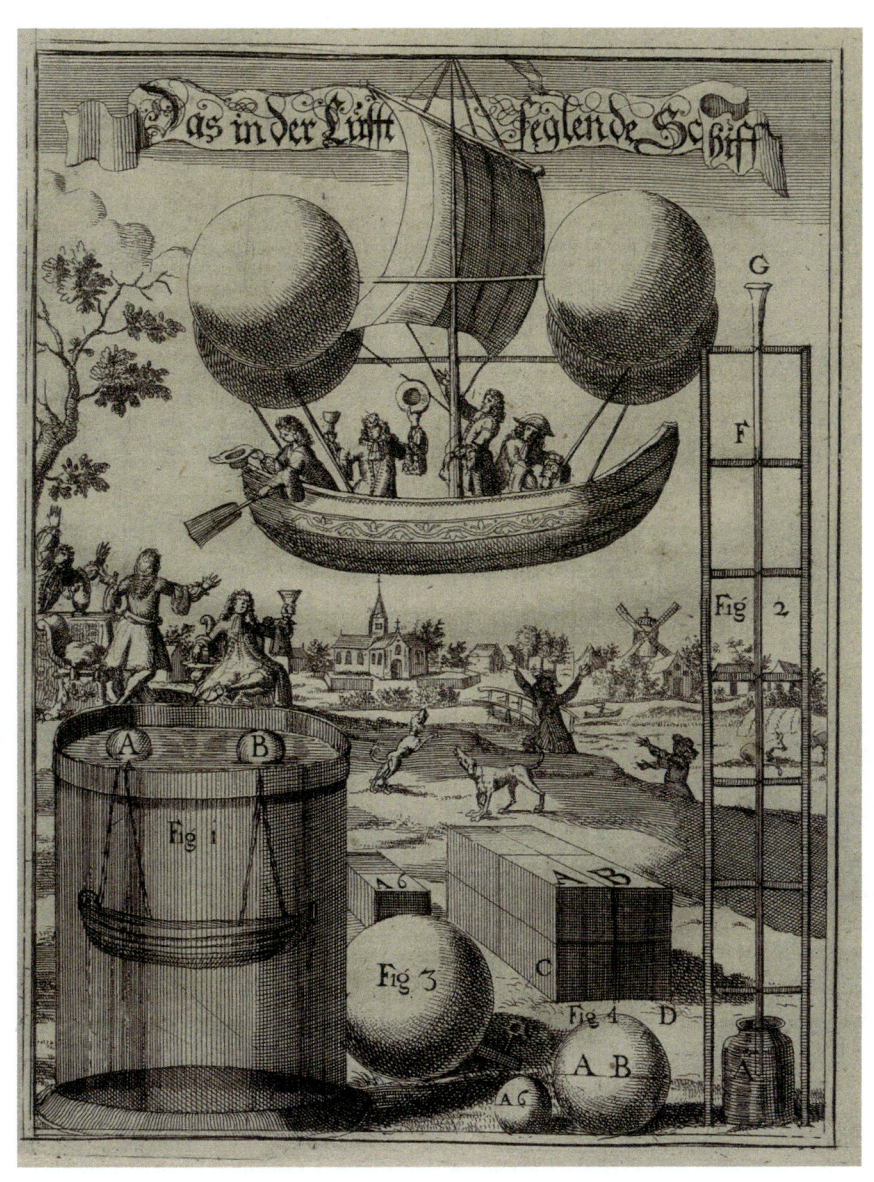

FIGURE 7.6 Engraving from Eberhard Werner Happel, Vierter Theil: Grösseste Denkwürdigkeiten der Welt oder so genandte Relationes Curiosae (Hamburg: Wiering 1689) USTC 2670460, plate after p. 309, Staatsbibliothek Berlin Ah 3122:R

That gravity could never be overcome with these constructions was immediately apparent.[8] Not so with Lana de Terzi, who designed a vacuum buoyancy for his airship. Inspired by Otto von Guericke's experiments with the Magdeburg hemispheres in 1663, Lana had developed a balloon theory.[9] The idea was good, but in reality no material proved suitable to compensate for the enormous pressure difference. Lana's rather schematic drawing appeals mainly to experts and colleagues. Nineteen years later, his invention, which was never realised, was to be popularised in text and image, in Eberhard Werrner Happel's *Denkwürdigkeiten der Welt oder sogenannte Relationes Curiosae* [Memories of the World or So Called Curious Relations].

In the foreground you can see an experimental set-up, on the bottom left a vat filled with water in which two vacuum balls make a submerged ship float. In the background, this principle is transferred from water to air: a pleasurable ship's balloon ride applauded by onlookers, which never took place in this form, despite being a potential precursor to the Montgolfier brothers.

2   Cutaways: Latterday 'How to Do Its'

If we fly forward to the twentieth century, the technology may have changed, but the 'look and learn' method is basically the same. In the example of 'the first four-jet air-liner in the world', the de Havilland Comet, we see the overall shape of the plane, but also its inner workings and how they relate to each

FIGURE 7.7   Eagle, 5 May 1950, from *The Eagle Book of Cutaways: L. Ashwell Wood*. With an introduction and edited by Dennis Gifford (London: Webb& Power, 1988), p. 58–59

8   Moritz Wullen, UFO 1665. Die Luftschlacht von Stralsund, exhibition catalogue, Staatliche Museen zu Berlin, Kunstbibliothek (Cologne: Wienand,2023), p. 52.
9   Natascha Adamowsky, *Das Wunder in der Moderne. Eine andere Kulturgeschichte des Fliegens* (Paderborn: Fink, 2010), pp. 129–134; Moritz Wullen, UFO 1665, p. 55.

other, with a text to give us a fuller explanation. This example is taken from a 1950 *Eagle* comic 'Cutaway'.[10] Other examples, from here and elsewhere, include early planes and planes of the future, rockets, hovercraft, chairlifts for alpine ski resorts, as well as airports themselves and space stations. Although there are general anthologising works providing accessible examples of this phenomenon, there has been comparatively little scholarly analysis given to the history or techniques of cutaways akin to our de Havilland example.[11] An overview here, essentially just flying through the subject, cannot do justice to a topic that could merit a full-length academic study.

FIGURE 7.8 Early Plane. Taken from Jon Richards and Alex Pang, *The Fantastic Cutaway Book of Flight* (London: Aladdin/Watts, 2001 [1998])

10   Eagle, 5 May 1950, from *The Eagle Book of Cutaways: L. Ashwell Wood*. With an introduction and edited by Dennis Gifford (London: Webb & Power, 1988), p. 58–59.

11   One relatively recent article however addresses the theme of cutaways in the context of ocean liners: Shawa Ross, 'Ocean-Liner Cutaways, Diagrams, and Composites: Technical Illustration as Mass Aesthetic in *Popular Mechanics* and *The Illustrated London News*', *The Journal of Modern Periodical Studies,* 8 (2017), pp. 1–33. Emphasis, as the title suggests, is on sectional drawings nearer to technical illustrations than the Cutaway artistry of the 1950s onwards. For examples specifically of hovercraft Cutaways, see Eric Sidney Hayden, *The Hovercraft* (Loughborough: Wills and Hepworth, 1969). For background information and reproductions of *Eagle* Cutaways, see Gifford (ed.), *The Eagle Book of Cutaways*.

FIGURE 7.9   Eagle, 23 September 1955, from *The Eagle Book of Cutaways. L. Ashwell Wood*. With an introduction and edited by Dennis Gifford (London: Webb & Power, 1988), pp. 90–91

'Cutaways', as they are generally called, are traditionally associated with the *Eagle* comic, founded by Marcus Morris (1915–1989), a Lancashire Anglican priest, with original inspiration from the parish magazine *Anvil*, thereby giving a religious background which, without being overbearing, nonetheless marked the publication. The *Eagle* initially ran from 1950 to 1969 and, as well as cutaways, reader participation pages and informative illustrated prose, included such strips as *Dan Dare* and *Captain Pugwash*.[12] The cutaways were generally by Leslie Ashwell Wood, born it would seem in 1913, although about whom very little is known, or by Walkden Fisher (possibly 1913 to 1979), likewise for whom bibliographical information is scarce.[13]

12   On the *Eagle* in the context of the history of comics, see, for example, Roger Sabin, *Comics, Comix and Graphic Novels: A History of Comic Art* (London: Phaidon, 1996), in particular pages 46–49. Several anthologies reprinting extracts are available, such as Daniel Tatarsky (ed.), *Eagle Annual: The Best of the 1950s Comic: Features Dan Dare, the Greatest Comic Strip of All Time* (London: Orion, 2007).

13   For what little is known, or can be hypothesised, see Steve Holland's posts for his *Bearalley* blog: Steve Holland, 'Leslie Ashwell Wood', https://bearalley.blogspot.com/2007

FIGURE 7.10   Haynes Service and Repair Manuals. Private collection

Aviation was a popular subject for Cutaways, but they also covered ships, cars, and trains, making transport the predominant theme, but by no means the only one. Other topics included a 'Den' or indeed a 'Windmill'. One other related adult form is the Haynes car manual.

Founded in 1960, these iconic guides would provide cutaways of specific makes of car so as to guide the user in the stripping down and repairing of the vehicle.[14] This do-it-yourself aspect does not play a role in the aircraft cutaways: here it is all about entertaining theory, how does something work?, but not about practical implementation. The guides, whether theoretical or practical, became so engrained in everyday consumer culture as to become the object of numerous pastiches, such as the Star Ship Enterprise or the Death Star. Complex technology reveals its interior, lifts it from the invisible into visibility and thus becomes emblematic.

FIGURE 7.11   Star Wars / Death Star. Hayne's pastiche. Private collection

3   And What Is There to Say about Rockets and Manned Spaceflight?

That interplanetary rockets also left their mark on the emblematic age is little known. Here, too, the globally missionary Jesuits set standards. Under the
guiding theme 'Unus Non Sufficit' in the sense of 'One World Is Not Enough',

we see in emblem 162 of Jacobs Bosch's *Symbolographia* how a rocket, with a stately tail of fire, flies from one planet to the next. The missionary work of the Jesuits is to gain galactic dominions in this way, propaganda that makes use of an utopian ideal was later to become a technological innovation.[15]

The twentieth century differs from the seventeenth in that metaphor became reality, but at the price of ever greater complexity that has to be explained. In the last century cutaways were often, but not always, aimed at children. They are also to be found in specific publications such as Jon Richards and Alex Pang's *The Fantastic Cutaway Book of Flight*, or Robert Russell and John Young's *Picture Reference Book of Aircraft*.[16] Interestingly, many of these popular visual habits and image formulas were taken up constructively by NASA years later, when it used striking shapes and pop colors to make the Skylab1 space station transparent.

In the space race, the United States had clearly overtaken the Soviet Union by the early 1970s. Twelve years earlier, the situation had looked very different when Yuri Gagarin became the first human to fly into space and orbit the Earth. It was also in 1961 when technology historian Doru Todericu made a sensational manuscript discovery in the archives of Hermannstadt (Siebenbürgen), now Sibiu (Romania), in which Conrad Haas (1509–1576) explained the principle of the multi-stage rocket for the first time. In 1969, the year of the moon landing by 'the enemy of the system', Todericu published a book on the subject introducing the early modern, hitherto completely unrecognised rocket pioneer as 'Conrad de la Sibiu'. The Romanian scholar called the work, written in German, which Haas himself entitled 'Kunstbuch' in the sense of craftsmanship 'Manuscriul de la Sibiu'.[17] In this way, even the Ceaucescu regime was able to appropriate this tradition, which was so relevant at the time, for communist nation building.

Conrad Haas came to Sibiu in 1551 with the army of the Roman-German Emperor Ferdinand I as armourer and gunmaster, where he took charge of the war arsenal. Perhaps it was the threat and permanent danger of this region

---

15   Sixty-two years earlier, it was not a rocket but an angelic genius who linked the 'Old World' and the 'New World', which are represented by two terrestrial spheres: see *Imago Primi Saeculi Societatis Iesu*, Antwerp 1640, p. 326. See also Wullen, *UFO 1665*, pp. 82–83.

16   Jon Richards and Alex Pang, *The Fantastic Cutaway Book of Flight* (London: Aladdin/Watts, 2001 [1998]); Robert Russell and John Young, *Picture Reference Book of Aircraft* (Leicester: Brockhampton Press, 1967).

17   Doru Todericiu, *Preistoria Rachetei Moderne. Manuscrisul de la Sibiu 1529–1569* (Bucuresti: Editura Academiei RSR, 1969). Sibiu was built as 'Hermannstadt' by German immigrants who settled in this part of Southern Carpathia from the 1140s onwards. Even towards the end of the Second World War, one third of the population was Lutheran and German-speaking.

FIGURE 7.12   Emblematic illustration (engraving) from Jacob Bosch, *Symbolographia, Sive De Arte Symbolica Sermones Septem* (Augsburg 1702), Tab. XIX

FIGURE 7.13   Artist's impression showing a cutaway view of the Skylab 1 Orbital Workshop
(OWS). Johnson Space Center, NASA, 1973. Anna Escardò, Julius Wiedemann
(ed.), *Science Illustration: A History of Visual Knowledge from the 15th Century
to Today* (Cologne: Taschen, 2023), p. 310

at the interface with the East that spurred his creativity to escape the earth's gravity, at least for a short time. Between 1529 and 1559, he completed an inherited manuscript on war technology, created by his ancestor Hans Haasenwein between 1450 and May 1459. Conrad Haas' 'Kunstbuch' consists of three parts, the first two of which contain practical advice on war craft and pyrotechnics. Only the third part was written by Conrad Haas, but it is this part that can claim particular originality. There, rockets with a multiple engine are shown, realised by successively inserting several rockets of different diameters. The text and illustrations depict a rocket with two firing sequences, executed from two rockets inserted into each other. Also shown are 'rocket arrows' with stabilising fins in the shape of a delta, as they were also to be used in the Concorde supersonic aircraft.

Again and again, Haas gives free rein to his creativity under the cue of concrete questions such as 'Wie du schöne Raketen machen sollst, die von selbst in die Höhe fahren und auf ebener Erde hin und her' [How to make beautiful rockets that go up by themselves and back and forth on level ground].[18] Haas has also thought of people as air passengers. On the reverse side of sheet 215 we see the 'flying house' – nothing less than a precursor of a space capsule.

The manuscript, which is now kept in Bucharest consists of 282 leaves, in the format 16 × 21 cm in the shape of a book and is littered with illustrations, to be precise 203 drawings, some of which are executed in several colours, red, blue, yellow, green, violet and brown, and also contains a number of blank pages. The exact time at which the work was bound could not be determined. The leather binding, with partially abraded embossing and remnants of the former clasps, probably worn to this form during the writing or during the activity of the last author, is of the type common for books in the first half of the sixteenth century.[19]

Conrad Haas' 'Kunstbuch' belongs to the genre that has been labelled as Firework Books.[20] In the exhaustive list in Chris Philip's *Bibliography of Firework Books* we also find *Künstliche und rechtschaffene Feuerwerk* [Artificial and Righteous Fireworks] by Johannes Schmidlap published 1590 in Nuremberg by Katharina Gerlachin. In this work, which comprises 77 pages in small format,

---

18   Doru Todericiu, 'Raketentechnik im 16. Jahrhundert. Bemerkungen zu einer in Sibiu (Hermannstadt) vorhandenen Handschrift des Conrad Haas', *Technikgeschichte*, 34 (1967), pp. 97–11, here p. 106.

19   Todericiu, 'Raketentechnik im 16. Jahrhundert', p. 98.

20   Chris Philip: *A Bibliography of Firework Books. Works on Recreative Fireworks from the 16th to the 20th century* (Winchester: C. Philip in association with St. Paul's Bibliographies, 1985), see also Simon Werrett, *Fireworks. Pyrotechnic Arts & Sciences in European History* (University of Chicago Press 2010).

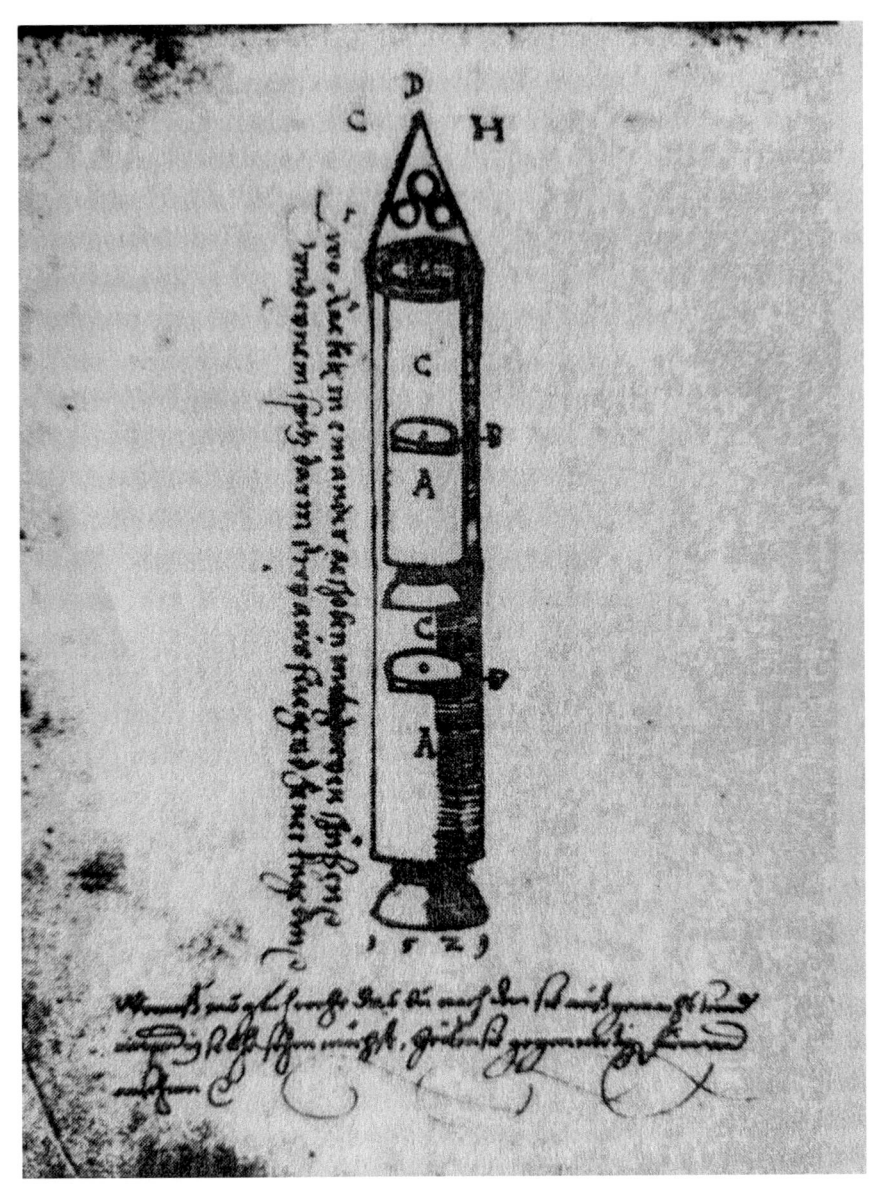

FIGURE 7.14   Rocket with two stages (drawing) from Conrad Haas, (Hermannstädter) Kunstbuch, Manuscript in the Bucharest, National Archives, Ms. 2286 (Todericiu, Rakentechnik, S. 104)

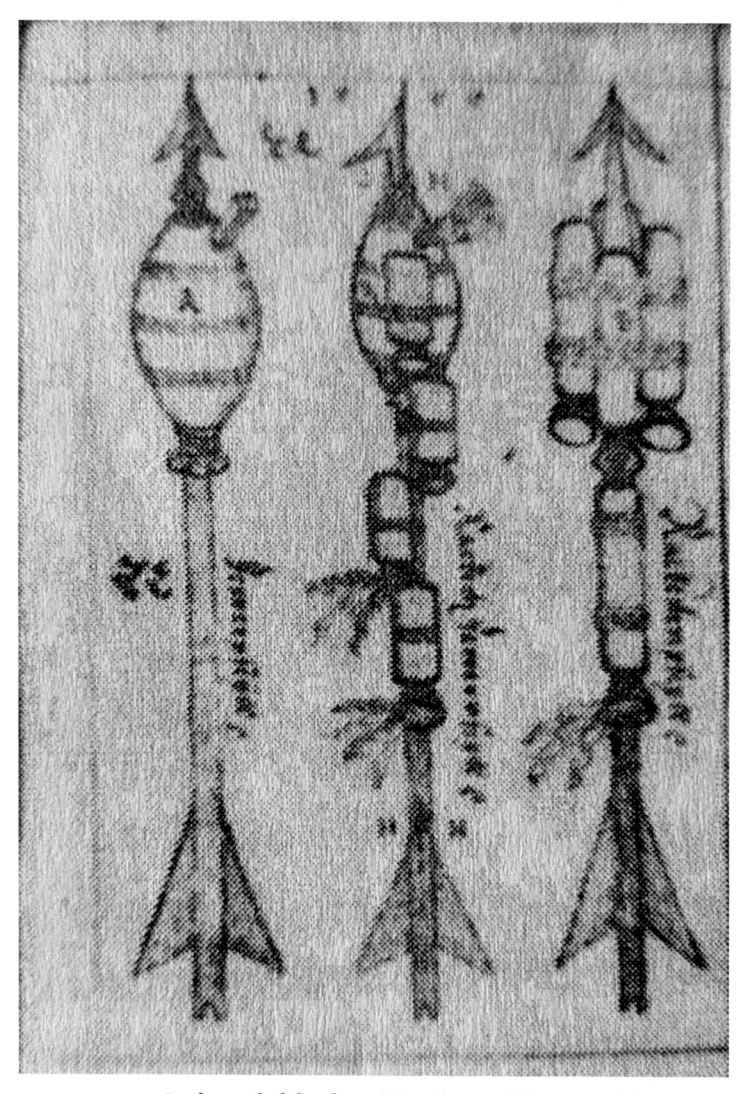

FIGURE 7.15   Rocket with delta shaped fins (drawing) from Conrad Haas,
                (Hermannstädter) Kunstbuch, Bucharest, National Archives,
                Ms. 2286 (Todericiu, Rakentechnik, S. 105)

one finds entire sections and graphic reproductions from Conrad's manuscript
without Schmidlap having acknowledged this reference, a typical example of
piracy in a time that was still largely alien to the idea of copyright.[21]

---

21   Todericiu, 'Raketentechnik im 16. Jahrhundert', p. 107; see also Adrian Johns: *Piracy. The*
      Intellectual Property Wars from Gutenberg to Gates (Chicago: The University of Chicago
      Press 2010).

FIGURE 7.16   The 'fliegende Haus' (drawing) from Conrad Haas, (Hermannstädter)
Kunstbuch, National Archives, Bucharest, Ms. 2286 (Todericiu, Rakentechnik,
S. 106)

4   Some Conclusions: Flying through Time

Haas visualizes technical processes in the style of an instruction manual, similar to Georg Agricola in his richly illustrated standard work *De Re Metallica*.[22] With Haas, the viewer is always the potential rebuilder. And from the difference between manuscript and print it follows inevitably that Agricola addressed thousands of the interested public with his know-how hints, while Haas's handwritten papers could reach only a very small inner circle in his practical ideas. With Schmidlap's printed tract, this was to change. And the cutaways of the twentieth century? They bring the anatomy of the aircraft to a mass audience with inviting, colourful illustrations and make their equipment and operation comprehensible. These aircraft seem far too complex to be recreated by interested amateurs. What remains is the 'alert mind' that only knows the theory behind the practice.

In the long-term perspective of the relationship between text and image the question is raised, why should the same, or at least similar, phenomena appear in the form of early modern 'How to Do Its', specifically with pedagogical orientation, and then in the twentieth century, in the form of Cutaways? The latter were then dropped, in the case of *Pilote* or the dying out of the *Eagle*, towards the end of the century, only to see a later revival in pastiche form.

On a first level I would refer to what I have called, in *Text/Image Mosaics*, 'parallel mentalities'.[23] In brief, whereas the Middle Ages might be seen as an age dominated by the image, the stained-glass windows of the great cathedrals, and the nineteenth century that of the cultural text – the lengthy novels of Dickens, Zola and Balzac – the transitional period between the two, the Emblematic Age, was that of text/image culture. The twentieth century, transitioning between the text-based culture of the positivist era and that of the cinema, television and internet image, was a new emblematic age. I would update by saying that the twenty-first century involves a new online text, a hyper-text that by-passes traditional gatekeepers, thus the vogue of nostalgia, sometimes expressed through pastiches, for old technologies.

In terms of 'How to Do Its' I think the key in our two parallel cases lies in the words of Joannes David, 'Invisibilium per visibilia contemplatio'. The examples we have considered function specifically through the technique of allowing us

---

22   Thus – to cite just one example – a hydraulic suction pump is depicted with letter indices in several stages of its composition; see Jasmin Meerhoff, *'Read me!'Eine Kultur- und Mediengeschichte der Bedienungsanleitung*, (Bielefeld: transcript, 2011), pp. 47–50.

23   Laurence Grove, *Text/Image Mosaics in French Culture: Emblems and Comic Strips* (Aldershot: Ashgate/Routledge, 2005).

to see what we normally could not see, the inside and outside of an object at once, so as to understand, with textual interaction, both the object itself – the outside – and what it represents – the inside.

Finally, why planes? Thinking about it personally, I can understand how a ship floats, or how a car moves forward, but I have never fully understood how a plane flies. For me, to understand that is a leap of faith.[24] Which according to the visual teachings of the Jesuits, is also how we find God.

---

24   Adamowsky, *Wunder in der Moderne*, passim.

CHAPTER 8

Playing with Recipe Conventions in *Den sack der consten*

Andrea van Leerdam

For whom, and for what purposes, did recipe collections appear in print?[1] Contrary to handwritten recipe collections, printed recipe books cannot usually be considered the result of the personal interests of an author or collector. Instead, we need to look for other factors to understand how and why these works were created and read. A key factor, in any case, was commerce: printed editions had to be commercially viable, they had to appeal in some way or another to a sufficiently large audience. To what extent did the appeal of printed recipes lie in their informative content and practical usability, and to what extent did other aspects weigh in? This paper uses the case of *Den sack der consten*, a collection of recipes and instructions printed in Dutch in 1528 and 1537, to demonstrate how purposes of instruction and entertainment could interact. Moreover, I aim to show how the concept of convention is helpful for unravelling how a printed recipe book may have been read. In this case, the book played with various textual and visual conventions, including genre conventions of the recipe. Moreover, the book invited the readers to engage in a play with conventions themselves. With a mixture of playful and practically applicable instructions, *Den sack der consten* aimed to provide entertainment for all ages. Thus, I will argue, if we consider printed recipes from a too narrow focus on practical usability, we risk to miss the essence of how a work like *Den sack der consten* will have been used.[2]

---

1   Parts of the analysis presented in this paper are also incorporated in my dissertation *Woodcuts as Reading Guides. How Images Shaped Knowledge Transmission in Medical-Astrological Books in Dutch (1500–1550)* (Amsterdam: Amsterdam University Press, 2024). This PhD research was conducted at Utrecht University, The Netherlands, with a grant from the Dutch Research Council NWO, and completed in 2022.

2   On entertainment functions of recipes, see also Laura Balbiani's contribution in the present volume and, regarding manuscripts, Marco Heiles, 'Das Wunderbare in der deutschen Rezeptliteratur des 15. Jahrhunderts', in Stefanie Kreuzer and Uwe Durst (eds.), *Das Wunderbare. Dimensionen eines Phänomens in Kunst und Kultur* (Paderborn: Fink, 2018), pp. 233–250.

Den sack der consten survives in two illustrated editions in Dutch from the first half of the sixteenth century, both of them printed in Antwerp: by Jacob van Liesvelt in 1528 and by Willem Vorsterman in 1537.[3] Both editions survive in a single copy; their low survival rate suggests that these books were heavily used.[4] The work continued to be printed (with further additions and alterations) in the later sixteenth century and even in the seventeenth and the eighteenth centuries.[5] My focus here is on the earliest two editions. *Den sack der consten* is a collection of practical as well as amusing recipes, tips and tricks for all kinds of domestic and medical issues, interspersed with some twenty woodcuts in each edition, which I will discuss in more detail below. It includes recipes and instructions to catch fish at night, to pull an egg through a golden ring, to remove unwanted hair, to make an ever-burning light, to know if a pregnant woman will have a boy or a girl, and much more. Vorsterman's 1537 edition contains eighteen recipes that were not yet included in Van Liesvelt's 1528 edition, and its woodcuts are nearly all different from those in the 1528 edition.[6] According to the 1528 title page, the content of the

---

3 *Den sack der consten* (Antwerp: Jacob van Liesvelt, 1528) USTC 437394. *Den sack der consten* (Antwerp: Willem Vorsterman, 1537) USTC 437907. In 1529, Willem Vorsterman also published a translation in French: *Le sacq des Ars et sciences* (Antwerp: Willem Vorsterman, 1529) USTC 80711. On the French edition, see Willy L. Braekman, *'Den sack der consten': een Vlaams volksboek, gereproduceerd naar de Antwerpse druk van Jacob van Liesvelt uit 1528* (Bruges: Van de Wiele, 1989), p. 23 and Wouter Nijhoff and M.E. Kronenberg, *Nederlandsche bibliographie van 1500 tot 1540* (3 vols., The Hague: M. Hijhoff, 1923–1971), nr. 3829 [NK 3829]. Like both Dutch editions, this French edition survives in a single copy (Paris, Bibliothèque nationale de France, RES P-R-341). It includes the same recipes as the 1528 Dutch edition, but in a different order, and nearly all of the woodcuts are different. The title page woodcut is closely copied after that of 1528. The existence of a French edition from 1529 makes it likely that Vorsterman already published a (now-lost) edition in Dutch around that time, as also suggested by Peter M.H. Cuijpers, *Teksten als koopwaar: vroege drukkers verkennen de markt. Een kwantitatieve analyse van de productie van Nederlandstalige boeken (tot circa 1550) en de 'lezershulp' in de seculiere prozateksten* (Nieuwkoop: De Graaf, 1998), p. 291.

4 Edition 1528: Amsterdam, Allard Pierson/University of Amsterdam, OTM: Ned. Inc. 290. Edition 1537: London, British Library, C.133.b.28.(3.). The only surviving copy of the 1537 edition misses the title page, but considering the edition's strong similarity to that of 1528, and considering the title of Vorsterman's 1529 French edition, it is likely that his 1537 edition was also titled *Den sack der consten*. On survival rates as indicators of use, see Andrew Pettegree, 'The Legion of the Lost. Recovering the Lost Books of Early Modern Europe', in: Flavia Bruni and Andrew Pettegree (eds.), *Lost Books. Reconstructing the Print World of Pre-Industrial Europe* (Leiden: Brill, 2016), pp. 1–27, here p. 2.

5 Braekman, *Sack der consten*, pp. 16–24 offers an overview of editions. After 1537 there is a substantial gap: the next surviving Dutch edition appeared in 1589.

6 Braekman, *Sack der consten*, pp. 57–58 on the added recipes in the 1537 edition and p. 18 on the woodcuts.

book is *ghecopuleert* ('copulated', i.e. compiled) from Latin, Italian, French, and German sources (Fig. 8.1).

In the preface, the printer (Jacob van Liesvelt) says that he found a book printed in Italy which he now prints 'in our language'.[7] Willy L. Braekman, an expert of Middle Dutch instructive literature and one of the very few scholars who have studied *Den sack der consten*, has observed that various recipes were taken from Hieronymus Brunschwig's *Die distellacien ende virtuyten der wateren* (Brussels: Thomas van der Noot, 1517) and the 'book of secrets' *Tbouck van wondre* (Brussels: Thomas van der Noot, 1513).[8] Brunschwig's distillation manual is commonly considered to provide serious knowledge rather than jestful entertainment. Conversely, *Tbouck van wondre* contains a substantial part of 'prescriptions from the tradition of "secrets" for joyful performance', as Arjan van Dixhoorn has pointed out.[9] *Den sack der consten* not only includes a number of these joyful tricks, but it also contains two mock recipes which make unequivocally clear that not everything should be taken seriously here. The preface of the 1528 edition says that the book contains 'some silly things for the youngsters and some other things' (*som wat sots voor die ionghers ende som anders*), thus explicitly indicating the presence of jestful content and explicitly including young readers among its target audiences.[10] Braekman notes that in 1621 the Antwerp bishop Malderus placed the work on a list of

---

7   The 1537 edition retains this prologue, written in the first person, thus suggesting it is now
         Willem Vorsterman who is addressing the reader.

8   Braekman, *Sack der consten*, pp. 13–14. Braekman confuses the 1517 Dutch translation of
         Brunschwig's *Liber de arte distillandi* (*Die distellacien ende virtuyten der wateren*, USTC
         400365) with the same-titled work that Van der Noot published in 1520 (*Die discelacien
         [sic] ende virtuyten der wateren*, USTC 437083), which is much smaller and contains a
         different text than the Brunschwig translation. Braekman refers to this edition of *c.*1520
         (which does not mention Brunschwig anywhere) as a source for *Den sack der consten* but
         the examples he provides are from the 1517 translation of Brunschwig.

9   On *Tbouck van wondre* (USTC 436878): Arjan van Dixhoorn, 'Nature, Play and the Middle
         Dutch Knowledge Community of Brussels in the Late Fifteenth and Early Sixteenth
         Centuries', in Bettina Noak (ed.), *Wissenstransfer und Auctoritas in der frühneuzeit-
         lichen niederländischsprachigen Literatur*, (Göttingen: V&R Unipress, 2014), pp. 99–121,
         esp. pp. 117–120, citation on p. 117. On Brunschwig's distillation book: Van Dixhoorn,
         'Nature, Play and the Middle Dutch Knowledge Community', pp. 116–117; Tillmann Taape,
         'Distilling Reliable Remedies: Hieronymus Brunschwig's *Liber de arte distillandi* (1500)
         between Alchemical Learning and Craft Practice', *Ambix*, 61 (2014), pp. 236–256; Tillmann
         Taape, 'Common Medicine for the Common Man: Picturing the 'Stripped Layman' in
         Early Vernacular Print', *Renaissance Quarterly*, 74 (2021), pp. 1–58.

10   *Sack der consten* 1528, fol. A1v.

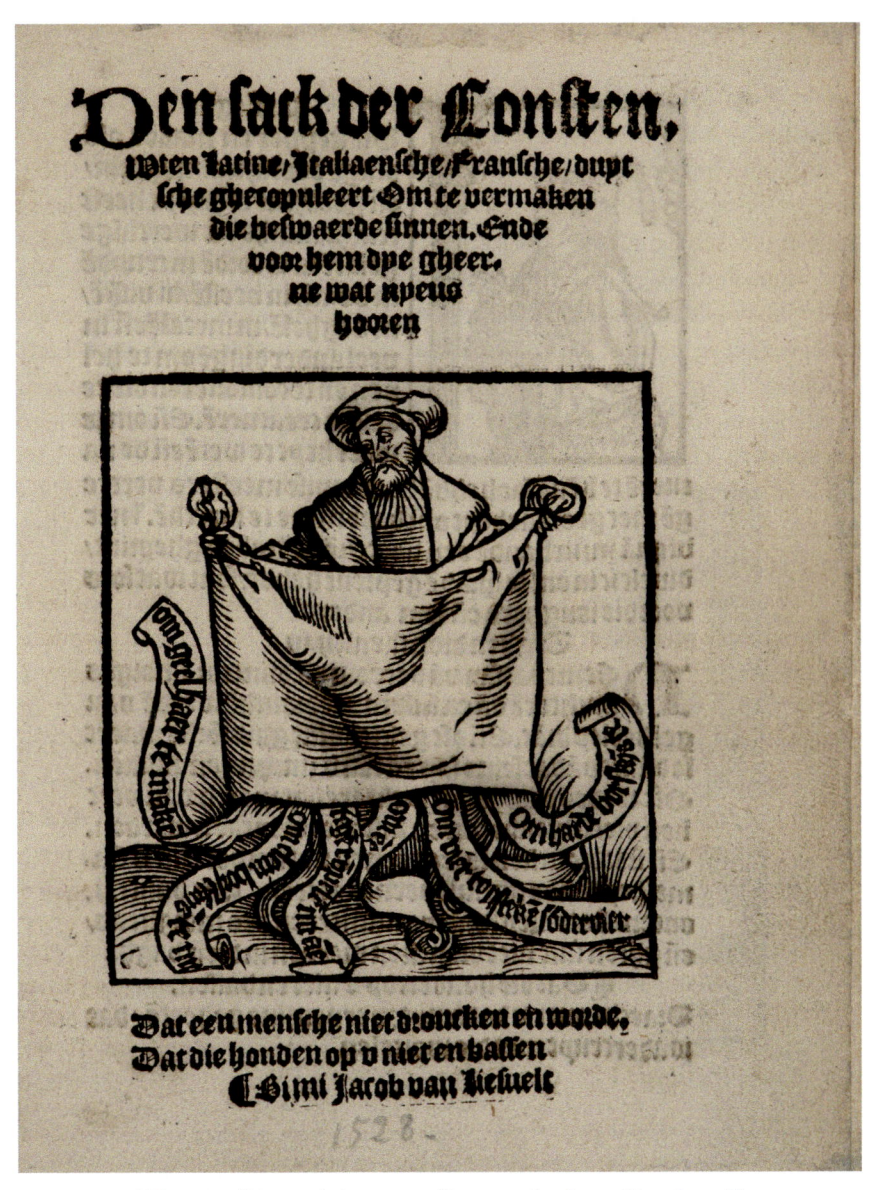

FIGURE 8.1   Title page of *Den sack der consten* (Antwerp: Jacob van Liesvelt, 1528).
Amsterdam, University of Amsterdam/Allard Pierson, OTM: Ned. Inc. 290

books deemed unsuitable for use in schools, implying that it was read there
until that time.[11]

---

11   Braekman, *Sack der consten*, p. 16.

1   Textual and Visual Conventions

Den sack der consten has been situated in the tradition of 'books of secrets'
and popular science.[12] Its content and appearance raise questions about our
assumptions regarding 'books of secrets' and other recipe collections. How
clearly delineated are these genres, to contemporary readers as well as to
present-day scholars? How 'practical' is the knowledge that recipes convey?
And what, indeed, makes a text identifiable as a recipe? In his influential
study of 'books of secrets', William Eamon describes the popularity across
Europe since ca. 1500 of printed 'treatises that professed to reveal the "secrets
of nature" to anyone who could read'.[13] These 'secrets', of nature itself as well
as of craftsmen who worked with natural substances, were presented through
recipes and technical prescriptions related to a vast variety of subjects, including medicine, painting, cookery, alchemy and magic. Although *Den sack der
consten* does not use the term 'secrets', its prologue draws on the same topos
that can be encountered in many 'books of secrets' as well as herbals and
distillery manuals, among others: God has endowed nature (herbs, stones,
animals etc.) with powers that humans can use to their benefit, and therefore
it is important to have knowledge of nature.[14] Moreover, the term *consten* –
'arts' – in the title was a key term, as Arjan van Dixhoorn has demonstrated, in
the discourse of the vernacular knowledge communities in the Low Countries
where a fascination with practical arts, experiment, and the manipulation of
nature had a central place.[15] The prologue of *Den sack der consten* points out
that 'wise masters' have made extensive study of nature to work with its powers. It also includes a section with recipes that are introduced as 'approbated

12   Braekman situates the work in the tradition of 'books of secrets'; Braekman, *Sack der
consten*, p. 7–12. Ria Jansen-Sieben categorises it under 'kunstboek' (i.e. 'arts book')
in her *Repertorium van de Middelnederlandse artesliteratuur* (Utrecht: HES, 1989),
p. 87. The anonymous contribution (dated 27 July 1992) on the website *Jeroen Bosch
Plaza* points to the work's ambiguous nature: 'Naar de vorm is *Den Sack der Consten*
een volksboek, naar de inhoud is het een zogenaamd 'secretenboekje' (onder te bren-
gen bij de artesliteratuur).' [In form, *Den sack der consten* is a chapbook, in content, it
is a so-called 'book of secrets' (to be classified as arts literature)], https://jeroenbosch
plaza.com/literaire-bron/sack-der-consten-ed-1989/ (accessed 19 July 2022).

13   William Eamon, *Science and the Secrets of Nature: Books of Secrets in Medieval and Early
Modern Culture* (Princeton: Princeton University Press, 1994), p. 3.

14   On this topos, see Van Leerdam, *Woodcuts as Reading Guides*, pp. 90–91, 130, 156–158.

15   Van Dixhoorn, 'Nature, Play and the Middle Dutch Knowledge Community', pp. 105, 113;
Arjan van Dixhoorn, 'Recreating Man's Cunning Virtues – The Philosophical Project of
Netherlandish Arts Culture', *Renaissance Studies* 32:1 (special issue on 'The Knowledge
Culture of the Netherlandish Rhetoricians', edited by Arjan van Dixhoorn, Samuel Mareel
and Bart Ramakers), pp. 23–42.

(*geapprobeert*) by masters such as Arnoldus de Villanova and Mesue and various others'.[16] Thus, on the one hand, the book clearly situates itself in this broader discourse of the quest for knowledge of nature, in which experiment and reliance on traditional authorities went hand in hand. On the other hand, such knowledge is intertwined in *Den sack der consten* with elements of jest and mockery to such an extent that they are hard to tell apart.

To get a better grasp of the reading experiences that the work may have incited and of the ways in which printed recipes could provide entertainment, I propose to use the concept of convention. From a communication perspective, conventions can be understood as social codes embedded in speech, text, or design that offer crucial grip for interpreting the messages that a speech act, a document or other artefact conveys.[17] Bold text signals importance, the presence of footnotes in a text makes us expect scholarly content, and when someone says 'Shhhhh' we understand they want us to be silent. Precisely because conventions are so common, we are not always aware of the strong extent to which they guide our expectations and interpretations. In addition to textual and linguistic conventions, readers/viewers are strongly guided by visual conventions, as Charles Kostelnick and Michael Hassett have foundationally demonstrated in an analysis of visual conventions in professional communication (documents, data displays, illustrations, etc.).[18] They argue that design (including information design) is inherently conventional: 'Information design is infused with conventional codes – local and global, textual and nontextual – which are blended in any given document to satisfy the needs and expectations of readers'.[19] Both textual and visual conventions, then, constitute the essence of (communicative or literary) genres: conventional features enable readers to situate a text in a certain genre (e.g. a newspaper, a letter, a novel, a scholarly article) and adjust their expectations accordingly, usually already before they have read a single word.[20] A key characteristic of

16   *Den sack der consten* 1528, fol. B4v; *Den sack der consten* 1537, fol. C1r.

17   Donald Davidson, 'Communication and Convention', *Synthese*, 59 (1984), pp. 3–17. Charles Kostelnick and Michael Hassett, *Shaping Information: The Rhetoric of Visual Conventions* (Carbondale, IL: Southern Illinois University Press, 2003); Gunther Kress and Theo van Leeuwen, *Reading Images. The Grammar of Visual Design* (London/New York: Routledge, 2006); Andrei Marmor, *Social Conventions: From Language to Law* (Princeton University Press 2009), esp. chapters 3 and 4, pp. 79–130.

18   Kostelnick and Hassett, *Shaping Information*.

19   Kostelnick and Hassett, *Shaping Information*, p. 17.

20   Jeanne-Louise Moys, 'Visual Rhetoric in Information Design. Designing for Credibility and Engagement', in Alison Black, Paul Luna, Ole Lund and Sue Walker (eds.), *Information Design. Research and Practice* (London/New York: Routledge Black, 2017), pp. 204–220, here p. 206; Jürgen Spitzmüller, *Graphische Variation als soziale Praxis: Eine soziolinguistische*

conventions is their deeply social nature: what is considered conventional evolves and differs across cultures and periods.[21] For this reason, it is important to identify and analyse conventions critically for the early period of print and to avoid taking our own assumptions about genres, book design, and image-text relations for granted.

Conventions, I'd like to argue, are excellently suited as an analytical concept for the study of recipes. On the one hand, recipes are a text type that is strongly tied to textual as well as visual conventions. Even though the precise content of a recipe may vary greatly every time it is written down, the structure and format of a recipe mostly follow conventions: a recipe text describes practical actions required to achieve a certain result with the aid of certain ingredients and tools.[22] Early printed recipes are often demarcated from each other visually, for example through white spaces, initials, or paragraph signs, and they commonly start with a specification of the desired result, often formatted as a header (for a smooth skin, against toothache, to know whether a pregnant woman will have a boy or a girl, etc.).[23] On the other hand, conventions for collections of recipes are much less well-defined, as recipes occur in a range of different text types that each have their own conventions, including 'books

Theorie skripturaler 'Sichtbarkeit' (Berlin/Boston: De Gruyter Mouton, 2013), esp. p. 278; John A. Bateman, *Multimodality and Genre: A Foundation for the Systematic Analysis of Multimodal Documents* (Basingstoke etc.: Palgrave Macmillan, 2008), esp. pp. 9–11 and 177–178; Irma Taavitsainen, 'Genres and the Appropriation of Science: *Loci Communes* in English in the Late Medieval and Early Modern Period', in Janne Skaffari, Matti Peikola, and Ruth Carroll etc. (eds.), *Opening Windows on Texts and Discourses of the Past* (Amsterdam/Philadelphia: John Benjamins Publishing, 2005), pp. 179–196, here pp. 183–184; Kostelnick and Hassett, *Shaping Information*, pp. 96–99.

21   Kostelnick and Hassett, *Shaping Information*. Marmor, *Social Conventions*.

22   Carrie Griffin, 'Reconsidering the Recipe: Materiality, Narrative and Text in Later Medieval Instructional Manuscripts and Collections', in Emma Cayley and Susan Powell (eds.), *Manuscripts and Printed Books in Europe 1350–1550: Packaging, Presentation and Consumption* (Liverpool: Liverpool University Press, 2015), pp. 135–149; Martti Mäkinen, 'Efficacy Phrases in Early Modern English Medical Recipes', in Irma Taavitsainen and Päivi Pahta (eds.), *Medical Writing in Early Modern English* (Cambridge University Press, 2011), pp. 158–179, here pp. 160–161; Irma Taavitsainen, 'Middle English Recipes: Genre Characteristics, Text Type Features and Underlying Traditions of Writing', *Journal of Historical Pragmatics*, 2:1 (2001), pp. 85–113.

23   On the uses of white space and paragraph signs (also known as pilcrows) to visually demarcate paragraphs, see Keith Houston, *Shady Characters. The Secret Life of Punctuation, Symbols and Other Typographical Marks* (New York/London: Norton & Company, 2013), pp. 3–25; Frans A. Janssen, 'The Rise of the Typographical Paragraph', in: Karl A.E. Enenkel and Wolfgang Neuber (eds.), *Cognition and the Book: Typologies of Formal Organisation of Knowledge in the Printed Book of the Early Modern Period* (Leiden: Brill, 2004), pp. 9–32.

of secrets', health regimens, surgery manuals, and herbals.[24] The concept of convention may thus help to establish with precision in what respects recipes are presented similarly or differently across different works, and to identify where and why breaches of genre conventions occur. *Den sack der consten* adheres to various conventions of 'books of secrets' and popular science; for example in terms of its visual presentation as a collection of individual recipes (each marked by an indented first line and a paragraph sign, without any visual distinction between serious and jestful recipes) and its discourse of wise masters who have uncovered the powers of nature – while it also betrays a play with conventions, as we will now see, through the presence of mock recipes and images.

2 Mockery and 'Impropriety'

Let us take a closer look at the mock recipe at the end of *Den sack der consten*, as it signals most overtly that practical use was not the book's sole purpose (Fig. 8.2).[25] By parodying conventional recipes, it draws on the reader's knowledge of these conventions: the joke can only be appreciated by those who are familiar with the common recipe format. The mock recipe proclaims to give a 'friendly' cure for toothache that contains ingredients such as 'a handful of vanity' and 'a little ignorance'. It instructs to cook them in 'a pot of transience' with 'the fire of profligacy' and then mix them with 'two ounces of anger', 'a pound of adultery', and a range of other mock ingredients in 'a vessel without discretion' and apply it to sore teeth for nine nights and a day. The recipe is attributed to *meester Arnout vander hagen prouoost van Commerkercken etc* ('ordinated and issued by master Arnout van der Hagen, provost of Sufferkirk etc.').[26]

Thus, the recipe follows the conventional format, including an authority reference to underline the recipe's reliability and efficacy, but the ingredients as well as the authority are parodied.[27] To contemporary readers, master Arnout's provenance of Commerkercken will have been an evident signal of ridicule:

24   See also Griffin, 'Reconsidering the Recipe'.
25   In both editions, the recipe is on fol. C3v–C4r.
26   In the 1537 edition, the master is called *arnout vander niethagen*.
27   On authority references in recipes: Andrea van Leerdam, 'Beproefde medicamenten', in Dineke van Krimpen, Mirjam van Velzen-Barendsen etc., *Pro memorie. Het geneeskundig receptenboek van Christina Poppincks, 1613* (forthcoming); Ville Marttila, 'New Arguments for New Audiences. A Corpus-Based Analysis of Interpersonal Strategies in Early Modern English Medical Recipes', in Taavitsainen and Pahta, *Medical Writing in Early Modern English*, pp. 135–157, here pp. 148–151.

salmen oochlaumaken ende doecken daer inne net
ten ende flaenfefolau om die boiften fo enfullenfefo
groot niet worden. Oor water vā wilde peeren ofte
hout peren is oocgoet voor maechden dye haer vor-
ften te groot en te flap werden die fullen neme doer-
ken en netten die in dat water en legghen die twee
of drie werfdes taechs op die boifte/fo bluue de boifte
daer af te cleender en werden hart

℧Om te maken harde boiften
Reemt water van wilde peeren en net doechte daer
in/en flaet die om die boiften twee oft dye werf des
daechs fo werden die boiften hart

Oft neemt water van onrype fteen ende netret
daer doecken in/en flaet die om die boiften/dat doet
die flappe boiften hart werden

℧Om gheelhaer te maken.
Reemt die wortel vā Aubea of Cleb crupt in duitfce
en fiet dat in looge en wafcht v haer daer met.

℧Teghen die hitte der peftilencien
Blau violertten water gedroncken en den brāt dair
mede gemenget is goet daer tegen. Oft kēpē werc
genet in huyfloot water en daer op geleit een luttel
gemengelt met roofwater en die leden dair met ge
wreuen is feer goet tegen die hitte der peftilencien.

℧Defe wateren vvoetfept fijn al ghedistilleert of
gebrande wateren van crupden en ander vruchten

℧Een vriendelijcke medecine voor die pijne der
tanden gheoordineert/ende wt ghegheuen bi meester Arnout vander haghen provost van Commer-
kerchen. ꝛc.

Reemt een hant vol pdelhept en fo
veel van vergetenthept/twee han
den vol van onwetenthept/en daer
toe een luttel van onwijfhept. Dan
neemt een halfpinte van haeftich;
en twee pont van vermetenthept/
een quaerte van onrepnichept.iij.
quaerten van fortfe en gewelt. Hie
bet dit flamen in eenen pot van ver
ganchelijchept/net dat vier vā ver
quilten/fchupmt dat metten lepele
der valfcher fupuerhept/ente ftapt
dat inden mortier der meenedich;
met een half onche der ongeloouir.
hept/twee oncen van boofhept.iiij.
onchen van woeckerie/ente fo veel
van fimonie ende flatterie/ce pont
van ouerfpel/vier pont van ontwpfhept/ander hal
ue quaerte van traechept/ende fo veel van verfun-
menthept/menghelt defe al tfamen met een luttel
verftante in een vat fonder difcretien/dan doet die
aen vfeer tanden ende vfeert dat neghen nachten/
ende eeuen dach/en uwen tantfweere fal vergaen,

℧Van alle medecinen
is dit die befte
Alle eerfame lefers die dit fien oft verftaen
Aliffer fomtijts bupten fweerchs ghegaen
Maert geen vermaē/maer wilt doch int befte ftaē.
Tis gedaen om durs verflaen int iaer ons heeren,
Als nu van.ꝛꝛviij.om vruechts vermeeren
Bi Jacob van Liefuelt om conften te leeren

FIGURE 8.2   Mock recipe against toothache 'ordinated by master Arnout van der Hagen provost of
Sufferkirk' at the end of *Den sack der consten* (1528), fols. C3v–C4r. Amsterdam, University
of Amsterdam/Allard Pierson, OTM: Ned. Inc. 290

this fictitious place appears in other contemporary parodic texts as well.[28]
In the 1528 edition, the mock recipe is even illustrated with a purported portrait of master Arnout. This stock image of a standing man who wears a long,
fur-lined gown with wide arms recalls conventional depictions of scholars and
medical professionals.[29]

The mock recipe thus typifies one of the three key sources of laughter as
distinguished in humour studies: incongruity. Simply put, incongruity theory

---

28   On Commerkercken: Hinke van Kampen, Herman Pleij, Bob Stumpel etc., *Het zal koud
zijn in 't water als 't vriest. Zestiende-eeuwse parodieën op gedrukte jaarvoorspellingen* (The
Hague: Martinus Nijhoff, 1980), pp. 120 and 191.

29   Stock figures in similar clothing appear, for example, in *Den groten herbarius met al sijn
figueren der cruyden* (Utrecht: Jan Berntsz, 1538, USTC 421086) to mark the end of a collection of remedies ('Anthidotarius', fol. V2v) and in *Chyromantia Ioannis Indagine* (Utrecht:
Jan Berntsz, 1536, USTC 421069) to mark the beginning of a treatise on how to take astrology into account when treating diseases ('Regulen van Cranckheyden', fol. P3v). In both
editions of *Den sack der consten*, stock images representing scholars appear on the page
of the prologue and at the beginning of the section that presents recipes approved by
Arnoldus de Villanova and other masters.

states that laughter can be incited when we are surprised by a sudden violation of our expectations.[30] The essence, then, of what makes the recipe funny lies in its play with convention, with what readers would expect of a recipe.

Following the mock recipe, a short disclaimer in verse requests the 'honourable readers' not to make any reproaches, 'even though there may have been some impropriety'.[31] It is surely not a coincidence that the most evident element of jest in the entire book is positioned at the end, right before this disclaimer, echoing the prologue's signals that the reader is not to take everything in this book seriously. The work leaves open just what the impropriety is and which elements may in fact be practically useful. Thus, the readers are challenged to decide this for themselves.

The ambiguity is already present on the title page (see Fig. 8.1). The woodcut there shows a bearded man (again in a fur-lined coat) emptying a sack. Text scrolls that are falling out of the sack indicate the type of light-hearted content the reader could expect: 'To make yellow [blond] hair', 'To ignite fire without fire', and 'For hard breasts …', among other things.[32] Though light-hearted, such life hacks undoubtedly enjoyed a genuine curiosity among various readers, as did many other recipes within the book, for example those to prevent mould on bread, to keep embers burning for a long time, to make a withering tree green again, to catch fleas, or to cure nosebleeds.

At the same time, the joint presence of such recipes with those for removing unwanted hair or wrinkles, or turning marital discord into peace, holds a mirror up to the human condition, to the many ailments and discomforts of life and the never-ending human pursuit of health and happiness. This comic mirror effect comes to the fore quite incisively in a moralising mock recipe halfway through the book.[33] It addresses perhaps the most universal human desire 'to live a long life' and instructs to achieve this by drinking a good sip every morning of the juice of patience mixed with quite some grace of God. Its positioning in between ordinary recipes for preserving pears and cherries enhances the surprise effect of incongruity all the more strongly.

---

30   John Morreall, 'Philosophy of Humor', in Edward N. Zalta (ed.) *The Stanford Encyclopedia of Philosophy* (Fall 2020 Edition), https://plato.stanford.edu/archives/fall2020/entries /humor/ (accessed 19 July 2022); Lisa Glebatis Perks, 'The Ancient Roots of Humor Theory', *Humor*, 25:2 (2012), pp. 119–132. The other two commonly accepted theories of laughter are superiority theory (we laugh at others out of a sense of our own superiority) and coping or relief theory (we laugh away anxieties).

31   Fol. C4r in both editions (*Al isser somtijts buyten sweechs ghegaen*).

32   *Den sack der consten* 1528, fol. A1r. The only surviving copy of the 1537 edition lacks the title page.

33   Fol. B3r in both the 1528 and the 1537 edition.

3 Reused Images: Reinterpreting Iconographic Conventions

The woodcuts in both editions reinforce the effect of a mirror of common human concerns, and they also play with conventions in doing so. It must have been a deliberate choice of the printers to add images in the first place and thus deviate from the genre conventions of 'books of secrets' and recipe collections.[34] Like virtually all choices made in the print shop, this must have been done with an eye to the target audience, possibly in this case to appeal to a broader or indeed different readership (including youngsters, as we saw). What is more, as I want to argue, the printers' choice of illustrations may also be interpreted as a play with conventions, full of allusions to familiar visual motifs that readers may have encountered in other contexts and that they were now challenged to interpret in new ways. Apart from the 1528 title page woodcut, none of the illustrations in the 1528 and 1537 editions seem to have been made specifically for *Den sack der consten*: they are true stock images, reused or copied from other works and again reused in later works. They depict, among other things, single figures of men and women, and scenes of eating, people lying in bed (a sick person in some images, a couple making love in others), defecating, old age, riding on horseback, making music, playing chess, and cooking fresh-caught fish. Many of these scenes, then, display everyday activities and situations of conversation. They reflect the kind of settings in which the presented recipes may be applied, while together they also reflect, as it were, a cross-section of human life.

Tellingly, many of these woodcuts reappear in contemporary editions of works of fiction as well as popular works on health, nature and astrology. They include images (copied or reused) that also appear in the stories of *Ulenspieghel* (a lost edition),[35] *The parson of Kalenborowe* (Antwerp: Jan van Doesborch,

---

34 For some book types that include recipes, such as herbals and distillation manuals, the insertion of images in the text was not uncommon, but in most cases these are predominantly epistemic images that focus on the particular characteristics of plants and instruments. Conversely, not a single image in the editions of *Den sack der consten* can be qualified as epistemic, i.e. intended to convey or demonstrate knowledge.

35 Loek Geeraedts (transl., ed. and intr.), *Het volksboek van Ulenspieghel. Naar de oudste, bewaard gebleven druk van Michiel Hillen van Hoochstraten te Antwerpen uit de eerste helft van de 16de eeuw* (Kapellen: De Nederlandsche Boekhandel/Uitgeverij Pelckmans 1986), pp. 60–61. Multiple 'Ulenspieghel' images recur in the 1528 edition of *Den sack der consten* and at least one in the 1537 edition.

1520s?)[36] and *Frederick van Jenuen* (Antwerp: Willem Vorsterman, 1531),[37] and in the almanac-like *Der scaepherders kalengier* (Antwerp: Willem Vorsterman, c.1514 and 1516),[38] the animal encyclopedia *Der dieren palleys* (Antwerp: Jan van Doesborch, 1520; a translation of chapters on animals from the *Hortus sanitatis*),[39] various editions of *Der vrouwen natuere ende complexie* (earliest known edition Utrecht: Jan van Doesborch, c.1531; a translation of the first two books of the *Liber physionomiae* by Michael Scotus (1175–c.1232) with added humorous elements),[40] and the medical-astrological compendium *Tscep vol wonders* (first printed in Brussels: Thomas van der Noot, 1514),[41] among many others. The interplay of practical usefulness and entertainment is thus reflected in the combination of sources where the selected woodcuts recur.

The reuse of image motifs (or indeed of the physical woodblocks) that also appear in other works can be interpreted as a way of playing with conventions. While the widespread practices of reusing and copying woodcuts may have had economic benefits to the book producers, as a matter of course they will also have had an effect on readers' interpretations. When readers encountered iconographies with which they were familiar from other contexts, they were challenged to forge new meanings for these images and perhaps even draw new connections between different works.[42] The 1528 edition of *Den sack der*

---

36   USTC 437148. Images that recur in *Den sack der consten*: a composite woodcut showing a kneeling man holding up a cup to another man (or woman?) and a winged figure above a wine barrel (ed. 1537: the two blocks appear separately); a naked couple in bed with a man hiding underneath the bed (ed. 1537).

37   USTC 437599. Images that recur in *Den sack der consten*: a man on horseback (ed. 1528); a woman lying in bed (ed. 1537), a naked, long-haired woman (ed. 1537, discussed below); a standing man holding a battle axe (ed. 1537).

38   Discussed below.

39   USTC 410142. Images that recur in *Den sack der consten*: a gathering of different bird species (ed. 1537), an old couple (ed. 1537; representing the melancholic complexion in *Der dieren palleys*).

40   Recurring images include the naked long-haired woman that also appears in *Frederick van Jenuen* (see above, note 37) in *Der vrouwen natuere ende complexie* (Utrecht, Jan Berntsz, c.1535, USTC 421110 and subsequent editions), the old couple that also appears in *Der dieren palleys* (see above, note 39) in *Der vrouwen natuere ende complexie* (Utrecht: Jan van Doesborch, c.1531, USTC 421109 and subsequent editions), and the naked couple being spied on that also appears in *The parson of Kalenborowe* (see above, note 36) in *Der vrouwen natuere ende complexie* (Utrecht, Jan Berntsz, c.1535, USTC 421110 and subsequent editions).

41   USTC 407305. Woodblocks that recur in *Den sack der consten*: purging (ed. 1537), the phlegmatic and melancholic complexions (ed. 1537).

42   See e.g. Daniel Bellingradt, 'The Dynamic of Communication and Media Recycling in Early Modern Europe: Popular Prints as Echoes and Feedback Loops', in Massimo Rospocher, Jeroen Salman and Hannu Salmi (eds.), *Crossing Borders, Crossing Cultures: Popular Print*

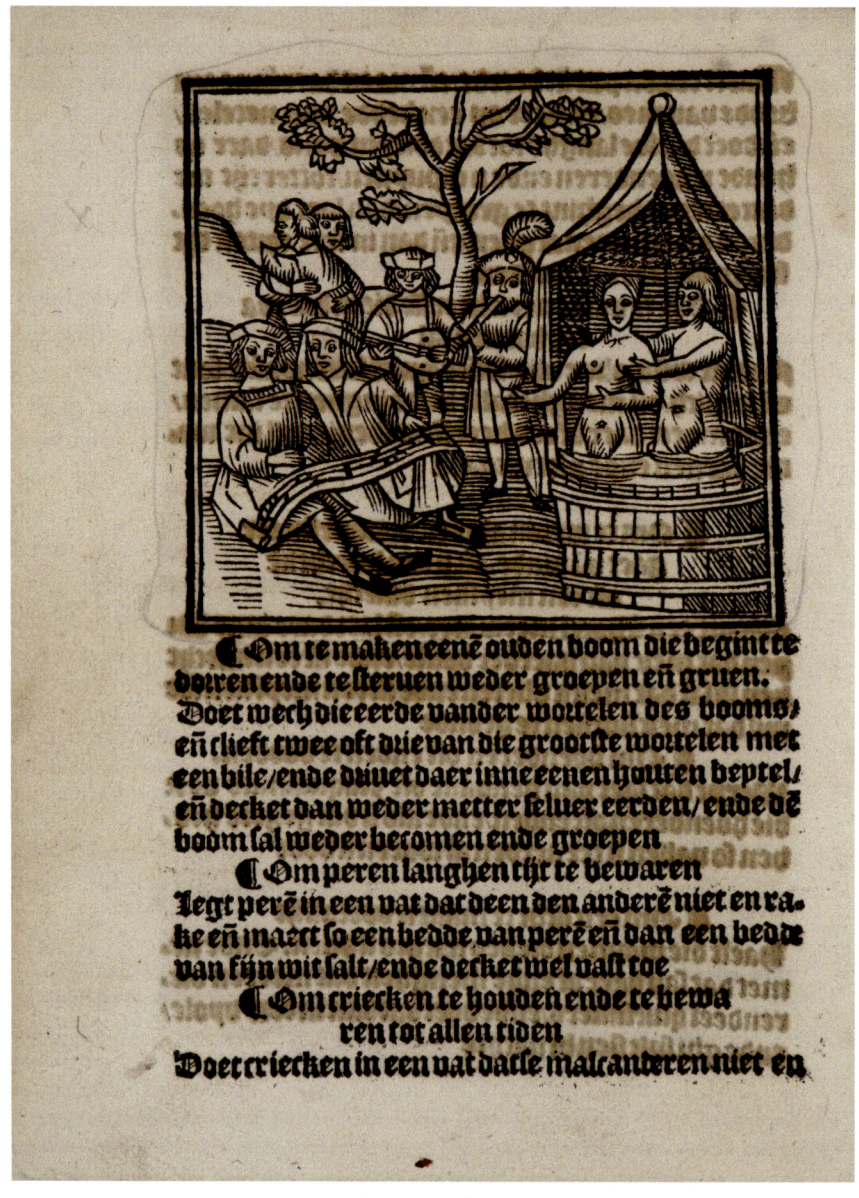

FIGURE 8.3 A woodcut representing Children of Venus accompanies an instruction to make
          an old dying tree green again. *Den sack der consten* (1528), fol. B2v. Amsterdam,
          University of Amsterdam/Allard Pierson, OTM: Ned. Inc. 290

Dit machmen aen venus kindern mercken
Schoone lichamen inder waerhept
Hebben si alsoe ons dorocius sept
Een ront aensicht seer schoon ooghen
Clepne wanghen mocht hi' geedooghen
Meer die waerhept der ooghen dan van node is
Hebben venus kinderen sijt dies ghewis
⁓⁓⁓⁓ ¶ander planeten Mercurius
Mercurius soe is minen name
Seer supuerlijck ende bequame
Ende ick ben ghemepn inder statueren
Metten heeten heet inder natueren
Ende metten couden cout dit moet ghi weten
Mijn hoochept en moechdi niet verghetẽ
Twee hondert dupsent milen hooghe

FIGURE 8.4 Children of Venus, woodcut in *Der scaepherders kalengier* (Antwerp: Willem Vorsterman, 1516), fol. h3v. Washington, DC, Library of Congress, Rosenwald 1137

consten includes a woodcut copied after the Children of Venus in *Der scaepherders kalengier*.[43]

It shows a bathing couple, the man embracing the woman and touching her breast, a group of four musicians, and two people embracing (Fig. 8.3). In the background is a tree of which some branches are bare and others have leaves. In *Der scaepherders kalengier*, the image serves to illustrate the sensuality and keenness on pleasure that was ascribed to people born under the influence of the planet Venus, while the tree refers to the springtime period when Venus was dominant (Fig. 8.4). This image, that draws on common motifs in the fifteenth- and sixteenth-century representation of the Children of the Planets, is used here in *Den sack der consten* to illustrate an instruction to make an old dying tree grow again (by splitting two or three of its largest roots). While the direct connection between text and image thus lies in the tree in the background, the prominent scene of merrymaking in the foreground will have added connotations of spring, fertility and love to any practical desire to revive a withering tree.

Another example is an image in the 1537 edition of *Den sack der consten* of a naked, long-haired woman who covers her genitals with a scarf-like cloth (Fig. 8.5).[44] She appears next to a choice of recipes to obtain smaller and firmer breasts. Earlier, she had been a key image in the narrative of *Frederick van Jenuen* (Antwerp: Willem Vorsterman, 1531), in the scene where 'Lord Frederick' reveals to the king that she is actually a woman (Fig. 8.6).

At first glance, the figure serves in *Den sack der consten* simply to signal 'breasts' (and perhaps to make the reader indulge a bit in some impropriety). At a deeper level, to readers familiar with *Frederick van Jenuen* (which was printed, after all, by the same printer and only a few years earlier than *Den sack der consten* of 1537), the image may have sparked further reflections on

---

      in Europe (1450–1900) (Munich: De Gruyter Oldenbourg, 2019), pp. 9–32; Katie Sisneros, 'Early Modern Memes: The Reuse and Recycling of Woodcuts in 17th-Century English Popular Print', *The Public Domain Review*, 6 June 2018, https://publicdomainreview .org/2018/06/06/early-modern-memes-the-reuse-and-recycling-of-woodcuts-in-17th-century -english-popular-print/ (accessed 19 July 2022); Patricia Fumerton and Megan E. Palmer, 'Lasting Impressions of the Common Woodcut', in Catherine Richardson, Tara Hamling, and David Gaimster (eds.), *The Routledge Handbook of Material Culture in Early Modern Europe* (London/New York: Routledge, 2016), pp. 383–400.

43   *Den sack der consten* 1528, fol. B2v. The woodcut closely resembles but is not identical to the block used in Willem Vorsterman's editions of *Der scaepherders kalengier* of c.1514 (USTC 403070) and 1516 (USTC 436942) and the block used in the 1520 *Der scaepherders kalengier* printed in Antwerp by Adriaen van Berghen (USTC 437082).

44   *Den sack der consten* 1537, fol. C3r.

Men sal die borsten bestrikē met winterlinc water of Cicuta int lath eñ dat water salmē ooc lau makē eñ doeckē daer in nettē/eñ slaē die so lau ō de borsten so en sullen si niet so groot werdē
¶ Ooc water vā wilde perē/ oft hout perē is ooc goet voor meechdē die hare borstē te groot eñ te slap werdē die sullē nemē doeckē eñ netten die in dat water eñ leggen die twee of driewerf tes daechs op de borstē so bliuē de borsten daer af te cleendr eñ werde hart.
¶ Om te makē harde borsten.
Neēt water van wilde peren eñ net daer doeckē in eñ slaet die om die borsten twee of driewerf des daechs/so werde die borstē hart.
Oft neemt water vā onrijpe sleen/eñ net daer in doeckē eñ slaet die om die borstē/dat doet die slappe borstē hart werdē.
¶ Dese wateren voorsept sijn al ghedisteleert oft ghebrande waterē vā crupdē eñ ander vruchten.
¶ Teghen den stanck vanden tanden.
Eedt een crupt dat fagus heet.
¶ Om die ghene die npet droncken en wil werden.
Hp sal eeten tsmorghens nuchteren vinckel saet
¶ Teghen die bloetsucht.
Neemt wperooc eñ tempert met witte van een ep eñ doeter van een hase bp ende nuttet.
¶ Teghen den steen inde blase.
Neemt cenen leuende hase ende doeten in eenen nauwen pot ende barnt hem te puluer ende dat puluer salmen houden in herten leer ende alsment wil orboren/so salment temperen met warme water ofte met wijne/ende men salt gheuen te drincken den gheenen die den steen heeft ende hp sallen wt pissen.

FIGURE 8.5 A woodcut of a naked woman accompanies recipes for small and firm breasts in *Den sack der consten* (Antwerp: Willem Vorsterman, 1537), fol. C3r. London, British Library, General Reference Collection C.133.b.28.(3.)

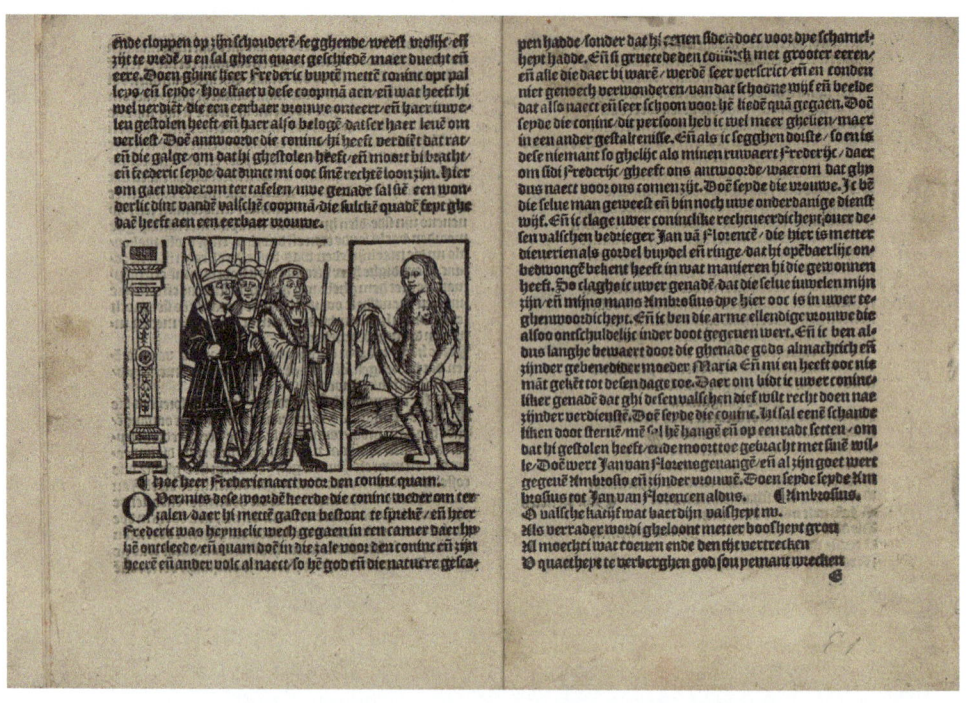

FIGURE 8.6 A woodcut of a naked woman as part of a composite illustration to the scene where 'Lord' Frederick van Jenuen reveals to be a woman in the prose romance *Van heer Frederick van Jenuen* (Antwerp: Willem Vorsterman, 1531), fol. D4v. Ghent, University Library, BHSL.RES.1070

gender relations (another domain imbued with conventions, some of which 'Frederick' evidently turned upside down), on what it means in everyday life to have breasts (socially, physically), and why a woman would want to have smaller and firmer breasts. As these two examples illustrate, this repurposing of iconographic conventions in a recipe context moves well beyond any practical purposes: the images do not have any instructive value, but they likely added to the readers' experience of entertainment and they situated the recipes in a social context.

The selections of images are largely different in both editions. This is remarkable, as in various contemporary Dutch works we see that once a title had been published with a certain set of images, these woodcuts were closely copied in subsequent editions, even if the images had initially been gathered from a variety of sources.[45] Although Vorsterman's 1537 edition of *Den sack der*

45 This happened for example in editions of *Der vrouwen natuere ende complexie* and of *Thuys der fortunen ende dat huys der doot*. See Van Leerdam, *Woodcuts as Reading Guides*, pp. 58–59, 372, 387.

consten does not copy the woodcuts of Van Liesvelt's 1528 edition, Vorsterman did take guidance from this previous edition for the positioning of the wood-cuts: several of them are inserted in the same place in the text. An instruction 'to cause that a horse does not want to go through a street' is illustrated in both editions with an image showing a horse, but they are different images in each case. Moreover, as this example and those discussed above illustrate, virtually all images, in both editions, bear some kind of connection to the text, if only loosely. Vorsterman evidently did not care to retain the exact motifs from the 1528 edition, but he did care to use similar motifs and, importantly, to visually create a similar mood.

4   Teaching the Reader to Play with Conventions

Conventions thus play various roles in how *Den sack der consten* entertains and indeed challenges its readers: recipe conventions are parodied, conventional iconographies and motifs from different contexts invite new interpretations, and the intertwinement of jestful and serious information leaves it up to the reader to determine whether and where any 'impropriety' in the sense of a deviation from social conventions occurs. What is more, the work challenges readers to play with conventions themselves, by means of tricks and practical jokes. Instructions to pull an egg through a ring, 'to make people at your table appear to be black', or 'to light a candle on the mouth of a painted or wooden image', however doubtful their practical use may be, all focus on defying expectations and achieving something that is highly unconventional, indeed deemed impossible.[46] These recipes and instructions thus also underscore the social nature of conventions and expectations: the tricks are to be performed in company, 'at your table' or in other social settings. Such tricks reflect similar ideas on the manipulation of nature and a fascination with experiment that underlie many contemporary 'serious' recipe collections. Through a conventional format, these trick recipes and technical instructions stimulate readers to achieve unconventional results.

---

46   For future research it would be interesting to attempt to reconstruct some of these recipes, succinct as they may be. This method might reveal whether any further (practical)
jokes may lie hidden in such recipes. On historical reconstruction, re-enactment and
replication as a research method, see Thijs Hagendijk, *Reworking Recipes. Reading and
Writing Practical Texts in the Early Modern Arts*, dissertation Utrecht University 2020,
https://dspace.library.uu.nl/handle/1874/397503 (accessed 19 July 2022); and the website of *The Making and Knowing Project* led by Pamela H. Smith at Columbia University,
https://www.makingandknowing.org/the-lab/ (accessed 19 July 2022).

5   Conclusion

To conclude, *Den sack der consten* exemplifies how printed recipe collections can serve different purposes than just providing practical instruction or a store of useful remedies and life hacks. The work evinces how 'practical' knowledge, whether or not practically useful, and its conventions were at the same time a source of mockery, occasional moralisations, and of what we might call domestic play.[47] As a result of the wide dissemination of the recipe format, as part of a variety of texts ranging from 'books of secrets' to cookery books, many readers must have been familiar with its conventions. This made it possible to play with these conventions in a way that readers could enjoy. The precise nature of this play can be elusive to us, modern readers, because there is a thin line between an interest in genuinely practical knowledge and somewhat more improper curiosity (including for practical jokes). Approaching recipes from the perspective of textual and visual conventions can help us obtain a clearer view of the intended readership of printed recipes in various contexts.

The unconventional presence of images in *Den sack der consten* might in fact provide a key to understanding the work's readership. According to Braekman, the images in *Den sack der consten* 'serve in the first place as decorations; their illustrative value can be qualified at best as minimal and highly vague'.[48] This observation seems to miss the point of the book, however. It is true that the images are not in any way instructive, nor are they related to the texts in any literal sense, but they are related in spirit. The recipes themselves are a hodgepodge, too, without any clear coherence in their ordering. Precisely this varied mix of texts and images establishes a certain overall coherence in tone and style that perhaps recalls present-day lifestyle magazines. Together, the texts and images convey a lively and relatable impression of the quest for a merry and healthy life, that must have appealed to a wide audience, young and old.

---

47   To this day, the format of practical instruction continues to hold potential for providing amusement as well as stirring reflection among a wide readership; see for example Randall Munroe, *How To. Absurd Scientific Advice for Common Real-World Problems* (London: John Murray, 2020).

48   Braekman, *Sack der consten*, p. 17 (my translation).

PART 4

Prescription and Improvisation

∵

CHAPTER 9

'That's How You Do It!' or Better not? Early Modern Recipes and Their Readers

Laura Balbiani

Recipes and recipe literature are a very popular topic that has been examined from different perspectives, both in terms of medical history and text linguistics. The same applies to books of secrets, which became the subject of numerous studies after the pioneering work of William Eamon and have been the focus of scholarly attention ever since.[1] The semiotician and co-founder of the Paris School Algirdas Julien Greimas also dealt with recipes and illustrated the unfolding of his structural semantics with the example of a cooking recipe. At the end of his semiotic reflections, which made the Provençal pesto-soup world-famous, Greimas dealt with the processes of transforming matter and producing 'cultural objects' in cooking recipes, and in doing so he wished to gain a deeper insight into the work of the alchemists, since '[elle: l'oeuvre théorique des alchimistes] pourrait y apporter probablement quelque lumière'.[2]

Greimas thus wished to build a bridge from today's cooking recipes to the alchemical recipe collections of the Early Modern Age. I would like to take up his suggestion and on the basis of his model of analysis I will scrutinise early modern recipe collections. The semiotic approach promotes an interpretation

---

1 On the concept and dissemination of so-called 'literature of secrets', cf. inter alia John Ferguson, *Bibliographical notes on histories of inventions and books of secrets* (2 vols., London: Holland Press, 1959). Here Ferguson also attempts a thematic grouping of the literature of secrets (vol. 1, part 1, pp. 6–7). 'Books of secrets' came to the fore with the relevant study by William Eamon, *Science and the secrets of nature. Books of secrets in medieval and early modern culture* (Princeton University Press, 1994). Since then, countless studies have been devoted to these early modern works – an overview of the now sprawling bibliography on the subject is omitted here.

2 Algirdas J. Greimas, *La soupe au pistou ou: la construction d'un objet de valeur* (Paris: Groupe de recherches sémio-linguistiques, 1979), p. 14; later in: *Du sens II* (Paris: Seuil, 1983), pp. 151–163. – The connection to alchemy is also emphasised by others, e.g. by Gianfranco Marrone, 'Cuisiner après Greimas: de la soupe au pistou au texte gastronomique', in *Greimas aujourd'hui: l'avenir de la structure*, Actes du congrès de l'Association Française de Sémiotique, 30 mai–2 juin 2017 (Paris: AFS Edition, 2017, pp. 570–581), p. 575. http://afsemio.fr/publications/greimas-aujourdhui-lavenir-de-la-structure-actes-du-congres-de-lafs-2017/.

that goes beyond the purely functional and praxeological dimension of the texts in search of a deeper level of meaning, and from this point of view, which complements and extends the studies carried out so far, it becomes possible to understand how these texts bring about the valorisation of their own inner elements. Indeed, the semiosic processes inherent in these works offer numerous points of reference for presenting these texts not only as a mere output of a body of knowledge, but themselves as forms of production of a particular body of knowledge.

1   Books of Secrets

In the Middle Ages and Early Modern Times, recipes were widespread in every area of everyday life, not only in the kitchen or in medical practice, as the recipe collections of the time clearly prove: they offer recipes for cultivating plants, for curing animals, for farming, for dyeing cloth, for working with metals, beauty recipes and much more. That is, the recipe was the 'Grundform wissenschaftlicher Prosa', the usual form of writing for the transmission and communication of action-oriented knowledge.[3]

The recipe collections that circulated under the generic term 'books of secrets', known in Germany as 'Haus- Kunst- und Wunderbücher', were very popular in the sixteenth century and so widespread that Tomaso Garzoni had to create a separate professional category for their authors in his *Piazza universale di tutte le professioni del mondo*: the 'Professors of Secrets'. Among the most famous representatives of this group, according to Garzoni, were Plinius, Albertus Magnus, Paracelsus, Della Porta, Agrippa, Alessio Piemontese, Isabella Cortese and many others more.[4]

Unlike treatises dealing with single, highly specialised arguments, 'books of secrets' were intended for a broad audience, not for experts in the strict sense; they were usually a florilegium or encyclopaedic collections that catered to a wide range of interests. As an 'aggregative type of text',[5] they consisted of groups of recipes that could deal with a wide range of subject areas, such as

---

3   See Joachim Telle, 'Das Rezept als literarische Form. Bausteine zu seiner Kulturgeschichte', *Berichte zur Wissenschaftsgeschichte*, 26 (2003), pp. 251–274, here p. 251; Mechthild Habermann, *Deutsche Fachtexte der frühen Neuzeit. Naturkundlich-medizinische Wissensvermittlung im Spannungsfeld von Latein und Volkssprache* (Berlin: de Gruyter, 2001).

4   Tomaso Garzoni, *Piazza universale di tutte le professioni del mondo* (Venetia: Giovan Battista Somascho, 1585) USTC 831901, Discorso 22, 'De professori de' secreti'.

5   Gundolf Keil, 'Pathologie und Reihung: Der abnehmende Schweregrad als serielles Gliederungsprinzip der Rezeptliteratur', in Christoph Friedrich etc. (eds.), *Pharmazie in Geschichte und Gegenwart*, Festgabe für Wolf-Dieter Müller-Jahncke (Stuttgart: Wissenschaftlicher Verlag, 2009, pp. 229–245), p. 229.

Giovan Battista Della Porta's *Magia naturalis*, or they could be monographic, such as the *Secrets* of the Venetian lady Isabella Cortese, which dealt mainly with beauty recipes, i.e., the preparation of fragrant oils, creams, and soaps. These two works are the basis of my remarks.

The collection of Isabella Cortese[6] already announces its thematic focus on the title page, because among the '400 Secrets pertaining to all the arts' (the first to be mentioned are alchemy and medicine), the author immediately names 'many wonderful waters, ointments, and perfumed soaps of all kinds'; the Italian edition explicitly mentions the 'arte profumatoria' and recommends the work to every respected lady. Written in 1561 in the vernacular, the work was aimed at a broad audience that did not know Latin, and through a clever marketing strategy, the author[7] attempted to expand his readership considerably by seeking to attract a female audience. The collection is a colourful, typographically unpretentious hodgepodge of short recipes loosely strung together; thematically related items are roughly grouped together but not systematically arranged.[8]

---

6 *I secreti de la signora Isabella Cortese ne' quali si contengono cose minerali, medicinali, artefi-ciose, & alchimiche, & molte de l'arte profumatoria, appartenenti a ogni gran signora* (Venetia: Bariletto, 1561) USTC 824295. Second edition 1565 ('con altri bellissimi secreti aggiunti') USTC 824296, then constantly growing in successive editions; German version: *Verborgene heimliche Künste unnd Wunderwerck Frawen Isabella Cortese in der* Alchimia, Medicina *und* Chyrurgia (Hamburg: Binder, 1592) USTC 704264; another edition was published in Frankfurt in 1596, USTC 658221; of this work there are no English translations. I quote from the second Italian edition (1565); translations into English are all my own.

7 The authorship of the work is disputed. John Ferguson wrote in his *Bibliotheca Chemica*: 'The authoress is called Cortesa, Cortese, Cortesi, but I have not met with any account of her' *Bibliotheca chemica: a catalogue of the alchemical, chemical and pharmaceutical books in the collection of the late James Young of Kelly and Durris* (Glasgow: Maclehose and sons, 1906, 2 vols.). Ferguson's comment remains true, for to this day it has not been possible to prove the existence of an Isabella Cortese. It was probably a *nom de plume* (the anagram of '*secreto*') as Garzoni himself suggested, also naming a possible author: 'il nome si tiene esser mentito insieme con quel di Don Alessio [Piemontese] dal Ruscelli'. See also Claire Lesage, 'La litterature des 'secrets' et *I secreti d'Isabella Cortese*', *Chroniques italiennes*, 1993, Université de Paris III. http://chroniquesitaliennes.univ-paris3.fr/PDF/36/Lesage.pdf; Meredith K. Ray, 'The *Secrets* of Isabella Cortese. Practical Alchemy and Women Readers', in *Daughters of Alchemy. Women and Scientific Culture in Early Modern Italy* (Cambridge: Harvard University Press, 2015), pp. 46–72; Mariacarla Gadebusch Bondio, 'Fragmente einer weiblichen Wissenschaftsgeschichte: Isabella Cortese und ihre *Secreti*', in Angelika Ebrecht-Laermann, Irmela Lühe, Ute Pott, and Cettina Rapisarda (eds.), *Gelehrsamkeit und kulturelle Emanzipation* (Stuttgart: Metzler, 1996), pp. 123–141.

8 The usual organising principles of the time, which enabled the reader to find recipes quickly (clear structuring, marginalia, alphabetical indexes, index of disease names, etc.) are not to be found here; see Gundolf Keil, 'Organisationsformen medizinischen Wissens', in Norbert Richard Wolf (ed.), *Wissensorganisierende und wissensvermittelnde Literatur im Mittelalter. Perspektiven ihrer Erforschung* (Wiesbaden: Reichert, 1987), pp. 221–245; idem: 'Pathologie und Reihung'.

FIGURE 9.1 *I secreti de la signora Isabella Cortese* (Venetia 1561), Title page
Early European Books

Most of the recipes are short and compressed, divided into numerous chapters; each chapter is functionally determined, i.e., the heading states the purpose to be achieved. If it contains several recipes, then only the first text is recognisable as a full text, while the following ones, through their lexically 'empty' headings ('another way' / 'Altrimenti'), present themselves as a series and describe alternative procedures for achieving the same purpose.

Della Porta's work looks quite different. The very fact that his *Magia naturalis* was first printed in Latin (in 1558) and in large format indicates that he was addressing a predominantly learned audience.[9] A manageable Italian translation came out in 1560 and both versions were reprinted again and again until a larger edition with the same title but expanded to twenty books replaced them on the book market (1589).[10]

In the first book, Della Porta offers the theoretical foundations for the exploration of natural phenomena (micro-macrocosm analogy, theory of signatures, etc.), while the following books deal with the several areas of knowledge which, according to the understanding of the time, constituted the 'magia naturalis': from agriculture to alchemy, from the art of cooking to optics and hydraulics.[11] The 'marvels of nature' are presented in the form of recipes and thus made reproducible, although their causes were not always precisely known. The recipes are usually commented on: First, the opinions of ancient writers are cited and compared, then the author reports on his own experiments and endeavours to find explanations and comparisons with similar phenomena. Such transitional sections, in which the author takes the floor, help the reader move from one group of recipes to the next, so that the single pieces of the text appear as a coherent whole and are inserted into a narrative framework.

Although these two works reflect strongly divergent authorial intentions (Isabella was a commercial enterprise of not too high a standard; Della Porta,

---

9 Giovan Battista della Porta, *Magiae naturalis sive de miraculis rerum naturalium libri IIII* (Neapoli: Cancer, 1558) USTC 826301. The work was quickly translated into Italian (Venice: Avanzi, 1560) USTC 826302, translations into Dutch (Antwerpen: Plantin, 1566) USTC 403260, French (Paris: de Roigny, 1570) USTC 75790 and German followed (Magdeburg: Rauscher, 1612) USTC 2002979, and were many times reprinted. Cf. Laura Balbiani, *La Magia naturalis di Giovan Battista Della Porta. Lingua, cultura e scienza in Europa all'inizio dell'età moderna* (Bern-Frankfurt/M.: Peter Lang, 2001).

10 Giovan Battista della Porta, *Magiae naturalis libri XX* (Neapoli: Horatius Salviani, 1589) USTC 826318. – There were also several editions and translations of this expanded version, including an English one (London: T. Young and S. Speed, 1658) and a German translation, translated and annotated by Christian Knorr von Rosenroth (Nuremberg: Johann Zieger, 1680, 2 vols.). Quotations are taken from the English edition [*Magia* 1658].

11 The materials are neatly and consistently presented and the author took pains to list the recipes according to a logical principle of order. An example is Book 9, which is structured according to the usual order *a capite ad calcem*: '... we shall set down the Art of Painting; and how to beautifie Women from Head to Foot, in many Experiments.' (*Magia* 1658, p. 233).

FIGURE 9.2 G.B. Della Porta, *Natural Magick in XX Bookes* (London 1658), Title page of the English translation. Boston Public Library (shelf-number *7969.5) urn:oclc:record:1049896135

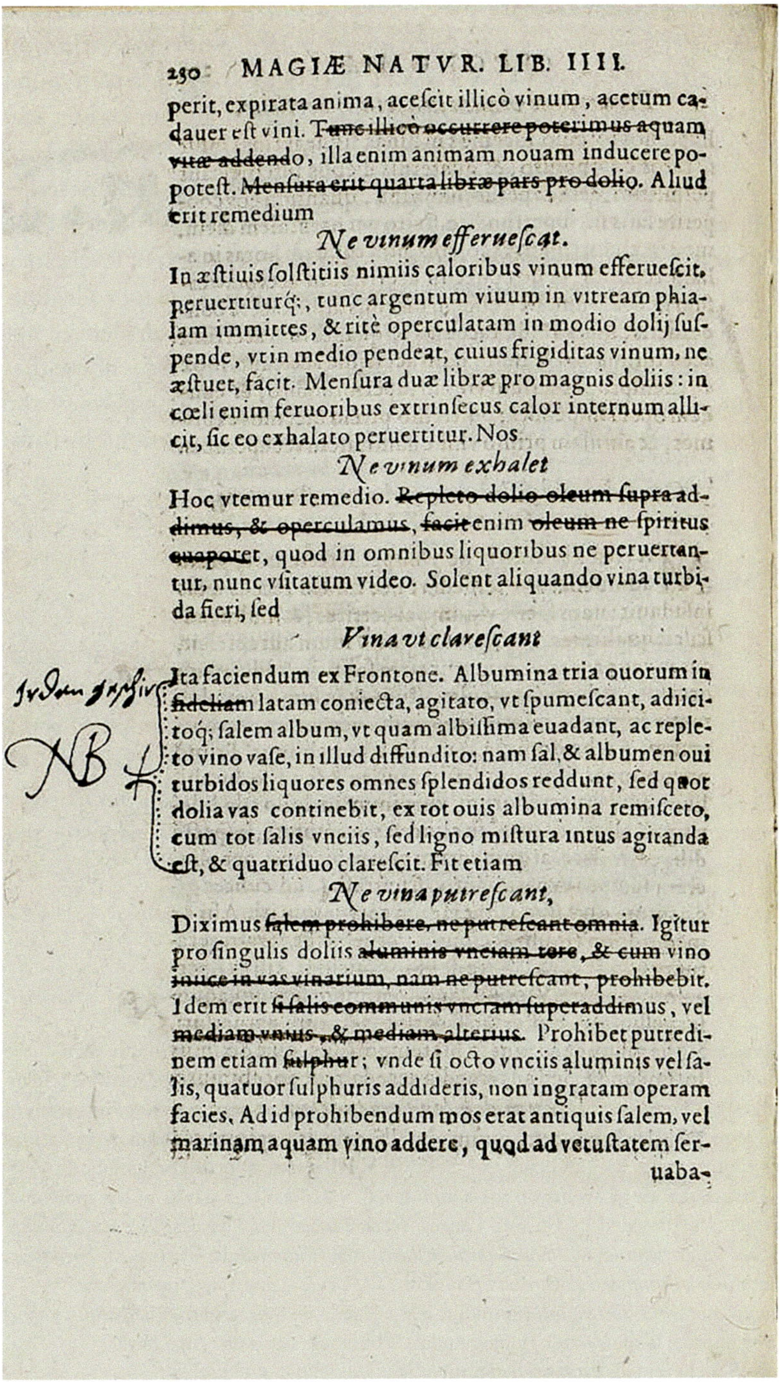

230   MAGIÆ NATVR. LIB. IIII.

perit, expirata anima, acefcit illicò vinum, acetum ca-
dauer eſt vini. ~~Tunc illicò occurrere poterimus aquam~~
~~vitæ addendo~~, illa enim animam nouam inducere po-
poteſt. ~~Menſura erit quarta libræ pars pro dolio.~~ Aliud
erit remedium

Ne vinum efferuefcat.

In æſtiuis ſolſtitiis nimiis caloribus vinum efferueſcit,
peruertitur⁊, tunc argentum viuum in vitream phia-
lam immittes, & ritè operculatam in modio dolij ſuſ-
pende, vt in medio pendeat, cuius frigiditas vinum, ne
æſtuet, facit. Menſura duæ libræ pro magnis doliis : in
cœli enim feruoribus extrinſecus calor internum alli-
cit, ſic eo exhalato peruertitur. Nos.

Ne vinum exhalet

Hoc vtemur remedio. ~~Repleto dolio oleum ſupra ad-~~
~~dimus, & operculamus, facit~~ enim ~~oleum~~ ne ſpiritus
~~euaporet~~, quod in omnibus liquoribus ne peruertan-
tur, nunc vſitatum video. Solent aliquando vina turbi-
da fieri, ſed

Vina vt clareſcant

Ita faciendum ex Frontone. Albumina tria ouorum in
~~fideliam~~ latam coniecta, agitato, vt ſpumeſcant, adiici-
toq; ſalem album, vt quam albiſſima euadant, ac reple-
to vino vaſe, in illud diffundito: nam ſal, & albumen oui
turbidos liquores omnes ſplendidos reddunt, ſed quot
dolia vas continebit, ex tot ouis albumina remiſceto,
cum tot ſalis vnciis, ſed ligno miſtura intus agitanda
eſt, & quatriduo clareſcit. Fit etiam

Ne vina putreſcant,

Diximus ~~ſalem prohibere, ne putreſcant omnia.~~ Igitur
pro ſingulis doliis ~~aluminis vnciam tore, & cum~~ vino
~~iniice in vas vinarium, nam ne putreſcant, prohibebit.~~
Idem erit ~~ſi ſalis communis vnciam ſuperaddimus~~, vel
~~mediam vnius, & mediam alterius.~~ Prohibet putredi-
nem etiam ~~ſulphur~~; vnde ſi octo vnciis aluminis vel ſalis, quatuor ſulphuris addideris, non ingratam operam
facies, Ad id prohibendum mos erat antiquis ſalem, vel
marinam aquam vino addere, quod ad vetuſtatem ſer-
uaba-

FIGURE 9.3   G.B. Della Porta, *Magiae naturalis libri xx* (Francofurti 1591), p. 230 with
annotations of Duke August. Herzog August Bibliothek Wolfenbüttel
(A: 74 Phys.) http://diglib.hab.de/drucke/74-phys/start.htm?image=00270

on the other hand, wanted to provide a scholarly contribution as a member of the learned élite), both can be considered prototypical of early modern how-to books. Without a doubt, Garzoni recognised their macro- and microstructural similarities and classified them accordingly. Both collections consist of a thematically structured sequence of small text modules, the recipes, which have similar linguistic features;[12] thematically, both aimed to reveal and describe the secrets and wonders of nature. As an encyclopaedic aggregate that could be expanded at will, they could satisfy early modern man on different levels: they stimulated his curiosity, his thirst for knowledge and his passion for collecting.

'Books of secrets' found countless readers and users. This is evidenced not only by their numerous editions and reprints, but also by the traces of use that often occur, indicating intensive engagement with the various parts of the text; the copy of the *Magia naturalis* with marginalia and annotations by Duke August preserved in Wolfenbüttel is just one example.[13]

2 'Misreading' Recipes

If we take a closer look at the reception of these works, we can distinguish between two levels: first, the level of the transmission of knowledge, i.e. the communicative level. Here, the actors are a writer (author or compiler) and a reader who interact with each other on the basis of a narrative strategy. Second, the level of execution, of the practical implementation of this knowledge. Here there are functional actants and a praxeological strategy, i.e. a master 'mit imperativischem Habitus'[14] who induces a subject to act.

---

12 Characteristic features of the text type 'recipe' are: short text length; compression of the whole action in a single paragraph; simple typographical design (only the heading is highlighted); coherence of the verb forms, which indicate individual action steps by means of the requesting imperative; structuring of the content through temporal determinations (as complements they indicate the duration of an action step, as connectors they signal the sequence of events on the action level). – A detailed analysis of the individual elements is provided by Gudrun Langer, *Textkohärenz und Textspezifität: textgrammatische Untersuchung zu den Gebrauchstextsorten Klappentext, Patienteninformation, Garantieerklärung und Kochrezept* (Frankfurt a.M.: Peter Lang, 1995), pp. 269–292.

13 *Magiae naturalis libri viginti* (Frankfurt a.M.: Claude de Marne und Johann Aubry, 1591) USTC 667007; Wolfenbüttel, Herzog August Bibliothek, signature: A: 74 Phys.

14 Telle, 'Das Rezept als literarische Form', p. 253.

On the communicative level, the reader feels no need to put recipes into practice; he appreciates them as purely informative or entertaining texts,[15] as erudite, curious and witty constructs for their own sake. Recipes can develop their full impact also on this level, i.e.: there is a narrative program behind the recipe, so that it also works without any practical implementation. This is because the recipe is enriched with an added value that places it in a broader program of social and cultural nature: to entertain, instruct, impart knowledge, arouse and satisfy curiosity, stimulate further research;[16] last but not least, such collections served for self-representation, to show off the erudition of the author. Let us take as an example the recipe for the very famous *aurum potabile*, still sold in pharmacies today.

How to make Aurum potabile.

Take ten pounds of good wine and distil it in the alembic as long as it is reduced to one pound; take it out of the still and put new wine in it, again ten pounds as before. Add to it the pound you have already distilled and distill it again till you obtain only one pound. The same you will do for a third time, with new wine. Then take a recipient with a very long neck and pour the water into it; place it under the manure for four days. From this liquid you shall take three ounces and put it in another vessel, add an ounce of candy sugar and it will be even better. Afterwards put this water in the alembic again, add 60 pieces of gold leaf and let it rest for 4 hours; distil it in bain-marie, and when it is done, do not dry the deposit but store it in two vessels.[17]

In order to bring out its narrative character, one could read a recipe considering it not as an instructional text but as genuinely narrative text, e.g. as a kind

---

15   I refer to the classification of text types, which was specifically coined for the early modern period from Oskar Reichmann and Klaus-Peter Wegera, *Frühneuhochdeutsches Lesebuch* (Tübingen: Niemeyer, 1988). Recipes usually count as instructional or procedural texts [*anleitende Texte*].

16   Telle ('Das Rezept als literarische Form', p. 253) has convincingly pointed out the 'Multifunktionalität der Gebrauchsform Rezept' and presented numerous examples of its literary power. Della Porta's recipes provide a good example of this functional diversity. As an introduction to Book 14, he writes, for example: 'The Cooks Art hath some choice Secrets, that may make Banquets more dainty and full of admiration: These I purpose to reveal, not that so I might invite Gluttons and Parasites to Luxury, but that with small cost and expence, I might set forth the curiosities of Art, and may give occasion to others thereby to invent greater matters by these.' (*Magia* 1658, p. 313).

17   Isabella Cortese 1565, Book 2, pp. 62–63.

of fairy tale. In the light of the morphological theory of the tale, one actually finds that many of the basic structural elements that Vladimir Propp identified as constitutive of folktales occur in recipes in numerous combinations:[18]

- The trigger is an adverse or a deficiency situation: the intention is to cure a disease, to fulfil a wish or to produce a certain effect;
- the hero or agent takes on the task of removing the evil;
- there is a kind of contract, a pact, which determines the conditions of the action;
- the actant has difficulties to defeat, often several trials to pass (the various steps of preparation with the corresponding action sequences);
- certain situations repeat themselves with small variations (the distillation repeated three times);
- helpers (in the recipe quoted above: fire, dung and rock sugar) and opponents (often it is air or impurity);
- elements for temporal (frequency and duration of the action steps, often with symbolic numbers) and spatial control (the different pots and vessels that have to be used or stored in certain places);
- alchemical vessels are a kind of utopian space like the magic circle, separate from the real, where miraculous phenomena occur.

This short list is enough to show that these basic functions in the case of the recipe are expressions of the interaction between the actantial roles involved in the text.[19] Recipes hide a deep narrative level, which from this point of view can be considered as the typical dynamic of knowledge transfer. This dynamic is based on the alternation of cognitive and pragmatic demands and sets in motion the processes described in the recipe.

3   Sequences, Processes, Flowcharts

The 'Kunst- und Wunderbücher', as books of secrets are usually titled in German, are also books of skills and doing (*Kunst*, from the verb *können*: being able to do something), not just of saying, and their characteristic feature is the instructing function, which implies a 'being-able-to-do'. A pact is made between the actants: the author/addresser is recognised as an expert and by entrusting himself to his instructions and carrying them out carefully,

18   Vladimir J. Propp, *Morphology of the folktale* (Austin: Texas UP, 1968). – Such a programming strategy can be equated to a narrative strategy in every respect: so Paolo Fabbri, 'Istruzioni e pratiche istruite', *E|C*, 2005, http://www.ec-aiss.it/biblioteca/biblioteca.php.

19   Greimas took Propp's invariants as a starting point and then reduced them to basic elements, to functional categories: *Sémantique structurale. Recherche et méthode* (Paris: Larousse, 1966), A la recherche des modèles de transformation, pp. 192–204.

the addressee is enabled to translate his aspiration into concrete action and thereby achieve the desired goal. The acceptance of this implicit pact triggers the action and it shifts from the cognitive to the pragmatic level, from competence to performance. In other words, the expectation is bound to a cognitive effort, that is, the desire to unravel the mysteries of nature: a 'wanting-to-know' that is often expressed in a conditional formulation ('if you will ...'), and this effort manifests itself entirely in the performance, in the acquisition of certain skills.

From a praxeological point of view, recipes could be considered as a flow-chart in which each work step (or sentence or enunciate) represents an element of a narrative program that unfolds entirely on the syntagmatic level – Greimas talks about a 'semio-narrative syntax'.

A recipe establishes a chain of operations that aims at a transformation through a linguistically and praxeologically codified procedure – precisely, a transformation on the objective and on the subjective level. On the objective level, recipes aim to bring about a change of state, a transformation of matter, and thus a natural product becomes a cultural product.[20] On the subjective level, on the other hand, the situation of the acting subject changes, because it passes from a condition of deficiency to a condition of union with the value-object (by removing the deficiency). And even if the transformation is operated on a third party, the actant in any case acquires authority, prestige and the manipulative power of the 'magus', the skilled master of nature, since he has accomplished the transition from 'wanting-to-know' to 'being-able-to-do'.

The result of this transformation is always a value-object, i.e. something to which one ascribes a value. It is not only a question of material value, more often are involved immaterial, socio-cultural values: beauty, prestige, health, courage, an extraordinary memory, fruits without pits, delicately scented flowers, etc.; connected to this is the social appreciation of the acting subject. Fundamental is the category of desire that produces an action and manifests itself in the 'practical and at the same time mythical form of the 'quest".[21] Thus, the desired purpose, which is verbalised in the recipe heading, is as well the object of desire as the object of communication.

The end point of the process is usually announced in the heading; here either the goal is stated (by a final clause: 'to make their Hair yellow'), or the means to the end (in this case usually formulated by a nominal phrase: 'an oil

---

20 Along the sequence, several transformations of matter usually take place, which are sometimes actual changes of state in the physical sense (melting, evaporating, subli-mating, solidifying), sometimes the result of basic actions such as: pounding to powder, mixing, distilling, boiling, see Françoise Bastide, *Le traitement de la matière: opérations élémentaires* (Paris: Groupe de Recherches Sémio-linguistiques, 1987).

21 Greimas, *Sémantique structurale*, p. 176.

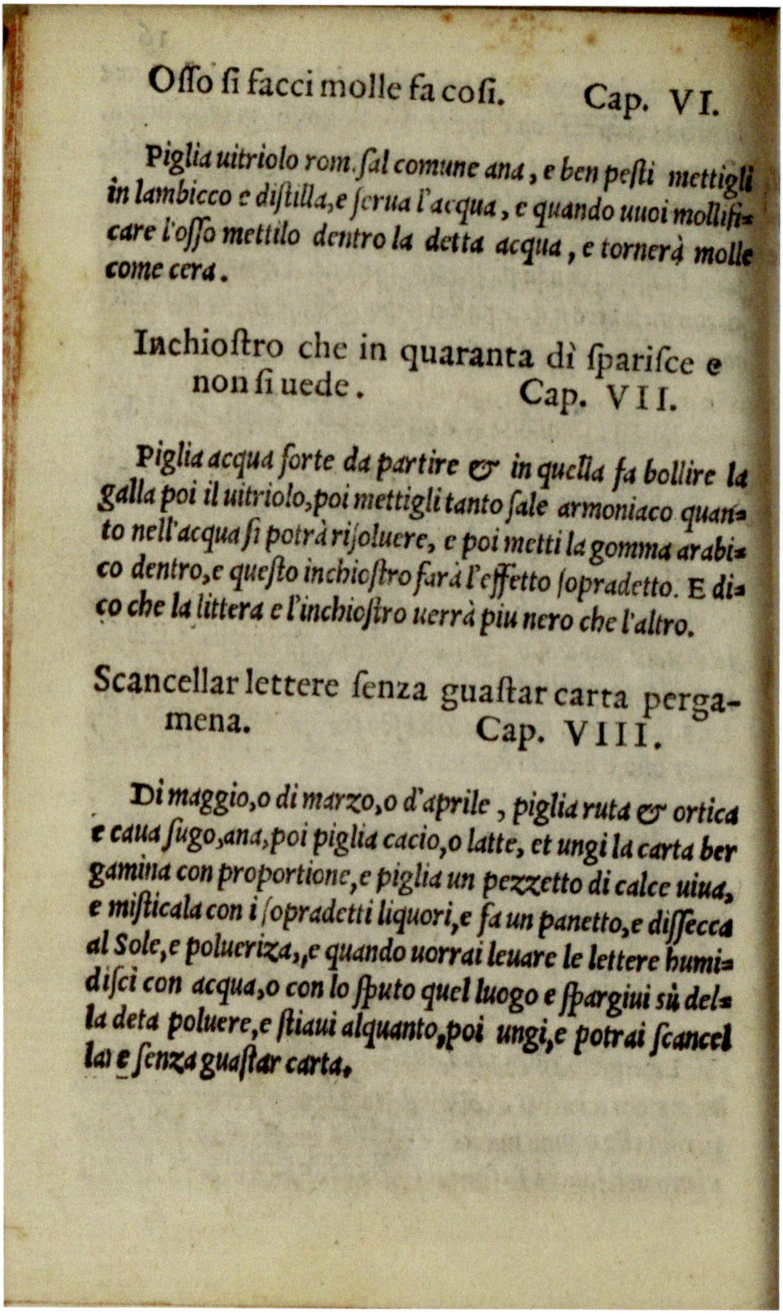

Osso si facci molle fa cosi.   Cap. VI.

Piglia uitriolo rom. sal comune ana, e ben pesti mettigli
in lambicco e distilla, e serua l'acqua, e quando uuoi mollifi-
care l'osso mettilo dentro la detta acqua, e tornerà molle
come cera.

Inchiostro che in quaranta dì sparisce e
non si uede.   Cap. VII.

Piglia acqua forte da partire & in quella fa bollire la
galla poi il uitriolo, poi mettigli tanto sale armoniaco quan-
to nell'acqua si potrà risoluere, e poi metti la gomma arabi-
co dentro, e questo inchiostro farà l'effetto sopradetto. E di-
co che la littera e l'inchiostro uerrà piu nero che l'altro.

Scancellar lettere senza guastar carta perga-
mena.   Cap. VIII.

Di maggio, o di marzo, o d'aprile, piglia ruta & ortica
e caua sugo, ana, poi piglia cacio, o latte, et ungi la carta ber
gamina con proportione, e piglia un pezzetto di calce uiua,
e misticala con i sopradetti liquori, e fa un panetto, e dissecca
al Sole, e polueriza, e quando uorrai leuare le lettere humi-
disci con acqua, o con lo sputo quel luogo e spargiui sù della deta poluere, e stiaui alquanto, poi ungi, e potrai scancel
la e senza guastar carta.

FIGURE 9.4 *I secreti de la signora Isabella Cortese* (Venetia 1561), fol. 16v Early
European Books

against pestilence', 'the best Soapes for women').[22] Sometimes the focus is not on the goal to be achieved, but on the procedure, on the 'how' to reach the goal; here a know-how (knowing-how-to-do) is imparted.

How to artificially remove letters from paper or parchment without damaging it

> In March, April or May take rue or nettle, in equal quantities, and press a juice out of them; than take fresh cheese [cacio] or milk and grease the parchment paper proportionally, then take a piece of quicklime, mix it with the above mentioned juice, form a lump and leave it to dry in the sun. Reduce it to powder, and when you wish to erase the letters, moisten the place with clear water or spit and sprinkle that powder over it, let it rest for a while, then grease the paper or parchment and you will erase everything without damaging it.[23]

In this recipe, the desired transformation is retrograde, i.e. something is brought back to its initial state.[24] This characteristic heading is fundamental also to the textual level and provides a significant contribution to the coherence of the text, because the recipe always starts from its end point: the heading is strongly cataphoric, because it anticipates the goal,[25] while the closing formula ('That's how you do it', 'so it will be done' or similar formulations that underline the result achieved), for its part, contributes to the high semantic density and to the unity of the recipe through the repetition and confirmation of the successful procedure. The last sentence is introduced usually either by the anaphoric framing adverb 'so', or by the demonstrative 'that's how', both referring to the whole procedure described, while the thematic pronoun refers back to the value object announced in the heading.

---

22 Della Porta, following scholarly models, often introduces the complement of argument with the preposition 'of' on the Latin model (*de* + ablative): 'Of the Production of new Plants'; 'Of making smalt or Ennamel'. – On recipe headings cf. also Elvira Glaser, 'Die textuelle Struktur handschriftlicher und gedruckter Kochrezepte im Wandel', in Rudolf Große and Hans Wellmann (eds.), *Textarten im Sprachwandel – nach der Erfindung des Buchdrucks* (Heidelberg: Winter, 1996, pp. 225–250), pp. 233–241.

23 Isabella Cortese 1565, Book 2, pp. 34–35.

24 This is often the case with beauty recipes: 'How to make a Sun-burnt Face white'; 'To take off spots from the Face'; 'To take away wrinkles from the Body' etc. (*Magia* 1658, Book 9, *passim*).

25 As Greimas notes in his analysis of the pesto-soup recipe, 'la programmation globale s'effectue à partir du point terminal du processus imaginé et consiste, en partant du but fixé, dans la quête et l'élaboration des moyens pour y parvenir'. Greimas, *La soupe au pistou*, p. 15.

The beginning of the text is traditionally marked by the imperative verb form: 'Take/Nimm/Piglia ...' with the corresponding accusative objects; the small number of sentences and limited lexical material are typical. The verb opens the sequence of action, which is concretised in a linear sequence of operations that could be also represented graphically by a flowchart; the emphasis is on modality (a 'wanting-to'), that sets the text in motion ('But if you desider to cast flame a great way, do thus'[26]).

Characteristic is the prompting tone, which is realised linguistically through imperative;[27] in this way, the enunciator wants to directly induce the addressee to act, while the second person singular addresses the reader personally and involves him/her directly in the text as an acting instance. This form reflects or simulates the original communication situation, when both actants were present and transmitted their knowledge and skills through practice and showing. The personal style of address that characterised this first phase of writing down recipes is then lost over time as the verb mode adapts to the communicative distance; through passive or impersonal constructions, the agent gradually disappears and the action moves to the centre.[28]

---

26   *Magia* 1658, Book 12, p. 301.

27   In Isabella Cortese's work, it is mostly so, exceptions are extremely rare, and this is true for the vast majority of 16th century recipes: according to the estimate quoted in Glaser, 80 to 90% of verb forms are imperatives. Elvira Glaser, 'Fein gehackte Pinienkerne zugeben! Zum Infinitiv in Kochrezepten', in David Restle, Dietmar Zaefferer (eds.), *Sounds and Systems. Studies in Structure and Change.* A Festschrift for Theo Vennemann (Berlin: de Gruyter, 2002, pp. 165–184), p. 167. This is not the case with Della Porta, who often uses a narrative style. He alternates the imperative with other forms such as the impersonal pronoun and the inclusive 'we', which unites addresser and addressee; descriptive passages in which the actions of a third party are reported are also frequent. Therefore, directive speech acts are here realised in different ways, for example through the future tense, indicative, impersonal sentences.

28   Trude Ehlert also cites other reasons to explain the shift from direct to indirect forms of solicitation, including the 'slow democratisation of manners': Trude Ehlert, "Nehmet ein junges Huhn, ertränckets mit Essig'. Zur Syntax spätmittelalterlicher Kochbücher', in Irmgard Bitsch, Trude Ehlert, and Xenia von Ertzdorff (eds.), *Essen und Trinken in Mittelalter und Neuzeit* (Sigmaringen: Thorbecke, 1990, pp. 261–276), p. 275. On the same topic cf. Hermann Cölfen, 'Vom Kochrezept zur Kochanleitung. Sprachliche und mediale Aspekte einer verständlichen Vermittlung von Kochkenntnissen', *Unikate: Berichte aus Forschung und Lehre*, 30 (2007), pp. 84–93; Elke Donalies, 'Man nehme ... Verbformen in Kochrezepten, oder Warum das Prototypische nicht immer das Typische ist', *Sprachreport*, (2012), 2, pp. 25–31; Glaser, 'Fein gehackte Pinienkerne zugeben!'; Nicola Hödl, 'Vertextungskonventionen des Kochrezepts vom Mittelalter bis in die Moderne', in Eva-Martha Eckkrammer, Nicole Hödl, and Wolfgang Pöckl (eds.), *Kontrastive Textologie* (Wien: Praesens, 1999), pp. 47–75.

4 The 'Professor of Secrets' as Communication Expert

The author is not only someone who wants to pass on a know-how, but also an enunciator who must first construct his own communicative act. That is, he must first establish his authority and identify himself as an expert and trustworthy teacher. To this end, different credential strategies are employed. By quoting from ancient sources, the author usually declares himself to be the bearer of an older experience that he has inherited; he reports how he came into possession of a certain, valuable 'secret' and how much time and effort he has devoted to researching the mysteries of nature; he claims that he has checked each recipe himself or personally experienced its effectiveness (*probatum est!*). Through such narrative framework, on the one hand the value of the recipe is increased, on the other hand the author claims an authority that makes him not only an expert master but also a credible author, who carries on the knowledge acquired from the ancients.

At the same time, he constructs not so much the material as the cultural value of the recipe. In the narrative prelude that introduces each group of recipes or accompanies the transitions, a certain goal is often asserted as socially recognised and desirable, and by emphasising the rarity or difficulty of the procedure, the addresser challenges the addressee to put his mastery to the test. The author creates a need, triggers a desire, and by asserting its importance, he motivates the addressee ever more strongly to act. In this way, the text becomes an actual manipulation of the reader, a technique that Della Porta masters very skilfully:

> First, I will shew you to adorn the Hair, and next the Countenance. For Women hold the Hair to be the greatest Ornament of the Body; that if that be taken away, all the Beauty is gone: and they think it the more beautiful, the more yellow, shining and radiant it is. We shall consider what things are fit for that purpose.[29]

Thus the text gradually constructs, even before the object itself is dealt, its cultural, social and in this case aesthetic value. This gives rise to desire, so that a 'wanting-to-know' (even before the 'wanting-to-do') is the actual trigger of reporting. This enables the author to keep a firm grip on the communicative

---

29 *Magia* 1658, Book 9, p. 233. – These narrative, manipulative interventions by the author are very frequent in Della Porta; rather rare in Isabella Cortese, who simply lines up recipes.

FIGURE 9.5 G.B. Della Porta, *Magia Naturalis oder Haus- Kunst- und
Wunder-Buch* (Nürnberg 1680), illustration for Book 9: 'Von
Schmincken und Weiber-Zier' ['Of Beautifying Women']. Halle
(Saale): Universitäts- und Landesbibliothek Sachsen-Anhalt
(Hb 5005 d (2)) urn:nbn:de:gbv:3:1-379330

relationship, to stimulate it and re-semantise it again and again by captivating the reader step by step, despite the somewhat meagre algorithm of the recipes:

> Other Women endeavour to make their Hair yellow thus: (*Magia* 1658, Book 9, p. 234)
> But these are but ordinary; the most famous way is … (ivi, p. 234)
> Because there are many men and women that are ruddy Complexions, and have the Hair of their Heads and Beards Red; which, should they make yellow-coloured, they would not agree with their Complexions: To help those also, I set down these Remedies. (ivi, p. 235)[30]

His communication strategy is particularly effective because it does not operate with concrete objects but with the social values associated with them. After all, it is not the objects themselves that interest people, and their production does not deserve the effort unless they are the *locus* where certain values are inscribed.[31] In this sense, the logical-semantic level at which values are recognised and are spreading is much deeper than the praxeological level at which objects are produced or exchanged. It is at this deeper level that the 'Professor of secrets' as communication expert argues.

5   Readers and Apprentices

The narrative main program is usually a production program that leads to the attainment of the value-object and thereby satisfies a need or brings pleasure. The recipe is thus dynamic implementation of an elementary structure that leads from the negative (lack) to the positive (value-object, recognition) under the direction of an acting subject. In order to successfully complete the main program, one must correctly carry out several action steps in the intended sequence; some in turn consist of smaller, subordinate chains of actions that are organised according to a clearly defined temporal sequence and can be considered as secondary narrative programs.

Although there is usually a competence gap between addresser and addressee, the second nevertheless has a certain knowledge that is to be

---

30   Here another value is introduced: If at the beginning the ideal of beauty was identified with the blond hair *tout court*, the harmony of appearance now comes to the fore, where the skin colour is supposed to harmonise with hair, beard and eyebrows.

31   What one acquires with the material object, 'c'est aussi un peu de prestige social ou un sentiment de puissance plus intime. L'objet visé n'est alors qu'un prétexte, qu'un lieu d'investissement des valeurs, un ailleurs qui médiatise le rapport du sujet à lui-meme'. Algirdas J. Greimas, 'Un problème de sémiotique narrative: les objets de valeur', *Langages*, 31 (1973), 3 (pp. 13–35), p. 15.

activated. He must have the necessary equipment, pots and vessels and be familiar with the graduation of fire and the dosage of the different substances, because quantity specifications are often very vague or left to his discretion (e.g.: some, a little bit, as much as you like). In addition, there are terms that sometimes denote sophisticated procedures and require complex knowledge ('distil it in bain-marie').

The chronological sequence is usually divided by punctuation marks (mainly commas) or by the connector 'and'. It is used to establish temporal relations by stringing together individual actions in an additive manner, thus explicitly fixing a certain progression. Sometimes the progression is supported by temporal connectors and indications (as long as, afterwards, when), while the sequence of short main clauses is from time to time interrupted by indicators that define the scope of action more precisely, for example by restrictive or descriptive relative clauses.[32]

The procedure, which can be characterised by recursivity rules (i.e. can be repeated x times by any actor), leads to a ritualisation of the actions. Due to its multiple proving, the recipe thus acquires a superior value based on social expectation. As a matter of fact, at the end of each recipe, the last sentence announces the achievement of the purpose and confirms the successful production of the desired value-object; the contract between addresser and addressee, between master and apprentice, is fulfilled and the acting subject receives its reward. The final statement reinforces the tacit agreement between sender and receiver and thereby establishes a correspondence between the discourse level and reality, between saying-to-be-true and being-true ('veridiction contract'). This correspondence is historically conditioned because it has its root in the socio-cultural context in which procedural texts are ascribed a truth claim and reliability: follow them correctly and you achieve the desired purpose. What is asserted as certain at the discourse level (believing-to-be-certain) is assumed to be true (knowing-to-be-true) due to a 'fiduciary ratification'[33] between the communication participants. In this way, the authority of the enunciator remains inviolable: any failures in achieving the purpose or in producing the value-object are not due to the enunciator or to the text itself, but rather to omissions or lack of competence on the part of the acting subject.

But the recipe is not only an instructional text: It is also the directing script of a more complex ritual staging of skill; the settings are the kitchen of the famous cook, the workshop of the alchemist, the laboratory of the experimenting

---

32   See also Elke Donalies, "Das Rezept war super! Es stand nur leider nicht dabei, ob die Kartoffeln roh oder gekocht verwendet werden sollten". Sprachmanagement für Kochrezepte', *Aptum*, 7 (2011), pp. 193–223, here pp. 210–211; Langer, *Textkohärenz und Textspezifität*, p. 273.

33   Algirdas J. Greimas, 'The Veridiction Contract', *New Literary History*, 20 (1989), pp. 651–660, here p. 659.

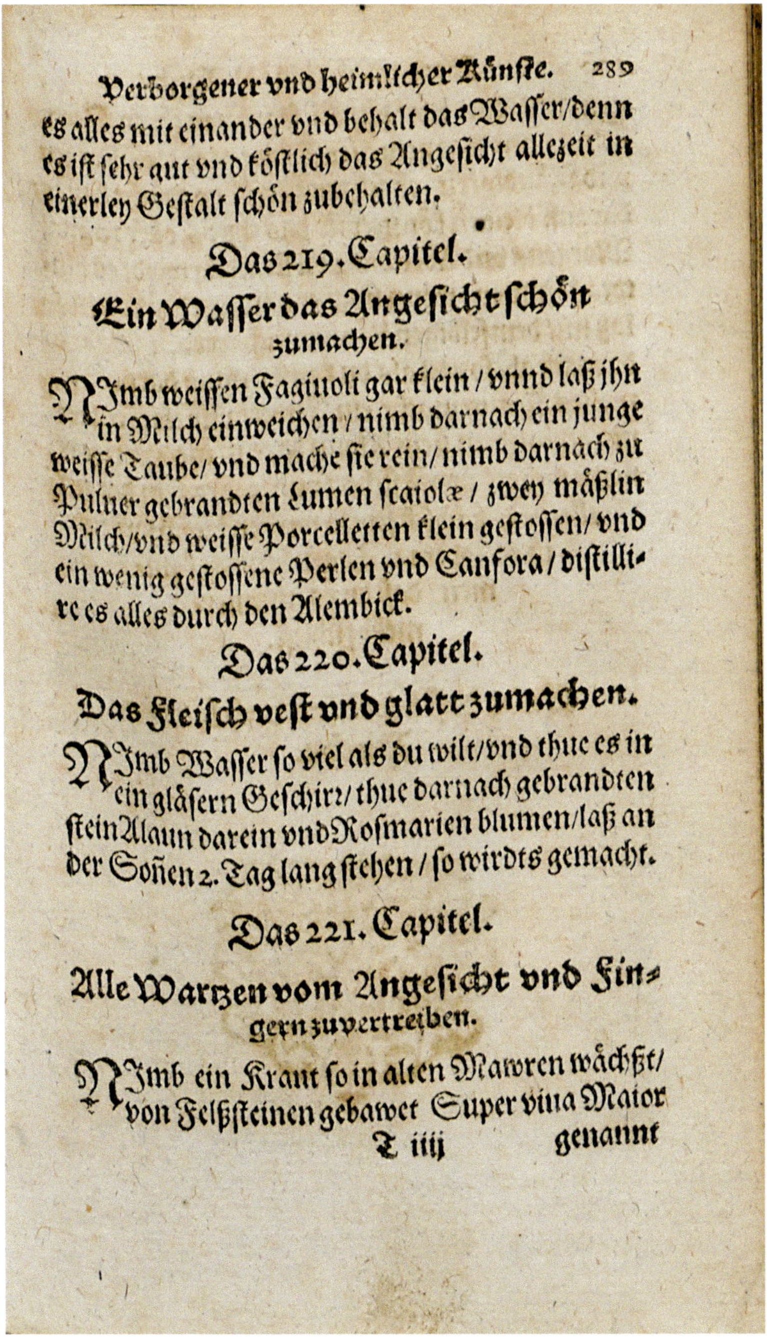

Verborgener vnd heimlicher Künste. 289

es alles mit einander vnd behalt das Wasser/denn
es ist sehr gut vnd köstlich das Angesicht allezeit in
einerley Gestalt schön zubehalten.

Das 219. Capitel.

Ein Wasser das Angesicht schön zumachen.

NImb weissen Fagiuoli gar klein/vnnd laß jhn
in Milch einweichen/nimb darnach ein junge
weisse Taube/vnd mache sie rein/nimb darnach zu
Pulner gebrandten Lumen scaiolæ / zwey mäßlin
Milch/vnd weisse Porcelletten klein gestossen/vnd
ein wenig gestossene Perlen vnd Canfora/distilli-
re es alles durch den Alembick.

Das 220. Capitel.

Das Fleisch vest vnd glatt zumachen.

NImb Wasser so viel als du wilt/vnd thue es in
ein gläsern Geschirr/thue darnach gebrandten
stein Alaun darein vnd Rosmarien blumen/laß an
der Sonnen 2. Tag lang stehen / so wirdts gemacht.

Das 221. Capitel.

Alle Wartzen vom Angesicht vnd Fin= gern zuvertreiben.

NImb ein Kraut so in alten Mawren wächßt/
von Felßsteinen gebawet Super villa Maior

T iiij   genannt

FIGURE 9.6 *Frawen* Isabellae Cortese *verborgene und heimliche Künste und wunderwerck* (Franckfort am Mayn 1596), p. 289. Halle (Saale): Universitäts- und Landesbibliothek Sachsen-Anhalt (AB 155293 (2)) https://opendata2.uni-halle.de/retrieve/4c0deb55-528b-452c-be11-40d1 eb261703/00000299.jpg

FIGURE 9.7 G.B. Della Porta, *Magia Naturalis oder Haus- Kunst- und Wunder-Buch* (Nürnberg 1680), illustration for Book 6: 'Von gemachten Edelgesteinen' ['Of counterfeiting precious Stones']. Herzog August Bibliothek Wolfenbüttel (Xb 9206:1) http://diglib.hab.de/drucke/xb-9206-1b/start.htm?image=00863

scholar, of the apothecary; they form the visual framework of the recipe. The actant plays the main role; his/her operations are favoured or hindered by different factors and are realised in the hero's ability and non-ability. Ingredients and tools appear like actors on a stage (also with surprise effects, since they are not listed at the beginning, as is usual today) and one can perceive a kind of crescendo in the stringing together of syntagms, in the repetition of actions, which creates suspense. Human and non-human actors are equally at work, be they simple substances (plants, minerals or animal matter) or tools and technologies (pots, spoons, mortars, stills, ovens).[34] The transformation of matter takes place with the help of water, fire and air, but always under the direction of the actant, who regulates the duration and intensity of the basic elements: If the elements get out of control, then they become adversaries and endanger the result.

The figurative and symbolic level is an integral part of the action. Symbolic are the repetitive work phases (the triple distillation of 'aurum potabile', reminiscent of the triple test of the hero in the folktales), their duration (40 days, 24 hours) and the names of numerous preparations (dragon's blood, sperma aquae lucis, spiritus). The vessels in which the trasformations take place are often anthropomorphic (neck-shaped, stomach-shaped), and spherical recipients where the microcosm is reproduced are also frequent. In the recipe 'How to artificially remove letters from paper or parchment', in fact, the process consists of three phases, each of which provides for the contribution of a natural kingdom (a plant, milk and lime).[35] In the pot they are mixed together, and the value-object emerges from the primordial chaos: the actant becomes a second creator, and what happens in the alembic or pot is the image of cosmic processes.

6   Concluding Remarks

Early modern how-to books offer the written fixation of a practical knowledge that until then had been transmitted orally while the addressee watched and acted himself. These skills were originally handed down as a non-verbal experience through people's actions; it was not until the late Middle Ages that

---

34   Claude Lévi-Strauss, *L'origine des manières de table* (Paris: Plon, 1968).

35   On the selection of medicines in the early modern period cf. Irmgard Müller, 'Arzneien für den 'gemeinen Mann'. Zur Vorstellung materieller und immaterieller Wirkungen stofflicher Substrate in der Medizin des 16. und 17. Jahrhunderts', in Joachim Telle (ed.), *Pharmazie und der gemeine Mann. Hausarznei und Apotheke in deutschen Schriften der frühen Neuzeit* (Weinheim : Acta Humaniora, 1988), pp. 27–34.

recipes were written down for the first time, at first only as a memory aid.[36] By being written down, the recipe turned away from its concrete operative context and has become one of the most popular text genres of written communication. The visual component and the co-presence of both interlocutors were then 'entexted' and produced the fictional embedding of the text, while the original scenario is evoked by the performative verb forms. Today, we are witnessing another remarkable transformation of this text genre: in television programmes, cooking shows, in the procedural YouTube-videos and internet tutorials for all kinds of purposes.[37] Here there is a massive return to the visual transmission of the recipe, but it is passed on in a monologue, since on the addressee side oral interaction is not possible. As with written texts, the addressee retains a temporal and spatial distance, can consult the recipe (or watch the tutorial) at any time and as often as he needs. Contact with other readers/users remains possible; in the past through the notes written in the margins of the books, now through the comments of internet users, which act as a 'sanction', i.e. as an evaluation of the successful or unsatisfactory execution of the instructions.

'Books of secrets' were from the beginning conceived as written collections and intended to be read; the authors were well aware of this. It was only at a second stage, if at all, that they were put into practice. This is confirmed by the fact that the lack of immediacy, the impossibility of seeing with one's own eyes,

---

36   Several studies highlight the situational context of such texts as the primary transmission channel, with the written fixation of procedures coming later. So Michael Giesecke, "Volkssprache' und 'Verschriftlichung des Lebens' im Spätmittelalter – am Beispiel der Genese der gedruckten Fachprosa in Deutschland', in Hans Ulrich Gumbrecht (ed.), *Literatur in der Gesellschaft des Spätmittelalters* (Heidelberg: Winter, 1980), pp. 39–70; Idem, 'Überlegungen zur sozialen Funktion und zur Struktur handschriftlicher Rezepte im Mittelalter', in Brigitte Schlieben-Lange and Helmut Kreuzer (eds.), *Fachsprache und Fachliteratur* (= *LiLi. Zeitschrift für Literaturwissenschaft und Linguistik*) (Göttingen: Vandenhoeck & Ruprecht, 1983), pp. 167–184. The importance of vernacular languages and the oral character of recipes are emphasised also by Giuli Liebmann-Parrinello, 'Einblicke in eine Textsortengeschichte: Kochrezepte seit frühneuhochdeutscher Zeit bis heute', in Hartwig Kalverkämper and Klaus D. Baumann (eds.), *Fachliche Textsorten. Komponenten – Relationen – Strategien* (Tübingen: Narr, 1996), pp. 292–320, here p. 296.

37   On television and on the WorldWideWeb, immediate visual perception becomes possible again, but without spatial contiguity. On recipes and new media see Hermann Cölfen, 'Vom Kochrezept zur Kochanleitung'; Markus Nickl, 'Die Zukunft der Anleitungstexte', in Marianne Grove Ditlevsen, Peter Kastberg, and Christiane Pankow (eds.), *Sind Gebrauchsanleitungen zu gebrauchen? Linguistische und kommunikativ-pragmatische Studien zu skandinavischen und deutschen Instruktionstexten* (Tübingen: Narr, 2009), pp. 8–28.

was not sufficiently taken into account and compensated for.[38] The difficulties that the apprentice had to overcome were innumerable: sometimes important information was missing, such as quantities or the shape of the vessels; sometimes complex actions were only described approximately or craftsmanship was simply assumed. And there was the tedious problem of the lack of codification of many ingredients, especially plants and alchemical preparations.[39] Another difficulty was dosage, which early modern recipes often left to the performer or quantified by unconventional, culture-based indications ('as long as a *miserere*'; 'as much as fits on a *carlino*', a local coin); and further still the coded instructions that were typical of many alchemical recipes.

In performative terms, the consequence is that the cognitive gap is never completely overcome and the acting reader often does not achieve the desired result, because the 'doing' of the performing subject can not be only inferential and cognitive (acquiring and storing knowledge), but has also an interpretative-pragmatic component: he has to feel his way forward, to try this way or that, to interpret the information as he thinks best, with more or less accuracy. Often it is the texts themselves that grant creative freedom to the agent ('as much as you think is enough'; 'according to your liking'), or suggest alternatives ('in March, April or May'; 'with clear water or spit'), i.e. there is an expectation in the recipe itself that it will be adapted to a particular situation. The text refers to the incompleteness of the rules as its own constitutive definition; the addressee is well aware of this and accepts it as part of the communicative contract.

Most authors of books of secrets, however, did not argue on the praxeological but on the cognitive level. They were learned collectors, excerpted dozens of works, copied from the writings of ancient authors and tirelessly searched for further 'secrets' with which they would enrich the next edition. They were

---

38   When describing an action, many details are lost. The art of writing, Donalies summarises, 'ist also die Kunst des Zerstörens. Wobei planvoll bedacht werden muss, wie viel erhalten und wie viel zerstört werden soll'; see Donalies, 'Das Rezept war super!', pp. 210–211. Although Donalies is concerned with internet recipes and online reviews, her reflections on missing or inaccurate instructions are also applicable to early modern texts.

39   Pronounced synonymy relationships in terminology led to numerous misunderstandings, as Bunsmann-Hopf also noted: Sabine Bunsmann-Hopf, *Zur Sprache in Kochbüchern des späten Mittelalters und der frühen Neuzeit. Ein fachkundliches Wörterbuch* (Würzburg: Königshausen & Neumann, 2003), Einleitung, p. LIII. – Della Porta, who was concerned with a scientific approach, often gave the scholarly Latin or Greek name alongside the vernacular one, and his translators behaved similarly: '… the Oxyacantha, or the Barbery-tree, is nothing else but …' (*Magia* 1658, p. 72). Not infrequently, however, the problem lay with the translations, which made the execution of many recipes impossible due to omissions or incorrect rendering of the original texts.

more concerned with the limitless expansion of knowledge, not so much with the practical feasibility of the individual recipe.

The adverb 'so' that introduces the concluding sentence of many recipes provides both a cognitive and pragmatic confirmation of the procedure: The close interlocking between the cognitive aspect (manipulation-sanction) and the pragmatic aspect (competence-performance) is perhaps the decisive feature of such collections of recipes and also explains why books of secrets had so many readers who did not necessarily want themselves to undertake experiments. Recipes promised miracles and were already satisfying on the level of knowledge, because they successfully conveyed a know-how, an 'art' that endowed the reader with the ability to manipulate the real, even if the transformation was not actually carried out. In the foreground was the awareness of being-able-to-do: I now know that I can do this.

By establishing themselves as procedural texts, how-to books became at the same time encyclopaedic works that promised to reveal the secrets of culture, as well as those of nature. In this way, they satisfied and at the same time nourished the clearly widespread need to influence reality, to dominate nature bending it to one's needs.

As a procedure for producing an (immaterial) value-object, the recipe actually offers the solution to a problem; it is a cultural construction and thus linguistic expression of social needs. From this point of view, such recipes collections exercise an identity-forming function, they create and consolidate the respective reference values and the identity of the social groups that recognise themselves in them. For this reason, they are particularly informative for the historian, because they enable him to reconstruct the corresponding 'reference worlds'. Through its components (substances and practices), recipes thus reveal a lot about the people and the society in which they are practised.

CHAPTER 10

Smelling Good While Conjuring the Spirits

Use of 'Perfumes' in Medieval and Early Modern Magic Books

Sergei Zotov

Olfactory studies of history flourish these days, and the editions and translations of grimoires (magic books) come more and more frequently.[1] These topics have never been brought together. Aromas were used in many magical treatises of Middle Ages and early modern period. Sometimes perfume manuals were within the same collection as the books on alchemy or magic.[2] Consequently, one may find many incense recipes in the alchemical or magical miscellanies. It should not surprise the researcher of manuscripts, who could easily see astrological charts, recipes for cooking cucumbers, calculations of the cost of alchemical ingredients, anatomical drawings, magic squares, images of medicinal herbs, drawings of various devices, fortifications, cannons, measuring instruments, within the confines of one book collection, or sometimes even within the same miscellany.

We do not only have the recipes of different incenses grimoires, but we also can read directly in the magical books about the theory of aromatic interaction. Scents are found to be already classified by governing planets, stars, and such, giving us a hint that they were a part of the great chain of being, as well as plants, stones, and animals. But the world of aromas was built upon all these three natures, as suffumigations (aromatic fumes, produced during a magic ritual of burning certain substances) often consisted of animal or other unusual ingredients. Some were pleasant, while others were stinking, and they were used according to their properties. We will see further that some of the ingredients were the basis for fragrances that have been used and are still used in the creation of perfumery. The other ones were 'symbolical' components, acting as an apotropaic agent, or a mediator of contagious/sympathetic magic.

---

1 Mark M. Smith, *Sensing the Past: Seeing, Hearing, Smelling, Tasting, and Touching in History* (Berkeley: University of California Press, 2007); Julia Seeberger, *Olfaktorik und Entgrenzung. Die Visionen der Wienerin Agnes Blannbekin* (Göttingen: V&R unipress, 2022); Brian Copenhaver, *Magic in Western Culture from Antiquity to the Enlightenment* (Cambridge: Cambridge University Press, 2015).

2 Perfumes collection in Wolfenbüttel, HAB, Cod. Guelf. 342 Helmst., or a miscellany in Glasgow, UL Ferguson Ms. 15 with recipes of pickling gherkins and making ink.

© KONINKLIJKE BRILL BV, LEIDEN, 2024 | DOI:10.1163/9789004683389_012

In this paper, I will try to summarize for the first time the most important mentions of aromas in different grimoires, especially in *Picatrix, Liber Razielis,* and some Solomonic treatises. But before delving into the wondrous, and sometimes, perhaps, illogical for our modern understanding, the world of medieval and early modern magic, it is worth starting with a brief introduction to the topic of grimoire magic.

1   Introduction: European Grimoires and Their Owners

The history of grimoire in Europe can be counted from the tenth or eleventh century when an Arabic treatise *Ghāyat al-Ḥakīm* was compiled, and then translated into European languages under the title *Picatrix* in thirteenth century with serious alterations. It was the first harmonious and comprehensive magical system in Europe, based on the creation of astrological amulets. This type of magic comes to Europe through Islamic influence, thanks to the cross-cultural contact in Moorish Spain. The other type of magic, summoning angels and demons, was associated with Jewish and Greek magical traditions, which came from Hellenistic Egypt, Spain, and Byzantium after the fall of Constantinople.[3]

At least in the Middle Ages, magic books were used mainly by the lower ranks of the church hierarchy, as well as students and people who helped the priests, i.e., those who already knew Latin and about the liturgy, with which magic rituals often look like. During rituals, the magician created a protective circle, either drawn on the ground with a magic wand or sword, or made from paper, skin, parchment or fabric. Of central importance was that the European mage had a written source, a grimoire, as well as a number of attributes: among them, there could be an altar, clothes, a magic wand, a staff, knives, a sickle, pipes, whistles, candles, and other tools, as well as special incense and suffumigations.

One of the first genuine European grimoires was the book *Ars Notoria, sive Flores Aurei* (c.1225). It explained how to instantly gain knowledge in a variety of subjects, namely the trivium and quadrivium, medicine, philosophy, and theology, as well as learn chastity, magic, and astrology.[4] It was believed the

---

3 See Dan Attrell and David Porreca, *Picatrix. A Medieval Treatise on Astral Magic* (University Park: Penn State Press, 2020); Stephen Skinner and Daniel Clark, *Ars Notoria: The Grimoire of Rapid Learning by Magic, with the Golden Flowers of Apollonius of Tyana,* 2 vols (Singapore: Golden Hoard Press, 2019), p. 16.

4 This book starts the genre of Ars notoria. It was believed that for the first time, this knowledge was received by the biblical king Solomon. The inquiry of the society to instantly gain

magician received all the knowledge he was in the hunt for through special images, 'notae'.

In the thirteenth century, in the *Liber Razielis* the magician was already offered a ritual to invoke the vision of an angel, which includes prayers, austerity, and sacrifices. Then the angel himself can teach a person the magical art.[5] So angelic magic appears in Europe. In the fourteenth century, in the *Sworn Book of Honorius* it is proposed to call the angels, and sometimes the demons controlled by them, with the subsequent fulfilment of the desires and orders of the magician. Among other desires that they could fulfil was the ability to control the forces of nature, the thoughts of other people, invisibility, building castles, creating ghosts, finding out the time of one's own death, foreseeing the future or past, turning day into night.[6]

In parallel with the tradition of summoning angels, the tradition of summoning demons, or necromancy developed. The word necromancy defined the summoning of spirits, angels, and especially demons (in very rare cases, also dead people). It was formed both by a medieval interest in the liturgical ceremonies, and by a passion for visions, stories about demons, and the structure of the infernal world.[7] In the early modern period, grimoires begin to be written in languages other than Latin, and they become more and more simple, after which they end up in print. Later magical books were begun to be used by the common people. Many of these readers copied grimoires or created new versions of them, experiencing the rituals and spells first-hand and adjusting them.[8] Two large traditions of demonic magic, or necromancy, existed in the late medieval and early modern grimoires: Solomonic and Faustian.

---

education was due to the fact that learning and books were very expensive. In order to acquire the expertise, the owner of the grimoire needed to perform the ritual. At first, it was required to be cleansed of sins by confession and fasting, and then to conduct a special ceremony with drinking water, in which the names of angels written on the leaves were dissolved. After that, an angel appeared to the magician in a dream and approved of his intentions. Then it was necessary to continue to practice similar rituals for three months, as well as to pray and fast in a specific way. In the fourth month, one could begin to read the book itself and contemplate the 'notae'. There were more than 80 kinds of 'notae' in total. Most often, their iconography is obscure, but some are directly related to the sciences they are supposed to teach – for example, the 'nota' of astronomy shows images of the planets and signs of the zodiac.

5   Don Karr and Stephen Skinner, *Sepher Raziel: Liber Salomonis. A Sixteenth Century English Grimoire* (Singapore: Golden Hoard Press, 2010).

6   Joseph Peterson, *Sworn Book of Honorius. Liber Iuratus Honorii* (Lake Worth: Ibis Press, 2016).

7   Frank Klaassen, *The Transformations of Magic. Illicit Learned Magic in the Later Middle Ages and Renaissance* (University Park: Penn University Press, 2013), p. 118.

8   Richard Kieckhefer, *Magic in the Middle Ages* (Cambridge: Cambridge University Press, 1989), pp. 153–156.

The belief in magic was a perennial throughout Europe. As late as 1710, a collection of 140 magical manuscripts was offered for sale in Leipzig for the immense sum of 4,000 riksdaler.[9] Dark forces were considered to be the keepers of underground riches, since they lived underground. Thus, the main task of the magician was to find treasures. It must be remembered that the majority of grimoire users were male. Many necromantic rituals were performed just to impress a woman,[10] others were to show a woman naked or make her dance for a magician.[11] *The Munich Codex* contained spells to seduce young girls with invocations to the Mother of God.[12] And while some of the goals of the grimoires included the study of various sciences or the creation of thermal springs for healing, many more spells were devoted to purposes such as casting corruption, finding thieves with a sieve, creating a flying carpet, building a defence fort, creating a ship, or experiencing invisibility with help of a wax figure.

The most common demon-summoning books were Solomonic grimoires, allegedly written by the biblical king himself.[13] Solomonic grimoires give detailed instructions for summoning. Demonic magic, like angelic magic, included long and complex rituals. Ideally, the magician had to personally forge all the tools, carve staves and wands, make writing utensils, incense, perfumes, candles in moments corresponding to certain astrological conditions so that these materials can be called 'virgin', never previously used for another purpose. Then it was necessary to decorate all the attributes with special inscriptions and get the blood, skins, and organs of sacrificial animals, among which could be chickens, goats, moles, and others.[14]

The magician who used a Solomonic grimoire often had to perform ritual washing, shaving, burn incense and use perfume before the ritual. The spirit was coaxed or tortured with different sets of tools, depending on its nature and behaviour, and rarely appeared earlier than on the ninth attempt, but even then, it could be completely invisible, or only a virgin child could see it. The

---

9   Daniel Bellingradt, Bernd-Christian Otto, *Magical Manuscripts in Early Modern Europe. The Clandestine Trade in Illegal Book Collections* (Cham (CH): Palgrave Macmillan, 2017). This 'Magica-Sammlung' is accessible in the university library of Leipzig.

10   Klaassen, *The Transformations of Magic*, p. 126.

11   Eliza Marian Butler, *Ritual Magic* (Cambridge: Cambridge University Press, 1949), p. 71.

12   Richard Kieckhefer, *Forbidden Rites. A Necromancer's Manual of the Fifteenth Century* (University Park: Penn State Press, 1998).

13   They were mentioned by Josephus Flavius in the first century AD. According to legend, Solomon imprisoned seventy-two demons, which he commanded with a magic ring, with a magic seal in a copper vessel. But people broke the seal of the jug, and the spirits were freed – so they can still be called.

14   Butler, *Ritual Magic*, pp. 53–54.

summoning of demons was once allegedly witnessed by Benvenuto Cellini himself, who mentions this in his autobiography.[15] What they did was possibly the ritual inspired by the Solomonic grimoire, with suffumigations as an integral part of invoking spirits. But in its turn, early modern Solomonic grimoires were inspired by famous *Picatrix*, and other medieval magical books.

I would try to trace the history of magical fragrances in grimoires from the thirteenth up to the nineteenth centuries in following sections, certainly not more than of prolegomenic nature, since this topic is truly infinite.

2   Use of Suffumigations in Medieval Grimoires: *Picatrix*, *Ars Notoria*, *Liber Razielis*, *Book of Honorius*

In contrast to the more theoretical-philosophical occult literature, which of course also existed, spell books are practical ritual texts, how-to texts, that give very specific instructions on how the magician can harness spiritual and demonic powers for himself. Subtle substances, such as scents and smells, play an important role in communicating with the supernatural powers. 'Grimoires' – the word is a malapropism of the French 'grammaire' – are highly performatively grounded. If one is serious about revenge magic, love magic, damage magic and treasure hunting, etc., these books can never be received apathetically.[16]

Grimoires not only contained magical invocations; they were magical objects themselves, which is often highlighted in long enumerations of the sorcerer's tools, among which there is always a book. The possession of the grimoire or its part was believed to be a magical act, and indeed it was enough for the court to the accusation of witchcraft. In some books, there were special empty spaces where the owner of the manuscript or the printed book should put their signature. Most of the magic books were in pocket size, which made it easier to carry the book during rituals. In the eighteenth century, we see more grimoires

---

15   We come across a passage about a necromancer, who tries to help Cellini and ask demons to unite him with his beloved Sicilian girl, Angelica. In this chapter we see that 'precious perfumes', as well as fetid odours were used during the ritual, and two people took care of the aromatic part of the process (including Cellini himself, and next time the same did his friend Vincenzio Romoli), looking after the perfumes and fire, obviously needed for giving off the fragrance See: George Anthony Bull (translator), *The Autobiography of Benvenuto Cellini* (Harmondsworth, Middlesex: Penguin, 1986), pp. 118–122.

16   Marco Frenschkowksi, 'Zauberbücher. Die Leipziger Magica-Sammlung im Schatten der Frühaufklärung', in *Zauberbücher* (Leipzig: Universitätsbibliothek, 2019), p. 10; see also Claude Lecouteux, *Le Livre des Grimoires: aspects de la magie au Moyen Âge* (Paris: Imago, 2008).

of bigger size: it made their look more solid, the book was perceived to be more authoritative, and reliable. Late magic books appeared closer to encyclopaedias or modern scientific manuals, filled with commentaries, illustrations, and charts. Some grimoires were full of glossa and marginalia, which shows us that their owners tend to make corrections, additions, and omissions to their copies. The visual aspect of the grimoire was also of the utmost importance. Images in magic books were prototypes for producing talismans, pentacles, or figurines for using the power of specific angels and demons or invoking them. Sometimes illustrated pages from grimoires, especially with sigils, were used in rituals instead of being only the exempla. Often luxuriously adorned with golden, silver, versicoloured, and iridescent illuminations, grimoires could give the reader the impression of magic only by means of decorations. The physically perceived shine of sigils, magic squares, and spells created a magical atmosphere.

If the imagery inside the books could be lavishly embellished, their covers were rarely as splendid. In later grimoires (18–19 centuries) we sometimes see golden cover ornaments, some images on binding spine,[17] or a completely black cover (this colour was seldom used in illumination because of its high cost), also decorated with a sigil and ornaments.

Probably, with such covers, protective/apotropaic and magical potential of grimoires were increased. I never succeeded in finding a single copy with a significantly 'magical' cover among the early magic books, which also rarely used frontispieces. Both probably were connected to censorship considerations, and the dangers of keeping such a book, as well as its visibility.

In addition to this, mainly the visual side of the materiality of grimoires, there was another, olfactory side. Grimoires, along with many other magical instruments, were fumigated with special concoctions, recipes of which they almost never failed to mention in abundance. Medieval grimoires were not the first to mention suffumigations and their recipes. One of the earliest indications of use of scents in magic is found of Papyri Graecae Magicae, where ink, perfumed with myrrh was used in the ritual of healing by drinking the water where special names written by this ink were dissolved, like later in *Ars notoria*.[18] Ancient Greek literature features many examples on witches preparing

17   Francis Barrett: The Magus, or Celestial Intelligencer (London: Lackington, 1801), Glasgow, University Library, Ah-y.5.

18   Stephen Skinner and Daniel Clark, *Ars Notoria: The Grimoire of Rapid Learning by Magic, with the Golden Flowers of Apollonius of Tyana*, 2 vols (Singapore: Golden Hoard Press, 2019), p. 119.

FIGURE 10.1   Glittering sigil of the Moon from Pseudo-Solomon's 'Les Clavicules de
R. Salomon', 1796. London, Wellcome Collection, Ms. 4670, p. 85

FIGURE 10.2   Cover of Pseudo-Solomon's 'Les Clavicules de R. Salomon, 1796
London, Wellcome Collection, MS. 4670

special herbs for fuming them.[19] Bad smelling suffumigations as offerings to demons were alluded to in Zosimos' writings, which are also closely related to alchemy.[20] In Byzantine magic use of incenses was as natural as of magic cir-

---

19   Britta Ager, 'Magic Perfumes and Deadly Herbs: The Scent of Witches' Magic in Classical Literature', in *Preternature: Critical and Historical Studies on the Preternatural*, 8 (2019), pp. 1–34.
20   David Rankine and Stephen Skinner, *The Veritable Key of Solomon* (Singapore: Golden Hoard Press, 2008), p. 346.

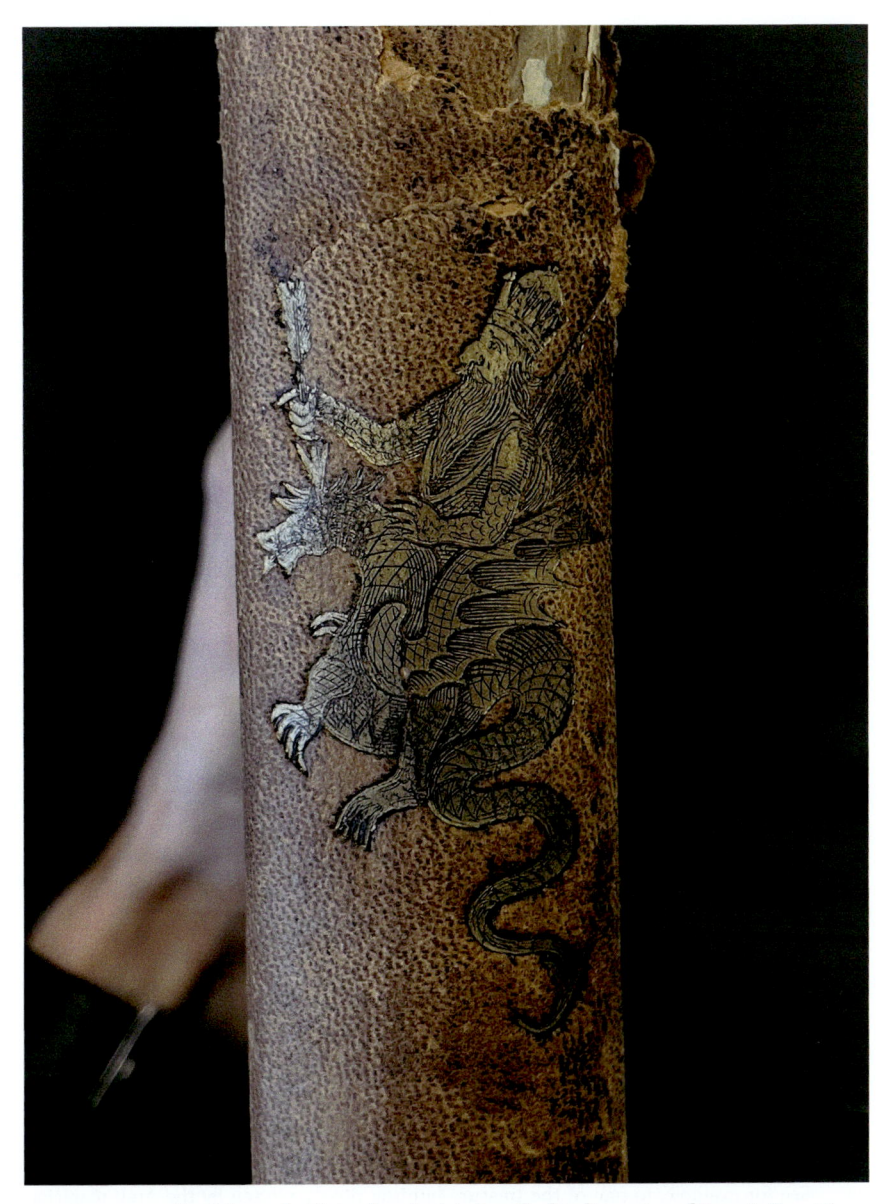

FIGURE 10.3   Cassiel, angel of Saturday, depicted on the binding spine of Francis Barrett's
              'Magus', 1801. Glasgow, University Library, Ah-y.5

cles or sacred names.[21] In Islamicate world treasure hunting and other magical
or alchemical operations were not rarely connected with special compounds
which meant to be burned for the glory of jinns and other supernatural

---

21   Peterson, *Sworn Book of Honorius*, p. 16.

FIGURE 10.4   Cover of the grimoire 'Imprecationes Fausti. Dr. Fausts Höllen-Zwang', *c.*1750.
                Leipzig, Universitätsbibliothek, Cod.mag.77

beings.[22] Probably some of these practices are also rooted in Indian knowledge, imported via Silk routes.[23] The latter example is especially relevant, since
it was close to the roots of the book created in the Islamic world, which then
were translated and became the first European grimoire: *Picatrix*.

---

22   See for example, to one of the treasure-hunting rituals, written by the Arab magician
     al-Maghrabi in the fourteenth century Okasha El Daly, *Egyptology: The Missing Millennium.
     Ancient Egypt in Medieval Arabic Writings* (London: UCL Press, 2005), pp. 36–37.

23   More on connections between East and West: Ronit Yoeli-Tlalim, *ReOrienting Histories of
     Medicine. Encounters along the Silk Roads* (London: Bloomsbury Academic, 2021). See the
     recipe for care for the body during the winter, similar to sweet-smelling suffumigations in
     grimoires, in a seventh century ayurvedic book Aṣṭāṅgahṛdayasaṃhitā: "smear [the body]
     with saffron mixed with musk and fumigate with aloeswood (Anya H. King, *Scent from the
     Garden of Paradise. Musk and the Medieval Islamic World* (Leiden: Brill, 2017), p. 104.

In *Picatrix* among descriptions of talismans, remedies, celestial circumstances, clothing, sacrifices, prayers, and rituals we find formulas for suffumigations, which are connected with seven planetary gods and could attract spirits to their magical images. It was believed that the ritual accompanied by suffumigations was more effective.[24] In book 3 chapter 5 we see a description of how and why suffumigations are able to invoke spirits:

> Air is a body without which other bodies are incapable of life since it is the medium for receiving bodies, influences, or the planetary effects, by the agent's will arranged through a combination of his own air with the air in general. It takes effect through suffumigations placed according to the limbs of the human body, and these suffumigations are composed from plants and other kinds of things. These suffumigations move the spirits of men toward their desires. The works of magic have many wonders and manifest effects.[25]

In *Picatrix*, the suffumigation affects the magician himself, not the objects, as in later Solomonic grimoires: 'Then inhale the suffumigations according to the chosen planet's nature, burn it in the fire of that censer'.[26] It is often advised to 'suffumigate yourself' during the prayer.[27] But also, the suffumigation will affect the spirits of the planet: 'the smoke of this suffumigation ought to reach the sphere of the signs'.[28] Sometimes there are direct invocations to the planetary gods about their aromas: 'O spirits of Mars, this is your sacrifice! Come, and smell this suffumigation'.[29]

There are detailed descriptions of what areas are governed by which god/planet. For example, Venus is responsible, among the other, for selling perfumes. Book 3, chapter 3 briefly describes the suffumigations of the planets.[30] It is important that the planets' aromas are here also characterized as

---

24   Attrell/Porreca, *Picatrix. Astral Magic*, p. 28.
25   Ibid., p. 145.
26   Ibid., p. 149.
27   Ibid., p. 187.
28   Ibid., p. 149.
29   Ibid., p. 187.
30   'Suffumigation of Saturn comprises all foul-smelling things, like asafoetida, gum, bdellium, hemlock. Suffumigation of Jupiter comprises all good and balanced scents, such as amber, aloewood. The suffumigation of Mars comprises everything hot, like pepper and ginger. The suffumigation of the Sun comprises all things with a balanced and good scent, like musk, amber, and similar things. The suffumigation of Venus comprises everything that smells balanced, like the rose, the violet, the green myrtle. The suffumigation of Mercury comprises everything with composite odours, such as narcissus, violets, myrtle,

'foul-smelling' or 'good', 'cold' or 'hot', 'balanced' or 'composite'. That denoted allegorical meaning in the relationships between planets and fragrances I will describe below. As we also can see from this and other recipes, suffumigations in *Picatrix* frequently consist of psychoactive substances such as opium, wormwood, mixed with traditional aromatic components (mastic gum, frankincense, storax, balsam, nutmeg; the latter could be psychoactive in certain amounts, too).[31] Other aromas could also be stinking or even deadly, as hemlock.

In book 3 chapter 7 there are two suffumigation recipes for each planet (only Mercury and Moon have one). One of the recipes for Saturn's suffumigations includes 'equal parts of opium, storax (which is a herb), saffron, seed of laurel, carob, wormwood, lanolin, colocynth, and the head of a black cat'.[32] The mage has to grind and mix them with the urine of a black she-goat and then make tablets of it, to place them on the coals in the censer. Some recipes have very precise dosages, but the majority are very approximate.

I gathered all the variations of the planetary suffumigation recipes in Table 10.1.

Many ingredients in these 31 recipes are the same, but it is striking, that rarely the same ingredient is present in different recipes for the same planet.[33]

Ingredients are usually somehow associated with the planet's deity properties, colours, or attributes. Saturn, the planet of the god of death, associated with black and tawny colours, is represented by bitter, dangerous, and hallucinogenic substances like wormwood, hemlock, opium, or asafoetida. Asafoetida in Europe was considered as a dangerous, evil, even blasphemous scent. In Luca Landucci's Florentine diary from 1450 to 1516 is mentioned, that once in the 1490s on the night of the Nativity in many churches asafoetida was put in the censers instead of incense as an act of vandalism.[34] Old dates also should be of unpleasant odour. Bellium is collected from black trees, juniper's

---

and similar things. The suffumigation of the Moon comprises all the cold scents, like camphor, lily, and so on'. See: Ibid., p. 139.

31   Ibid., p. 27.

32   Ibid., p. 159.

33   Wormwood, hemlock, and the head/brain of a black cat are mentioned twice in the recipes for Saturn, aloe, wine, and incense – for Jupiter, pepper, mustard, and aloe – for Mars, incense, nutmeg, saffron, and spikenard – for Sun, rose, chicory, and incense – for Venus, and frankincense, elecampane, myrrh, and lily for Moon. There are no matching ingredients for Mercury. All the other ingredients are either unique for all the recipes, like pomegranate flower or such usual component as musk (!), or, vice versa, are present in many other recipes, like storax, appearing in seven formulas, or aloe, appearing in eight.

34   Luca Landucci, *A Florentine diary from 1450 to 1516* (London, New York: J.M. Dent & Sons, 1927), pp. 152–153.

berries and carob's fruits are black as well. In chapter 3 recipes it is very rare to mention animal or human body parts as components, so the head of a black cat and the urine of a black she-goat definitely allude to death and decay associated with Saturn.

Jupiter's suffumigation consists exclusively of pleasant scents like aloe wood, amber, or myrrh. It also uses grapes and 'pure and old wine aged for many years', perhaps as references to the highest cuisine and respectively to the highest rank of this god. Mars as the planet of the god of war is associated with hot and bright red substances like mustard, pepper, ginger, holly, spikenard, wine, and also with violence and fights, which gives the human blood in the composition. The Sun is associated mainly with yellowish-coloured or reddish-coloured ingredients such as litharge, saffron, terebinth fruits, fleabane, elecampane, sonchus, cinquefoil, pine nuts, as well as of noble scent, as myrrh, clove, incense, or both, as yellow and red sandalwood, red cinnamon, honey, and wine. Venus is closely associated with love. In the images of Venus in astrological manuscripts we know that her chariot carriers were doves: in *Picatrix*, the dove's body has to be placed on the charcoals together with the suffumigation itself. The colours of this planet could be associated with red because this is the colour of love, and with blue or gold, as it also stated in *Picatrix*. There appear such ingredients as rose, rosewater, poppy, grapes, saffron, and violet, some of these plants were believed to be aphrodisiacs. Moon is associated with yellow in *Picatrix*, but also as we can see from the list of ingredients, with white colour, because of its obvious visual likeness with the visible planet's surface. That is why camphor, lily, poley germander, white snake grease, body of calf, and St. John's Wort, elecampane appear in this list.

There are also many references to the use of suffumigations by Indians (see Table 10.1) or Chaldeans in *Picatrix*. It is told that the latter made Saturn's suffumigation 'of old hides, fat, sweat, dead bats, and mice'.[35] The planetary recipes of old wise men from distant lands are usually far more 'symbolic' than the others. If animal/human ingredients are used in their recipes (book 4, chapter 6) thirty times, in all the other recipes of *Picatrix* there are only six mentions, the majority of which are in fact part of the burned sacrifice, and not the suffumigation itself.

There are also twelve suffumigations for the signs of the zodiac and twenty-eight suffumigations for the mansions of the Moon, some of them even containing cannabis resin. In other aromatic recipes, not connected with astrology, usually simple mixes of incense and galbanum are used, sometimes with the addition of hairs of a wolf tail or other 'symbolic' ingredients. Occasionally

---

35   Attrell/Porreca, *Picatrix. Astral Magic*, p. 182.

TABLE 10.1   Planetary suffumigation ingredients in *Picatrix*[a]

	Saturn	Jupiter	Mars
Picatrix 3.3	asafoetida, gum, bdellium, hemlock	amber, *aloe wood*	*pepper*, ginger
Picatrix 3:7 (1)	opium, **storax**, **saffron**, seed of **laurel**, carob, *wormwood*, lanolin, colocynth, ***head of a black cat***, urine of a black she-goat	classe, **storax gum**, columbine, peony, aromatic calamus, **pine resin**, hellebore seeds, pure and old *wine aged* for many years	**wormwood**, *aloe*, **squina**, cywort, spurge, large *pepper*, watercress, human blood
Picatrix 3:7 (2)	southern *wormwood*, bericus seed, juniper root, **nut**, old dates, thistle, good **wine aged** for many years	fleabane, *incense*, hackberry, **myrrh**, skinned grapes, *wine aged* for many years	storax gum, incense of **nutmeg**, holly, *aloe wood*, spikenard, **mastic**, the be wine
Picatrix 3:9	*brain of a black cat*, euphorbia, **hemlock**, **myrrh**, St. John's Wort	mastic gum, *aloe wood*	**myrrh**, *mustard*, sarcocol
Picatrix 4:6	mandrake fruits, dried olive leaves, black myrobalan seeds, dried black chickpeas, **black crow's brains**, dried crane brains, pig blood, dried monkey blood, **whipped honey**	balsam, dried **myrtle** flowers, *frankincense*, shelled **nut**, shelled and dried hazelnuts, dried brains of cock, **dove**, goose brains, dried blood of peacock and camel, **nutmeg**, camphor, whipped honey	red **asafoetida**, mustard, **terebinth**, **pine resin**, red orpiment; **brain of sparrow**, dried brain of scorpion, leopard blood, red **snake grease**, whipped honey

a   Bold are ingredients which are also present in any other recipes and italicised are ingredients that are the same for one planet in different sets of recipes. The ingredient is grey-coloured if it coincides only with the same planet recipe in *The Keys of Rabbi Solomon*, but not with other recipes in *Picatrix*. In brackets are the names of the sacrifices burned along with the incense.

n	Venus	Mercury	Moon
..sk, amber	*rose*, violet, green myrtle	narcissus, **violets, myrtle**	**camphor**, *lily*
...mmon **fleabane, bdellium, myrrh,** ..danum, elecampane, cicely, nettle ..e, **poley germander, cleaned pine** ...ts, **lily root,** sonchus, **cardamom,** ...matic reed, *incense, nutmeg* **shell,** ...ied roses, *saffron, spikenard,* root caper, cinquefoil, **clove, balsam** ...ed, cuscuta, **squinancywort;** ..cumber seed, amomum, **tere-** ...nth, **date** powder, **skinned grapes,** ...immed **honey,** the best **wine**	(dove's body, **turtledove's** body), **aloe wood,** *chicory,* **costus, saffron, labdanum, mas-** **tic gum,** poppy husks, willow leaves, **lily root,** *rosewater*	**nutmeg,** holm oak, **cumin,** dried **cloves,** myrtle branches, bitter almond husks, acacia, seeds of tamarisk, **grapevine** branches, **squinancywort,** pure and delicate **wine**	**mastic gum, cardamom,** savin, **storax gum,** peppered thistle, *elecampane, myrrh,* squinancywort, dar sessahal, **spikenard, costus,** *frankincense,* **saffron,** cucumber, **cucumber seeds,** henna root, *lily root,* Celtic nard, Indian **poley germander,** shelled **cleaned pine nuts,** St. John's Wort, **labdanum,** apple leaves, **dried roses,** jelly, cleaned **grapes, dates,** the subtlest **wine,** (body of a bovine calf, or a sheep)
..ffron, **storax gum,** *incense, nutmeg,* ..harge, pomegranate flower, **aloe** ...od, saxifrage	*chicory,* **peppered thistle, grapes,** *frankincense,* **mastic gum,** rain water	-x-	-x-
..	-x-	**Aloe wood,** incense, myrrh, **hemlock,** elecampane	*frankincense,* hemlock, *elecampane, myrrh,* aloe wood
..ikenard flowers, yellow and red ndalwood, sedge, thyme, red **cinna-** ..on bark, **costus,** eagle brain, eagle ...ood, **cat brain,** cat blood, **whipped** ..oney	**laurel** berries, **nut** kernels, *frankincense* grains, **mastic gum, henbane** stalks, **poley germander** stalks, **storax gum,** borax, **brain of sparrow,** dried hawk brain, dried horse blood, **whipped honey**	**henbane** flowers, indigo leaves, hazelwort, **amber,** toad testicles, red ammonia, **brains of crow,** hoopoe, tortoise, blood of donkey, **whipped honey**	peach tree, **cinnamon** leaves, iris, dried **storax gum, cumin,** white **snake grease,** dried brain of rabbit, **brain of black cat,** fox blood, **whipped honey**

these recipes could be quite complex, almost fully consisting of 'symbolic' and exotic ingredients, like hair from a woman's comb or hairs from her clothes, wolf's vulva, black dog's penis, rabbit cheese, toad brain, hedgehog blood, eyes of a white cock, gazelle brain, black cat's gallbladder, claw of a leopard, tortoise fat, donkey urine, dung, or such 'alchemical' components as bezoar stone, sulphur, arsenic, sublimated mercury, wine vinegar. Some of these suffumigations are made to blind, immobilize or kill people or animals, the others are love potions, sometimes it is recommended for a magician to cover their nose with silk and not inhale the smoke due to the deadly nature of these mixes. Some ritual describes a suffumigation made of sesame oil, opium, and human blood for seeing everything one wishes, the other illustrates the ritual of the ultimate power over nature, demons, and people which includes making a suffumigation of 'man's seven properties (namely, blood, semen, saliva, ear wax, tears of the eyes, excrement, and urine)'.[36]

Definitely, the astrological recipes in *Picatrix* were the ones that made the most use of traditional perfume ingredients. That is probably because planetary gods were considered the most powerful spirits, and the magician had to use the finest means, the subtlest substances to invoke them. Conveniently, the scents rose vertically to the very top, where the planetary gods were also believed to reside. On the other hand, these ingredients were also connected with the great chain of being through the established system of planetary associations with stones, animals and aromatic ingredients here were just implemented in the existing relationships. Non-astrological recipes were not strongly attached to any systems, so they often contained components of pure symbolical nature, probably inherited from folk magic or other local traditions. We see, that *Picatrix* was a huge inspiration for the subsequent tradition of suffumigations' magic, as it was the first authoritative source of it, and contained hundreds of recipes with a variety of 164 species of plants mentioned in them.[37] Many of these recipes will migrate to the later medieval grimoire tradition.

As we already know, the first grimoire fully conducted in Europe, of course not without some continuity of knowledge and influence of other regions, was thirteenth-century *Ars Notoria, sive Flores Aurei*. There are only a few mentions of aromatic substances in this treatise, including the remark that the mage has to suffumigate themself with frankincense. This tradition is clearly connected with *Picatrix*, where auto-suffumigations were a part of the ritual.

---

36   Ibid., p. 255.
37   Shalen Prado, 'Esoteric Botanical Knowledge-scapes of Medieval Iberia', in *Archaeological Review from Cambridge*, 35 (2021), pp. 98–111, here p. 101.

But already in a sixteenth-century copy of thirteenth-century *Liber Razielis* (British Library Sloane MS 3826) we find the entire system of suffumigating the spirits. It is stated that St. John's wort (Corona regia) or rosemary is able to 'chase away devills', as well as peony, or calamintha.[38] The suffumigation of the horns of a hart has to chase away serpents and devils. Chicory is used for performing an exorcism. On the contrary, parsley or wild celery 'gathereth togither divells when suffumigacions is made with' it, as well as henbane and mugwort.[39] The same herb together with some other ingredients is able to make the magician 'see fantasyes and devills of divers maners'.[40] Similar recipe contains asafoetida, water hemlock, henbane, red sandalwood, black poppy, and 'sapss barbate' (usnea?), and can give visions of 'devills and things and strannge figures', which is highly probable, given that it is a pure drug cocktail.[41] Amber suffumigation of tombs should gather the spirits above it. Another ritual implies that among other actions suffumigation of the dead body with costus, musk, and succory will rise the body and it will speak. The other compound, made of coriander, saffron, black henbane, parsley, black poppy, water hemlock, chicory, and musk is to hide treasure from any other person. Frankincense, musk, succory, aloe, and costus will empower treasure guard with devils and evil winds.[42]

After these simplistic and practical recipes, the treatise elaborates, that according to Solomon, an angel said to Adam, and then God to Moses, to make 'thymiamata' (Greek name for fumigations[43]), i.e. good odour to glorify the Creator.[44] This suffumigation 'maketh to be opened the gates of the aire and of the fyre and of all other heavens', and then the mage could 'see heavenly things and privatyes of the Creator'.[45] One of the ways to make a sacrifice are fumigations with good odours, and that 'ouercometh in all'. That is why the wise man has to know the nature of suffumigations: with the right confection they could also summon the spirits and speak with them, including spirits of four elements ('angells & spirits of the ayre and the soules of dead men and divels and windes of spelunke and of deepenes and fantasies of desert place'), as well as remove sicknesses or vice versa, and many other.[46] Angel Raziel also

38   Karr and Skinner, *Sepher Raziel: Liber Salomonis*, p. 168.
39   Ibid., p. 76.
40   Ibid.
41   Ibid., p. 173.
42   Ibid., p. 170.
43   Rankine and Skinner, *The Veritable Key of Solomon*, p. 390.
44   Karr and Skinner, *Sepher Raziel*, p. 185.
45   Ibid., p. 91.
46   Ibid., p. 95.

develops that a good suffumigation should be in accordance with specific days and planets: 'suffumicacion is bread of which spirits liveth'.[47] In the end there are also lists of the suffumigations for twelve signs of the zodiac (which are completely different from the ones in *Picatrix*) and thirty-six 'faces of them', i.e. decans, as well as four seasons and four cardinal directions.[48]

According to *Liber Razielis*, there are seven kinds if suffumigations: sharp/ penetrative, sweet, stinking, simple, gentle, of grief, and of peace.[49] Solomon further explains that the odour of the clean suffumigation comes to clouds, next to higher clouds, then to wind, and the high wind, and afterward 'of this the spirit is made higher and of the spirit and angell of heaven'. Using this logic, if the human aromatic sacrifice could be of use for spirits/angels, maybe they will help in return?

Liber Razielis is among the earliest grimoires which explain how the suffumigation works on the 'body' of spirits (in *Picatrix* there was only an explanation of how they affect the human body). There are biblical references to the use of incense by Adam and Moses for the glory of God.[50] Consequently, the magician could in principle reunite with the Creator, due to suffumigations only. Their use is almost only limited to invoking spirits, which can assist in hiding treasures or speak with the dead. A certain Christianization of the practise of aromatic magic is visible in this text. What considers the recipes they are simplified compared with *Picatrix*, and do not use any 'symbolic' ingredients, but only herbs.

In the fourteenth-century *Sworn Book of Honorius* there is a new tendency in aromatic magic. The magician suffumigates not only themself or spirits, but magic attributes necessary in various rituals: the magic circle is fumed with pearls, the altar is fumigated with incense,[51] there is also a special suffumigation for the magician himself.[52] Only one suffumigation for demons is

---

47   Ibid., p. 191.
48   Ibid., p. 99.
49   It is also mentioned, that different temperaments of the aromatic compound will invoke spirits of different colours.
50   Bernhard Kötting, 'Wohlgeruch der Heiligkeit', in *Jenseitsvorstellungen in Antike und Christentum*. Gedenkschrift für Alfred Stuiber, ed. Theodor Klauser (Münster in Westfalen: Aschendorff, 1982), pp. 168–176; Ulrike Bechmann, 'Duft im Alten Testament', in *Die Macht der Nase. Zur religiösen Bedeutung des Duftes: Religionsgeschichte – Bibel – Liturgie* [zum Gedächtnis an Helmut Merklein], ed. by Joachim Kugler (Stuttgart: Katholisches Bibelwerk, 2000), pp. 49–98.
51   Peterson, *Sworn Book of Honorius*, p. 131.
52   Ibid., p. 209. Compare: "Rather than associate a suffumigation with the nature of the magical activity, the Rawlinson scribe links them to the days of the week and, most tellingly, assigns a final one to the operator (Subfumigatio tua)! Suffumigating the operator might

mentioned: the Labadau's consists of sulphur.[53] A pleasing suffumigation is offered to a spirit when it is placated after the conjuration. During the ritual of the Seal of God, which includes fasting, cleaning, praying, and writing in blood, the Seal of God is also fumed.[54] This composition seems to be quite standard in medieval or Renaissance perfumery, and we can spot some mentions of similar ingredients bought by ambassadors in a diary of Florentine spice vendor.[55] Assuming that the ambassadors were using these spices for making a perfume for official visits, there could be an interesting parallel between the mage, waiting for the visit of demon, angel, or God himself, and ambassadors, visiting the king. Certainly, there is also an immediate association with the Christian liturgy, which the grimoire tradition directly inherited, deriving many attributes and ceremonies from it, including suffumigations.

In the late medieval period we see Heinrich Cornelius Agrippa's attempt to classify magic and create a harmonious system of rituals, connected with an almost mathematical understanding of associations between planets and metals, letters and numbers, natural ingredients and supernatural spirits.[56] In his *Three Books of Occult Philosophy* (1533) we also see scents of planets ranked like in *Picatrix*. After this book, printed, and well-known and actively debated, suffumigation art in magic in the sixteenth century became more popular. We can see how Agrippa's book, deeply funded in the legacy of many important and authoritative treatises, mainly existing in manuscript form and unknown to a mass reader, renovated this field together with a general increasing interest in grimoires.

3   Solomonic 'Perfumes'

In the early modern period Solomonic magic was on the rise. If we see that many medieval grimoires were rediscovered only at the end of the nineteenth or beginning of the twentieth century (like *Book of Abramelin*), grimoires

---

well derive from the use of incense in the Mass, since Arabic magic characteristically only purifies or intensifies the effect of the image by holding it in the smoke" (Klaassen, *The Transformations of Magic*, p. 144). In *Picatrix* there are mentions of auto-suffumigations (see earlier).

53   Peterson, *Sworn Book of Honorius*, p. 279.

54   With a confection of 'amber, musk, aloe, white and red labdanum, mastic, frankincense, pearls, and incense'. See Ibid., p. 75.

55   I am grateful for this remark and the inspiration for this article to Allen J. Grieco.

56   Anna Marie Roos, 'Magic Coins' and 'Magic Squares': The Discovery of Astrological Sigils in the Oldenburg Letters', in *Notes and Records of the Royal Society of London*, 62 (2008), pp. 271–288.

connected with the name of Solomon were constantly copied and even printed later. Around 150 manuscript copies of Solomonic grimoires have come down to us, with the earliest surviving book created in the sixteenth century, but with the text of the thirteenth or fourteenth century.[57] The *Lemegeton Clavicula Salomonis* [Lesser Key of Solomon] was especially famous because it contained seventy-two sigils of the infernal lords: knights, dukes, marquises, earls, princes, presidents, and kings of hell (the hierarchy of otherworldly beings given in this book is similar to the social strata that existed in the late medieval Europe). Manuscripts were dispersed all around Europe and were translated into vernacular languages, like French, Italian, German, English, etc.

A great deal of texts of these grimoires is dedicated to aromatic magic. Working with perfumes implied that they were laid and lit in a special apparatus, most often a censer was used. In a W.H. Ibbett's *Treatise on magic* from the University of Manchester John Rylands Library English MS 44, written in 1854–1857, we find detailed description of creation of such a 'thurible'.

I have transcribed it and show it here in its entirety:

> This Thuribulum and Tripod should be of the following proportions and forme, The vase consisting of three parts, as A The Cover which has a tube up it and a hollow ball on the top, perforated with 9 crosses to let the perfume escape, The body B has a small grate as E on which the fuel rest on when put into the Body B. The Button C is a vacume for the admission of the air to keep the fine burning, therefore from the passage or currancy of air from C to A answers as a pair of Bellows, The Tripod or stand D the top and bottom must be an exact triangle, and the sides must be a perfect square equal to the triangle each way and may be made either solid or hollow of some hard wood as pane tree.[58]

The use of 'perfumes' inside of the censer/thurible is described in detail in the Solomonic grimoires. In *The Keys of Rabbi Solomon* (1796) from the manuscript from London, Wellcome Library MS 4670, translated and edited by Paul Harry Barron, Peter Forshaw, and Stephen Skinner, we find many references to scents, fragrances, odours, perfumes, incenses, fumigations, and suffumigations. In nine parts of this book out of twenty-two, we find mentions of perfumes.[59]

57 Owen Davies, Grimoires, A History of Magic Books (Oxford: Oxford University Press, 2009), pp. 14–15; David Rankine and Stephen Skinner, *The Veritable Key of Solomon* (Singapore: Golden Hoard Press, 2008), p. 15–26.

58 Manchester, John Rylands Library, English MS 44, p. 47.

59 In preface, chapters 6, 8, 10, 12, 15, 19, 20, and appendix 'The Talismans or Characters'. Already in the Preface it is stated that the reader will learn not only about conjurations and prayers but also about perfumes and incenses. In chapter 6 the mage has to sprinkle

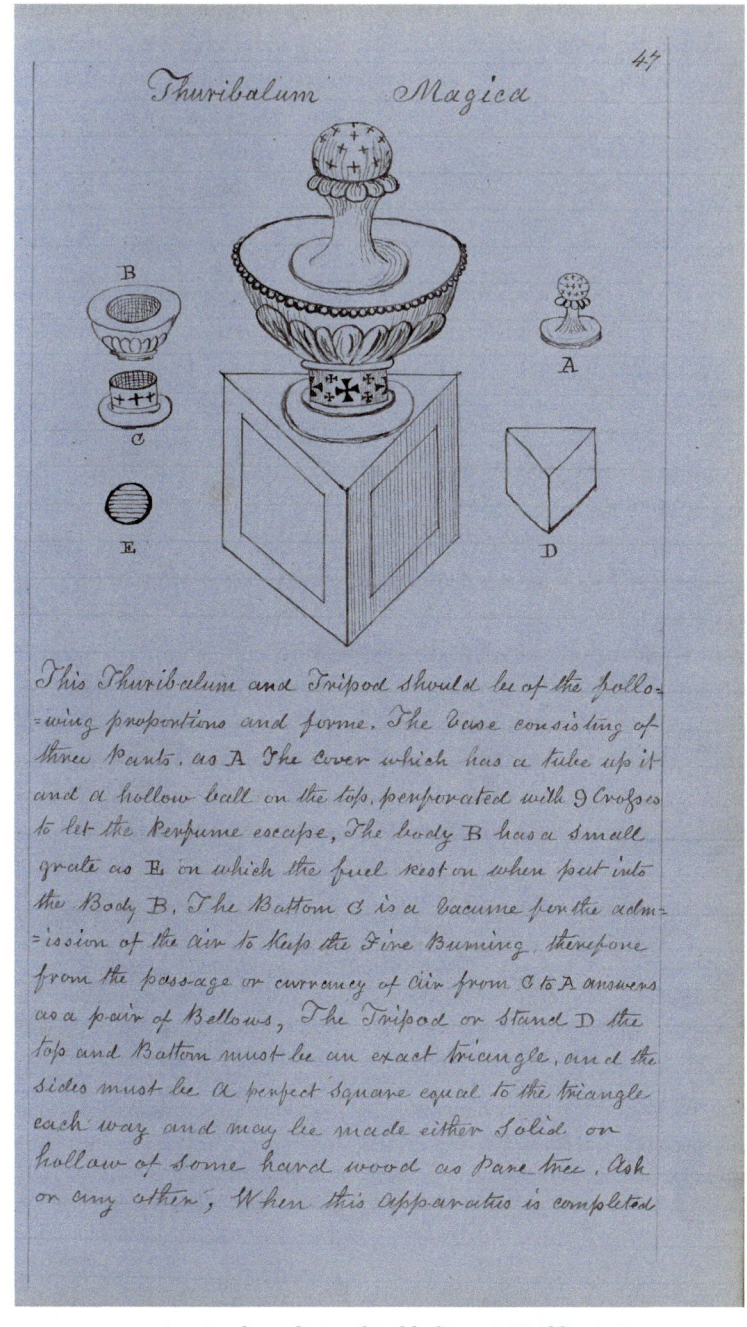

FIGURE 10.5   A recipe for making a thurible from a W.H. Ibbett's 'Treatise on magic', 1854–1857; Manchester, John Rylands Library, English MS 44, p. 47

As one can think, it seems that there is no distinction between perfume and incense here, but later it is clearly stated that incense is only an ingredient, and the perfume consists of many ingredients, including frankincense. The meaning of the word 'perfume' in the early modern period was to fill with smoke or vapor, essentially, it was what we call today incense, or what *Picatrix* and other medieval grimoires called suffumigation. There is no wonder that 'perfume' as described in grimoires was mostly used as a paste formed into pellets and then burned.

Chapter 8 is the more representative in terms of perfume recipes: it is fully dedicated to 'Perfumes appropriate to the Seven Planets' and 'method for Crafting them'. The main instrument for the distribution of fragrances was a small clay or iron thurible. The grimoire explains in detail when, how and with what exactly the fire in it should be lit but does not describe its construction. The thurible must be sprinkled with the purifying water (obviously, as all the other instruments of the magician), and only then it is possible to 'throw a pinch of incense or perfume', which associates with a particular planet. At the end of this chapter, there are advised specific seven 'simple perfumes' for each of the seven planets.

Airy Spirits could be attracted by this operation, and simultaneously it has the apotropaic function of warding off evil spirits. This is recommended, because in the biblical story of Tobias, angel Raphael (one of the three angels who has names in the Bible besides Michael and Gabriel) advised Tobias, who wanted to marry a cursed woman, to throw a perfume made from the liver of fish (sic!) on the glowing coals in order to defend himself against the demons,

---

'instruments and materials of Operation with purifying water', and afterward also 'burn some perfumes' in honour of Spirit. There is a similar operation in chapter 10 about the consecration of the room of the magician. Storax and benzoin are placed in the fire, and the room is censed with the perfume, the composition of which is not indicated. Consecrated water and perfumes that are appropriate to Venus are used for making a love charm in chapter 12. In a similar way burning in a small vase a perfume, connected to specific planets, is used to create a mystical ring in chapter 15, or to gain golden coins ('pistoles') in chapter 20. In an appendix called 'The Talismans or Characters' it is told how to create 12 different rings associated with the signs of the zodiac. The magician has to enclose a perfumed parchment (with magic words written with the blood of a white dove) into in the hollow of the stone. Perfumes varied from aloe wood or orange peel to flies, or the hair of the one who is making it. Flies could be the reference to biblical Ecclesiastes 10:1, 'A dead flye doth corrupt sweete oyntment, and maketh it to stinke: Euen so oft tymes he that hath ben had in estimation for wysdome and honour, is abhorred because of a litle foolishnesse'. Using hair as a perfume could refer to the biblical plot of the anointing of Jesus by Mary's hair, soaked in the pint of pure nard (John 12:1–8).

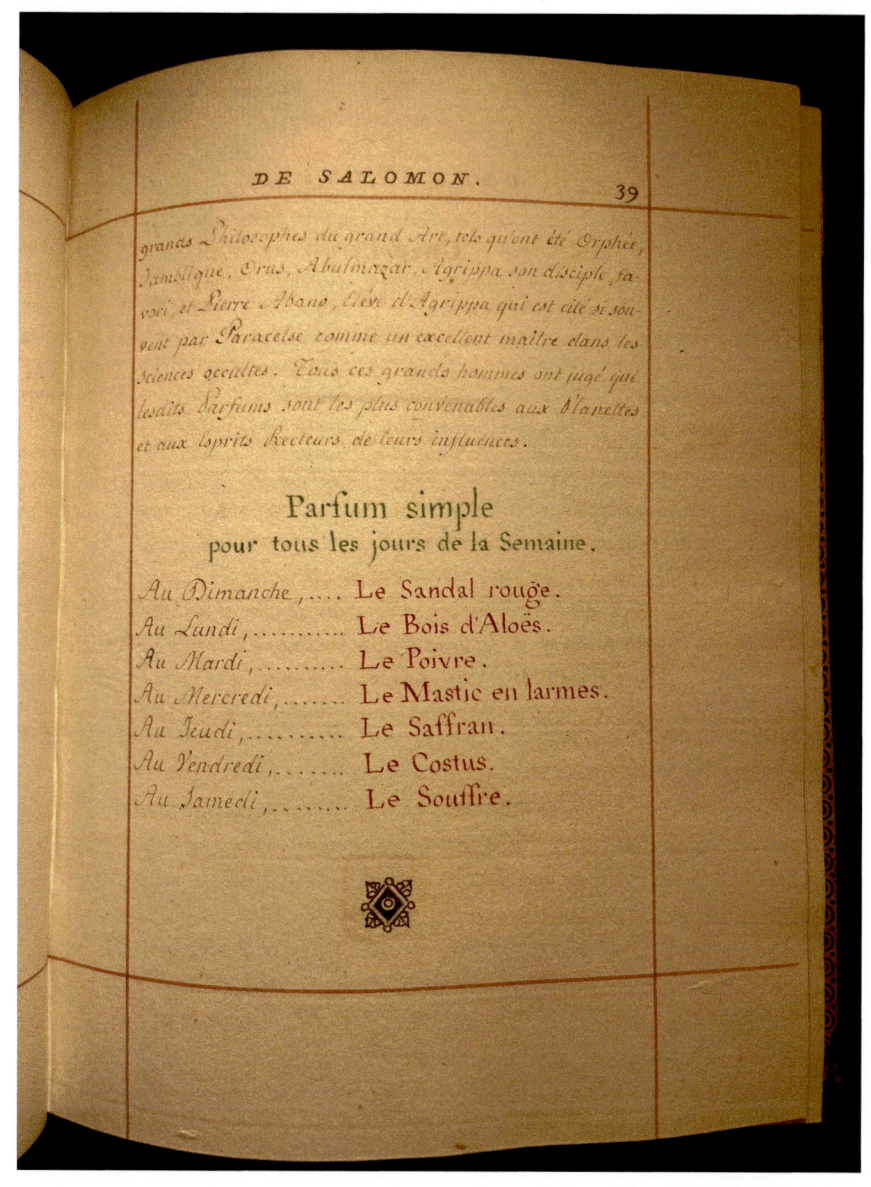

FIGURE 10.6 A page with 'simple perfumes' from Pseudo-Solomon's 'Les Clavicules de R. Salomon', 1796 London, Wellcome Collection, MS. 4670, p. 39

TABLE 10.2   Planetary suffumigation ingredients in *The Keys of Rabbi Solomon*[a]

The Keys of Rabbi Solomon 8	brimstone (sulphur)	**saffron**	*pepper*	red sandalwood	**ginger** or *costus*	*mastic* resin	*aloe wood*
The Keys of Rabbi Solomon 12	black **poppy** seed, henbane seed, root of *mandrake*, powder of magnet stone, powder of *myrrh*, blood of a bat, *brain of black cat*	rowan berry, *wood of aloes*, *storax*, benzoin, powder of lapis lazuli, *peacock* feathers, blood of swallows or the brain of a deer	euphorbia, belladonna, ammonia salt, hellebores roots, powder of magnetised stone, sulphur, blood of a black cat, brain of a crow	*saffron*, *amber*, *musk, aloe wood, balm* wood, **laurel seeds**, *cloves*, *myrrh*, *incense*, *brain of eagle* or blood of a white cockerel	musk, ambergris, *aloe wood*, dried *red roses*, red coral, blood of a *dove* or brain of a *turtledove*, brain of *sparrows*	oriental mastic, *incense*, *cloves*, pentaphylla flowers, powder of agate, brain of a fox, blood of a magpie	dried frog's head, bull's eyes, white poppy seed, the most exquisite *incense*, *camphor*, blood of a gosling or **blood of a turtledove**.

a   Bold are ingredients which are also present in any other recipes of *Picatrix*, italicised are ingredients that are the same for one planet in different sets of recipes of *Picatrix*.

who could choke him to death as they did with her previous husband. The text remarks that Porphyry attracted friendly spirits in the same way.

Iamblichus and Paracelsus are referred to in the description of the use of perfumes in the prevention of treasure hunting. After creating a special astrological talisman and under the specific astrological disposition, it is necessary to 'cense' (fume) the talisman with a certain perfume.[60]

It is implied that after that the spirits would help to protect the mage's treasure hidden underground or in a wall from thieves. After that, all the thieves would be repelled and insane. The ingredients here are mostly of aromatic or neutral nature, but hemlock was famous for its unpleasant and deadly smell, which is not a contradiction with the fact that it could (at least symbolically) assist in madding the treasure hunters.[61]

---

60   The recipe for this perfume, hugely influenced by Islamic thought (see earlier), is as follows: 'Take some coriander, saffron, some hyssop, some Lady Apple seeds and some black poppy seeds in equal amounts. Boil all these drugs together and make a paste with the juice or sap of hemlock and burn several pellets of this paste on the fire of the Art in the direction where the treasure lies'. See Rankine and Skinner, *The Veritable Key of Solomon*, p. 97.

61   But the patronage of superior spirits could also help with locating and expropriating the other's treasure. The ritual for that, as if taken in Hermes writings, is just a couple of lines

We see here that the aim of the second recipe, acquiring someone's treasure, is dressed up with a more noble first recipe of protecting the mage's own treasure, although apparently mage was certainly more interested in theft. Whale wax was used for making candles and cosmetics; galangal, storax, benzoin were ingredients of perfumes; adding blood of a hoopoe bird certainly has magic connotations, as it was used in grimoires for other purposes.[62] But in terms of the perfume properties, it is very doubtful that the smell was 'friendly' in any way, given that such fetid ingredients as fish liver or bird blood were used. Perhaps, this obnoxious smell could help to defeat an enemy spirit, but most likely these substances were listed primarily as symbolic ingredients, and not the ingredients important for creating a fragrance. As we can see, some of the components had a specific aromatic, cosmetic or perfume significance, while the others were of pure symbolic nature, as in *Picatrix*.

Chapter 12 shows the recipes for the manufacture of perfumes for each planet/day.[63] After mixing all the aromatic substances together, some special ingredients must be added, mostly of animal nature.[64] As we can see, the main

---

below, and includes, among creating a talisman, and reciting invocations, a perfume's recipe: 'Take in equal parts, some spermaceti [whale wax], a laurel seed, wood of aloes, some galangal, storax, benzoin, the liver of a morena fish [link with Tobias?], and having boiled them and mix these drugs together, make a paste from them with the blood of a hoopoe bird. Then make some pellets from the granules and you will have the most exquisite perfume to make you the master of enchanted treasure'. See Rankine and Skinner, *The Veritable Key of Solomon*, p. 97.

62   Robert Goulding, Illusion, in *The Routledge History of Medieval Magic*, eds. by Sophie Page and Catherine Rider (London: Routledge, 2019), pp. 312–331, here p. 318.

63   The perfume of Sunday, described as "pleasant odour" is made of saffron, amber, musk, aloe, wood, balm wood, laurel seeds, cloves, myrrh, and incense. For the first time in this treatise, an approximate amount of substance is indicated: a sixth of an ounce for everything except amber and musk, which needed to be only a grain. This composition, as well as six others, do not match the recipe of 'simple perfume' for the same day, moreover, sometimes substances are mixed up: Saturday's sulphur is mentioned in the chapter about Tuesday now. Only in case of Wednesday there is one similar ingredient: oriental mastic (its simple perfume was mastic resin).

64   For Sunday, it is brain of eagle or blood of a white cockerel; for Monday, a dried frog's head, bull's eyes, and blood of a gosling or of a turtledove; for Tuesday, almost all substances are unusual as for a perfume: 'euphorbia, belladonna, ammonia salt, roots from two hellebores, powder of magnetised stone and a small amount of sulphur', along with blood of a black cat and the brain of a crow. If euphorbia, hellebores, and sometimes belladonna could be used in the perfumery, all the others are specific for magic, including three substances more appropriate for an alchemical recipe (sulphur, magnetised stone, ammonia salt), than for a perfume. For Wednesday, special ingredients are powder of agate, the brain of a fox, and the blood of a magpie; for Thursday, powder of lapis lazuli, pieces of chopped up peacock feathers, and the blood of two or three swallows, or the brain of a deer; for Friday, red coral, the blood of a dove or of a turtledove, and the brain

aroma is created from traditional perfumery ingredients, such as white poppy seed, incense, camphor, cloves, ambergris, myrrh, and so on. Some of the ingredients are again of pure symbolic function, and hardly can add something to the fragrance, such as feathers, corals, ammonia salt, or stones powder. They are mostly associated with colours or attributes of the planetary gods roses and corals are red and linked with Venus, as well as doves (as in *Picatrix*), martial Mars is responsible for the hardness of the stone, and aggressiveness of sulphur, Jupiter is connected with his chariot carrier, peacock, and the stone of the colour of his sphere of influence, the sky. White poppy seed is related to Moon, as it also has white colour. These pages in manuscripts are usually also decorated with the images associate with the planetary symbolic.

We also see many animal components here. The aromatic substances could only disguise the terrible smell given off by 'special ingredients' such as dried head, brains, eyes, or blood. There are no instructions about the quantity of these ingredients: thus, it is possible that one drop of crow's blood or a small amount of deer's brain barely could negatively affect the fragrance. Most obviously nearly all of these ingredients were derived from the planetary scents of *Picatrix*, given that often (but not always, probably due to the influence of local traditions and other grimoires) they coincide with this treatise's components. In *The Little Key or Key of Solomon, King of the Hebrews* in Wellcome MS 4669, written also in 1796, we find slightly different use of perfume. There are no mentions of adding animal substances into perfumes throughout the entire treatise. We come across the description of why and how the perfumes are used during the ritual. In a special chapter entirely dedicated to perfumes and fumigations it is indicated that there are two sorts of them (they were first distinguished in *Liber Razielis*). The first kind of perfume is sweet-smelling, made to attract good spirits, usually based on wood of aloes, nutmeg, benzoin gum and musk.[65] The second kind of perfume is made to drive off harmful spirits, and is based on stinking odours, namely on poppy seeds, leather, old fabrics,

---

of two or three sparrows; for Saturday, root of mandrake (not flowers!), powdered magnet stone, blood of a bat (mentioned also in Picatrix in a Chaldean recipe for Saturn), and the brain of black cat.

65   It is accompanied with a prayer to God with the following words: 'deign to bless these perfumes so that they may receive and strength and virtue necessary to attract Good Spirits'. In chapter 7 it is revealed that special perfumes (benzoin, olibanum, storax) are used to quieten the good spirits, and in the prayer which is recited by the magician, they commands the spirits in the following way: 'smell the aroma of our perfumes, go in peace in the Name of the living God'. (Rankine and Skinner, *The Veritable Key of Solomon*, p. 302.). In the *Universal Treatise of the Keys of Solomon*, in chapter 6 is declared that perfumes made of aloes, musk, and balm are to be burned in a vase with a pierced lid. Perfumed items are then used during the magic rituals.

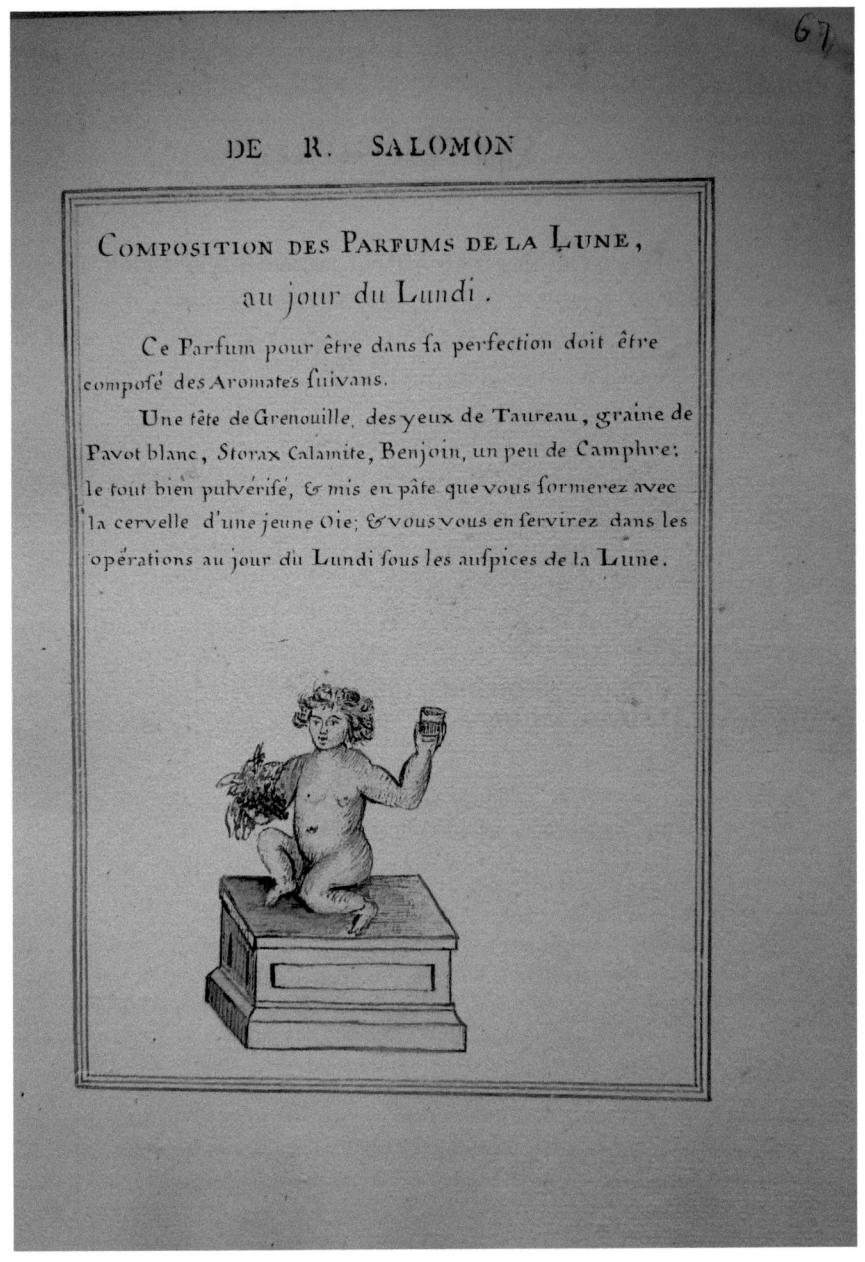

DE R. SALOMON

COMPOSITION DES PARFUMS DE LA LUNE,
au jour du Lundi .

Ce Parfum pour être dans sa perfection doit être
composé des Aromates suivans.

Une tête de Grenouille, des yeux de Taureau, graine de
Pavot blanc, Storax Calamite, Benjoin, un peu de Camphre;
le tout bien pulvérisé, & mis en pâte que vous formerez avec
la cervelle d'une jeune Oie; & vous vous en servirez dans les
opérations au jour du Lundi sous les auspices de la Lune.

FIGURE 10.7   A page with description of the Moon's perfume from Pseudo-Solomon's
'Les Clavicules de R. Salomon', late eighteenth century. London, Wellcome
Collection, Ms. 4661, p. 67

and rags.[66] For instance, the use of a special lamp filled with the oil of poppy seed against the infernal spirits is mentioned as part of a ritual of invoking the dead. Rags and old fabrics as ingredients of a suffumigation for Saturn, associated with evil and death, were already mentioned in *Picatrix*. Poppy was not associated in *Picatrix* with anything evil, but opium, made of poppy, was closely related to Saturn, so perhaps its use was mediated to poppy seeds in later grimoires.

As *The Little Key* states further, the magician has to perfume literally almost everything they has: garments, knives, swords, talismans, wax figures and images, magic apples, grimoire, magician's room, a special place for work in the mountains, and even a companion, who can be (if not an adult) either a dog, or a child.[67]

We see, that in Solomonic grimoires all types of aromatic magic come together. These are auto-suffumigations for the magician and suffumigations for spirits, like in *Picatrix*. There are also different types of scents for good and evil spirits, a feature inherited from *Liber Razielis*. There is a comprehended system of fuming every instrument used in the rituals, an influence of *Sworn Book of Honorius*. Solomonic grimoires concentrate on censing magical instruments; perhaps this is a part of a bigger trend in early modern magic books, which focus mainly on ceremonies and rituals, and the recipes become less and less important. Such grimoires as *Book of Abramelin* describe long and

---

66   In chapter 3 sweet-smelling perfumes are also opposed to 'all foul smelling and filthy materials' without any explanations about the use of it.

67   In the book 1 chapter 8 the magician learns how to incense and perfume their room and talismans with sweet-smelling fragrances and scents. In chapters 10, 11, and 14 – they perfume wax figures/images which give invisibility, love (the ritual also includes holding the image over the perfume), and destruct enemies respectively, in chapter 12 – an apple serving as a love charm (first thing to do after picking it from the tree is perfuming and suffumigating the fruit), in chapter 16 – the area of magic ritual, in chapter 22 – a writing/pact for favour and love. In book 2 chapter 3 it is advised to perfume the dog, which serves as a companion (with the prayer 'I wash and perfume thee in the Name of the Most High and Most Powerful Eternal God'), or even a young boy/girl, along with washing them and having their nails cut. In chapter 4 mage perfumes their garments, in chapter 6 – a secluded room for rituals in their house, as well as a knife or similar tools, in chapter 7 – also a black handed knife, along with dipping it into the blood of a black cat and sap of hemlock, and a hilt of the magic sword, in chapter 12 and 13 – a feather and inks for writing, in 19 – a needle for sewing and a burin for engraving, in chapter 20 – the grimoire itself during the entire week (each day they has to change the perfume appropriate to the governing planet). In the preface to the book 3 it is stated that the perfume is one of the magician's instruments, together with the circle, pentacle, sword, etc. In the Universal Treatise of the Keys of Solomon, which comes directly after this treatise, the perfuming of parchment and an excluded place in the mountains or forest for invoking spirits are also described.

tedious rituals, lasting for months if not years. The biggest role in them play instruments and incantations, and the recipe part is essentially downgraded to a minimum or greatly reduced to a simple description of suffumigations.

4 Conclusion

It could be stated that grimoires implied a kind of olfactory communication between the magician and demons or angels. In fact, using them was one of the ways for them to materialize spirits or to give them more power.[68] In almost all aforementioned magical books it is stated that the magician has to smell good (in Solomonic, as well as in later Faustian grimoires it is also directly indicated). Another thing is that if a good spirit is to be invoked, the mage applies sweet-smelling suffumigations. But the evil spirits could smell bad (in Faustian grimoires it is often mentioned along with frightening ruckus, noise, and weather conditions they produce). Respectively, fouling odours were used to attract evil spirits on a 'like attracts like' principle, or vice versa, drive them away (for example, pig excrement was used for that in Faustian grimoires). It is also implied that these scents are destructive or unpleasant for the evil spirits. In MacGregor Mathers' translation of one of the copies of *The Key of Solomon the King* there is a special curse against a disobedient spirit: his seal is put into a black box together with asafoetida as well as 'other stinking substances' and is then put over the fire.[69] It is implied that the demon shall choke from the smell of this sulphurous substances (as there were not enough of them in hell). The mage used different aromas to punish and placate spirits, building a communicative system of interacting with them and trying to transmit their desires to angels or demons.

Air was considered to be a transmitter of various diseases, and fumigations were often performed to clean the air or heal the patient. These beliefs are rooted in the Aristotelian philosophy of sight and also in Roman magic, which tells that the eye could convey some properties or thoughts to objects, and vice versa. Within this logic, in Middle Ages 'the scent of Saturn' or other planets was believed to affect people's fate. Norman nobleman Henri de Ferrières in *Livre du roy Modus et de la royne Ratio* (fourteenth century) mentions that poisonous mephitis generated by a conjunction of Saturn, Jupiter, and Mars, as well as of a certain eclipse, and a comet, caused the epidemic in France

---

68   "The use of incense was not only for purposes of appeasement and of punishment. It was also supposed to help the spirits to materialize" (Butler, *Ritual Magic*, p. 57).

69   Ibid., p. 75.

in 1347–1351.[70] In early modern period, for example during the plagues of 1603, 1609, and 1625, rosemary was used in England to counter the smell of the plague-infected bodies, and also to heal the plague, which was thought to be 'airborne'. This then partially led to the association of rosemary with a bad and dangerous smell.[71] So the magic suffumigations were believed to affect certain planets, illnesses, and even spirits through the air. That is why many grimoires took that for granted, that certain scents could influence the world around, and why the mage was advised to have prepared many suffumigations for every occasion.

A medieval or rarely modern magician, according to the exact and humorous remark of Eliza Marian Butler, a pioneer of magic studies, had to be a Jack of all trades, given that it was implied they prepares all the utensils and ingredients themself.[72] The mage who was capable of making use of hundreds of herbs and other ingredients needed for various magical confections and fumigations, was also a universal man, a polymath, mastering all the sides of nature. Consequently, their grimoire was a book of universal knowledge, close to the Bible itself, but composed as a tome of endless lists of recipes.

The article is based exclusively on handwritten books. Why? Only very occasionally such books, which contained 'black magic', i.e. illicit magic practices, could appear in print and then also, because of the censorship authorities, rather camouflaged.[73] Grimoires drew almost exclusively from the handwritten tradition, exploiting its advantages as a hermetic medium for the 'happy

---

70   Andrea Apostu, De la joute à plaisance à la guerre de pestilence: dynamiques de la confrontation dans quelques miniatures du ms. Fr 12399, in *Armes et jeux militaires dans l'imaginaire XII*ᵉ*–XV*ᵉ *siècle*, sous la direction de Catalina Girbea (Paris: Classique Garnier, 2016), p. 121–135.

71   Holly Dugan, *The Ephemeral History of Perfume. Scent and Sense in Early Modern England* (Baltimore: John Hopkins University, 2011).

72   Butler, *Ritual Magic*, pp. 53–54.

73   The indication of false places of printing was intended to conceal the origin of problematic printed works. In 1725, Peter Hammer in Cologne – according to the Germanized identification of a fictitious publisher from Holland with the imprint 'Cologne chez Pierre Marteau' – published a compilation whose title 'Sammlung der größten Geheimnisse außerordentlicher Menschen in alter Zeit' [Collection of the greatest secrets of extraordinary people in ancient times] electriefied. There were magical key texts united, see Paul Raabe, 'Pseudonyme und anonyme Schriften im 17. und 18. Jahrhundert', in *Der Zensur zum Trotz. Das gefesselte Wort und die Freiheit in Europa*, ed. by Paul Raabe, exhibition catalogue Wolfenbüttel, (Weinheim : VCH, Acta Humaniora, 1991), pp. 53–66; Michael Treadwell, 'On False and Misleading Imprints in the London Book Trade 1600–1750', in Robin Myers and Michael Harris (eds.), *Fakes and Frauds. Varieties of Deception in Print & Manuscript* (Winchester: St. Paul's Bibliography, 1989), pp. 29–47.

few'.[74] Moreover, it was possible for the scribe to pick up new aspects and integrate corrections with each new copy. A permanent process of additions and omissions, annotations and crossings out could take place, far more pronounced than was the case with early modern prints. This "constant flux"[75] could turn manuscripts into a creative field for spontaneous insertions.

Acknowledgments

I am grateful to the following funds and scholarships, as well as to librarians and scholars in visited institutions, for making my trips in search of manuscripts and secondary literature for this paper possible: DFG funds for travelling to Glasgow (via PD Dr. Stefan's Laube Project 'Bilder aus der Phiole') (2022), SHAC Research Travel Grant for travelling to Glasgow (2021), Dr Greg Wells Small Research Award for travelling to Manchester (2021).

---

74   Stefan Laube, 'Geister aus Papier. Magisches Schrifttum im Visier der Zensur', in Florian Gassner and Nikola Roßbach (eds.), *Zensur vom 16. bis zum 18. Jahrhundert: Begriffe, Diskurse, Praktiken*, in Jahrbuch für Internationel Germanistik Reihe A, Bd. 136 (Berlin, Lang: 2020), pp. 33–84.

75   Michael Johnston and Michael van Dussen: Introduction: Manuscripts and Cultural History, in Johnston and van Dussen (eds.): *The Medieval Manuscript Book. Cultural Approaches* (Cambridge: Cambridge University Press, 2015), pp. 1–16, here p. 5.

CHAPTER 11

The Duchess's Medicine Chest: Prescriptions and Medicines for Sophia of Brunswick-Lüneburg (1522–1575)

Britta-Juliane Kruse

After the death of her husband Duchess Sophia of Braunschweig-Lüneburg left the palace in Wolfenbüttel and moved into Schöningen, the widow's residence near Helmstedt.[1] In her many letters to contemporaries and physicians, she mentioned her own ill health. Furthermore, as a noblewoman, social expectations required her to engage in ensuring the medical welfare of those living on her estate.[2] Duchess Sophia commissioned a medicine chest for medical care at the widow's residence. Caspar Neefe (1511–1579), professor of medicine in Leipzig and personal physician to the Saxon electors, was the advisor when it came to the design and equipment of this chest.[3] The "house and field

1   This study was produced as part of the research project *Korrespondenznetzwerke am Wolfenbütteler Hof. Briefwechsel von Julius und Hedwig von Braunschweig-Lüneburg* (1550–1600): https://www.hab.de/korrespondenznetzwerke-am-wolfenbuetteler-hof-briefwechsel-von -julius-und-hedwig-von-braunschweig-lueneburg-1550%e2%80%921600/. (2 January 2023). The author's 'own post' is funded by the Ministry of Science and Culture of Lower Saxony. A study with further results of the research project is currently being finalised. I would like to thank my friends and colleagues, Prof. Stephanie Leitch (Florida State University of Tallahassee) and historian Marion Read for their invaluable help with the translation into English. Dr. Angela Jianu has enriched the translation with important notes. For the final review of the text and valuable advice, I would like to thank my friend Prof. Elisabeth Wåghäll-Nivre (Stockholm University).
2   See Almut Bues, *Zofia Jagiellonka, Herzogin von Braunschweig-Lüneburg (1522–1575)*, Akten zu Heirat, Tod und Erbe (Braunschweig: Braunschweigischer Geschichtsverein, 2018), pp. 75–86. Almut Bues, "Frictions in the lives of Polish princesses and queens consort, 1500–1800," in Almut Bues (ed.), *Frictions and Failures: Cultural Encounters in Crisis* (Wiesbaden: Harrassowitz Verlag 2017), pp. 105–132; Andrea Lilienthal, *Die Fürstin und die Macht: Welfische Herzoginnen im 16. Jahrhundert: Elisabeth, Sidonia, Sophia* (Hannover: Verlag Hahnsche Buchhandlung 2007), pp. 241–284.
3   Like his older brother Johann Neefe (1499–1574), he was also responsible for the medical care of members of the princely house of Braunschweig-Lüneburg. See Birgit Schubert and Tilmann Walter, 'Heilkunst und Diplomatie: Die kursächsischen Leibärzte Johann Neefe (1499–1574) und Caspar Neefe (1514–1579),' *Sudhoffs Archiv* 105 (2021), pp. 20–56. Research Project *Early Modern Physicians' Letters, 1500–1700*, Bavarian Academy of Sciences and Humanities: www

FIGURE 11.1
Portrait of Duchess Sophia. Lucas
Cranach the Younger (1515–1586),
*c.*1553. Czartoryski Museum Krakow,
Accession number XII-544

FIGURE 11.2   Current view of the widow's residence Schöningen
PHOTO: AUTHOR

pharmacy" ordered by Duchess Sophia was ready for transport to Schöningen at the turn of the year 1573/74.[4]

1 The Materiality and Functionality of the Medicine Chest

This elaborate apothecary box does not appear to have been preserved: its appearance and design can be reconstructed in detail on the basis of historical documents in an archive called Niedersächsisches Landesarchiv Wolfenbüttel.[5] Further details are contained in inventories of the duchess's estate compiled in Schöningen on 5 and 6 July 1575. These show that, in addition to the medicine chest, she possessed a second chest, which was inventoried three times: 1. "A large green drawer with iron fittings, also with green linen."[6] 2. "A large green drawer inside and outside with ornate iron mountings."[7] 3. "A green drawer with iron fittings and green cloth inside."[8] This was a letter case containing a handwritten book of remedies. The medicine chest is described somewhat differently, with an emphasis on its functionality: "A green drawer, therein a field

---

.aerztebriefe.de. Andreas Lesser, *Die albertinischen Leibärzte vor 1700 und ihre verwandtschaftlichen Beziehungen zu Ärzten und Apothekern* (Petersberg: Michael Imhof Verlag 2015), on the biographies of Johann Neefe p. 63–67 and Caspar Neefe pp. 71–74. Andrea Kramarczyk and Antonia Krüger (eds.), *Im Dienste von Kaiser und Kurfürst: Die Leibärzte Johannes und Caspar Neefe und ihre Familien.* Exhibition guide on the occasion of the 500th birthday of Caspar Neefe. Schloßbergmuseum Chemnitz 2014. Andrea Kramarczyk, Johannes Neefe, in Saxon Biography: https://saebi.isgv.de/biografie/Johannes_Neefe_(1499-1574). (18 August 2022). On doctors' correspondence see Michael Stolberg, *Gelehrte Medizin und ärztlicher Alltag in der Renaissance* (Berlin, Boston: De Gruyter 2021), pp. 102–109, 428–430.

4 This is documented in a letter dated 5 January 1574, Niedersächsisches Landesarchiv, Abteilung Wolfenbüttel (NLA WO), 1 Alt 23, no. 30, fols. 38r–39v.

5 https://nla.niedersachsen.de/startseite/landesarchiv/abteilung_wolfenbuttel/abteilung-wolfen buttel-197407.html. (6 January 2023). The medicine chest is mainly referred to in the file NLA WO, 1 Alt 23, no. 30. See Bues, *Zofia Jagiellonka*, p. 187. Heinrich von Schennis chose the designation "Haus und Reiseapotheke" for his "Spagyrische Hausz und Raysz Apotheca", which was published in 1628 by Johann Jacob Bodmer in Zurich.

6 NLA WO, 1 Alt 23, no. 69, fol. 50v. The inventory in fair copy is preserved on fols. 37r–73v, title: "Inuentarium oder Verzeichnus, was in der Hertzogin zu Schoningen Gemach am 5. Julý Anno 75. befunden worden …", fol. 37r. Duke Julius of Braunschweig-Lüneburg commissioned the inventory on 4 July 1575, NLA WO, 1 Alt 23, no. 69, fols. 29rv. The edition of the inventory in fair copy in Bues, *Zofia Jagiellonka*, p. 173–210. NLA WO, 1 Alt 23, Nr. 69, fols. 74r–114v, records a second version of the inventory written in Schöningen.

7 NLA WO, 1 Alt 23, no. 69, fol. 52v. Bues, *Zofia Jagiellonka*, p. 188.

8 NLA WO, 1 Alt 23, no. 69, fol. 70r. Bues, *Zofia Jagiellonka*, p. 206. This green chest contained, in addition to many bundles of letters, a prayer book with a red and green velvet cover and a handwritten medicine book, ibid. fol. 70v.

pharmacy [Velt Coryns or Apothecken]."[9] The duchess owned the letter case, the medicine chest, which contained a removable field apothecary, and a second field apothecary case – the appearance is not documented in more detail. 'Field pharmacies' were travel cases whose contents were adapted to the care of sick or wounded soldiers. The designation of the duchess's medicine chest as a "home, travel and field pharmacy" seems to have been chosen to characterize all possible applications of its contents. Written instructions for treatments and medical prescriptions were compiled for the use of the medicine chest by Caspar Neefe, who referred to them as "records" [Bericht] and "directives" [Regiment]. Both of these can be found in the inventory of her estate.[10]

Further details about the materiality of the medicine chest at the center of this study can be reconstructed on the basis of a price list in which all the craftsmen involved in its manufacture are named. The medicine chest was made of wood by a cabinet maker and painted green. It is not possible to say from the records whether the interior was also colored. A locksmith decorated the box with fittings and installed a lock. The list of invoiced costs includes the following items:[11]

> 3 thaler to the cabinet maker who made the chest
> 2 gulden to the locksmith who shod it with iron
> 1 thaler to the turner who turned the small round boxes made of wood
> 1 thaler to the painter who painted the small round tins made of wood[12]
> 2 gulden for painting the outside of the chest
> 19 gulden, 2 groschen (20 pennies), 6 pennies to the jug maker according to his invoice
> 1 thaler as tips for the jug maker's journeyman
> 1 thaler to the writer of the book and the regiment
> 6 pennies for the straps on the chest
> 4 pennies for the canvas cover of the chest

9   "Eine gruene Laden, darin ein Velt Coryns oder Apothecken. Noch eine ander Velt Apotheken", NLA WO, 1 Alt 23, no. 69, fol. 62r. Bues, *Zofia Jagiellonka*, p. 196.

10   This inventory was compiled in Wolfenbüttel on 1 April 1584 and is preserved in two versions: NLA WO, 1 Alt 23, no. 78, concept with additions, fols. 92r–95v, and the fair copy on fols. 96r–100r. Fol. 96r: "Noch No: 1. Ettliche Apotekereȳ Concept. An der Zall 6 stuck" and fol. 98r: "Noch No: IX. dar auff geschrieben auß der Landtgraffischen Lade. Ein bundt jn. 8to, darin D Neven [Dr. Neefe] bericht von der Hauß oder Veldt Apoteken, vnd D. Gervasȳ Marstallers [Dr. Gervasius Marstallers] bedencken, sein dreȳ stuck." At the end of the inventory: "Noch 5 kleine Zettel vnd Recepta etc", fol. 100r. Bues, *Zofia Jagiellonka*, pp. 252, 255, 258, 351.

11   NLA WO, 1 Alt 23, no. 30, fol. 36v.

12   Painted medicine vessels.

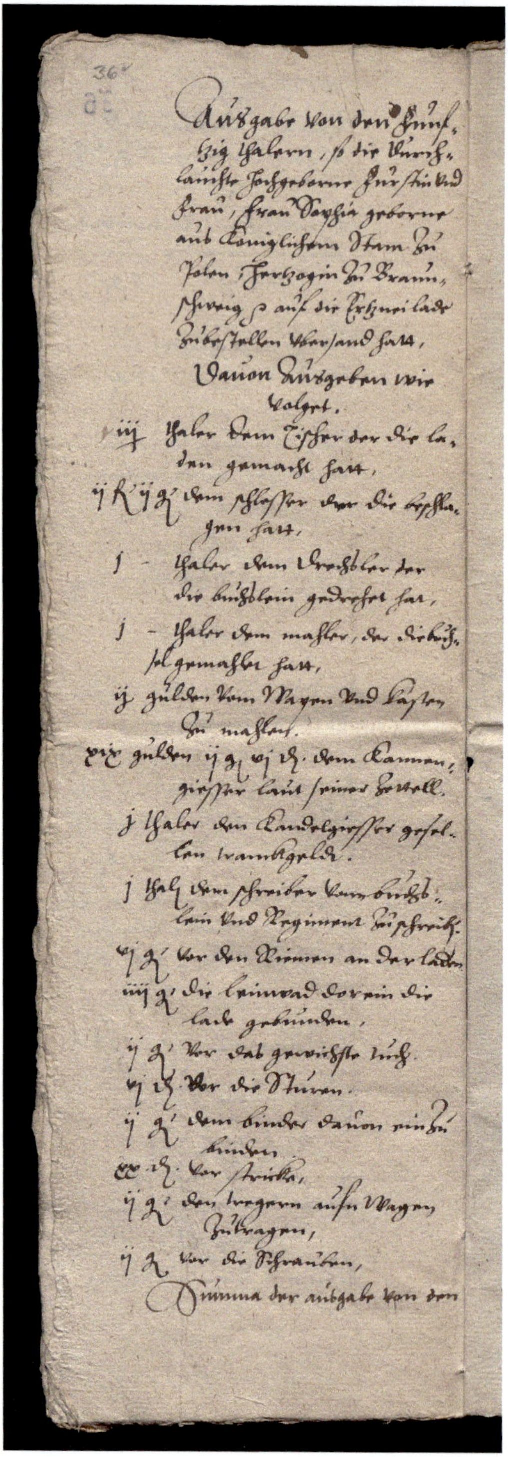

FIGURE 11.3

Cost breakdown for the production
of the medicine chest. NLA WO,
1 Alt 23, No. 30, fol. 36v
PHOTO: LOWER SAXONY STATE
ARCHIVE WOLFENBÜTTEL

2 pennies for the oilcloth of the chest

2 pennies for the Sturen[13]

2 Groschen (20 pennies) for the bookbinder

20 pennies for the ropes to tie down the chest

2 Groschen (20 pennies) for the porters who carried the chest to the wagon

2 pennies for the screws to fix the chest.[14]

The original invoice from the pot founder Bendix Keßeler mentions the material and the production prices in the pricelist for the medicinal vessels made of pewter.[15] Commissioned by Doctor Caspar Neefe, he produced bottles, square vessels, and round jugs that were turned on a lathe. For this he charged 19 gulden, two groschen (20 pennies) and six pennies.[16] In addition to these pewter vessels, the chest also included containers made of wood. The different materials made it possible to store tinctures, ointments, powders, pills, and crushed herbs. Their shape, perceptible at first glance, and the numbers written on them increased their functionality and prevented prolonged searching: pewter medicine vessels were marked with Roman numerals and the wooden vessels with Arabic numerals.

These were:

19 large pewter bottles

38 square pewter vessels

19 round screwed pewter jugs

85 turned round wooden containers

A removable square box with nine compartments.

Together with the medicine chest, the cabinet maker delivered the removable square box.[17] This box could be taken out of the medicine chest and was intended, as already stated, as a travel and field pharmacy.[18] It contained nine

---

13 The meaning is still not clear.

14 NLA WO, 1 Alt 23, no. 30, fols. 36v–37r. The translations were by the author of the chapter.

15 There is a direct reference to the invoice of the cannon founder Bendix Keßeler, NLA WO, 1 Alt 23, no. 30, fol. 18r.

16 Ibid.

17 Comparable turned medicine vessels are on display in the museum of Wienhausen Monastery, see Britta-Juliane Kruse, "Medizin im Kloster", in Katja Lembke and Jens Reiche (eds.), *Schatzhüterin: 200 Jahre Klosterkammer Hannover* (Dresden: Sandstein, 2018), pp. 292–295.

18 Claudia Selheim, "Für den Notfall gerüstet: Die Reiseapotheke", in Claudia Selheim and G. Ulrich Großmann (eds.), *Reisebegleiter: Mehr als nur Gepäck* (Nürnberg: Verlag des

compartments for different medicines, a small mortar and an enema.[19] When the medicine chest was filled, helpers carried the heavy object – the pewter vessels inside weighed 73 pounds – to the cart with the leather straps attached to the outside.[20] Screws mentioned in the invoice indicate that the chest was screwed down in the carriage during transport. In addition to the green linen cover they covered it with oilcloth to protect the precious cargo from moisture.[21]

2   Caspar Neefe's Instructions for the Preparation and Use of the Medical Recipes

Caspar Neefe's instructions were noted down by a professional scribe.[22] The medicine chest contained three pieces of writing. Firstly, an overview of 18 illnesses for whose cure the medicinal vessels contained ingredients. Secondly the "Report" on how medications could be used, an instruction manual. Thirdly the booklet, in which the content of all medicine jars and the compartments of the field pharmacy are summarized.

The overview of 18 illnesses, for which diseases and ailments the medicines in the home and field pharmacy could be used, is divided into three columns.[23]

Alternative treatment concepts for each disease offer greater variability in the application of prescriptions. The precision of the formulations guaranteed a quick grasp of the content when reading and led to the uncomplicated preparation and application of the medicines:

1. Against fainting (6 recipes)
2. Against strokes (5 recipes)
3. Serios diseases (2 recipes)

Germanischen Nationalmuseums, 2010), pp. 42–47. Online: Heidelberg: arthistoricum .net 2019 https://doi.org/10.11588/arthistoricum.453 (25 May 2022).

19   A travel or medicine chest from the second half of the 18th century, now in Germanisches Nationalmuseum Nuremberg, contains fold-out side wings with drawers, further drawers in the middle of the box and additional compartments into which medicine jars could be inserted; see Selheim, *Reiseapotheke*, pp. 42–43, fig. 17.

20   1 pound was 12 ounces, about 357.66 grams. Gabriele Wacker, *Arznei und Confect: Medikale Kultur am Wolfenbütteler Hof im 16. und 17. Jahrhundert* (Wiesbaden: Harrassowitz Verlag, 2013), p. 535.

21   The green color of the linen cover is mentioned in the inventory of the estate; see Bues, *Zofia Jagiellonka*, p. 185. Linen covers were also common in the early modern period to protect painted globes.

22   This is evident from the invoice of the craftsmen involved in the production.

23   "ZV WIEVIEL GEBRECHEN VND KRANCKHEITEN DIE ARTZNEI IN DER HAVS ODER FELT APOTEKEN GEORDNET SEỸ". NLA WO, 1 Alt 23, no. 30, fols. 14r–17r; the numbering corresponds to the original.

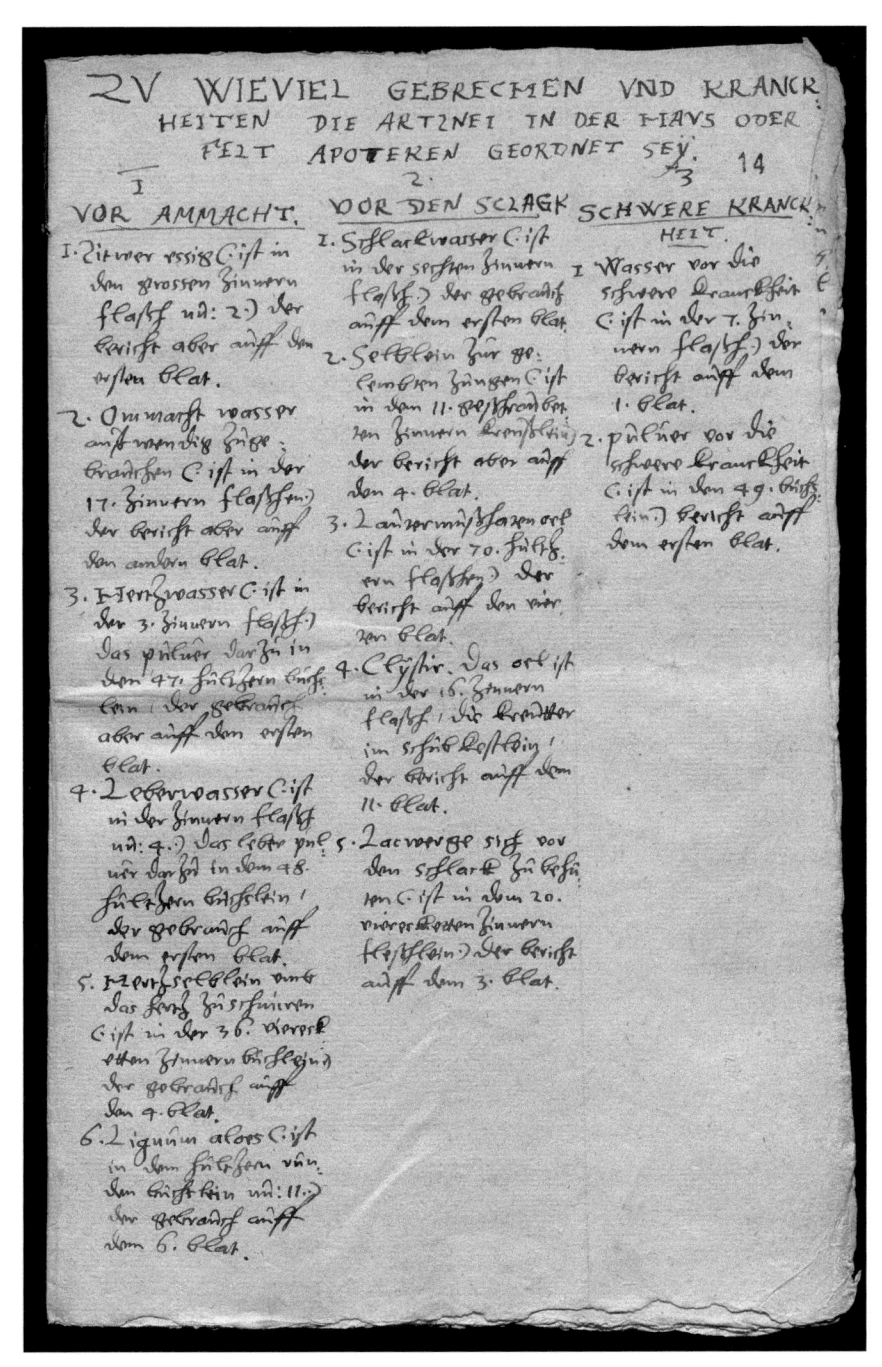

FIGURE 11.4   Overview of 18 diseases for whose therapy the medicinal vessels contained
ingredients. NLA WO, 1 Alt 23, No. 30, fol. 14r
PHOTO: LOWER SAXONY STATE ARCHIVE WOLFENBÜTTEL

4. For protection against the plague (3 recipes)
5. To cure the plague (4 recipes)
6. To regulate menstruation before it begins (4 recipes)
7. About the womb (4 recipes)
8. For the stomach (2 recipes)
9. Against the stone (3 recipes)
10. Against colic (2 recipes)
11. Sleeping aid (1 recipe)
12. Against inflamed gingivae (1 recipe)
13. Against chapped lips and warts[24] (1 recipe)
14. Against clotted blood on the chest (1 recipe)
15. Against intestinal worms (1 recipe)
16. During a difficult birth (1 recipe)
17. To stimulate menstruation (1 recipe)[25]
18. To stop menstruation (1 recipe).

The systematic arrangement of the recipes and the precise instructions on how to use the ingredients in the medicinal vessels can be illustrated with two selected examples: 2. Against strokes: the potion against strokes whose use is described on the first page is to be found in the pewter bottle with the number 6; 4. Enema: the oil is in the pewter flask with number 16, the herbs in the sliding chest, the "Report" is located on the second leaf.[26] Caspar Neefe evidently favored general medical needs when selecting the recipes. As a nod to contemporary circumstances, he placed a special emphasis on instructions for avoiding infection with the plague. Since he was commissioned by a princess on a widow's estate with many female residents, he also integrated recipes for gynecology and pediatrics. His recipe collection geared towards general readers offers a precise insight into the medical practice of the early modern period, a topic which is still little researched.[27]

3 On the Social Scope of the "Home, Travel and Field Pharmacy"

The second document, probably compiled by Caspar Neefe in Leipzig and not dated, is the "Report" with the operating instructions.

---

24 Probably for herpes on the lips.
25 To induce abortion.
26 NLA WO, 1 Alt 23, no. 30, fol. 14r.
27 Stolberg, *Gelehrte Medizin*, pp. 2–3.

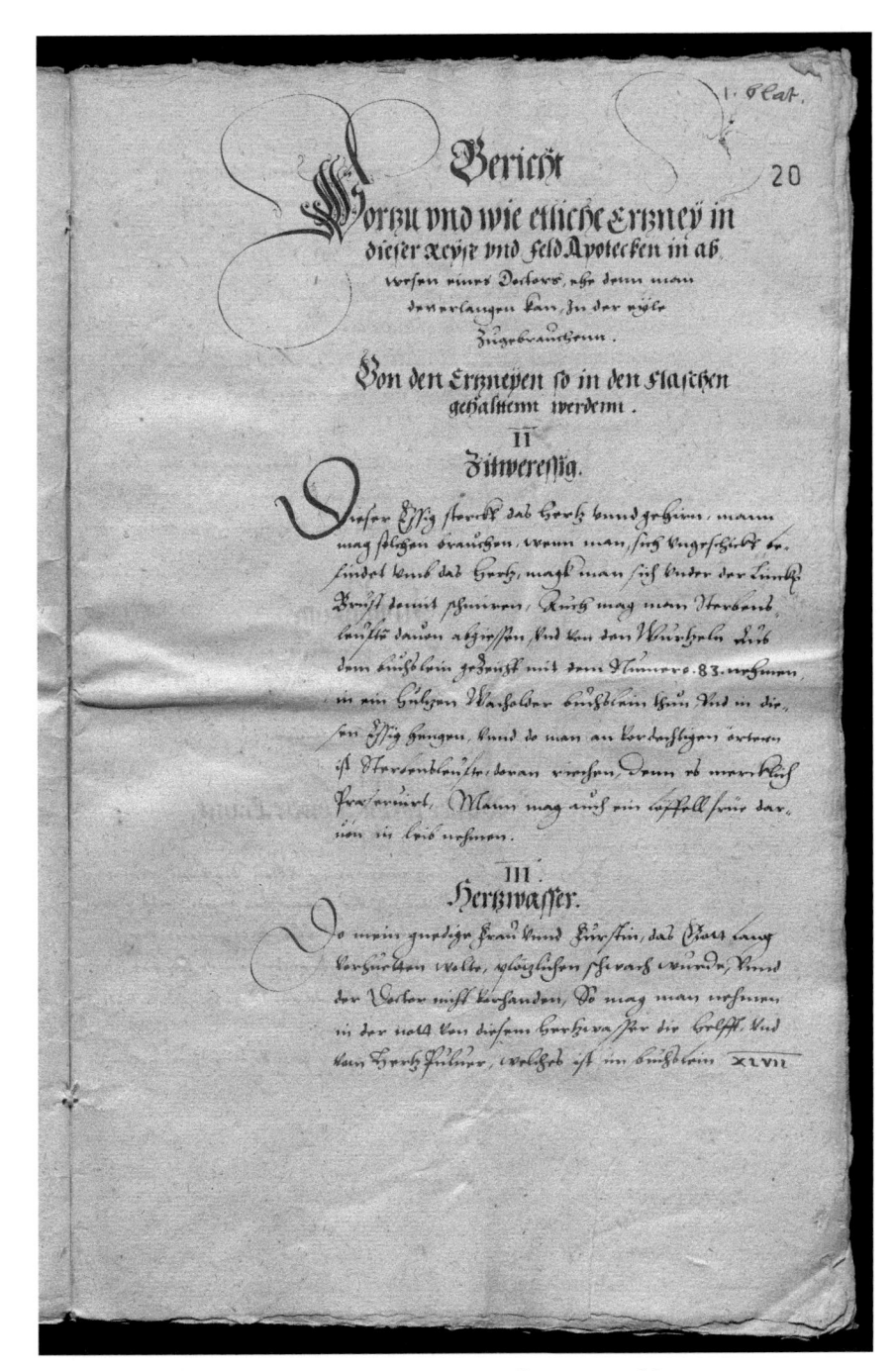

FIGURE 11.5   Beginning of the "Report". NLA WO, 1 Alt 23, No. 30, fol. 20r
PHOTO: LOWER SAXONY STATE ARCHIVE WOLFENBÜTTEL

It is entitled: "Report of how medications in this travel and field pharmaceutical cabinet can be used in the absence of a doctor, or before you can reach a doctor, to be used in a hurry".[28] In Schöningen, the guide was to be used primarily by the court lady or the chambermaid. When the duchess was travelling and there was no doctor nearby, it was available in case of emergency.[29] Duchess Sophia often travelled to the residence of Duke Julius (1528–1589) and Duchess Hedwig (1540–1602), née Margravine of Brandenburg, in the Wolfenbüttel residence. She also undertook other journeys and visited her sister Hedwig/Jadwiga (1513–1573), Electress of Brandenburg, in Berlin, who was bedridden after an accident. At the beginning of January 1570 she travelled on from there to Küstrin for the wedding of her stepdaughter Katharina of Brandenburg-Küstrin (1549–1602) to Elector Joachim Friedrich of Brandenburg (1546–1608).[30] Several times she visited Landgrave Wilhelm IV of Hesse, a good friend of hers.[31] From the beginning of May to the middle of July 1570, she went with her widowed stepdaughter Margareta von Münsterberg (1516/17–1580) to Bad Ems for a cure, in order to enjoy the warm baths.[32] The spa treatment seems to have had an effect, because the two women repeated the trip in 1571.

In Schöningen there were also opportunities for Duchess Sophia to take therapeutic baths. This is indicated by the mention of the bath recipe from Dr. Pellitius in an estate inventory compiled in her chamber after her death.[33] Justus Pellitius (Jodocus Pilirius et al.) was town physician in Lüneburg from

---

28   "Berichtt Wortzu vnd wie etliche Ertzney in dieser Reyse vnd Felld Apotheken in abwesen eines Doctors, bevor denn man den erlangen kann, in der eyle zu gebrauchenn." NLA WO, 1 Alt 23, no. 30, fols. 19r–29v.

29   "Haus vnd Reißapotecken wurt auf die not gemacht vnd zu gericht." NLA WO, 1 Alt 23, no. 30, fol. 29v.

30   NLA WO 1 Alt 23, no. 8, fols. 52r–61v. 1 Alt 23, no. 9, fols. 4r–5v.

31   The landgrave gave her a yellow drawer with inlays, in which she kept bundles of letters. Mentioned in NLA WO, 1 Alt 23, no. 69, fol. 51v. Presumably the material was yellowish wood.

32   NLA WO 1 Alt 23, no. 9, fol. 18r. Pirozynski, *Herzogin Sophie*, p. 91.

33   NLA WO, 1 Alt 23, no. 69, fols. 37r–73v, the recipe is recorded on fol. 38r. A revealing insight into the bathing culture and functionality of the only completely preserved bathing facility from the second half of the 16th century in Ambras Castle near Innsbruck is provided in the essay by Margot Thun-Rauch: "Die Badewanne der Philippine Welser: Gesundheit und Genuss," in Kristina Deutsch, Claudia Echinger-Maurach, and Eva-Bettina Krems (eds.), *Höfische Bäder in der Frühen Neuzeit: Gestalt und Funktion* (Berlin, Boston: de Gruyter, 2017), pp. 191–203. The 'padwannen für ihr Gnaden', Philippine Welser (1527–1580), is mentioned in an inventory that can be dated around 1571/72: Vienna, Austrian National Library, Cod. 7998, fol. 198v. See Thun-Rauch, p. 191, note 3. Alisha Michelle Rankin, *Panaceia's Daughters: Noblewomen as Healers in Early Modern Germany* (Chicago: The University of Chicago Press, 2013), pp. 163–165 contrasts Philippine Welser with Electress Anna of Saxony. For Anna of Saxony and her Medical 'Handiwork' see pp. 128–167. See also Katrin Keller, *Kurfürstin Anna von Sachsen* (1532–1585) (Regensburg: Pustet, 2010).

1557 to 1571, later also in Hamburg. He was first court physician to Duke Heinrich the Younger and Duchess Sophia, later to Duke Julius and Duchess Hedwig.[34] The presence of personal physicians as permanent member of the court was not a fundamental requirement in the principality of Braunschweig-Lüneburg. Caspar Neefe therefore developed a realistic concept for the functionality of the medicine cabinet. The personal physicians, who were often city physicians from Hamburg or Braunschweig, were only summoned to provide medical care in the residential palace of Wolfenbüttel, the summer residence of the Hesse Palace or the widow's residence of Schöningen when necessary.[35]

The treatment of Duchess Sophia of Braunschweig-Lüneburg with the contents of the medicine chest had top priority. She was also responsible for providing medical care on the widow's estate and in the town of Schöningen.[36] Around 1575, about 90 people lived in the widow's residence. The pharmacist Bartholomäus Seiffart and his assistant were involved in their medical care.[37] Duchess Sophia conformed to conventional expectations of her conduct by ordering the expensive medicine chest. The role of aristocratic women in early modern society included their involvement in the medical care of the court, their servants, maids, farmhands, and the needy population in their political sphere of influence.[38] Caspar Neefe seems to have taken this into account when planning to equip the medicine chest: a square tin box contained an ointment ready for use against inflamed gums. The physician informed his client that it was suitable for the treatment of servants: "I have also ordered a salve for ailing gums for your F.G. [Princely Grace] … in the event that this affliction befalls one of the servants."[39] He recommended rinsing the mouth after getting up and before going to bed with common stonecrop (sedum acre) water mixed with a little rose honey and alum. In addition, the gums should be rubbed with the ointment.[40] In a recipe for a "children's powder", Caspar

---

34   Wacker, *Arznei und Confect*, pp. 114–115.

35   Wacker, *Arznei und Confect*, pp. 108–170. Pirozynski, *Herzogin Sophie,* pp. 88–89; see Hans-Uwe Lammel, 'Hofmedizin als interdisziplinäre Forschungsaufgabe: Eine Bilanz', *Medizinhistorisches Journal*, 53 (2018), pp. 197–216.

36   "on E.F.G. gewonliche schwacheitten gereichet, auch vor derselben Hoffgesinde, vndt domit E.F.G. andern leutten behilfflich sein können." NLA WO, 1 Alt 23, no. 30, fol. 26v.

37   Pirozynski, *Herzogin Sophie*, p. 89.

38   Britta-Juliane Kruse, "Adelige Witwen im Netz frühneuzeitlicher Verhaltensdiskurse: Standesgrenzen und Aktionsradien," in Dirk Schleinert and Monika Schneikart (eds.), *Zwischen Thronsaal und Frawenzimmer: Handlungsfelder pommerscher Fürstinnen* (Cologne: Böhlau Verlag 2017), pp. 37–64. On widows in healthcare see Britta-Juliane Kruse, *Witwen. Kulturgeschichte eines Standes in Spätmittelalter und Früher Neuzeit.* (Berlin, New York: Walter de Gruyter, 2007), pp. 340–362.

39   NLA WO, 1 Alt 23, no. 30, fol. 23r.

40   Ibid.

Neefe referred to the qualities of charity and social commitment, which had a particularly positive connotation in Protestantism: "so that they may also be beneficial to other people."[41] The niece of Duchess Sophia, Duchess Hedwig of Braunschweig-Lüneburg, acted in accordance with such expectations of the care of princesses: the wife of Duke Julius, founder of the court library (Bibliotheca Julia), established a princely house pharmacy in Wolfenbüttel, which was closely linked to the court pharmacy.[42]

4   Selected Examples of Caspar Neefe's Recipe Compilation
     from the Medicine Chest: Contents, Possible Models, and
     Comparable Traditions

On the first page of the "Report" on the practical use of the medicine chest, the title is repeated: "Report on how to use some remedies in this travel- and field-pharmacy case in the absence of a doctor, before one can obtain one, to be used in a hurry." The text that follows is divided into 84 sections with Roman numerals. The scribe copied the recipes from one or more templates. Judging by the numbering, some of the recipes were omitted: Number 56 is followed by prescriptions numbered 78, 79, and 84.[43] Then follows an overview, divided into seven subsections, of the use of the medicinal substances in the travel and field pharmacy already mentioned within the medicine chest.[44] The nine compartments of the box mainly contained dried herbs.[45] From the list can be concluded that medicines for common illnesses could be prepared with them. These included: gargling, enema for colic, herbs for urinary and kidney stones, an electuary for purging, bandages for treating the uterus and medicinal water for the care of the heart and liver. This curative water should be applied to the skin above the organs with the sponge provided.[46] This part concludes with explanations on the use of an enema, to which I will return. Caspar Neefe put his signature under the finished text and in this way confirmed to the princess that the contents were legally binding.

---

41   NLA WO, 1 Alt 23, no. 30, fol. 28r.
42   Wacker, *Arznei und Confect*, on the Duchess's pharmacy pp. 62–64, 177–178, 308–327; on
      the laboratory and the distillers pp. 179–184; on the court pharmacy and the court apoth-
      ecaries pp. 53–62, 185–198.
43   NLA WO, 1 Alt 23, no. 30, fols. 28arv.
44   NLA WO, 1 Alt 23, no. 30, fols. 28av–29r.
45   NLA WO, 1 Alt 23, no. 30, fols. 35v–36r.
46   Ibid.

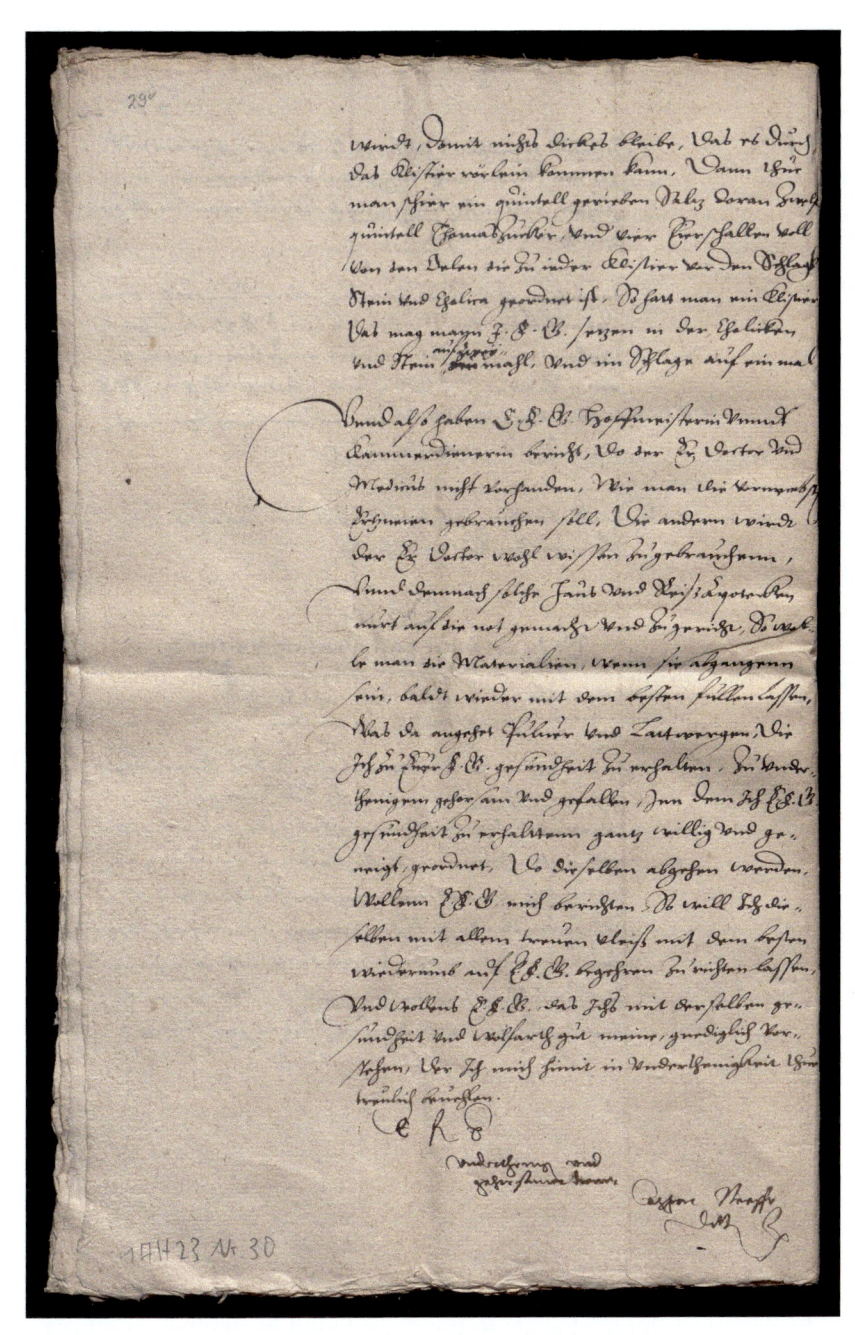

FIGURE 11.6   Caspar Neefe authorized the "Report" with his signature. NLA WO, 1 Alt 23,
No. 30, fol. 29v

It can be assumed that Caspar Neefe's concept for the selection of medicines took into account, on the one hand, more common diseases and, on the other hand, placed an emphasis on physical ailments of the duchess. The templates for his prescriptions may have originally been handwritten and later printed. Ideally, we could find cross-references to the handwritten and printed prescription literature from the second half of the 16th century. This probability will be examined on the basis of the content of some selected publications from this period.

The applications of a provided medicine, a basic medicinal substance or required utensils for each illness are already articulated in the headings. In the corresponding text, the symptoms are explained and the application of the remedy or object used is described. To his duchess, Caspar Neefe pointed out the rarity of some ingredients and emphasised the high quality of the substances contained in the medicine chest. Purgative remedies in the square tin boxes do not always seem to have been offered in Saxon pharmacies. To ensure that the dosing was not too strong and to prevent overdoses, the physician had ordered high-quality ingredients from other places in order to guarantee reliably effective medications. His empirical knowledge is documented by the note that if the basic medicinal substances were not exposed to too much cold or heat, they could be used for between one and four years.[47]

> From the use of several Medications
> that have been held in the square pewter containers
> XXXVIII.

> In these square pewter containers, there are some purgatorial remedies that can be used in E.F.G. [Your Princely Grace] weaknesses, and which I did not prepare as they cannot be found in the apothecaries in Saxony. But because it is very important that they are made of good materials, so that they do not do too much during purgation, which entails risks, and not every pharmacist can be trusted in every pharmacy. And also, if they do little with each other, they should not let themselves be mixed in this way. So that E.F.G. Medicus [personal physician] knows to rely on them, I have had them prepared from the best materials, of which we have the choice here, so that E.F.G. may be provided for. Thus, they are not all common in the apothecaries' shops. And because of this, it could easily be dangerous for aristocrats to use those found in common apothecaries, which has caused me to have them prepared here, because they can

---

47   On experiential knowledge see Stolberg, *Gelehrte Medizin*, pp. 348–350.

last a year, three, or even four years, if they are kept away from frost and great heat.[48]

Caspar Neefe often adopts a confidential tone towards his client, who in her early fifties was in an advanced age. The recipe for making the heart water is a good example of this.

III.

Heart water

As my dear mistress and princess, whom God had long protected, suddenly became weak, and the doctor was not available. So, in the emergency one may take the half of this heart water, and from the heart powder, which is in booklet XIVII [fol. 20v] two lots, mix it well, and dip the red cloth into it, which is only in the ninefold [Addendum: No. 7] box, which one may put on Your Grace in the emergency to strengthen the heart. However, the heart water, when used, should always be warmed up. And it can be used during the night if required. During the day, it should be used at seven in the morning and at two or three in the afternoon. Likewise, the liver water may be used with the help of bottle No. IIII with two lots of liver powder in the wooden container with the number 48.[49]

---

48 'Von gebrauch ettlicher Ertzneÿ so in den viereckketen zinen gefeslein gehaltten worden seind XXXVIII. Jn diesen viereckketen zinen gefeslein seind etliche purgirend Ertzneÿ, die man in E.F.G. schwacheitt gebrauchen kan, die Jch derhalben nicht habe zurichten lassen, das sie in den Apotecken in Sachsen nicht zufinden. Sondern dieweil doran viel gelegen, das sie recht vnndt aus guten Materialien zugerichtet worden, domit die im Purgiren nicht zuuiel thun mugen, darin denn grosse gefahr, vnnd nicht allen Apoteckern in ieder Apotecken zuuortrauen. Vnnd auch, so der wenig mit einander gemacht, sich nicht also mischen lassen. Domit nuhn E.F.G. Medicus [Leibarzt] wisse, sich auf solche gewis zuuerlassen, Als habe Jch die aus den besten Materialien, der wir dann alhir die wahl haben, zurichten lassen, domit E.F.G. vorsehen sein möchten. So seind sie auch nicht alle in den Apotecken dorunden gebreuchlich. Vnnd kann leichtlich aus diesen ein gefahr entstehenn, vnd hohen Furstlichen Personen soll billich bedencklich sein, solche aus gemeinen Apotecken zu gebrauchenn [fol. 22r] welches mich vorursacht hatt, solche alhie zurichtenn zu lassen, dieweill sie auch ein Jhar dreÿ aber vier, wenn sie ohne frost vnnd grosse hitze gehaltten werden, dauren vnd wehren können.' NLA WO, 1 Alt 23, no. 30, fols. 21v–22r.

49 "III. Hertzwasser / Do mein gnedige Frau vnnd Furstin, das Gott lang vorhueten wolte, plötzlichen schwach wurde, vnnd der Doctor nicht vorhanden. So mag man nehmen in der nott von diesem Hertzwasser die helfft, vnd vom Hertz Puluer, welches ist im buchslein XIVII [fol. 20v] zweÿ lot, wolle es wohl mischen, vnnd tuncke das rote tuch darein, welches einzig (?) im Neunfechichten [Nachtrag: No 7] kestlein ist, das mag man Jhr F.G. [Fürstliche Gnaden] in der not auflegen zu sterckung des Hertzens. Es soll aber

5   Enemas: Treatment in Compliance with Standards of Decency

Probably because of reasons of decency, no doctor was called in to treat Duchess Sophia with an enema, which was used mainly for colic or gall stones pain. In these cases, the women kept to themselves. An enema syringe made of ivory lay in the field pharmacy within the large medicine chest. It could be taken out by the court mistress Katharina Metsch († after 1575) or the chambermaid Margarete and used according to the instructions in the guide.[50] Caspar Neefe anticipated an emergency situation for which he made provisions by writing instructions for use:

> Report
> If the need to use such enemas arises. How to use them in the absence of the doctors, so that the treatment of Your Princely Grace is not neglected.[51]

One takes the herbs that belong to each disease, put them into a pot, pour[52] boiled clean warm water through a small cloth a good *Nössell*[53] or more on it, let them boil in a boiled out pot,[54] which is covered with an elevated cover, until the third part boils. Then strain the broth through a cloth. Take a good half *Nössell* of this broth, and beat the electuary that

---

das Hertzwasser, wenn man es gebrauchet, allzeit warm gemacht werden. Vndt man mag solches brauchen im fall der not die nacht. Am tage aber früe vmb Sieben vnd nach mittage vmb zweÿ aber dreÿ. Desgleichen mag man auch das Leberwasser die Helffte aus der Flaschen no. IIII mit zweÿ lot des Leber Puluers im buchslein gedreht mit der Ziffer 48. gebrauchen." NLA WO, 1 Alt 23, no. 30, fols. 20rv.

50   Enema syringes of various formats made of ivory mentioned in Piners, *Haus- und Reiseapotheken*, p. 21. Katharina Metsch was the widow of the court master Ludwig Baumbach († before 1567). The names of the court mistress and the valet or chambermaid Margarete can be reconstructed from the list of the staff's dispatches after the death of Duchess Sophia: NLA WO 1 Alt 23, No. 78, fols. 102r–103v, see 103r; Pirozynski, *Herzogin Sophie*, p. 89. Bues, *Zofia Jagiellonka*, p. 212.

51   Bericht Do die not solcher Klistier vorfiele zu gebrauchen Wie mann die soll in abwesen des Herrn doctors zurichten, Also, das Jhr F.G. nicht vorseumet werden.

52   This is another indication that the text was copied from an original: after an eye movement, the previously mentioned 'do' was corrected by 'pour'.

53   Nößel, Nösel, Notsel, Nocel, Oessel, or Pinte is a historical unit of measure for liquids that denoted about 450 to 500 milliliters. A mug comprised half a liter. Jars in the early modern period often had a capacity of two Nößel, about one liter. August Lübben, *Mittelniederdeutsches Handwörterbuch* (Darmstadt: Wissenschaftliche Buchgesellschaft, 1995), p. 250. Christa Baufeld, *Kleines frühneuhochdeutsches Wörterbuch* (Tübingen: Max Niemeyer, 1996), p. 180.

54   The example of the boiled pot documents empirical knowledge on the subject of sterility.

belongs to it with a whisk, so that it becomes very thin, so that it passes unhindered through the tube of the enema. Then one adds almost a pinch (quint)[55] of grated salt to it, twelve tiny bits of Thomas sugar,[56] and four eggshells full of the oils that are ordered for each enema for stroke, gallstones, and cholica. Thus, one has a clyster that may be[57] secreted by my Princely Grace in the cholica and stone at two times and in the beater at one time.[58]

And so Your Princely Grace, the court mistress and chambermaid have reported that the doctor and Medicus are not present. How to use the most noble remedies. The doctor will probably know how to use the others. Accordingly, such medicine chest is made and equipped for emergencies. When the ingredients are used up, they should be replenished with the best substances. This especially concerns the powders and electuary which I have provided for the preservation of Your Princely Grace's health, which I am willing and inclined to do. When these have been used up, may Your Princely Grace inform me. So, I will refill them with all the best that can be obtained, according to the wishes of Your Princely Grace. And if Your Princely Grace wishes me to continue to do the best I can for your health and welfare, I am ready to do so in subservience and loyalty. Sincere and obedient Caspar Neefe Doctor.[59]

---

55 'Ein quintell', 1 quint, denotes a quart, about 3.65 grams. Baufeld, *Wörterbuch*, p. 186; Wacker, *Arznei und Confect*, p. 535.

56 Thomas sugar is described as soft, brownish-reddish sugar of simple quality, obtained from the island of St Thomas; *Pierer's Universal-Lexikon*, vol. 17, 1863, p. 535.

57 'One' corrected to 'two times'.

58 'Mann [sic!] nehme die Kreutter die zu jeder Kranckheit gehoren, thue sie in ein topf, giesse rein gesottenn warm wasser durch ein tuchlein ein gut nössell aber mehr dorauf, lasse die sieden in eim ausgesottenem topf, der mit einer geheben sturtzen bedeckt ist, bis der dritte theill versottenn. Dann seihe man die brüe durch ein tuch. Dieser brue nehme mann ein gut halb nössell, vnd zurtreibe die Lattwerge die dortzu gehöret, mit eim quirl, das sie gar Dünne [fol. 29v] wirdt, damit nichts dickes bleibe, das es durch das Klistier rörlein kommen kann. Dann thüe man schier ein quintell gerieben Salz doran zwelff quintell Thomaszucker, vnd vier Eierschallen voll von den Oelen die zu ieder Klistier vor den Schlagk Stein vnd Cholica geordnet ist. So hatt man ein Klistier das mag mayn J.F.G. seczen in der Cholicken vnd Stein auf zwey̆ mahl vnd im Schlage auf ein mal.'

59 'Vnnd also haben E.F.G. Hoffmeisterin vnndt Kammerdienerin bericht, so der Er doctor [sic!] vnd Medicus nicht vorhanden. Wie man die vornembst Ertzneien gebrauchen soll. Die andern wirdt der Er doctor wohl wissen zu gebrauchenn. Vnnd demnach solche Haus vnd Reiß Apotecken wurt auf die not gemacht vnd zu gericht. So wolle man die Materialien, wenn sie abgangenn sein, baldt wieder mit dem besten fullen lassen. Was da angehet Puluer vnd Lattwergen, die jch zu Euer F.G. gesundheit zu erhalten. Zu vnderthenigem gehorsam vnd gefallen, jnn dem Jch E.F.G. gesundheit zu erhalttenn gantz willig vnd geneigt geordnet. Do dieselben abgehen werden. Wollenn E.F.G. mich

For the application of a "water against serious diseases" the personal physician recommends a dosage corresponding to the age of the person being treated.

VII.
Water in case of severe illness

This water may be given to an old person, if one notices symptoms of the illness coming on, or if it has already presented itself, pour a spoonful of this, not heated. It may also be applied under the nose. For a young person give a bit less, to a child give it with a very small wooden spoon, such as one used for herbs. In addition, a delicious powder in the recipe with the number 49 will serve against such illnesses. An old man should be given two spoonful of lime blossom but Lili Connalli water,[60] more than half a tiny bit, made warm, and a young man a third of a tiny bit, all before the next day. And if necessity requires it, every day early, but after midday about three-thirds, the head is also to be quenched. It has been tried by many who are well off. The doctor will know how to use the other herbs in the other bottles. Because the herbs for the enemas against the[61] stones, the cholica, and the beating which the Almighty will preserve, the doctor will also know how to put them together in an emergency. Which I have therefore left to be judged in our apothecary.[62] Therefore, some of the pieces are not used in pharmacies in Saxony.[63]

---

berichten. So will Jch dieselben mit allem treuen vleiß mit dem besten wiederumb auf E.F.G. begehren zu richten lassen. Vnd wollens E.F.G. das Jchs mit derselben gesundheit vnd Wolfarth gut meine, gnediglich vorsehen, der Jch mich hiemit in vndertheniglkeit thue treulich beuehlen. EFG vndertheniger vnd gehorsamer Caspare Neefe Doctor.' NLA WO, 1 Alt 23, no. 30, fols. 29rv.

60   For Lily of the valley water: 'lilium convalium, lilium conuallium', see Baufeld, *Wörterbuch*, p. 161.

61   'the' added.

62   This reference probably refers to the pharmacy in Chemnitz, Caspar Neefe's birthplace.

63   'VII. Wasser vor die Schwere Kranckheitt / Dieses Wasser mag man einer Alten Personen, wenn man merket, das sich die Kranckheit regen will, Aber auch schon reget, ein löffell also kalt geben. Auch damit vnder der Nasen bestreichen, einer Jungern Person weniger, einem kinde ein Wurtzlöfflein voll. Doruber so hat man auch ein gar köstlich Puluer vor solche Kranckheit dienende vnder den buchslein gezeicht mit der Ziffer 49. Dauon wolle man einem Alten geben in Zwelff löffell Lindenblüe aber Lili Connalli wasser, mehr als ein halb quintell, warm gemacht, eim Jungern ein drittheil eines quintels, alwege vor den andern tag. Vnd do es die not erfordert, alle tage frue aber nach mittage vmb dreỹ, pflegt auch das haupt zu stercken. Jst in vielen probirt worden, denen es wohl bekommen. Die ander Ertzneỹ, so in den andern Flaschen ist, wirdt der Er doctor wohl zu gebrauchen wissen. Denn die Kreuter zun Clỹstiern vor den Stein, Cholica, vnd Schlagk dorfur der

In one recipe, the number of the box containing the required herbs was forgotten. This omission was marked with a cross in the margin of the recipe.[64] An electuary (*Latwerg*), a boiled-down mixture of juice, medicinal drugs, and honey as a healing confection, should be produced.

XIX
Electuary for infected people

I have also decreed to Your Princely Grace a most exquisite electuary, if anyone has been charged with restlessness,[65] God save us from this,[66] the body is to be opened with a suppository[67] or an enema by the order of Your Princely Grace. This includes the herbs in the compartment with the number[68] in the square box with the nine compartments, together with the enemas that go with them. When the body is opened by the enema, if it is an old person, let him take this mixture warmed: four eggshells full of sorrel water, one eggshell with lemon water and a good quint of this electuary, then cover him and make him sweat. If someone vomits after giving the electuary, they should quickly be given another potion made in the same way, which they should keep with them. Your Princely Grace's personal physician has already received a report on this from me in the court camp [Schöningen].[69]

Allmechtige behutten wolle, Wirdt der Er Doctor auch zur notturfft wissen zu sammen zu fugen. Welche Jch derhalben alhir in vnser Apotecken habe lassen zu richten. Dorumb das ettliche Stück in den Sächsischen Apotecken nicht im gebrauch sein.' NLA WO, 1 Alt 23, no. 30, fols. 20v–21r.

64   NLA WO, 1 Alt 23, no. 30, fol. 22r.
65   The early New High German term 'unhulde' denoted restlessness or annoyance; Lübben, *Handwörterbuch*, p. 438. Possibly this is a synonym for syphilis.
66   What is meant is: God protect us from this.
67   Remedial suppositories for insertion. Baufeld, *Wörterbuch*, p. 256.
68   The digit was not entered.
69   'XIX Lattwerge den behaften Personen / Euern F.G. [Fürstlichen Gnaden] habe Jch auch geordnet ein gar Köstliche Latwerge, do iemand mit der Vnhuld, do Gott fur seÿ, behaft wurde, dem soll mann mit Reuerentz vor E.F.G. zu schreiben mit Zeplein aber dem gemeinen Klistier den leib öfnen. Dorzu die Kreutter gereicht mit der Ziffer im Neunfechichten viereckketten Kestlein gehorig, sambt beÿgeordneten Purgir Lattwergen. Do nuhn der leib geöfnet, dann wolle man in vier Eÿerschall voll Saurampfwasser vnnd ein Eÿerschal voll zittweressig durcheinander gemenget, zu treiben, dieser Lattwerge eim alten ein gutt quintell, Vnd wolle Jhn solches gar warm zu sich nehmen lassen, bedecken vnd schwitzen lassen, vnndt in fall iemand solche Lattwerge wurde weg brechenn, wolte mann jhm als bald ein ander trencklein also zu gericht geben lassen, vnnd jhnen sich darauf lassenn vorhaltten. Wie dann E.F.G. Medicus von mir einen bericht E.F.G. Hofflager zu beförderung albereidt entpfangen.' NLA WO, 1 Alt 23, no. 30, fols. 22rv.

6   Cultural Transfer of Medicines and Experiential Knowledge of the Medical Practitioner

Two medicinal jars contained the expensive universal remedies theriac and metridate, which were composed of many individual ingredients. In the Renaissance, theriac and metridate were made using snake meat, honey, powdered spices, and other animal and vegetable components. Silvaticus, who wrote a book on theriac and dedicated it to the medical college of the University of Milan in 1596, emphasizes the difficulty of making theriac with pure, precisely composed elements.[70] Caspar Neefe informed his client that these reliably effective medicinal preparations had been obtained in Venice or had been produced according to Venetian recipes and were purchased by him.

> XXIX vnnd XXX
> Theriac vnd Metridat.

> I have also bought a good Venetian Theriac and Metridat for your F.G. [Princely Grace] in both cases. E.F.G. [Your Princely Grace] may rely on this in the future.[71]

Venice and Nuremberg were the centers of production and trade of theriac for a long time. In the 16th century, the pharmacy of the Jesuit College in Rome was added as a production site, whose employees shipped Roman theriac (*Triaca Romana*) to many countries.[72] The wooden box with the number 20 contained pulverized horn from the antlers of deer that were hunted between two Marian days. Caspar Neefe mentions that he himself produced this medicine with particular diligence and sent some of it to the Elector Joachim II of Brandenburg (1505–1571). The Elector was the brother-in-law of Duchess Sophia of Braunschweig-Lüneburg and husband of her sister Jadwiga/Hedwig of Brandenburg. Powdered antler was considered an effective antidote for poison. It stimulated sweating and was thought to be particularly effective if the

---

70   See Gilbert Watson, *Theriac and Mithridatium: A Study in Therapeutics* (London: Publications of the Wellcome Medical Library vol. 9, 1966), pp. 100–109: 'ii. An International Panacea', p. 102.

71   NLA WO, 1 Alt 23, no. 30, fol. 23r.

72   Sabine Anagnostou, 'Theriak: Ein weltweites Antidot', in Christoph Friedrich and Wolf-Dieter Müller-Jahncke (eds.), *Gifte und Gegengifte in Vergangenheit und Gegenwart* (Stuttgart: Wissenschaftliche Verlagsgesellschaft, 2012), pp 45–70, see p. 48; Alisha Michelle Rankin, 'On anecdote and antidotes: poison trials in sixteenth-century Europe', *Bulletin of the History of Medicine*, 91 (2017), pp. 274–302.

burning process had already taken place some time ago. Elderly people should only be given a modicum of it as a precaution.[73]

For the treatment of rabies, crayfish eyes or crayfish stones were used interchangeably. These are two calcareous concretions situated below the head of crayfish, compared to eyes because of their round shape. Together with gentian, red myrrh, and frankincense, these calcareous deposits were pulverized.[74] To make a healing potion, a small amount of it was mixed with fennel water and some wine vinegar. The sick person was supposed to consume it frequently and as hot as possible, because it should make her sweat. In this context, Caspar Neefe again mentions his experiential knowledge: he had seen that two boys which bitten by a rabid dog had been cured with this medicine.

21.

Unboiled crayfish eyes

The unboiled crayfish eyes are better than those boiled with the crayfish, because the boiling takes away their strength, and they also serve the purpose served by the stag's horn. But if a person has been bitten by a raging dog, he shall be given a powder of these crab's eyes, gentian, red pine, and wine vapour. Poke them again and give the sick person a tiny bit of the same in fennel water with wine vinegar. He can drink it warm and let him sweat on it. If it does not help once, use it again. It will help. I have experienced it myself with instructions from two noble books.[75]

The most important ingredient of the following recipe was Armenian clay, whose origin is described precisely. A dram of the clay was mixed with fennel water and wine vinegar as an antidote[76] for spider bites, i.e., an injury caused

---

73   '20. Gebrant Hirschhorn, Jm buchslein 20 jst gebrand Hirschhorn, das zwuschen zweÿen Frauentagen geschlagen, vnd von mir mit sonderm fleiß zu gerichtet worden. Daruon Jch [Caspar Neefe] auch dem Churfürsten zu Brandenburgk [Joachim II. von Brandenburg] hochseliger gedechtnus gesand habe. Welches man pflegt zu nehmenn, so mann sich gifts befahret. Auch wenn man schwitzen will, denn es gar kostlich, vnnd ie elter es gebrand, ie tuchtiger es ist. Mann mag einer Alten Personen schier ein quintell geben.' NLA WO, 1 Alt 23, no. 30, fols. 23r, 25rv.

74   On frankincense and myrrh as medicines see Dieter Martinetz, Karlheinz Lohs, and Jörg Janzen, *Weihrauch und Myrrh: Kulturgeschichtliche und wirtschaftliche Bedeutung – Botanik, Chemie, Medizin* (Stuttgart: Wissenschaftliche Verlagsgesellschaft, 1989), pp. 125–151. Frankincense was already recommended by the ancient physician Hippocrates for wound healing, p. 126.

75   NLA WO, 1 Alt 23, No. 30, fol. 25v.

76   For the definition of the term antidote see Anagnostou, *Theriak*, p. 46.

by animal poison, or – like the burnt deer antler – for deliberate poisoning of food.[77]

7   Publications and Preparations for the Prophylaxis of the Plague

Plague epidemics were a recurring threat in the second half of the 16th century. In the Duchy of Braunschweig-Wolfenbüttel, the epidemic was particularly rampant in the 1570s, when the medicine chest was available for use. When the pandemic reached Wolfenbüttel, Duke Julius had the population supplied with free medicines as a preventive measure. There was not yet a town doctor at the court at this time.[78] Court, personal, and city physicians compiled treatment-oriented prescription literature such as plague tracts, plague regimens, and a large number of individual prescriptions. They appeared in Latin and German and were directed towards reading publics with different levels of education.[79] Gervasius Marstaller (1543–1578), one of Duchess Sophia's personal physicians, wrote a rhymed "Brief summary of how to act for protection against the plague or in times of need due to the plague."[80] The three-column pamphlet was published in 1577 by Michael Kröner in Uelzen. This cheaply produced work in a single-sheet print was intended to have a broad media

---

77   '26. Bolus Armenus, Jst ein Erde, kompt aus Armenien vnder dem Turcken gelegen, braucht man ein gifft, also, wenn einer ein Spinnen, aber ettwas anders im essen bekommen. So nimbt man solches schier ein quintell in Fenchell wasser mit Weinessig vermischet, wie oben vermeldet wordenn.' NLA WO, 1 Alt 23, no. 30, fols. 25v–26r.

78   On the care of the court in times of plague and the plague writings of the Wolfenbüttel personal physicians, see Wacker, *Arznei und Confect*, pp. 275–308. Ulf Wendler, 'Johann Bökel (1535–1605): Leibarzt, Professor und Kämpfer gegen die Pest', in Marina Hilber and Elena Taddei (eds.), *In fürstlicher Nähe: Ärzte bei Hof (1450–1800)* (Innsbruck University Press, 2021), pp. 149–169, see pp. 165–168.

79   See Erik A. Heinrichs, *Plague, Print and the Reformation: The German Reform of Healing, 1473–1573* (Routledge: Abingdon/New York, 2018), pp. 145–152. Diethelm Eikermann and Gabriele Kaiser, *Die Pest in Berlin 1576: Eine wiederkehrende Pestschrift von Leonhart Thurneisser zum Thurn (1531–1596)* (Rangsdorf: Basiliken-Presse, 2012), p. 15.

80   *Kurtze Summa / Wie man sich in Pestilentz zeitten zur Vorsorg vnd in der Not verhalten sol / in Reimen gefast / durch Geruasium Marstaller / der Artzney Doctorem, vnd Fürstlichen Lüneburgischen Medicum*: https://digital.francke-halle.de/urn/urn:nbn:de:gbv:ha33-1-149 288. (25 July 2022) There are three copies in the Herzog August Bibliothek, shelfmark: M: Mi 141 (2) and M: Mi 141.1. The third copy, H: M 63bb.4° Helmst (2), was part of the Helmstedt University Library; see Britta-Juliane Kruse, *Gelehrtenkultur und Sammlungspraxis: Architektur, Akteure und Wissensorganisation in der Universitätsbibliothek Helmstedt (1576–1810)* (Berlin, Boston, De Gruyter, 2023).

impact among the population, via its deliberately chosen rhyme scheme. For plague prophylaxis, for example, the personal physician recommends:

> Against the poison of the plague take something /
> That keeps your body pure /
> Such as pills / powder / and the like /
> That is prescribed against this plague:
> Electuary / metridat / theriac
> Of the golden egg, according to what
> Your supply and your purse allow.
> If you have much of it, take quite a lot of it /
> Of each a little / but above all
> Take well the pills /
> That are able to purify your body /
> And are also useful to you in other ways.[81]

In addition to this short guide Gervasius Marstaller compiled a 140-page treatise on pestilence.[82] Johann Neefe, Caspar Neefe's brother, also wrote a pestilence treatise, which was printed by Matthes Stöckel in Dresden in 1566 and again in 1577, three years after his death. This pestilence treatise for the inhabitants of Dresden and all others who needed rules for behavior before or during occurring epidemics had been commissioned by Duke August of Saxony (1526–1586).[83] It is possible that Caspar Neefe took his cue from his brother's publication, adopted rules of conduct from it and had jars in the medicine chest filled on the basis of the recipes. Johann Neefe's plague tract is divided into three parts. First, it explains how one could protect oneself

---

81 "Wider das gifft nim etwas ein / Das dein leib müge bleiben rein / Als Pillen / Puluer / vnd dergleichen / Geordnet wider diese seuchen: Latwergen / Mitridat / Theriack / Vom Güldeney vnd was vermag Dein vorrath vnd der beutel dein. Hastu jr viel / so nims recht ein / Eins vmbs ander / doch vor allem Las dir die Pillen wol gefallen / Die dich zugleich purgieren mügen / Vnd andre nutz auch mehr zufügen [...]."

82 *Kurtzer vnd einfeltiger Bericht / Wie man / so viel Gott gellig / sich für der grawsamen vnd schrecklichen Pestilentz bewaren / Oder so man damit behafft / sie vertreiben müge.* [...] by Geruasium Mar = staller / the Physician / and Princely Lüneburg Medicum at Zell. Uelzen: Michael Kröner 1576/77. https://opendata2.uni-halle.de//handle/1516514412012/1052 (2 August 2022). See Wendler, 'Johann Bökel', p. 163.

83 *Ein kurtzer Bericht: Wie man sich in denen jtzo vorstehenden Sterbensleufften / mit der Præseruation oder vorwahrungen / Dornach auch der Curation der Pestilentz / vnd etzlicher jrer accidentien, oder zufellen / verhalten soll.* See Lesser, 'Leibärzte', p. 66. The patron is mentioned in the short preface (Aijv), VD 16 N 41, Duke August Library, shelfmark M: Mi Kapsel 4 (13), Thuringian University and State Library Jena, shelfmark 4 Med. XXI, 54 (9).

from the plague with divine intervention, secondly, how to help those suffering from the plague and thirdly, how symptoms of the disease could be cured. According to the physician, six aspects in particular were important for avoiding infection: the first of these was keeping living spaces clean and fumigating them to avoid bad air. Here he followed a doctrine that had been handed down since antiquity, according to which miasmas, pathological secretions that entered the body by breathing polluted air, were considered to trigger the epidemic.[84] He considered the removal of waste to be just as important as the reduction of contact with peoples. Nutrition was the second aspect. A third was the maintenance of rhythms of day and night, and a fourth, the relationship between movement and relaxation. Bodily hygiene was the fifth aspect, and last was the mental state or "movements of the mind". These points of view are described in more details.[85]

As Giovanni Boccaccio (1313–1375) stresses in the *Decameron*, the safest approach to a pestilence was to flee the infected location. The *Büchlein der Ordnung der Pestilenz*, first published by Johannes Zainer in Ulm in 1473, the Ulm city doctor Heinrich Steinhöwel (1412–1482) follows this tradition in his recommendation to either flee or isolate oneself: "Fleuch bald, fleuch ferr, kom spat herwider" [flee quickly, flee far, come back late].[86] This was the practice of members of the patrician class of the imperial city of Nuremberg in the early modern period. In times of plague, they often retreated to their country estates for longer periods. Caspar Neefe integrated the administration of plague medication into his guidelines for using the medicine chest. Once a selection was made, the basic substances in the medicine jars could be mixed with additives to make a medication ready to use. The medicine chest contained ingredients that could be mixed with lemon water by the court mistress or chambermaid to make an ointment. A pea-sized portion of the ointment was to be spread around the left breast and on the wrists (pulse locations). Alternatively, a

---

84   Eikermann and Kaiser, *Pest*, p. 13. LWL-Museum für Archäologie Herne (ed.), *Pest. Eine Spurensuche*. Texte zur Ausstellung, dt./engl. (Darmstadt: Wissenschaftliche Buchgesellschaft, 2019).

85   Johann Neefe mentions these aspects in the introduction to the first part, Aiijv.

86   Heinrich Steinhöwel: *Büchlein der ordnung / wie sich der Mensch halten sol / zu dieser zÿten dieser grusenlichen kranckheit* (Nuremberg: Printer of the legend of St. Roch, ca. 1484): https://data.cerl.org/istc/is00764500. https://www.digitale-sammlungen.de/de/view/bsb 00032075?page=,1. (2 August 2022), 4v. Hans Dorn printed a Low German version of Steinhöwel's *Büchlein der Ordnung der Pestilenz*, title: *Een korth schon vnde gar trostelick regime[n]t wedder de swaren vn[de] erschreckliken Krancheit der pestilencie.* Braunschweig 1506. VD 16 S 8813. Herzog August Bibliothek, shelfmark A: 448.1 Theol. 2° (1). See Wendler, 'Johann Bökel', p. 161.

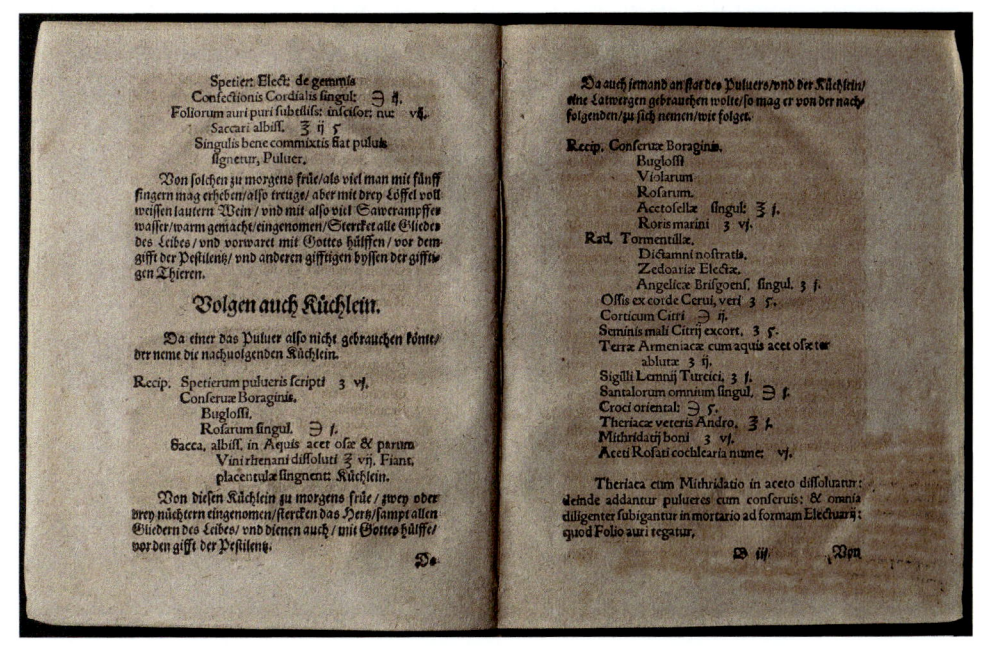

FIGURE 11.7   Double page from Johann Neefe's printed plague treatise, Bijv-Biijr
PHOTO: HERZOG AUGUST BIBLIOTHEK WOLFENBÜTTEL

pea-sized amount of the preparation could be swallowed at five o'clock in the morning to protect against the pestilence.[87]

The red myrrh contained in the wooden box number 12 could be consumed in small portions and gargled in the mouth when one was in danger of becoming infected with the plague.[88] Similar to the small portion of the medicine with red myrrh, three pieces of the "Liberantes Küchlein" were to be taken early in the morning against the plague. *Confectio liberantis* was an electuary consisting of many ingredients.[89] The little cakes are also mentioned in Johann Neefe's plague treatise. Two or three of these little cakes, taken early in the

---

87   "XVIII Praeseruativum vor die Pestilenz / Dieweill sich auch von wegen des Vngewitters der schweren Seuchten zu befahren, als habe E.F.G. Jch ein Præseruativo aber Vorwahrung geordnet, Dauon mag man nehmenn einer kleinen Erbes gros, vnnd mit Zittweressig machen zum Selblein, vnd sich teglich damit vnder vnnd vmb die lincke Brust schmieren, auch auf die Pulsadern. Man mag auch dauon früe nuchtern vmb funfe einer Arbes gros nehmen vnd hinein essen Praeseruiret mercklich." NLA WO, 1 Alt 23, Nr. 30, fol. 22r.

88   "12. Red gutte Mýrra. In the wooden box 12 is red good myrrha. When one travels through evil places and walks. Take a little on the tongue and wilt it in the mouth. It also protects against pestilence." NLA WO, 1 Alt 23, no. 30, fol. 25r.

89   Wacker, *Arznei und Confect*, p. 533.

morning, would sooth the heart, together with all the organs of the body, and also, with God's help, will serve as a protection against the pestilence.[90]

In equipping the medicine chest, his brother Caspar Neefe took care to include the pre-mixed "Liberantes Küchlein". They were in the medicine jar with the number 35.[91] A powder against pestilence can be found in the square tin vessel with the number 18. Instead of the electuary, it could be taken mixed in water. If the sick person vomited, he or she was to be quickly provided with a newly prepared healing potion.[92] Parallels between Johann Neefe's printed plague treatise and the written "Report" of his brother Caspar Neefe can be detected. While Johann Neefe described the composition of the recipes for plague prophylaxis, the medicine chest contained ready-made basic medicinal substances that could either be used directly or could be quickly produced. It is conceivable that the recipes contained in the medicine jars were based on the recipes in Johann Neefe's printed plague tract. Unlike his brother, who equipped the medicine chest for a wealthy princess, Johann Neefe differentiated between expensive medicines and preparations for poor people who could not afford them:

> For the poor, there is a latwerg made of rue and nuts in the pharmacies, which is also good for protection against the plague. An elderly person should take an amount of it equal to the size of a walnut, younger people less, depending on their age. Afterwards, one should fast for two or three hours. Those who cannot pay for this latwerg from the pharmacy take a little fresh wormwood with salt or some juniper berries that have previously been soaked in wine vinegar for a night or a bite of bread dipped in wine vinegar, otherwise two or three bites of fresh butter and bread.[93]

---

90 Herzog August Bibliothek, shelfmark M: Mi Kapsel 4 (13), B2v.

91 NLA WO, 1 Alt 23, no. 30, fol. 26r.

92 "55. Puluer vor die Pestilenz / Dieses Puluer mag man an stad der Lattwerge, welche oben im viereckten zinen gefes gezeicht mit der ziffer 18. gebrauchen, in ob vorzeichnetem wasser, Vnd do mans weg breche, wolle mann dem behaftenn wieder flugs ein anders geben." NLA WO, 1 Alt 23, no. 30, fol. 28v–28ar. Johann Neefe's printed plague tract contains a recipe for making a powder against the plague: Herzog August Bibliothek, shelfmark M: Mi Kapsel 4 (13), Biv–B2v.

93 'Vor die armen aber ist ein Rauten vnd Nußlatwerge in die Apoteken geordnet / seind auch zur vorwarunge / vor dieser plagen gar gut / Von welchen eine alte Person einer Welschen Nuß gros / die Jungen aber mügen nach gelegenheit jres Alters weniger zu sich nemen / vnd wolten etwan zwo oder drey stunden hernach fasten / Die aber solches nicht zubezalen / die nemen ein wenig frische Wermut mit Saltze / oder etzliche Wacholderbeere / so zuuorn eine nacht in Weinessig gebeitzet / oder einen bissen Brots

Then Johann Neefe mentions two more proven means of plague prophylaxis that should be used in the early morning: a potion made from one's own urine, mixed with a little saffron and drunk warm, or the ingestion of a large piece of salted horseradish.

8   Recipes for Women's Medicine

Duchess Sophia's female court (*Frauenzimmer*) included the aforementioned court mistress Katharina Metsch and the chambermaid Margarete. She was also surrounded by five ladies in waiting (*Hoffräulein*): Elisabeth von Weihe, Salome Kesselberg, Margarethe von Bodensee and Sophie von der Marwitz, as well as her secretary and confidante Agnieska, who was small in stature. The honored "Matron" Anna Leibinghausen was looked after by one of her own maids.[94] A further nine ladies-in-waiting, some of whom had moved to the principality of Braunschweig-Wolfenbüttel from Poland, can be traced as wives of court officials. In addition to the chambermaid, there were other servants in the vicinity of the princess[95] and there were many other women who lived and worked on the widow's estate. Their presence and the expectation of the duchess to be charitable were probably the reasons for the emphasis on prescriptions for women's medication.[96]

Since antiquity, medicinal theory had embraced the concept of uterine migration in medicine, especially the rising of the uterus in the female body, which was called 'suffocatio matricis' or hysteria. Among other things considered to be the triggers were accumulations of undrained menstrual blood or harmful liquids in the uterus. According to the medical thinking of that period, foul gases were formed when these substances decomposed, which caused the uterus to rise up to below the heart. A tried and trusted antidote was the use of incense, the vapors of which were supposed to drive the organ back to its original place.[97] The medicine jar with No. 2 contained a ready-made

---

in Weinessig getuncket / oder sonsten zweene oder drey bissen frische Butter vnd Brot.' Herzog August Bibliothek, shelfmark M: Mi Kapsel 4 (13), Biijv.

94   NLA WO, 1 Alt 23, no. 78, fol. 103r.

95   Details of the duchess's female court can be found in NLA WO, 1 Alt 23, no. 66, fols. 47rv. See Pirozynski, *Herzogin Sophie*, pp. 44–45, 88–89. On medical practice for women in Renaissance courts see Rankin, *Panaceia's Daughters*.

96   On gynecology in the early modern period see Stolberg, *Gelehrte Medizin*, pp. 317–347.

97   Monica Helen Green, *Women's Healthcare in the Medieval West: Texts and Contexts* (Aldershot: Ashgate 2000); Britta-Juliane Kruse, *Verborgene Heilkünste: Geschichte der Frauenmedizin im Spätmittelalter* (Berlin/New York: De Gruyter, 1996), pp. 91–94. Jan Pirozynski inadvertently interprets a prescription in the medicine chest against a rising

product, called 'Rauchpuschel'. It consisted of roots of unspecified plants.[98] After it had been lit, the woman was supposed to breathe in the rising smoke. In addition, the medicine chest contained a powder that was supposed to be effective against a rising uterus. One or two tiny amounts of this powder was to be mixed with eleven spoonfuls of mugwort water or of warm wine. It was expected that the uterus would move back to its usual place.[99] Uterine migration was considered a phenomenon that could have the most threatening effects on the female body. If the powder in medicine jar with no. 78 had no effect, one was supposed to take small amount of a different powder instead, which would make the uterus subside.[100]

Another powder was supposed to restart a menstrual cycle after a missed period, but this also means that it could have an abortive effect. In order to restart menstruation, this preparation was recommended: a tiny amount of the powder was to be mixed with eleven or twelve spoons of mugwort water or an extract of pole mint in water. Like mugwort, pole mint was known as an effective abortifacient.[101] The woman was to drink the mixture one to three days before the expected start of menstruation. Late medieval recipe books contain instructions to rub the abdomen with an extract of mugwort in wine, beer, or honey.[102] To stimulate menstruation, mugwort was to be boiled in a cauldron with water. After this, the cauldron was to be placed between the patient's spread legs to allow the steam entering the body.[103]

uterus ('vor das aufsteigen der Mutter') as a prolapse of the uterus and expresses the opinion that Duchess Sophia suffered from this organ weakness. However, there is no evidence for this. Pirozynski, *Herzogin Sophie*, p. 118.

98   '2. Rauchpuschell zur Mütter / Jst ein Puschell jm buchsell gezeicht mit der Ziffer .2. wenn die Mutter jemand aufsteiget, Vnd durch ander weise nicht mag gelagert noch gestillet werden. Als mag mann solchen buschell der Personen vber die Nasen haltenn. Wird die Mutter wiederumb stillen. Do ander dinge zuuor nicht haben helffen wollen.' NLA WO, 1 Alt 23, No. 30, fol. 24v–25r. The directory '*Vorzeichnus*' mentions 'Wurtzellen im Rauchpuschell': NLA WO, 1 Alt 23, No. 30, fol. 35r.

99   "78. Puluer vors auffsteigen der Mutter / Wenn die Mutter aufgestiegenn vnnd sich nicht legen will, demselben mag man von diesem Puluer geben schier ein quintell aber zwei teill eines quintels in eilf löffell Beifus wasser, ader aber warmen wein. So wirdt sich die Mutter lagern." NLA WO, 1 Alt 23, no. 30, fol. 28ar.

100 "84. Anderpuluer im aufsteigen der Mutter / So sich die Mutter vonn dem Puluer 78. nicht legen wolte, So mag man ann stad desselben dieses Puluers ein halb quintlein gebrauchen. So wirdt sich die Mutter lagern." NLA WO, 1 Alt 23, no. 30, fol. 28av.

101 See Larissa Leibrock-Plehn, *Hexenkräuter oder Arznei: Die Abtreibungsmittel im 16. und 17. Jahrhundert* (Stuttgart: Wissenschaftliche Verlagsgesellschaft, 1992); Kruse, *Verborgene Heilkünste*, pp. 173–182.

102 Kruse, *Verborgene Heilkünste*, p. 82.

103 Kruse, *Verborgene Heilkünste*, p. 106.

The wooden medicine jar with no. 52 contained a powder which, in contrast, was to be used to stop menstruation that lasted too long and could lead to physical weakness or fainting. At mealtime, the powder was to be sprinkled over six or eight portions of food. In addition, it was recommended that if the menstruating woman also abstained from soups or liquid foods, menstruation would stop.[104]

Only when a midwife had tried everything that was in her power during a difficult birth, and in cases of emergency, could a birth be induced with another recipe. The amount of "difficult birthing powder" that could fit on the tip of a knife was to be dissolved in nine spoonfuls of warmed white lily water, mixed with two spoonfuls of wine from the Malvasian grape and given to the pregnant woman. Her body was to be kept warm.[105] Eucharius Rösslin's tract *Der swangern Frauwen vnd hebammen Rosegarten* (*The pregnant women and midwives rose garden*), first printed in 1513, offers a possible model for this recipe. The fifth chapter describes medicines to ease the course of childbirth.[106] But the powder for a difficult birth in combination with Malvasia wine and water of white lilies is not included.

In 16th-century obstetrics, midwives used extracts of lily water in olive oil to make ointments for birthing.[107]

Johann Neefe included recipes and advice for pregnant women in his tract on the plague, entitled "Die Schwangern Weiber belangendt." He mentions several tonics and protective remedies such as "Liberantis Küchlein" or boiled down and sugared lemon or bitter orange peel. At the same time, he warns against taking some medicines against the plague to safeguard the child (the foetus). This is because their ingredients consist of plant components that are

---

104   '51. Puluer die Blume wiederzubringen / So in einer Weiblichen Personen die Blume nicht fort wolte. So mag solche dieses Puluer ein tag aber dreÿ vor der Zeit, denn es zu kommen pflegt, in eilf aber zwelf löffell Beifus aber Boleÿ wasser dieses Puluers schier ein quintell nehmen,' NLA WO, 1 Alt 23, Nr. 30, fol. 28r.

105   '79. Puluer zur schweren geburt / Do auch jemand in schwerer geburt ligt, vnnd man alles bei der Person gethan hatt, was die erfahrung mit sich bringet. So mag man in der eussersten not, denn ehe soll man es nicht brauchen, der arbeittenden Personen in der geburt geben, ein gutte Messerspitz aber anderhalb in neun löffell weis Lilgenwass, damit zwen löffell Maluasier vermischt sein, vnnd wohl warm, vnd sie sich lassen darauf warm haltenn.' NLA WO, 1 Alt 23, no. 30, fols. 28arv.

106   This standard work on obstetrics was first published in 1513 by Martin Flach in Strasbourg. The facsimile (Wutöschingen: Antiqua-Verlag, 1993), was based on the copy in the Herzog August Bibliothek, shelfmark 25.1 Med. See Theresa Hitthaler-Frank, *Hebammen, Ärzte und ihr 'Rosengarten': Ein medizinisches Handbuch und die Umbrüche in der Obstetrik des 15. und 16. Jahrhunderts*, Beihefte zur Mediaevistik vol. 26 (Berlin: Peter Lang, 2021).

107   White lily oil appears in the fifth chapter of Rösslin's *Rosegarten*, Fj. On lily oil see Kruse, *Verborgene Heilkünste*, p. 82.

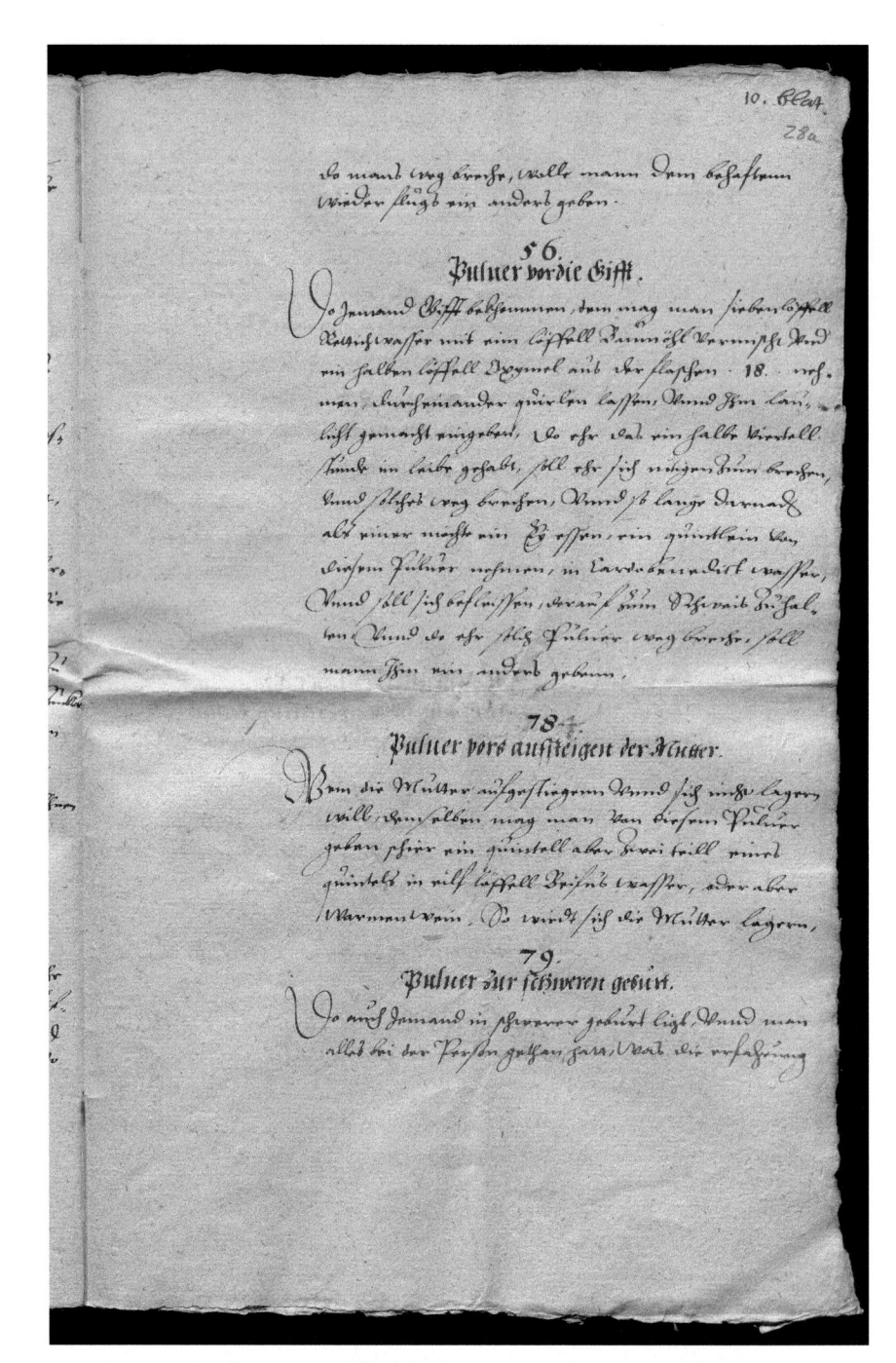

FIGURE 11.8   Powder against a difficult birth. NLA WO, 1 Alt 23, No. 30, fols. 28arv
PHOTO: LOWER SAXONY STATE ARCHIVE WOLFENBÜTTEL

suitable for stimulating menstruation: "Which promote the female 'bloom' / Therefore they would abstain / from the use of pestilent pills."[108] This implicitly alludes to abortifacients.

9   Two Prescriptions for Pediatrics

Gynecological prescriptions were traditionally combined with prescriptions for the care of infants and young children.[109] The printed source of two prescriptions for pediatrics in the medicine chest is the first manual printed in the German-speaking world for the nutrition, medical therapy, and instruction of children up to the age of seven. Bartholomäus Metlinger (after 1440–1491/92) was the author of this incunabulum, first published by Günther Zainer in Augsburg in 1473 with the title *Ein Regiment der jungen Kinder* [A guide to the medical treatment of young children]. It had been already available 100 years before the medicine chest was prepared.[110] The third part of this didactic text relates to children's illnesses. For equipping the medicine chest, Caspar Neefe took into account a "children's powder" and another powder that was supposed to be effective against worm infestation in children. Neither of these recipes can be found in Bartholomäus Metlinger's textbook so they can be excluded as master texts.

The medicine chest contained the "Margrave's Powder" (Pulv. Visci comp.) for the treatment of coughs and cramps that occurred in children. It consisted

---

108   Herzog August Bibliothek, shelfmark M: Mi Kapsel 4 (13), Ciijv.

109   Françoise Loux, *Das Kind und sein Körper: Volksmedizin – Hausmittel – Bräuche* (Frankfurt am Main: Ullstein, 1983).

110   On the author and content, see Frank Ursin, *Der Stadtarzt Bartholomäus Metlinger (nach 1440–1491/92) und die erste deutschsprachige Kinderheilkunde*, in Dietmar Schiersner (ed.), Augsburg – Stadt der Medizin. Historische Forschungen und Perspektiven (Regensburg: Verlag Schnell & Steiner, 2021), p. 10–119. Facsimile, with commentary by Peter Amelung (Dietikon-Zürich: Bibliophile Drucke von Josef Stocker, 1976). BSB-Ink M-357 (GW M23095): https://daten.digitale-sammlungen.de/~db/0004/bsb00040536/images/index .html?seite=00001&l=en. Until the year 1500, four more printed editions of the pediatric recipe book were published in Augsburg: Johann Bämler 1474 BSB-Ink-M-358 (GW M23083): https://daten.digitale-sammlungen.de/~db/0003/bsb00030000/images/index .html?id=00030000&groesser=&fip=qrssdaseayasdasfsdrxdsydsdaseayaeayaxdsydxdsyd &no=3&page=5. and 1476, BSB-Ink M-359 (GW M 23087): https://daten.digitale-samm lungen.de/~db/0003/bsb00034532/images/index.html?id=00034532&groesser=&fip =qrssdaseayasdasfsdrxdsydsdaseayaeayaxdsydxdsyd&no=3&page=5. Hans Schaur published the booklet in 1497 and 1500: BSB-Ink-M-360 (GW M23091) see https://daten.digitale -sammlungen.de/~db/0003/bsb00030002/images/index.html?id=00030002&groesser =&fip=qrssdaseayasdasfsdrxdsydsdaseayaeayaxdsydxdsyd&no=2&page=4. (9 June 2022).

of Viscum album, Magnes. Subcarbonic, Rhiz. Iridis, and Conchae praepara-
tae.[111] In Austria, the use of "Margrave's Powder" (*Pulvis contra epilepsiam*) can
be traced back to around 1570. It is not mentioned in printed pharmacopoe-
ias from the German-speaking world until the 18th century. Caspar Neefe's
"Report" thus contains remarkably early evidence for the written distribution
of this recipe.[112] It was customary to sprinkle the powder on a gold leaf, fold
it up and then swallow it. If a child had breathing difficulties (presumably
asthma, bronchitis), the powder was to be stirred into ragwort water (*Aqua
senecionis*) and given to children while the illness lasted.[113]

Worms appeared after eating raw or poorly cooked meat. They severely
damaged the organs of children and, after a long illness, could lead to death.[114]
Historical home and travel medicine cabinets contained "Corallina corsica seu
rubra", worm kelp, which was collected on the coasts of the island of Corsica
and exported as a worming remedy for treating children.[115] Johann Neefe's tract
on the plague provides a recipe for little children, which also refers to infestation with intestinal worms. According to this, parents should give their young
children 12 to 15 coated or otherwise prepared worm seeds (*Semen sanetum*)
half an hour before their morning soup, on an empty stomach. Older children
could take a higher dose.[116] According to his theory, mucus and moisture accumulated in the bodies of children, which could cause many diseases. Wealthy
parents should have had a special powder prepared for their children at a pharmacy to protect them against worm infestation. They could give them a knife
tip of this to eat early in the morning on two or three days on a piece of bread
soaked in chicken or beef broth, in rose water or in a little bit clear white wine.
An hour later the children could receive their morning soup.

In his "Report" against worm infestation in children, his brother Caspar
Neefe recommended washing a handful of rye grains four times, pouring a
pot of water over them and heating this concoction until the grains germi-
nated and broke open. Small children were to be given a spoonful of the rye
water and a good pinch of the powder. The ingredients of the powder are not

---

111   According to Piners, *Haus- und Reiseapotheken*, p. 21.
112   Peter W. Ditzel, 'Von Markgrafen- und Schwarzem Pulver', *Deutsche Apotheker Zeitung*
         No 4, 2006, p. 44.
113   "53. Kinderpuluer/ Ewr F.G. habe jch auch gar ein gut Puluer geordnet, damit sie auch
         andern leutten mugen förderlich sein. Wenn die Kinder dempficht vmb die brust sein.
         So pflegt mann Jhn solches in Kreutzkrautwasser, welches zu Latein Aqua Senecionis
         genandt wirdt zu geben in ein löffell voll machet sie luftig vmb die Brust. Mag jnen sol-
         ches geben etliche tage weill sie es bedörffen." NLA WO, 1 Alt 23, no. 30, fols. 28rv.
114   Loux, *Das Kind und sein Körper*, pp. 221–223. Stolberg, *Gelehrte Medizin*, p. 313.
115   Piners, *Haus- und Reiseapotheken*, p. 21.
116   Herzog August Bibliothek, shelfmark Mi Kapsel 4:13, Ciiv–Ciijr.

further specified, but it was ready for use. A boy could receive as much as a sixth part of a pinch, but at least a third. An older child could receive more. This treatment was supposed to be continued for several days as long as it was necessary.[117]

10   Statement of Costs for the Purchase of Basic Medicinal Products

The third document on the practical use of the medicine chest is a narrow booklet with the inscription "List of the medicines which have come into the medicine chest of the Serene and Highborn Princess and Lady Sophia, born of the Royal House of Poland, Duchess of Braunschweig-Lüneburg, etc. With an overview of the orders for medicines paid by Doctor Neefe in Leipzig from the 50 gulden received."[118] This passage is found in a somewhat different form on top of the pricelist. Here the duchess appears not only as the commissioner, but also as the recipient of the medical prescriptions of the honorable, respectable and highly learned Caspar Neefe, doctor of medicine.[119] This document includes the content of all the medicine jars and the medicines and items in the square box, i.e., the field pharmacy. The cost is listed for all the medicines contained in each case.[120]

---

117   '54. Puluer vor die wurme den Kindern / Es ist gar ein köstlich Puluer vor die Wurme, welches man also pflegt zu brauchenn. Mann nimbt ein Hand voll Rocken korn, vnnd wenn das aus vier wassern rein gewaschen ist, dann geust man schier ein kandell wasser doran, last das sieden, bis es keimet. Do das gesotten, dann nimbt man des wassers ein löffell voll in gar kleinen kinde vnnd ein gute messerspitze des Puluers. Vnd gibts jhm also ein. Dann die Wurme gerne nach diesem kornwasser pflegen zu kriechen. Vnd do dem kinde das kornwasser zu eckell zu nehmen. So mag mans jhm mit eine Zucker ein wenig süsse machen. Einem Knaben mag man geben den sechsten teill eines quintells aber schier den dritten theil. Einem altern mehr. Vnd gebe Jhnen das etliche tage weill sie es bedurffenn.' NLA WO, 1 Alt 23, no. 30, fol. 28v.

118   'Vorzeichnus Der Ertzneÿ so in die Laden aber Hausapothecken. der Durchlauchtigen vnnd Hochgebornen Furstin vnd Frauen, Frauen Sophien, gebornen aus Konig Stamme zu Polen, Hertzogin zu Braunschweig vnnd Luneburgk etc. kommen, sambt der Ausgabe von den entpfangenen funftzig thalern, so doctor Neeffen zu Leiptzigk die zubestellen zugesandt worden, wohin die gegebenn.' NLA WO, 1 Alt 23, no. 30, fol. 30r.

119   'Die Artzneÿ fur die Durchlauchte vnnd Hochgeborne Furstin vnnd Fraw, Frau [sic!] Sophiam, geborne aus koniglichem Stam zu Polen, Hertzogin zu Braunschweig vnnd Luneburgk etc.' 'So der Ernuest achbar vnnd Hochgelartte Herr Caspar Neeff, der Artzneÿ D. etc. Jhr F.G. verordnet hatt, kost wie volget.' NLA WO, 1 Alt 23, no. 30, fol. 31r.

120   NLA WO, 1 Alt 23, no. 30, fols. 31r–37r.

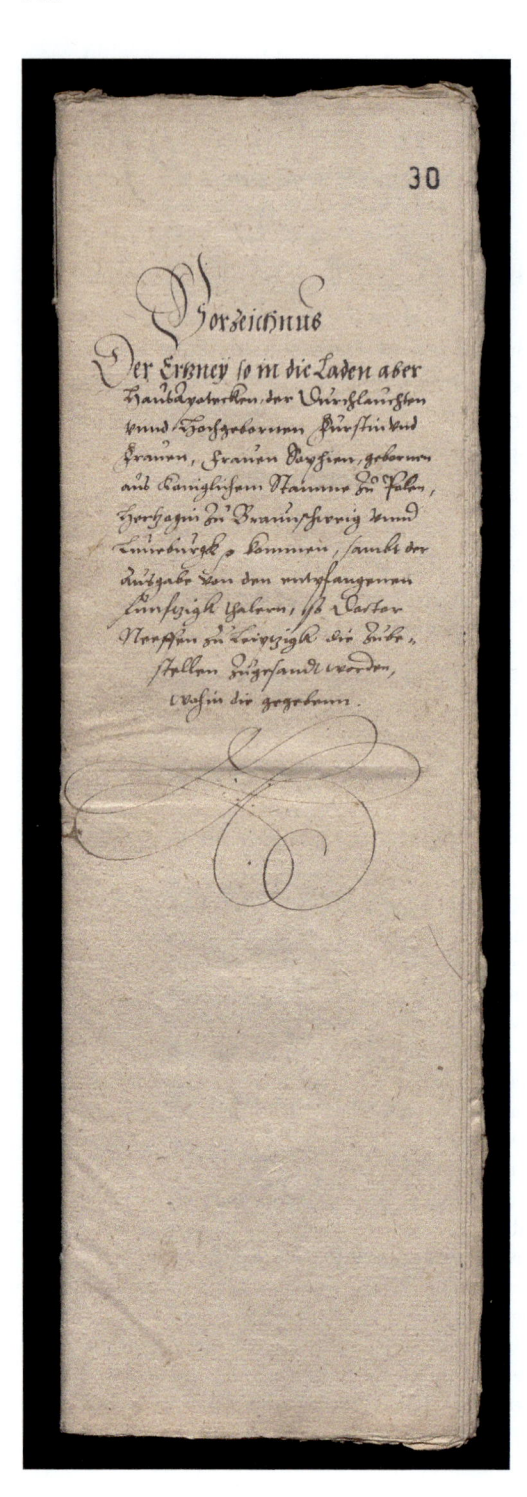

FIGURE 11.9
List of remedies in the medicine
chest. NLA WO, 1 Alt 23, No. 30,
fol. 30r
PHOTO: LOWER SAXONY STATE
ARCHIVE WOLFENBÜTTEL

Below the lists, an outstanding invoice of two gulden is noted for the personal physician Dr. Elias Butticher (Bötticher, 1532–1579).[121] Some of the medication for the medicine chest had been ordered from the pharmacist Jeronimus Hoffmann in Chemnitz, who charged 92 gulden, 19 groschen and two pfennige for them.[122] Because Caspar Neefe's family came from Chemnitz it can be assumed that personal relations had led to the commissioning of the delivery. Things not available in Chemnitz were procured elsewhere: on 14 February 1574, Elias Butticher confirmed that Duchess Sophia's treasurer Hans Gebert († before 1583) had paid him 58 thalers for medicines that were still missing.[123] It therefore can be concluded that both Caspar Neefe and Elias Butticher were involved in the acquisition.

11   The Dietetics of the Personal Physician Gervasius Marstaller

Gervasius Marstaller, the author of the two aforementioned pamphlets on the plague, compiled special dietary instructions for Duchess Sophia. They are divided into six subheadings and were recorded in Schöningen on 26 January 1574.

His patient suffered from bladder stones and stomach complaints.[124] According to his recommendation, she was to avoid cheese, milk, and fish. As a dessert she was to take roasted or preserved quinces or pears with some wine to settle the stomach. Alternatively, he suggested a potion of quince, currant, or cherry juice with or without the addition of wine. He reminded her that he had already given her this advice orally. A potion was made for her from fruit juice, with an addition of the so-called "Duke Henry's stomach powder"[125] from a pharmacy located in Braunschweig. To keep her stomach functioning, she was to swallow the usual stomach pills called Alphangin at least once a week in the morning or evening; these were available in the medicine chest in two different doses as simple and powerful Alphangin pills (*Gemeine und*

---

121   NLA WO, 1 Alt 23, no. 30, fol. 36r.

122   NLA WO, 1 Alt 23, no. 30, fol. 37r.

123   NLA WO, 1 Alt 23, no. 30, fol. 37r. On Johann Gebert see Pirozynski, *Herzogin Sophie* p. 89. Bues, *Zofia Jagiellonka*, p. 146, 173, 195.

124   The dietetic guidelines have been handed down in: NLA WO, 1 Alt 23, no. 30, fols. 7r–13v. It is recorded in the estate inventory NLA WO, 1 Alt 23, no. 69, fol. 60r: 'D. Gerwasý Arzneý Regiment an essen vnd trinken' and was in a small red cabinet at the time when the inventory was notes down.

125   Duke Henry II. (1489–1568) was her deceased husband.

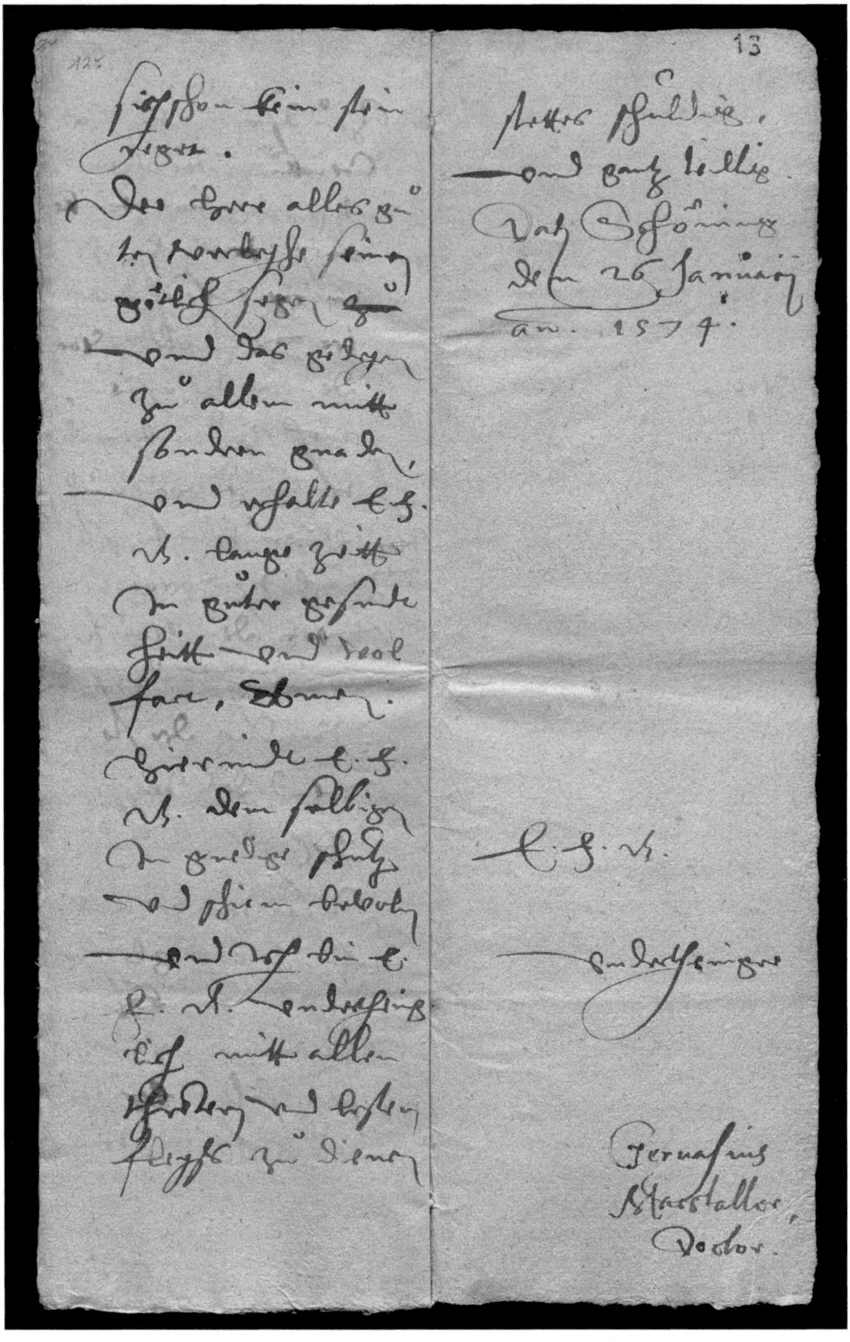

FIGURE 11.10 Double page from the dietetic guidelines of the personal physician Gervasius Marstaller. NLA WO, 1 Alt 23, No. 30, fols. 12v–13r
PHOTO: LOWER SAXONY STATE ARCHIVE WOLFENBÜTTEL

Gescherffte Alphangin pillen).[126] When she was in bed in the morning or in the evening, her loins were to be rubbed with red sandal ointment. If she had no complaints from urinary stones, these medical and dietary measures were not required. If she had problems with the urinary stones, she should take an enema in the morning or evening. After that, her back and lap should be rubbed with the ointment against the stones. This could be performed in a warm location, but not by an open fire or near a tiled stove, because the heat would not have helped. In the morning, in the evening, at midnight and when the urinary stones did not cause any problems, the princess should drink the prophylactic potion that the personal physician had prescribed for her. The recipe for this potion was written down by someone other than Gervasius Marstaller on a slip of paper that was placed with the documents relating to the medicine chest.[127]

For this purpose, two portions of aniseed, fennel, licorice, and sugar were to be pounded to powder in a mortar, mixed with finely chopped licorice and then boiled in a covered pot in two measures of water for one hour.[128] The healing potion was warmed up and served to the Duchess in the morning and in the evening.

Duchess Sophia died at the age of 53, less than a year and a half after the home, field and travel pharmacy arrived in Schöningen, on 28 May 1575. Before her burial in the upper sepulcher of the main church in Wolfenbüttel – next to her late husband and his two sons Karl Viktor (1525–1553) and Philipp Magnus (1527–1553), who were killed in the Battle of Sievershausen – Dr Andreas Bacher embalmed her body.[129] Her gravestone has been preserved and was restored a few years ago.

Margareta von Münsterberg, with whom she had gone to Bad Ems for a cure, attended the funeral and was given a sum of money from her inheritance in the settlement.[130] The inventories of the deceased's estate include bundles of medical prescriptions and boxes of medicines in various containers.[131] It can

---

126 Recipes no. 36 and no. 37, NLA WO, 1 Alt 23, no. 30, fols. 26rv.

127 NLA WO, 1 Alt 23, no. 30, fol. 15r.

128 One portion was about 14.6 grams (half an ounce), Wacker, *Arznei und Confect*, p. 535.

129 The embalming took place several weeks after her death, on 23 June 1575, Pirozynski, *Herzogin Sophie*, p. 124.

130 Bues, *Herzogin Sophia*, p. 211.

131 Medicines contained in the red box are mentioned in: NLA WO, 1 Alt 23, no. 69, fol. 6or: 'Ein schachtel mit manus Christi die D. Solinander verordnet' – a box with 'Manus Christi', a remedy prescribed by Dr. Solinander; 'Another box of *knuflein* of calamus'– small 'knobs', pieces of *Calamus aromaticus*, an Asian marsh plant; "A box of zucats" – meaning succade, cubes of lemon peel candied in sugar (citronate); 'Ein Schachtel mit Marsellen' – these were *morsellen*, a confection made from a boiled-down sugar solution enriched with chopped nuts or almonds and spices such as cinnamon, nutmeg, cardamom, ginger,

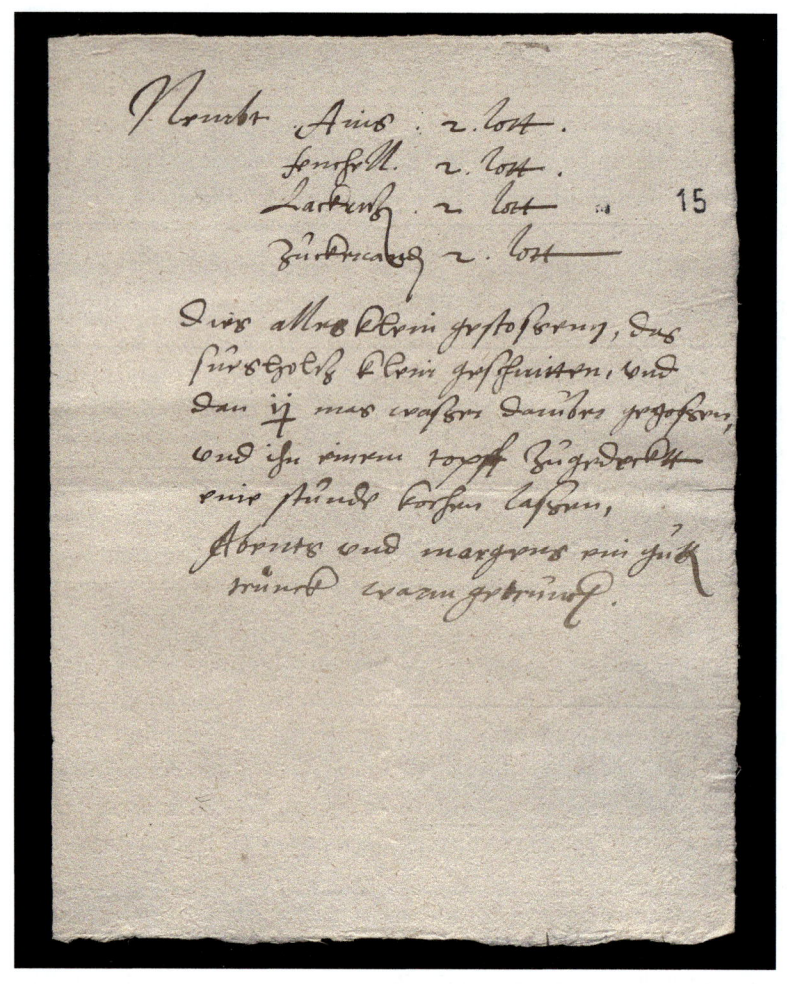

FIGURE 11.11   A note with the recipe for the potion against urinary stones from the
personal physician Gervasius Marstaller. NLA WO, 1 Alt 23, No. 30,
fol. 15r
PHOTO: LOWER SAXONY STATE ARCHIVE WOLFENBÜTTEL

be assumed that in addition to the medical manuscript, her library contained other medical works and presumably also printed herbal books in Polish and German.[132]

galangal, or cloves; 'Ein Christir Beütel' – an enema preserved in a bag; 'Ein buchsseln Jngemachte hegebotten' – a tin of boiled down rose hips; 'Sechs gleser mit allerhandt wasser' – six glass jars that contained distilled waters; 'Sieben schechtlein mit allerhand medicinalien Puluer vnnd ander ding' – seven boxes of medicinal powders; 'Sieben erden buchssen vnnd begen, darin auch medicinalia'– seven vessels of clay with medicines.

132   Pirozynski, *Herzogin Sophie*, pp. 225–226. The OPAC of the Herzog August Bibliothek does not list any books previously owned by Herzogin Sophie (accessed on 25 July 2022).

FIGURE 11.12   Grave sculpture of Duchess Sophia, her husband Duke Henry II. and his sons
PHOTO: AUTHOR

Index